CETA IMPLEMENTATION
AND IMPLICATIONS

McGILL-QUEEN'S/BRIAN MULRONEY INSTITUTE OF GOVERNMENT STUDIES
IN LEADERSHIP, PUBLIC POLICY, AND GOVERNANCE

Series editor: Donald E. Abelson

Titles in this series address critical issues facing Canada at home and abroad
and the efforts policymakers at all levels of government have made to address
a host of complex and multifaceted policy concerns. Books in this series receive
financial support from the Brian Mulroney Institute of Government at St Francis
Xavier University; in keeping with the institute's mandate, these studies explore
how leaders involved in key policy initiatives arrived at their decisions and what
lessons can be learned. Combining rigorous academic analysis with thoughtful
recommendations, this series compels readers to think more critically about
how and why elected officials make certain policy choices, and how, in concert
with other stakeholders, they can better navigate an increasingly complicated
and crowded marketplace of ideas.

CETA Implementation and Implications

Unravelling the Puzzle

Edited By

Robert G. Finbow

McGill-Queen's University Press

Montreal & Kingston • London • Chicago

© McGill-Queen's University Press 2022

ISBN 978-0-2280-1191-0 (cloth)
ISBN 978-0-2280-1192-7 (paper)
ISBN 978-0-2280-1275-7 (ePDF)
ISBN 978-0-2280-1276-4 (ePUB)

Legal deposit third quarter 2022
Bibliothèque nationale du Québec

Printed in Canada on acid-free paper that is 100% ancient forest free
(100% post-consumer recycled), processed chlorine free

This book has been published with the help of a grant from the Jean Monnet
Erasmus+ Program in support of the CETA Implementations and Implications
Project at the Jean Monnet EU Centre of Excellence at Dalhousie University.

Funded by the   Financé par le
Government   gouvernement   Canada   Canada Council   Conseil des arts
of Canada   du Canada   for the Arts   du Canada

We acknowledge the support of the Canada Council for the Arts.

Nous remercions le Conseil des arts du Canada de son soutien.

Library and Archives Canada Cataloguing in Publication

Title: CETA implementation and implications: unravelling the puzzle /
  edited by Robert G. Finbow

Names: Finbow, Robert G., 1956- editor.

Series: McGill-Queen's/Brian Mulroney Institute of Government studies
  in leadership, public policy, and governance; 8.

Description: Series statement: McGill-Queen's/Brian Mulroney Institute
  of Government studies in leadership, public policy, and governance; 8 |
  Includes bibliographical references and index.

Identifiers: Canadiana (print) 20220218889 | Canadiana (ebook)
  20220218978 | ISBN 9780228011910 (cloth) | ISBN 9780228011927 (paper) |
  ISBN 9780228012757 (ePDF) | ISBN 9780228012764 (ePUB)

Subjects: LCSH: Comprehensive Economic and Trade Agreement
  (2016 October 30) | LCSH: Foreign trade regulation—European
  Union countries. | LCSH: Foreign trade regulation—Canada. |
  LCSH: European Union countries—Foreign economic relations—Canada. |
  LCSH: Canada—Foreign economic relations—European Union countries.

Classification: LCC HF3228.E97 C48 2022 | DDC 382/.97104—dc23

This book was typeset by Marquis Interscript in 10.5/13 Sabon.

Contents

Tables and Figures

TABLES

FIGURES

Acknowledgments

The CETA Implementation and Implications Project (CIIP), funded by an Erasmus+ Jean Monnet project, developed linkages with scholars and stakeholders across Europe and North America to analyze and evaluate the implementation and impacts of the Comprehensive Economic and Trade Agreement between Canada and the European Union (CETA). This involved the dissemination of presentations and papers following two key events held at the Dalhousie University in 2018 and 2019, centring on the implementation and impacts of CETA. These activities successfully brought together a network of emerging and established scholars, civil society actors, and government officials to analyze and discuss the programmatic and legislative changes required to bring CETA to fruition in Canada, at the EU level, and in member states. The two events featured several panels focused on the critical issues underpinning the CETA agreement as it is ratified and implemented.

The areas covered throughout the project included the regulatory process, labour mobility and rights, trade, business, procurement, investment, environment, agriculture, and geographic indicators, as well as intellectual property rights. Experts in these key areas from academic and policy backgrounds came together to begin establishing a baseline for the implications of CETA. Many of these scholars participated in the Conference on CETA Implementation, the culminating event of the CIIP, held at the Dalhousie University on 27 and 28 September 2019. The conference brought together a range of scholars from Europe, Canada, and the United States to examine various aspects of CETA and assess early evidence from the first two years of provisional implementation. This volume represents the cumulation of knowledge in this project, including revised versions of the conference papers covering many areas of this complex and wide-ranging economic and trade agreement. The logistical problems and delays induced by the Covid crisis notwithstanding, it provides a basis for understanding some of the early accomplishments and challenges of putting such a complex economic framework into practice.

The editor wishes to acknowledge the generous support of the Erasmus+ program and the European Commission toward funding the CIIP and providing financial support for this publication. The project was also assisted by the Jean Monnet European Union Centre of Excellence at Dalhousie University; its director, Ruben Zaiotti; and the centre coordinator, Madeleine Coffen-Smout, who provided important logistics for the project. The project administrator, Alanna Taylor, was exceptional in organizing the events and managing the complex budgets and was essential to the success of the project. The editorial assistance of Susan Manning in the preparation of this volume has also been invaluable.

Abbreviations

ACE	Architects' Council of Europe
Art.	Article
BIT	bilateral investment treaty
CACQ	Coalition of Quebec Consumer Associations
CAFTA	Canadian Agri-Food Trade Alliance
CALA	Canadian Architectural Licensing Authorities
CARIFORUM	Caribbean Forum of the Organisation of African, Caribbean, and Pacific States
CBA	community benefits agreement
CELA	Canadian Environmental Law Association
CETA	(Canada–European Union) Comprehensive Economic and Trade Agreement
CFSP	common foreign and security policy
CIPP	Erasmus+ CETA Implementation and Implications Project
CJEU	Court of Justice of the European Union
COMESA	Common Market for Eastern and Southern Africa
CPTPP	Comprehensive and Progressive Agreement for Trans-Pacific Partnership
CSF	civil society forum
CSI	Committee on Services and Investment
CSR	corporate social responsibility
CTE	Committee on Trade and Environment
CTS	Crosslinx Transit Solutions
DAG	domestic advisory group
DG	directorate-general

DG GROW	Directorate-General for Internal Market, Industry, Entrepreneurship and SMEs
ECHR	European Court of Human Rights
ECJ	European Court of Justice
ECT	Energy Charter Treaty
ECT	Treaty on European Community
ED	environmental defence
EDC	Export Development Canada
EP	European Parliament
EPA	economic partnership agreement
EPRS	European Parliamentary Research Service
ETUC	European Trade Union Confederation
EUJEPA	EU-Japan Economic Partnership Agreement
EUSFTA	EU-Singapore Free Trade Agreement
EUZBBG	Law on the Cooperation between the Federal Government and the German Bundestag in matters of the European Union
FDI	foreign direct investment
FET	fair and equitable treatment
FIPA	foreign investment protection agreement
FIRA	foreign investment review agency
FQD	Fuel Quality Directive
FTA	free trade agreement
FTC	Free Trade Commission
GATS	General Agreement on Trade in Services
GATT	General Agreement on Tariffs and Trade
GDP	gross domestic product
GHG	greenhouse gas
GG	Grundgesetz
GMO	genetically modified organism
GPA	Agreement on Government Procurement
GRP	good regulatory practices
GVC	global value chains
IBA	International Bar Association
ICO	inter-corporate ownership
ICM	investment court mechanism
ICS	investment court system
ICSID	International Centre for Settlement of Investment Disputes
i.c.w.	in conjunction with

IDEaS	Innovations for Defence Excellence and Security
ILO	International Labour Organization
IMF	International Monetary Fund
INTA	Committee on International Trade
IPR	intellectual property
IRC	international regulatory cooperation
ISDS	investor-state dispute settlement
ITB	industrial and technological benefits
LRT	light rail transit
MASH	municipal, academic, schools, and hospitals
MEA	multilateral environmental agreements
MEP	member of the European Parliament
MFN	most favoured nation
MRA	mutual recognition agreement
MRPQ	mutual recognition of professional qualifications
MST	minimum standard of treatment
NAFTA	North American Free Trade Agreement
NDC	nationally determined contributions
NGO	nongovernmental organization
NTB	non-tariff barriers
OECD	Organisation for Economic Co-operation and Development
PPE	personal protective equipment
PTA	preferential trade agreement
RAPEX	European Union Rapid Information System
RCB	regulatory cooperation body
RCF	regulatory cooperation forum
RFQ	request for qualification
SAP	single access platform
SDG	sustainable development goal
SDR	special drawing rights
SME	small and medium enterprise
SPA	single point of access
SPA	strategic partnership agreement
SPS	sanitary and phytosanitary measures
TAP	technology action plan
TBT	technical barriers to trade
TCBN	Toronto Community Benefits Network
TCS	trade commissioner services
TEU	Treaty on European Union

TFEU	Treaty on the Functioning of the European Union
TNA	technology needs assessment
TPP	trans-pacific partnership
TRIMS	trade-related investment measures
TRQ	tariff rate quota
TSD	trade and sustainable development
TTIP	Transatlantic Trade and Investment Partnership
TUC	Trade Union Congress
UNCITRAL	United Nations Commission on International Trade Law
UNCTAD	United Nations Conference on Trade and Development
UNFCCC	United Nations Framework Convention on Climate Change
USMCA	United States–Mexico–Canada Agreement
USTR	United States trade representative
WDBA	Windsor-Detroit Bridge Authority
WG III	Working Group III
WHO	World Health Organization
WTO	World Trade Organization

CETA IMPLEMENTATION
AND IMPLICATIONS

Introduction: Unravelling the Puzzle

Robert G. Finbow

The Comprehensive Economic and Trade Agreement (CETA) between Canada and the European Union (EU) is hailed as a gold standard for trade agreements. It reflects many of the EU's goals regarding trade policies in the wake of stalemate at the World Trade Organization (WTO) and the 2008 global financial crisis. CETA addresses a wide range of themes, going beyond tariffs on traded goods, favoured status for EU and Canadian exporters, trade in services and the so-called technical barriers to trade. It seeks, gradually, coordination between government agencies to promote regulatory cooperation, harmonization, or mutual recognition of standards. Via collaboration among professional associations on both sides of the Atlantic, CETA also incrementally promotes professional mobility and recognition of credentials and qualifications. In addition, it includes provisions related to intellectual property, notably extended patent protection and data exclusivity for pharmaceutical and other goods. It opens access to the parties' public procurement contracts above thresholds at all levels of government. Finally, it proposes an innovative investor-state dispute settlement (ISDS) system, with a permanent investment court system (ICS) in place of ad hoc arbitration of investment disputes as found in previous agreements.

The complexity of the deal necessitates a collaborative approach to analysis, with interdisciplinary scholars across law, economics, public policy, and political science, among other fields. It also requires experts from public sectors and academia, on both sides of the Atlantic. This volume reflects that diverse range of experts, with contributions from both established and emerging scholars. While not all of the immense range of matters covered in CETA are analyzed here, the Erasmus+ CETA Implementation and Implications Project (CIIP), on which it is based, did cover several of essential and contentious areas – investment, regulation, procurement, and social and environmental impacts. It also reflects on the complex issues in negotiation and innovative governance structures and approaches created by CETA. These are addressed in the various sections of this volume. The scholarly approaches are diverse as the project attracted participation from scholars at various career stages with very different disciplinary backgrounds and theoretical and methodological inclinations. Contributors varyingly used data drawn from EU databases, documents, and interviews with officials in the EU, as well as academic and civil society organizations. Given this variation in approach and substance, this volume speaks to both a scholarly and policy-oriented audience interested in CETA and EU trade and economic relations. The diverse national origins of contributors enable the project and volume to provide for "cross-fertilization," bringing together Canadian and European scholars, to examine the Canada-EU relations in light of CETA. Alongside similar contemporary works, this project helps to establish a baseline understanding of the implications of CETA in several policy fields.

This research was undertaken in a context of the slow-paced intricate implementation and ratification process for CETA which at times appears as if it might flounder on the shoals of multi-level governance after the Lisbon Treaty, and which remains incomplete. Provisions for EU Parliament's (EP's) increased involvement in treaty ratification introduced new complexities, which generated uncertainties as the various actors learned how to operate in the Lisbon regime. Some member states pressed for mixed agreements where not essential and "seem not to fully accept the consequences of the Treaties' reform and often rely on pre-Lisbon practices" where these no longer have a legal basis (Gatti and Manzini 2012, 1734). Despite the transfer of new competencies to the European Commission, there was a backlash, with national and sub-national governments insisting on playing a larger role (Bollen, De Ville, and Gheyle 2016). Economic crisis, increased nationalism and populism, and concern over migration also complicated matters.

For the EU, CETA was among a series of trade negotiations including the aborted Transatlantic Trade and Investment Partnership (TTIP) with the US and deals with Singapore, Japan, and Vietnam that provided early tests for this new ratification approach. Several national parliaments requested that CETA and TTIP be treated as "mixed" because they encompassed member state competencies such as services, transport, and investor protection. As chairs of EU parliamentary committees wrote to the trade commissioner: "In view of the important role national parliaments have in the democratic decision-making process of the EU, we feel that it is of great importance that trade agreements such as CETA and TTIP are ratified by the national parliaments" (Tweede Kamer der Staten-Generaal 2014). The Commission declined to accept that all economic agreements would be considered mixed (European Commission 2014). Under political pressure, in July 2016, the Commission finally agreed that CETA be submitted to the European Council as a "mixed agreement" so that the ICS provisions among other matters would require member state ratification. The European Court of Justice (ECJ) determined in the Singapore case that indirect portfolio investment and ISDS required member states' approval. After surviving varied challenges from member states and sub-national governments, CETA retained its ambitious scope with some matters requiring future work in committees and professional associations in future. Nonetheless, ongoing political change and complex litigation generated uncertainty about CETA ratification, as well as future EU economic and trade treaties.

The creation of ICS encountered challenges from member states, since disputes resolution and indirect investment were seen as member state competencies. This led to litigation which extended beyond the date of provisional implementation. With litigation outstanding on the ICS when CETA entered into force, only limited aspects of its Chapter 8 on investment were provisionally applied, relating only to foreign direct investment (FDI) (and not indirect or portfolio investment). These included Arts 8.1 to 8.8, relating to definitions, market access, and performance requirements; national treatment and most favoured nation (MFN) treatment; and senior management and directorships (CETA 2016). Also provisionally implemented were Arts 8.13 on investment transfers, 8.15 on reservations and exceptions, and 8.16 on denial of benefits. Investment disputes provisions were delayed by litigation and national political decisions and ratifications. For similar reasons, elements of Chapter 13 on financial services were not provisionally applied where they affected indirect portfolio investment, investment protection and investor-state disputes resolution. These exemptions affected Art. 13.2 (paras 3 and 4), and all of Arts 13.3, 13.4, 13.9, and 13.21. Hence many of CETA's innovative elements on investment disputes and the ICS remain in abeyance with an uncertain fate (see table 1.1).

The Court of Justice of the EU (CJEU) has affirmed the compatibility of the ICS with EU law, but given that the EU accepted member states assertions on the mixed competencies in the deal, it remains to be ratified by many states at time of writing. While most legal hurdles to the ICS have been removed, ratification by all states cannot be guaranteed. Table 1.2 indicates the ratification timeline for CETA.

Table 1.1
Limits on the provisional application of CETA

(a) Only the following provisions of Chapter 8 of the agreement (Investment) shall be provisionally applied, and only insofar as foreign direct investment is concerned:

Arts 8.1 to 8.8; Art. 8.13; Art. 8.15, with the exception of paragraph 3 thereof; and Art. 8.16

(b) The following provisions of Chapter 13 of the agreement (Financial Services) shall not be provisionally applied insofar as they concern portfolio investment, protection of investment, or the resolution of investment disputes between investors and states:

Art. 13.2 (Paragraphs 3 and 4), Art. 13.3, Art. 13.4, Art. 13.9, and Art. 13.21

(c) The following provisions of the agreement shall not be provisionally applied:

Art. 20.12, Art. 27.3, and Art. 27.4, to the extent that these articles apply to administrative proceedings, review, and appeal at member state level; and Paragraph 7 of Art. 28.7

(d) The provisional application of Chapters 22, 23, and 24 of the agreement shall respect the allocation of competences between the Union and the member states.

Source: Official Journal of the EU (2017).

Canada's CETA approval received royal assent in May 2017 with the provisional implementation date determined for 21 September of that year. Pursuant to Canada's commitments under the Vienna Convention on the Law of Treaties, this implied that CETA would have immediate legal effect in many areas. For instance, Section 3 of the CETA Implementation Act ensures that "any federal law that implements or fulfills the Agreement will be interpreted in a manner consistent with the Agreement ... With the passage of the CETA Implementation Act and related regulatory and administrative action, the Government of Canada will have taken the steps necessary to implement the Agreement in Canada at the federal level" (Government of Canada 2017a). In the first years of implementation, according to officials at the North America office at the Directorate-General for Trade of the European Commission (hereinafter DG Trade),[1] the Canada-EU Joint Committee was active, and some nineteen bilateral specialized committees and five bilateral dialogues were created. At the joint committee's first meeting in September 2018, agreements were reached on climate action to implement the Paris Accords, gender and trade, and small and medium enterprises (SMEs) in CETA.

Implementation is fairly advanced in some of the less-contested areas of the agreement, notably trade in goods. For instance, the federal government issued a notification in advance of preliminary application indicating

Table 1.2
Timeline of CETA ratification

15 February 2017	European Parliament approval
9 March 2017	Latvian notifies EU of ratification
16 May 2017	Canadian Parliament's bill on CETA received royal assent
1 June 2017	Denmark notifies EU of ratification
26 July 2017	Malta notifies EU of ratification
21 September 2017	CETA provisionally applied subject to limits
9 November 2017	Croatia notifies EU of ratification
10 November 2017	Estonia notifies EU of ratification
16 November 2017	Czech Republic notifies EU of ratification
13 December 2017	Spain notifies EU of ratification
31 January 2018	Portugal notifies EU of ratification
5 May 2018	Lithuania notifies EU of ratification
9 October 2018	Sweden notifies EU of ratification
8 November 2018	UK notifies EU of ratification
3 January 2019	Finland notifies EU of ratification
25 May 2019	Austria notifies EU of ratification
28 November 2019	Slovakia notifies EU of ratification
6 June 2020	Luxembourg notifies EU of ratification
2 December 2020	Romania notifies EU of ratification

Source: European Commission (2020).

the immediate effectiveness of tariff reductions or the beginning of phased-in reductions depending on the product. This move triggered a series of "regulatory amendments and new regulations under the Customs Act related to the CETA," notably the creation of a new Canada-EU Tariff (Government of Canada 2017b). In addition to phased-in provisions, specific rules applied to particular products, with limitations as outlined in detailed annexes to the CETA, for instance, regarding automotives, fish and seafood, and "quota textiles and apparel products," which had specific rules of origin as well as volume limitations on imports (CETA 2016, Annexes 5 and 6). Trade in automobiles and auto parts was subject to gradual tariff reductions with exemptions for sensitive lines, increased quotas for cars made with significant Canadian contributions, and gradual relaxation of rules-of-origins provisions, especially considering the deep integration of the US and Canadian automotive sectors.

Several other elements of the agreement were provisionally applied immediately. For instance, chapters relating to services and investment (except investor-state disputes via the proposed ICS) and intellectual property were given immediate effect. The accord as per CETA (2016) chapter 10 also permitted temporary entry of professional visitors and persons travelling for investment or business purposes or to provide specialized services and information. Access to government procurement at all levels of government (both Canada and the EU, including the respective provinces and muncipalities, and member states) was also quickly opened, for procurement contracts above specified thresholds of contract value (CETA 2016, Chapter 19). The development of common databases and information sources would follow; the parties were given five years to create a single point of access (SPA) for government procurement and coordination on judicial appeals procedures on procurement issues. Processes to address sanitary and phytosanitary issues (ibid., Chapter 5) and technical barriers to trade (ibid., Chapter 4) were also simplified, though with substantial work remaining as the parties agreed to work on recognition of equivalent standards using technical consultations backed by audit and verification processes and "conformity assessments." Work, under the auspices of a joint customs cooperation committee, also commenced immediately on customs and trade facilitation, working toward a system to create transparent, streamlined, and predictable customs processes (ibid., Chapter 6).

Many elements of CETA's implementation involve new organizations and communications channels put into practice over several years (see table 1.3). The overarching structure is coordinated by the Canada-EU Joint Committee, which involves the trade minister, the commissioner, and senior officials, to coordinate priorities and oversee specialized bilateral dialogues and committees for specific chapters of CETA. At its initial meetings, the joint committee indicated priorities for action – on gender-responsive trade policy, trade impacts on climate in light of Paris Accords commitments, and challenges facing SMEs in the complex, competitive, post-CETA markets. The joint committee also oversaw the initiation of bilateral dialogues on specific themes including forest products certification, sustainability, and bioenergy; motor vehicle emission, safety standards, and automation; biotechnology and controls, and labelling genetically modified meat and salmon; raw materials issues including critical resources, minerals and metals, and sustainable technology and practices; and electronic commerce which has yet to convene). Many of the other sub-committees are established and active and working through

Table 1.3
CETA governance and committees

Committee	Initial Meeting Dates	Location
CETA Joint Committee	26 September 2018	Montreal
Agriculture	19 September 2018	Brussels
Financial Services	19 June 2018	Brussels
	12 June 2019	Ottawa
Geographical Indicators	17 May 2018	by videoconference
Goods	29 November 2018	by videoconference
Government Procurement	22 February 2019	Brussels
	15 March 2018	Brussels
Joint Customs Cooperation	22 June 2018	Brussels
Pharmaceuticals	16 November 2018	by videoconference
Professional Qualifications	16 April 2019	Brussels
Regulatory Cooperation Forum	14 December 2018	Brussels
Sanitary and Phytosanitary	26 February to 7 March 2018	Ottawa
	25 January to 7 February 2019	Brussels
Services and Investment	18 September 2018	Brussels
Trade and Sustainable Development	13 September 2018	Brussels
Civil Society Forum	12 September 2018	Brussels
Wines and Spirits	5 July 2018	Brussels

Source: Government of Canada (2020).

particular issues of this nature. But some of these issues involved political decisions, which were the purview of the ministerial level and the Canada-EU Joint Committee, which takes the lead on the most sensitive and contentious matters. Table 1.3 shows the initial meeting dates of major committees; several have met regularly, including the agricultural committee that met annually, and some sub-committees have been very active through 2020, though virtually owing to the COVID-19 pandemic (Government of Canada 2020).

Some aspects of implementation have proceeded significantly, with 98 per cent of good trade for instance becoming duty-free at implementation on 21 September 2017, with some more gradual phase-ins for sensitive categories such as fish and seafood products, agriculture, and automobiles. But other aspects of the agreements were not implemented, awaiting the slow process of ratification by EU member states; these included the ICS, portfolio investment, protection of investment or the resolution of investment disputes between investors and states. Implementation was further complicated by the elaborate multi-level governance framework involved. Depending on the issue area, decisions and legal adjustments had to be undertaken by some combination of: the ministerial level Canada-EU Joint Committee; specialized committees between the partners around each chapter of CETA; bilateral dialogues on select themes; directives or decisions by the European Commission; regulations or legislation by the Canadian federal government, member states, or provinces; enactment and implementation of several essential changes and measures by the municipal, local, or regional government; professional associations' collaboration on qualifications and mobility; civil society dialogue on sustainability; and, business sector actions to put the deal into practice (see table 1.4). This all made for a rich arena for research, which collaborators of the project have broadly engaged.

In addition to the transnational governance dimension, there is also a complex multi-level governance element to CETA implementation in both of the parties. As table 1.4 indicates, many different agencies at multiple levels of governance will ultimately be involved in the implementation process, making this a complex and protracted process. The agenda for researchers is multifaceted, covering the complex range of subjects addressed in this comprehensive transatlantic accord.

CETA will inch forward as ratification processes in various EU states proceed. For many states, this may be relatively straightforward through parliamentary approvals. In other states, referendums are theoretically possible if mandated by the national constitution. Given the national importance of the deal, in some cases political decision-making may be required to work around these constitutional requirements to permit ratification. With more protectionist and nationalist forces represented in member state legislatures, the possibility of nonratification in some countries cannot be entirely discounted, especially where irritants remain in relations with Canada. Several major EU states have yet to ratify at the time of publication. Therefore, CETA itself remains somewhat tenuous, and ultimate complete ratification remains uncertain. However, provisional application by most member states in most areas of the deal could create irreversible momentum for eventual approval. ICS and the disputes resolution mechanisms could well be the primary orphan lost in the contentious trade and integration politics of the times or hived off to a parallel investment agreement as in subsequent EU economic negotiations.

Table 1.4
Sample implementation tasks

Actor	Sample themes	Sample implementation actions
Canada-EU Joint Committee	gender, climate, SMES and others TBA	identify priorities; discuss politically contentious areas (e.g. cheese, wines and spirits, meat tariff rate quotas, etc.)
Specialized committees	one for each chapter of the CETA agreement	information sharing; exchanges on regulatory developments and policy priorities
Bilateral dialogues	motor vehicles, biotech, raw materials, electronic commerce, market access	information sharing; standards setting; implementation guidance
EU Commission	ALL except indirect investment, investment disputes, marine transport, labour relations	implementing directives; ECJ referrals; creation of consultative bodies
Federal government	patent extensions, tariff reductions, agricultural quotas; generating new institutions	tariff notices; legislation or regulation; creation of consultative committees; civil society outreach; trade promotion
Member states	investment court participation; other mixed competences	ratification in parliament and sub-national levels
Provinces	labour mobility; labour relations; procurement	legislation or regulation; links to immigration and skills development policies
Municipal/local	procurement	adjusting tenders; preparing coordinated databases
Professional associations	professional qualifications	negotiated mutual recognition
Civil society groups	sustainability, labour, environment	participation in committees, consultations, lobbying
Business/ corporate	regulation, procurement, investments, marketing	cooperation on "behind-the-border" elements of integration

Source: Finbow (2019) – author's compilation.

CETA was born in times of crisis but adjusted in response to the social push back that occurred, especially after the failed TTIP negotiations, to some of its liberalizing elements. It is hailed as an example of social sensitivity by the EU and Canada in an era when populist alternatives are challenging the liberal international order. Canada and the EU depict CETA as the most progressive trade agreement adopted to date, with the right of government to regulate for health, environment, and safety guaranteed in the joint interpretive instrument, and with integrated chapters on trade and sustainability, labour, environment, and human rights. Critics assert that commercial interests are paramount, and liberalizing components of CETA remain pronounced. They question whether the changes made during negotiations reflect democratic responsiveness and if they will achieve their stated purposes. Provisional implementation provides a chance to investigate and test the specific balance in CETA and observe initial impacts – though without the critical investment component, which will eventually affect how the whole of CETA is put into practice. As implementation proceeds, analysts can perhaps gauge the possibilities and limitations of CETA as a model for future progressive trade deals.

This volume assesses many of the important areas of CETA in several sections. These studies reflect on the negotiation, early implementation, and consequences of CETA ratification. Part I addresses negotiation and governance complexities. Felix Stern (Munich) writes about "Legitimization and Control of Committee Bodies in EU Free Trade Agreements" using the CETA example. He notes that the new generation of EU free trade agreements (FTAS) includes committee systems with authority over regulatory cooperation "beyond the border," and with authority that goes beyond existing decision-making mechanisms in international law. These bodies could end up bypassing member state parliaments in ways which could run afoul of domestic constitutions, notably in Germany. Grants of discretionary power to such committees to solve problems and fill gaps left in this agreement could create legitimacy problems and a need to reconcile these committees with domestic laws and constitutions. Stern examines key court decisions, based on the German constitution, which pose potential challenges for CETA and discusses proposed solutions to balance efficient implementation of the deal with democratic legitimacy.

Wolfgang Weiß (German University of Administrative Sciences Speyer) argues in "Implementing CETA in the EU: Challenges for Democracy and Executive – Legislative Balance" that balance is complicated due to the limited role of the European Parliament (EP) in the treaty bodies' decision-making. The fact that joint committees that have binding decision-making competences to facilitate the implementation of CETA means they are involved in substantial decision-making power on issues and values, raising questions of political legitimacy. Despite the change in roles after Lisbon, the European Parliament exercises "very limited control over FTAS treaty bodies' decision-making." The committees go beyond "technical-administrative matters" to cover "fundamental issues." Structures such as the

ICS, committees for product standards, privacy protection, business secrets all delegate fundamental functions to external bodies not subject to normal democratic decisions making at the member-state level and only indirectly via the European Council. Weiß argues that this exercise of public powers takes place without sufficient parliamentary involvement and control. The increase of executive powers in rulemaking and treaty amendment exercised by CETA committees needs to be balanced against democratic legitimacy. This requires extended supervisory mechanisms, as proposed by the author, in favour of the parliament in the implementation and operation of trade agreements.

Part 2 focuses on CETA's implications for the regulatory process. Pia Acconci (University of Teramo) discusses "The Connection between the 'Right to Regulate' and 'Regulatory Cooperation' within the CETA, as a Possible Tool for the Prevention of Conflict of Interests." CETA is an ambitious agreement which offers companies new opportunities in trade and investment while safeguarding their respective standards of protection for the environmental, health, food, safety, labour, and consumers. To ensure that advanced competitor states do not use the investment and regulatory provisions of the deal to impinge on national policies in areas such as environment, public health, and/or cultural heritage (so-called legitimate public objectives), CETA includes a "right to regulate" provision similar to other EU treaties, which is meant to balance provisions on "regulatory cooperation" and to address differences in regulatory and technical standards and in protected values, to ensure these were not acting as "barriers" to the freedom of investment and trade. The balancing act between these provisions will prove challenging as legitimate regulatory objectives needed to be reconciled with the pursuit of regulatory convergence to facilitate economic objectives.

Mark Camilleri (Canada-EU Trade and Investment Association) discusses "Regulatory Cooperation under CETA: Facing Up to the 'Gorilla in the Room.'" He outlines the role of regulation in trade including its costs and provides an overview of regulatory cooperation under CETA with its "three novel aspects: mutual recognition of professional qualifications, the chapter on regulatory cooperation, and the overall IRC [international regulatory cooperation] architecture of CETA." He considers how CETA is working to date and calls for more effort "to ensure that regulatory cooperation" is being done in a coordinated, efficient, and transparent manner so it "can be better informed and understood by stakeholders, especially businesses and SMES." He advocates creation of a secretariat to coordinate this process and ensure that the stakeholders are adequately consulted.

Charell van Rooy (Cardiff University) talks about "A Cautionary Tale of Regulatory Cooperation in CETA: Executive Expertise and the Influence of Foreign Governments in Domestic Regulatory Processes." She discusses how CETA's wide-ranging regulatory cooperation provisions could impact democracy negatively by giving foreign governments and interests input into domestic policy decisions. Complex regulatory cooperation measures promote potential convergence between the two parties' regulatory frameworks. While regulatory cooperation activities are "essentially procedural and voluntary," provisions for sharing information and consultation on proposed regulations could necessitate consideration of the other party's positions in advance, requiring "the EU and Canada to discuss possible regulatory measures before proposing them to their respective bodies responsible for approving draft regulatory measures." This would have potentially far-reaching implications for policymaking to the extent that "national democratic processes might need protection from the future of regulatory cooperation."

Part 3 focuses on public procurement. Saul Schwartz (Carleton University) and Elizabeth Schwartz (Memorial University of Newfoundland and Labrador) ask "Is CETA a Major Threat to Municipal Autonomy?" During the negotiation phase, several Canadian municipalities passed resolutions opposing CETA for fear that its procurement provisions would limit the potential for local preferences designed for policy goals such as employment creation and sustainability. Particular concern was expressed about control of major contracts for public infrastructure and public services and prohibitions on preferences for local workers or firms. Their research finds that CETA's procurement provisions are unlikely to have significant constraining effects on municipal contracting systems. European firms have already been bidders on major projects and the negative list approach already exempts important public services from the agreement. While provisions preventing renationalization of public services once privatized are of concern, the officials interviewed did not consider this an imminent or significant threat in the near future. Thresholds for eligible contracts also will protect small local businesses from exposure to competitive bids form EU firms. Overall they conclude that CETA will not seriously limit Canadian municipal autonomy.

Agnès Ruffat and Patrick Leblond (University of Ottawa) discuss "Public Procurement under CETA's Chapter 19" with a focus on why barriers to procurement bids are so difficult to remove. They outline the provisions of the CETA chapter, which is designed to promote access to EU-Canada public procurement markets, without discrimination against firms from the other party (above certain contract thresholds), extension of procurement rights to the provincial, territorial and municipal levels, and agreement to create an SPA similar to what already exists in the EU, to increase transparency about opportunities for firms. But the annexes to the agreement present certain restrictions, and the CETA has weak institutional enforcement mechanisms to protect against discrimination, especially as the ISDS is not yet in place. The federal government in Canada can monitor but not sanction provinces for noncompliance as provincial and municipal procurement are outside Ottawa's constitutional purview. Notably procurement access for Canadian firms were hindered by "higher transaction costs that SMEs face relative to larger, multinational firms in monitoring the issuance of tenders and putting together competitive bids." Barriers persist after CETA's provisional implementation and the authors suggest solutions, including integrated public procurement support programs for SMEs.

Part 4 considers the still-uncertain ISDS area of CETA. David A. Gantz (University of Arizona) compares the different character of "Canada's Approaches to Investor-State Dispute Settlement: Addressing Divergencies among CETA, USMCA, CPTPP, and the Canada-China FIPA." In these agreements, Canadas ISDS and foreign investment rules significantly diverge. The Comprehensive and Progressive Agreement for Trans-Pacific Partnership (CPTPP) incorporates traditional ISDS using ad hoc arbitration under International Centre for Settlement of Investment Disputes (ICSID) or United Nations Commission on International Trade Law (UNCITRAL) rules. While still subject to member state ratifications, CETA Chapter 8 embodies the first effort by the EU to promulgate its investment "court"/appellate body system, substituting a standing investment court for more traditional arbitration. In the US-Mexico-Canada Agreement (USMCA), the United States and Canada have agreed to eliminate ISDS entirely after a three-year transition period, leaving it in place for bilateral US-Mexico complaints. The future implications for this "inconsistent" Canadian approach are explored, including the contribution to EU's efforts to conclude a broad-based multilateral agreement, or possible abandonment of ISDS altogether (given Canada's strong domestic legal processes). The potential for Canada to face diplomatic pressure from its larger EU and US trade partners in absence of a regularized ISDS may also increase.

Elizabeth Whitsitt (University of Calgary) considers the question "CETA Investor-State Dispute Settlement: Will Reform Enhance Legitimacy?" Her chapter discusses the "ISDS legitimacy crisis." Civil society has challenged the ad hoc ISDS system in which private arbitration firms make final and binding awards with no public input. The process produces inconsistent decisions with a lack of binding precedents and one-sided decisions, often pro-investor, with no right of appeal. This increased uncertainty for governments and promoted "regulatory chill," whereby legitimate public policy goals might be set aside to avoid potential ISDS claims. In response to political pressures, the EU proposed, and Canada accepted the ICS to replace ad hoc arbitrators with permanent judges and provide greater transparency and an appellate process, with ultimate recourse to political intervention via the CETA Joint Committee. The effectiveness of the new system in addressing various normative and sociological legitimacy claims remains to be seen once it is implemented, though she suggests reasons for concern that using the ICS may not solve ISDS's "legitimacy crisis."

Part 5 considers the environment, energy, and labour provisions of CETA. Aakriti Bhardwaj (University of Nottingham) investigates "Collaborative Integration for Climate Change: Evaluating CETA's Scope." She analyzes CETA in context of the WTO trading system and multilateral environmental agreements. CETA's Trade and Environment chapter and the recommendation on trade, climate action, and the Paris Agreement by CETA Joint Committee are "two pillars" to advance climate-resilient trade through the agreement. Concerns expressed by civil society and analysts about the impact of investment provisions on environmental commitments requires careful implementation, so that action plans in the sustainability chapters work effectively. Bhardwaj proposes that the public-private role in the implementation of CETA's climate action commitments should be looked at from the perspective of "collaborative integration" so that government and corporate actors progress on the action plan and "channel investment provisions toward climate change commitments." CETA is still in the initial stages of implementation insofar as its climate action provisions are concerned. Bhardwaj examines how collaborative integration may be applied in four key areas: technology, ecolabelling, forest products, and raw materials trade.

Emmanuelle Santoire (École Normale Supérieure of Lyon) addresses a critical subset of the environment file on the "The Effects of CETA on Energy Systems in Canada: Insights from a Critical Integrated Approach." Despite its importance in bilateral commerce, CETA does not explicitly address energy trade and treats it like any commodity product. In fact, the lack of explicit reference might be considered "strategic" given the difficulty in sidestepping the EU Fuel Quality Directive respecting Canada's heavy oil supplies. A textual analysis of the agreement reveals that it includes many implicit elements which affect energy, including many reservations respecting this commodity. An energy chapter was described as "unnecessary" by several interviewees despite its implications for sustainability. Drawing on a two-year investigation led in different parts of Canada (Ontario, Quebec, Alberta) and both quantitative (text analysis) and qualitative (thirty-one semi-structured interviews), this chapter develops an original geo-legal perspective and uses this to demonstrate why the definitions of energy provided in CETA, and the influence on the scaling of energy responsibilities and governance should be carefully assessed if CETA is to be considered a template for future international negotiations. Santoire formulates recommendations for the development of integrated protocols on energy in trade agreements and seeks a transferable model to encourage further energy and environmental research within trade law.

Finally, Isabella Mancini (City Law School) outlines her research on "Taming Regulatory Cooperation for the Protection of Labour Rights: The Case of CETA." Her case study involves the interplay between regulatory cooperation and fundamental labour rights. She examines the potential use of regulatory provisions to promote human rights through the role given to civil society actors in regulatory cooperation mechanisms and the extent to which they voice labour rights concerns as regulatory cooperation is pursued. She addresses the issues for labour rights in light of the EU's move toward "deep integration" in scope and levels of institutionalization in trade and economic agreements. This deepening creates potential issues involving fundamental human rights as these are affected by key chapters aimed at deepening integration. The chapter explores the place of labour rights in regulatory cooperation and provides an empirical account of the role of civil society actors in deliberations on labour rights in the implementation stage of CETA. The chapter suggests that regulatory cooperation under CETA should be used as a platform, by the EU and Canada, including civil society on both sides, to exchange views and table proposals on matters pertaining to trade and labour rights.

These chapters represent a compilation of impressive original studies on CETA's implications and early implementation. They do not encompass the full scope of this very complicated agreement – high-profile areas such as agri-food, pharmaceuticals, and intellectual property are not addressed here, though they are of vital importance in assessing the overall import and impact of CETA. These studies were also conducted before the onset of the COVID-19 pandemic which complicated the efforts to assemble the whole work and introduced challenges to the EU-Canada relationship. Nonetheless they constitute reflective expert assessments of the wide range of complex implementation challenges and tasks as specifics are worked out collaboratively in new institutions such as the committee structures, the joint interpretative instrument, and, as ratification advances, the ICS. They are illustrative of the detailed empirical and theoretical investigations awaiting academic and policy specialists as this complicated agreement comes to fruition in stages over the next years. Significant elements of the agreement, notably the innovative ICS, remain to be implemented pending member state assent. CETA's eventual impacts, and the opportunities and challenges these will produce, remain untested and will be an important field for analysis for some time to come.

NOTE

1 Respective private interviews with the author.

REFERENCES

Bollen, Yelter, Ferdi De Ville, and Niels Gheyle. 2016. "From Nada to Namur: National Parliaments' Involvement in Trade Politics, The Case of Belgium." Paper presented at the State of the Federation Conference, University of Ghent, 20 Decemeber 2016. https://biblio.ugent.be/publication/8506662/file/8506676.pdf.

Canada-European Union Comprehensive Economic and Trade Agreement (CETA). 2016. Accessed 21 July 2020. https://www.international.gc.ca/trade-commerce/trade-agreements-accords-commerciaux/agr-acc/ceta-aecg/text-texte/toc-tdm.aspx?lang=eng.

European Commission. 2014. "Letter to National Parliament Representatives." Accessed 9 March 2021. http://www.ipex.eu/IPEXL-WEB/dossier/files/download/082dbcc54b222e18014b6da663ed5531.do.

– 2020. "Treaties and Agreements Database: Comprehensive Economic and Trade Agreement (CETA) between Canada, of the One Part, and the European Union and its Member States, of the Other Part." Accessed 9 March 2021. https://www.consilium.europa.eu/en/documents-publications/treaties-agreements/agreement/?id=2016017.

Finbow, Robert. 2019. *Implementing CETA: A Preliminary Report.* Ottawa: EU-Canada Network. https://carleton.ca/canadaeurope/wp-content/uploads/Robert-Finbow-Implementing-CETA-A-Preliminary-Report-Policy-Brief-August-2019.pdf.

Gatti, Mauro, and Pietro Manzini. 2012. "External Representation of the European Union in the Conclusion of International Agreements." *Common Market Law Review* 49, no. 5: 1703–34.

Government of Canada. 2017a. "Canada-European Union
    Comprehensive Economic and Trade Agreement – Canadian
    Statement on Implementation." Accessed 9 March 2021. http://
    www.international.gc.ca/trade-commerce/trade-agreements-
    accords-commerciaux/agr-acc/ceta-aecg/canadian_statement-
    enonce_canadien.aspx?lang=eng.
– 2017b. "Implementation of the Canada-European Union
    Comprehensive Economic and Trade Agreement (CETA) Customs
    Notice 17–30." Accessed 9 March 2021. https://www.cbsa-asfc.gc.ca/
    publications/cn-ad/cn17-30-eng.html.
– 2020. "Canada-European Union Comprehensive Economic and
    Trade Agreement (CETA) - Governance and Committees." Accessed
    9 March 2021. https://www.international.gc.ca/trade-commerce/
    trade-agreements-accords-commerciaux/agr-acc/ceta-aecg/
    committees-comites.aspx?lang=eng.
Official Journal of the EU. 2017. "Notice Concerning the Provisional
    Application of the Comprehensive Economic and Trade Agreement
    (CETA)." Accessed 9 March 2021. http://eur-lex.europa.eu/legal-
    content/EN/TXT/?uri=uriserv:OJ.L_.2017.238.01.0009.01.
    ENG&toc=OJ:L:2017:238:TOC.
Tweede Kamer der Staten-Generaal. 2014. "Letter in the Framework
    of the Political Dialogue: The Role of National Parliaments in Free
    Trade Agreements." Accessed 9 March 2021. http://www.ipex.eu/
    IPEXL-WEB/dossier/files/download/082dbcc54b222e18014b6d9f06
    9154f8.do.

PART ONE

Negotiation and Governance Complexities

2

Legitimization and Control of Committee Bodies in EU Free Trade Agreements

Felix Stern

INTRODUCTION

CETA Committee Bodies as a Legal Problem

Because of the deadlock in the Doha Round since 2006, the European Union (EU) has been pursuing the negotiation and conclusion of a new generation of comprehensive bilateral free trade agreements (FTAS) (European Commission 2006). This new class of treaties, which includes the Comprehensive Economic and Trade Agreement (CETA 2016) with Canada, combines novel regulatory cooperation frameworks with the delegation of multiple tasks to entire systems of international treaty bodies. The bodies set up in this way are endowed with a scope of authority that goes far beyond the decision-making mechanisms which are already known under international law (Weiß 2018a, 533). The EU is a contracting party to the trade agreements of this new type.[1] Taking the case law of the European Court of Justice (ECJ) into account, it is argued that the decisions of the committees described above may become part of European law via Art. 216(2) of the Treaty on the Functioning of the European Union (TFEU) (2012) and can thus have legal effects within the legal systems of the EU member states, even though a direct application within the national legal systems is excluded by Art. 30.6 of CETA (Weiß 2018a, 542; Wessel and Blockmans 2014, 20).[2] The EU's participation in international bodies in which it is entitled to vote is, in most cases, governed by Art. 218(9) of TFEU (Nettesheim 2017; Weiß 2018a). In this process, a common EU position is to be established in advance in the council of ministers. Under Arts 218(9) and 218(10) of TFEU, the European Parliament is only informed if the common EU position is on a subject matter in which the parliament would be actively involved in cases of internal law-making (Weiß 2016a, 288; 2018a). Furthermore, it is largely unclear how the EU member states will participate in the CETA bodies (Krajewski 2017; Weiß 2018a). For these reasons, there are far-reaching reservations regarding the democratic legitimacy of these committees. In the Federal Republic of Germany, several proceedings have been considered by the federal constitutional court.[3]

Committee Bodies and the Principal-Agent Approach

This research aims to critically take up the jurisprudential discussion unfolding on the CETA committee system and use a principal-agent model in analyzing that issue. The aim is to functionally distinguish the delegation of tasks to the committees in CETA, and to examine their different need for democratic control under European law and the German constitution.

The basic idea of a principal-agent approach is to break complex social (or political) systems down into hierarchical relationships between two actors. A principal-agent model consists of the binary hierarchies between a principal and an agent entrusted with a task. It is assumed here that the behaviour of all actors is based on their preferences and interests, because they strictly pursue their given goals in a way that maximizes their own benefit (Delreux and Adriaensen 2018). This makes the principal-agent theory a part of the school of rational choice institutionalism (Hall and Taylor 1996, 944–5).

A principal-agent model necessarily consists of individual acts of delegation, each of which places two actors in a hierarchical and mutual relationship to each other (ibid.). The principal(-to-be), as a utility maximizer, faces the problem of having to perform all tasks necessary to maximize their utility with limited resources at disposal. If they succeed in delegating individual or bundled tasks to an agent, they can achieve a higher benefit with the same amount of resources (Damro 2007, 885).

A delegation in this sense is a conditional assignment of the power to act in place of the delegating one. It is revocable in principle. It makes the delegating actor conceptually the principal and the actor entrusted with powers through the delegation the agent (Hawkins et al. 2006). For the delegation to be useful, the agent must be given discretion in the exercise of their powers. If the principals were to dictate or supervise every decision taken by the agent, they would not need the delegation and would carry out the associated tasks themselves (ibid.). A very appropriate illustration of this is a comparison by David Epstein and Sharyn O'Halloran (2009, 7, 34) between the delegation of legislative powers by the US

Congress and the entrepreneurial decision as to whether a required good should be produced or purchased (a "make-or-buy" decision). The delegation will regularly be limited in terms of time or subject matter. The act of delegation is, therefore, a reciprocal, binary, and hierarchical relationship between a principal and an agent. In terms of theory, it is irrelevant whether the delegation act is formalized in any way or whether it is an express agreement (Delreux and Adriaensen 2017; Hawkins et al. 2006; Niemann and Huigens 2011). The agent does not have to exist as an entity before the act of delegation is established. The act of delegation can also create the agent. The principal delegates an authority to the agent, and only the principal retains the right to take the delegated authority back (Delreux and Adriaensen 2018; Hawkins et al. 2006).

This chapter serves to present an early stage of development of the conducted principal-agent research. In the next section, the theoretical approach to the problem is presented from the perspective of German constitutional law. Afterwards, the different fields of activity will be dealt with, with a clear focus on the reduction of transaction costs. This will be followed by a brief overview on planned further research in the final section.

CHAINS OF DELEGATION: FROM THE GERMAN BUNDESTAG TO THE CETA COMMITTEE BODIES

When analyzing complex political systems, such as the EU, or the relationship between international institutions and their member states, it is useful, if not essential, to consider several binary principal-agent relationships in succession as a chain of delegation. The individual links in the chain fulfill the function of an agent in one direction and that of a principal in the other (Delreux and Adriaensen 2017; Bergman, Müller, and Strøm 2000).[4] If a delegation chain is to be tracked and described, it must be clarified which actors or instances are involved and identify the legal basis for determining the respective act of delegation (Delreux and Adriaensen 2018).[5]

Searching for the Ultimate Principal

If the entire course of a delegation chain with an international treaty body at the end is to be examined, the sovereigns of the participating states and the EU are at the beginning of the delegation chain as "ultimate principals" (Nielson and Tierney 2003). Since the study is conducted from the perspective of the Federal Republic of Germany, the German federal structure must also be taken into account. However, this aspect would exceed the scope of this chapter. Therefore it is reduced to brief references in the relevant places. For the purposes of this study, the search for the highest-ranking principals is based on the democratically legitimized legislative (state) organs of the EU and the Federal Republic of Germany as a member state. The Bundestag,[6] the parliaments of the federal states of Germany (Länder), and the European Parliament are themselves "only" the collectively composed representation of the respective electorate and thus their agent as well. In the case of the Federal Republic of Germany, however, the Bundestag is the central authority that legitimizes the exercise of sovereignty. A direct-democratic consultation of the people themselves is not excluded but remains of subordinate importance given the almost complete absence of direct-democratic elements in the German constitution (Grzeszick 2020, "Art. 20 GG" [Grundgesetz], paras 111–5). This dominance of the Bundestag means that the will of the sovereign can (almost) only be expressed through this one channel. For this reason, the present principal-agent model, at least as far as the ultimate principal of the Federal Republic of Germany is concerned, is linked to the Bundestag as a state organ. With regard to the European Parliament and the parliaments of the German federal states, this approach will also be considered in the further course of the project and needs further investigation. For this chapter, the author focuses on the chain of delegations starting from the German Bundestag.

Starting from the German Bundestag

The Bundestag is elected by the people in accordance with Art. 38 of GG.[7] In turn it elects the federal chancellor in accordance with Art. 63 of GG.

According to Art. 64(1) of GG, the federal chancellor is responsible for the composition of the federal government. The federal government represents the Federal Republic of Germany in the EU executive bodies, namely the Council (Scholz 2020, paras 133–6), in which the formation of the Union's decision-making in the affairs of the CETA treaty bodies takes place. The Bundestag retains the tasks of monitoring the federal government and the ratification of international treaties following Arts 59(2) and 24(1) of GG or, in the case of European primary law, Art. 23(1) of GG.

The constitutional assessment of the delegation of the powers (mentioned earlier) to the federal government also depends on whether matters are affected whose regulation has already been transferred to the EU or not.[8] However, it is highly controversial whether the conclusion of CETA is covered by the current version of the European treaties, the Treaty on

European Union (TEU), and the TFEU (Grzeszick 2016, 1760–1; 2017, 92–3), or whether the conclusion of this new type of FTA – in particular, due to the establishment of international committee systems – amounts to a change in primary law within the meaning of Art. 23(1) of GG (Nettesheim 2017; Weiß 2016a, 290; 2016b, 35; 2017). As far as subject matters, which have remained with the EU member states are concerned, there is no agreement as to whether the committee competences contained in the CETA are to be measured against Art. 23(1) of GG, or, as with other international treaties, also against Art. 59(2) and/or Art. 24(1).[9] In any case, insofar as an FTA covers subject matters that have already been transferred to the Union by the EU member states, Arts 23(2) and 23(3) of GG are the relevant regime under German constitutional law. These provisions presuppose that the federal government exercises the power of representation of the Federal Republic of Germany in the EU executive bodies. Besides, Arts 23(2) and 23(3) of GG and the "Law on the Cooperation between the federal government and the German Bundestag in matters of the European Union" (EUZBBG) contain provisions which specify the delegation made by the Bundestag.

On the level of European law, the representation of the Federal Republic of Germany (as well as of the other member states) by its governments in the Council is further elaborated. The TEU expressly requires the power of delegated members of the government to represent the respective member state bindingly, including the exercise of voting rights. The subsequent procedure under Art. 218(9) of TFEU was also incorporated into the national law of the Federal Republic of Germany. With the ratification of the Lisbon Treaty, the Bundestag (and the Bundesrat) delegated the representation of the federal republic within the bodies of the EU to the federal government or confirmed the delegation that had already taken place. At this point, it is necessary to return to the already-mentioned point of contention whether the conclusion of CETA is covered by the current version of the European treaties (TEU and TFEU), or whether the conclusion of the agreement amounts to an amendment of primary law within the meaning of Art. 23(1) of GG.

From the point of view of a principal-agent investigation, the federal government becomes an agent of the Bundestag with the ratification of an international agreement such as CETA, which is including procedures of intergovernmental decision-making. This delegation is pre-designed by the regulations mentioned above. On behalf of the Bundestag, the federal government represents the federal republic in EU matters and in the EU's executive bodies, in particular in the Council in the procedure laid down in Art. 218(9) of TFEU. The conditions for the delegated representation of the Federal Republic of Germany in EU matters is referred to in constitutional law and the jurisprudence of the federal constitutional court as "integration competence," which is also attributed to external affairs. Within this framework, the federal government is granted a far-reaching prerogative. As already noted, the Bundestag remains responsible only for the democratic control and legitimization of the federal government. This is laid down in Arts 23(2) and 23(3) of GG and EUZBBG (Scholz 2020, paras 133–4). Within this statutory context the principal (the Bundestag) only retains the control of the agent (the federal government) and the possibility in principle of future retrieval of the delegated tasks.

The Council of the European Union is at the heart of cooperation between the governments of the member states at EU level. It is the body in which, according to Art. 218(9) of TFEU, the common EU position to be introduced in the CETA Joint Committee is formally adopted. Common EU positions, in that sense, are drafted by the EU Commission. In principle, the federal government sends one of its members to the meetings of the individual Council formations following Art. 16(2) of TEU. Since the Federal Republic of Germany has adopted this regulation into its own law by ratification, the secondment of a federal minister or one of the other relevant persons is to be seen as an act of delegation. The federal government, for its part, becomes the principal and the German representative in the Council its agent. The Council itself thus becomes a collective agent of the national governments, which are not to be unified in their entirety but rather a collection of multiple principals. According to Art. 218(9) of TFEU, it is empowered to adopt the positions prepared by the EU Commission.

The Council's decision to be adopted under Art. 218(9) of TFEU establishes the positions to be adopted on behalf of the EU. Corresponding decisions are regularly addressed to the EU Commission (see Council of the European Union 2018, Art. 2 for example) and instruct it to represent the given position in the specific individual case. This makes the Commission an agent of the Council, for which it will have to represent the position adopted in the relevant committee meetings. The Council is to be characterized as a collective principal. The Commission will regularly decide on the more precise composition of the EU delegation and delegate the representation of the EU position to it accordingly. In particular, the CETA contains only a few personnel requirements for the composition of secondments to the committees.

LOGIC OF DELEGATION

Transaction Costs, Credible Commitment, and Blame-Shifting

Strictly benefit-maximizing actors will only delegate tasks if they expect to gain an advantage from doing so. Just as an investment is expected to generate a profit, an expected problem- solving potential precedes a possible delegation of tasks to an agent (Keohane 1984, 80; Pollack 1997, 102). Majone (2001, 103), when discussing a fundamental distinction between reasons for the delegation of tasks, wrote "there is no single logic of delegation." This still has a decisive influence on principal-agent theory today. While early contributions to the principal-agent approach had mainly concentrated on the reduction of transaction costs through a delegation, Majone (2001) decisively referred to an additional problem: the credible commitment. Another current is examining the question of the extent to which the delegation of tasks can also serve to blur the consequences of politically unpopular decisions ("regulatory lottery"), to pass on the responsibility for unpopular policies and, in this way, to keep them away in particular from the directly elected representatives of the legislatures ("protection racket").[10] "Blame-shifting" and blame avoidance" are also common terms for this (Mortensen 2016; Thatcher and Stone Sweet 2002, 4).

In the following section, the designed principal-agent model will be further elaborated with a focus on reducing transaction costs.

Focus: Transaction Costs

Epstein and O'Halloran (2009) describe transaction costs as a quantitative deviation from a Coasian system. This concept, which goes back to Coase (1960), consists of a theoretical test arrangement in which agreements can be made and implemented without any conceivable loss in terms of time, financial, or other resources. This presupposes in particular that all actors have the same level of information at all times and adhere to agreements made under all circumstances (Epstein and O'Halloran 2009, 35–6; North 1993, 18). The theory of comparative cost advantages by Ricardo (1817), as the most prominent plea for an international division of labour between the world's economies, would function perfectly under this premise.

The transfer of the concept of transaction costs to political processes is problematic especially with regard to the quantification of such costs (Epstein and O'Halloran 2009). On the other hand, there are similarities between a contract under private law that can be characterized as an act of delegation and sovereign delegation of authority. For instance, a sovereign delegation of authority (e.g., by law, administrative act, or other sovereign instrument) determines which task is assigned to the recipient of the delegation and what obligations this entails. The rights and obligations of the recipient of the delegation, as well as those of the delegating body within the scope of the delegating act, are determined. The intervention of authorized third parties (such as a court) to enforce the contained requirements is also regulated. In addition, a body endowed with sovereignty also faces the question of when to outsource tasks instead of performing them itself, just as a private company has to decide when to buy a (preliminary) product or service on the market instead of self-sufficing through its own (production) capacities (Epstein and O'Halloran 2009, 45–6).

In the following discussion, two categories of such delegable tasks are presented against the background of CETA. These are the facilitation of cooperation in case of incomplete information and the handling of incomplete contracts. For illustration, several (not exhaustive) examples for both categories are taken from CETA. Further types of tasks, which will be examined in more detail in the further course of the project, are, in particular, the accomplishment of an ordered agenda setting and the processing of highly complex subject matters (Pollack 1997, 2003).

Cooperation and Incomplete Information

As described earlier, actors defined as strict benefit maximizers often face the reality that they can achieve a higher benefit through cooperation in the medium to long term than if everyone "struggles" alone. The establishment of a medium- to long-term advantageous free trade for all participants, however, often threatens to be sabotaged by participants who want to gain an even bigger advantage at the expense of their partners by short-term, and possibly concealed, defection. Besides, principals who have a more or less large intersection of shared interests may be unable to communicate about the same. In game theory those *cooperation* and *coordination* problems are illustrated with different thought experiments, in particular the "Prisoner's Dilemma," the "Battle of the Sexes," and the "Chicken Game," which are transferable to international trade relations (Hawkins et al. 2006; Kuhn 2019; Martin 1992). In a situation where it makes sense to cooperate, but the necessary exchange of information is complicated or requires a common intermediate, the most important thing an agent should achieve is to clarify the preferences and especially the behaviour of the different actors (the later principals) (Pollack 2003, 21–2).[11]

Examples for committee competences to monitor the implementation of contracts can be found both as regards the CETA Joint Committee and the special committees subordinate to it. The Joint Management Committee for Sanitary and Phytosanitary Measures (SPS), in particular, has many tasks in its area of responsibility to ensure mutual information between the contracting parties. According to Art. 5.14(2)(e) of CETA, the committee supervises the implementation and the execution of amendments to the appendices to Chapter 5 (SPS) of CETA. In Art. 5.14(2)(f), the body is assigned the task to offer a permanent platform on which information about the regulatory system of each contracting party (including the scientific and risk assessment bases for SPS measures) can be exchanged.

The Joint Committee on Mutual Recognition of Professional Qualifications ("MRA Committee") is also concerned with several competencies to promote the flow of information within its area of responsibility. According to Art. 11.5(d) of CETA, the committee has the task of facilitating the exchange of information on the legal situation and policy regarding standards and criteria for the approval, accreditation, or certification of regulated professions. Art. 11.5(e) of CETA gives the MRA Committee the task of making information on the negotiation and implementation of mutual recognition agreements publicly available. According to Art. 11.5(f) of CETA, the MRA Committee has to inform the CETA Joint Committee about progress in the negotiation and implementation of such agreements.

CETA as an Incomplete Contract

The problem of incomplete contracts arises in (almost) every conceivable subject of a jurisprudential investigation. In economics and political science, an incomplete contract is understood as an agreement that does not take into account all eventualities that may occur in the future, but rather establishes a framework for the future relations between the parties (Milgrom and Roberts 1990, 62). This includes, in particular, agreements on general expectations as well as decision-making and conflict resolution processes. In order to facilitate the implementation of such an agreement, corresponding tasks can be delegated, thus creating a principal-agent relationship (Kassim and Menon 2003; Pollack 1997). When implementing an incomplete contract, the agents involved are often given the task of concretizing the content of the agreements within the given framework.[12]

In this sense, the law of European integration, from the connecting points in the GG to European primary law to the most specialized areas of European law, is also shaped by the problem of dealing with what is called an "incomplete contract" in economics and political science. The same applies to agreements (co-)concluded by the Union. Especially if considerable progress toward integration is intended, a large part of the developments covered by the agreement in its application over decades cannot be regulated in detail.[13] As shown above, in the case of incomplete agreements there is a particular need for ongoing interpretation, supplementation, and settlement of disputes in connection with the agreement reached. It is also noticeable that, in addition to corresponding competences for the implementation and adaptation of the content of the agreement, such competences are also transferred for the further concretization or even reform of the underlying institutional regulations.

Subsequent changes to the agreements made under CETA are made possible by Art. 2.4(4). Here it is stipulated that the CETA Joint Committee may decide on an acceleration of the tariff dismantling if the contracting parties have agreed on this beforehand. This competence, therefore, makes it possible to accelerate the tariff dismantling provided for in Appendix 2-A of CETA retrospectively, if this appears to make sense after the conclusion of the agreement.

The CETA Joint Committee can subsequently add geographical indications to be protected to the list contained in Appendix 20-A, or to delete such indications, as per Art. 20.22 of CETA. This competence serves to subsequently adapt the protection mechanism for geographical indications established by CETA by delegating to the CETA Joint Committee the competence to keep the protection list up to date.

In Arts 4.7(1)(f) and 26.1(5)(c), CETA entrusts the CETA Joint Committee with the task of further developing Chapter 4 of the Agreement with regard to future developments of the World Trade Organization (WTO) law in the field of technical barriers to trade (TBT) – namely, results of the work of the relevant WTO Committee and developments in the field of the TBT agreements.[14] The CETA Joint Committee may, on the recommendation of the Committee on Trade in Goods, amend Chapter 4 accordingly.

The investment protection chapter contains various competences to the CETA Joint Committee for continuous further development. In Art. 8.1 of CETA, the committee is given the task of including further categories of intellectual property in the investment protection chapter that have not yet been considered in CETA. A corresponding extension of the concept of intellectual property would have to be applied in subsequent investor-state dispute settlements (ISDS) by the investment court provided for in the agreement. Art. 8.10(3) of CETA enables the CETA Joint Committee to subsequently extend the standard of conduct of the fair and equitable treatment (FET) of foreign investors. Such a decision would lead to a change in the obligations of the participating states as well as the EU toward foreign investors as provided for in the CETA. In both cases, these are competences for the further development of the investment protection agreements concluded in CETA in the light of future developments which the contracting parties cannot yet overlook at the time the agreement is concluded.

A competence which is already controversial in its scope[15] is provided for in Art. 30.2(2) of CETA. According to this article, the CETA Joint Committee may amend the Protocols and Annexes of the agreement, which are equivalent to the agreement pursuant to Art. 30.1. The provision constitutes a simplified procedure in relation to the general procedure for the amendment of treaties under Art. 30.2(1). Its function is the subsequent completion of the content of the agreement by the CETA Joint Committee as an agent.

The Joint Management Committee for SPS is also given powers to adapt the content of the agreement subsequently. According to Art. 5.11(3) of CETA, it has the task to adapt the procedures for the exchange of information in SPS matters provided for in Arts 5.11(1) and 5.11 (2). According to Art. 5.14(2)(d), future changes of the appendices of the SPS chapter are assigned to it (according to Art. 30.1 of CETA, equated to the agreement). These competences also serve the subsequent completion of the content of the agreement.

In addition to the competences to interpret and adapt the content of the agreement, CETA also contains committee competences to change the working methods of the committees themselves or of other bodies established by it. In both categories, the possible intensity of the competences conferred differs and ranges from the precise internal procedure to comprehensive institutional reforms.

So the CETA includes certain powers of the committees to issue rules of procedure or rules of procedure for the respective body itself. Art. 26.1(4) (d) of CETA provides for such a power for the CETA Joint Committee. Similar competences are provided in Art. 11.5(c) for the MRA Committee, in Art. 5.14(7) for the Joint Management Committee for SPS and in Art. 21.6(4)(a) for the Forum for Regulatory Cooperation.

Competences of the CETA Joint Committee for the further delegation of tasks and even a comprehensive reform of the committee system provided for in CETA are covered under Arts 26.1(5)(a), 26.1(5)(g), and

26.1(5)(h) of CETA. According to Art. 26.1(5)(a) of CETA, the CETA Joint Committee may delegate competences to the other special committees set up under the agreement. According to Art. 26.1(5)(g), the body may amend or take over tasks delegated to its subordinate special committees. The CETA Joint Committee may also dissolve special committees. Art. 26.1(5) (h) of CETA also allows the CETA Joint Committee to establish special committees and bilateral dialogue forums.

Another far-reaching competence for a possible future reform is stipulated under Art. 8.29 of CETA. Here the contracting parties reaffirm their efforts to establish a multilateral investment court with an appeal instance. If such a multilateral ISDS mechanism is set up one day, the CETA Joint Committee has the power to decide to transform the investment protection system provided for in the CETA into the new framework and to adopt appropriate transitional arrangements.

Authorizations for such a far-reaching transformation may be granted by the contracting parties, to the CETA committees, to subsequently make modifications to the committee system that appear necessary or useful, without a formal treaty amendment procedure being adopted. This can also be helpful in resolving any reform blockades in the national political systems of the participating states and in preventing an informal change in the free trade regime established by the agreement that would be much more difficult to control in the medium to long term. Especially if the contracting parties do not have sufficient instruments available to them to restructure a treaty, the introduction of additional agreements in addition to or beyond an agreement (so-called layering) can often be observed in international policy practice. A change in the practical significance of a treaty and the institutions established by it (so-called drift) can also be the consequence if the contracting parties do not (cannot) react adequately to changes in the environment of the treaty (Hanrieder 2014). On the other hand, it is in particular this kind of far-reaching competence that has evoked the criticism and concerns referred to in the beginning of this chapter.

FURTHER RESEARCH:
DELEGATION LOSSES AND CONTROL MECHANISMS

In further analyses, the principal-agent model will be further developed used to evaluate the CETA committee system as it evolves. The federal structure of the Federal Republic of Germany and the role of the European Parliament, which could only be hinted at in this chapter, will be increasingly included in the research. The described categories of delegations will be significantly extended, with a strong focus on the reduction of trans-action costs. Furthermore the risks associated with the delegation of tasks to international contractual bodies will be dealt with. Generally, the efficiency gains to be obtained by the delegation can only be achieved if the agent is granted a certain degree of discretion (Damro 2007). Therefore, the delegation of powers to international treaty bodies entails potentials for agency slack (da Conceicão-Heldt 2013, 24). On the other hand side, it is possible to set up suitable control mechanisms (Delreux and Kerremans 2010; McCubbins and Schwartz 1984; Nielson and Tierney 2003), which are capable of tackling the underlying dilemma of governmental efficiency and democratic legitimacy.

CONCLUSION

This chapter outlined a possible application of the principal-agent approach to the treaty bodies envisaged in CETA. The analysis started with the political system of the Federal Republic of Germany as a member state of the EU. Starting with the electorate of the Federal Republic of Germany as an ultimate principal, a chain of delegation was traced up to the treaty bodies provided for in CETA. On the level of the EU, the simpli-fied procedure for the establishment of common Union positions according to Art. 218(9) of TFEU was the focus of jurisprudential interest.

In a second part, the reasons for delegating tasks to international treaty bodies were outlined. Here, the focus was on the reduction of transaction costs, as they arise in particular from the solution of cooperation and coordination problems, as well as in the implementation of incomplete treaties. For both problem areas, several competencies that are transferred to the committees provided for in CETA were identified as examples. Against the backdrop of the legal debate on the democratic legitimacy of the bodies established by CETA, a number of the competencies transferred to the CETA Joint Committee for the further development of CETA as an incomplete treaty, in particular, were identified as problematic.

NOTES

1 In the case of CETA, this refers to a "mixed agreement" with the EU member states.
2 Before the current wording of Art. 216(2) of TFEU was introduced, compare to Lavranos (2004, 237–8), Martenczuk (2001, 141–63, 161–2), and the ECJ case laws *S. Z. Sevince* v. *Staatssecretaris van Justitie*

(1990, para. 9) and *Hellenic Republic* v. *Commission* (1989, para. 13). As a recent development, see also ECJ (2020) and Advocate General Kokott (2020).

3 The Federal Constitutional Court rejected a number of lawsuits against the provisional application of CETA without a substantial discussion of the committee system (see Federal Constitutional Court 2022).

4 Compare, for example, the concept by Nielsen and Tierney (2003, 249–51).

5 Delreux and Adriaensen (2018) describe the questions about the participants and the content of a transfer of tasks as a necessary precondition for a principal-agent investigation. In the present chapter, the content is determined on the basis of the relevant provisions or agreements for the respective delegation of tasks.

6 The Bundestag is the Chamber of the Parliament of the Federal Republic of Germany, which is elected directly by the voters on the federal level. Besides this there is the Bundesrat, in which the sixteen federal states (Länder) are represented by members of their respective governments (see Art. 51(1) of GG).

7 Constitution of the Federal Republic of Germany, in English literature also known as "Basic Law."

8 See ECJ (2017, para. 276) and Krajewski (2017, 16).

9 Compare on this point of controversy on the one hand: Grzeszick (2016, 2017); Grzeszick and Hettche (2016); and on the other hand: Nettesheim (2017); von Arnauld (2016), and Weiß (2016a, 2017, 2018b).

10 For a critical summary, see Epstein and O'Halloran (2009, 29–33).

11 For an accurate description with theoretical explanation, see Luce and Raiffa (1957, 90–4). On the "Chicken Game," see a well-known exemplification from Russell (1959, 30). See also Poundstone (1992, 198–201) and Hawkins et al. (2006, 15).

12 With the EU institutions as an example, see Pollack (1997).

13 See, in this sense, the judgment of the German Federal Constitutional Court (Bundesverfassungsgericht) (2009, 351–2).

14 Agreement on Technical Barriers to Trade (1980).

15 Compare on this point of controversy Grzeszick (2016, 2017) on the one hand, and Weiß (2016a) on the other.

REFERENCES

Advocate General Kokott. 2020. Opinion C-66/18 of the Advocate General (ECLI:EU:C:2020:172). 5 March.

Agreement on Technical Barriers to Trade. 1980. UNTS 1186, 276. New York: United Nations.

Bergman, Torbjörn, Wolfgang C. Müller, and Kaare Strøm. 2000. "Introduction: Parliamentary Democracy and the Chain of Delegation." *European Journal of Political Research* 56, no. 2: 255–60. https://doi. org/10.1023/A:1007088002419.

CETA (Canada-European Union Comprehensive Economic and Trade Agreement). 2016. Accessed 21 July 2020. https://www.international.gc.ca/ trade-commerce/trade-agreements-accords-commerciaux/agr-acc/ceta-aecg/ text-texte/toc-tdm.aspx?lang=eng.

Coase, Ronald. 1960. "The Problem of Social Cost." *Journal of Law & Economics* 3, no. 1: 1–44.

Council of the European Union. 2018. "Decision (EU) 2018/1062 on the position to be adopted within the CETA Joint Committee established by the Comprehensive Economic and Trade Agreement between Canada and the European Union," OJ L 190/13. Accessed 4 August 2020. http://data. europa.eu/eli/dec/2018/1062/oj.

da Conceicão-Heldt, Eugénia. 2013. "Do Agents 'Run Amok'? A Comparison of Agency Slack in the EU and US Trade Policy in the Doha Round." *Journal of Comparative Policy Analysis* 15, no. 1: 21–36. https://doi.org/10.1080/ 13876988.2012.754152.

Damro, Chad. 2007. "EU Delegation and Agency in International Trade Negotiations: A Cautionary Comparison." *Journal of Common Market Studies* 45, no. 4: 883–903. https://doi.org/10.1111/j.1468-5965.2007. 00752.x.

Delreux, Tom, and Johan Adriaensen. 2017. "Introduction: Use and Limitations of the Principal-Agent Model in Studying the European Union." In *The Principal-Agent Model and the European Union*, edited by Tom Delreux and Johan Adriaensen, 1–34. London: Palgrave Macmillan. https:// doi.org/10.1007/978-3-319-55137-1_1.

– 2018. "Twenty Years of Principal-Agent Research in EU Politics: How to Cope with Complexity?" *European Political Science* 17, no. 2: 258–75. https://doi.org/10.1057/s41304-017-0129-4.

Delreux, Tom, and Bart Kerremans. 2010. "How Agents Weaken Their Principals' Incentives to Control: The Case of EU Negotiators and EU Member States in Multilateral Negotiations." *European Integration* 32, no. 4: 357–74. https://doi.org/10.1080/07036331003797554.

Epstein, David, and Sharyn O'Halloran. 2009. *Delegating Powers: A Transaction Cost Politics Approach to Policy Making under Separate Powers* (online edition). Cambridge: Cambridge University Press.

European Commission. 2006. "Global Europe: Competing in the World." COM(2016) 567 final. Accessed 21 July 2020. https://eur-lex.europa.eu/LexUriServ/LexUriServ.do?uri=COM:2006:0567:FIN:EN:PDF.

European Court of Justice (ECJ). 2017. Opinion 2/15 of the Court (ECLI:EU:C:2017:376). 16 May.

– 2020. Judgment C-66/18 of the Court (ECLI:EU:C:2020:792). 8. October.

Federal Constitutional Court (Bundesverfassungsgericht). 2009. Case 2 BvE 2/08, Judgment (Lisbon Treaty) (ECLI:DE:BVerfG:2009:es20090630. 2bve000208), 30 June.

– 2016. Case 2 BvR 1368/16, Judgment of the Second Senate (ECLI:DE_BVerfG:2016:rs20161013.2bvr136816). 13 October

– 2022. Case 2 BvR 1368/16, Order of the Second Senate. (ECLI:DE:BVerfG:2022:rs20220209.2bvr136816), 9 February.

Grzeszick, Bernd. 2016. "Völkervertragsrecht in der parlamentarischen Demokratie: CETA als Präzedenzfall für die demokratischen Anforderungen an völkerrechtliche Verträge." *Neue Zeitschrift für Verwaltungsrecht* 35, no. 24: 1753–61.

– 2017. "Statement on behalf of the German Bundestag in the proceedings concerning CETA (2 BvR 1368/16, 2 BvR 1444/16, 2 BvR 1482/16, 2 BvR 1823/16, 2 BvR 3/16) before the German Federal Constitutional Court." Accessed 4 August 2020. https://www.mehr-demokratie.de/fileadmin/pdf/2017-09-27_Stellungnahme_von_Prof._Dr._Bernd_Grzeszick_im_Namen_der_Bundesregierung.pdf.

– 2020. "Article 20 GG." In *Grundgesetz-Kommentar* (91st edition) (online edition), edited by Theodor Maunz and Günter Dürig. Munich: C.H. Beck.

Grzeszick, Bernd, and Juliane Hettche. 2016. "Zur Beteiligung des Bundestages an gemischten völkerrechtlichen Abkommen: Internationale Freihandelsabkommen als Herausforderung des deutschen Europa- und Außenverfassungsrechts." *Archiv des öffentlichen Rechts* (141): 225–67.

Hall, Peter A., and Rosemary C.R. Taylor. 1996. "Political Science and the Three New Institutionalisms." *Political Studies* 44, no. 5: 936–57. https://doi.org/10.1111/j.1467-9248.1996.tb00343.x.

Hanrieder, Tine. 2014. "Gradual Change in International Organisations: Agency Theory and Historical Institutionalism." *Politics* 34, no. 4: 324–33. https://doi.org/10.1111/1467-9256.12050.

Hawkins, Darren G., David A. Lake, Daniel L. Nielson, and Michael J. Tierney. 2006. "Delegation Under Anarchy: States, International Organizations, and Principal-Agent Theory." In *Delegation and Agency in International*

Organizations, edited by Darren G. Hawkins, David A. Lake, Daniel L. Nielson, and Michael J. Tierney, 3–38. Cambridge: Cambridge University Press.

Hellenic Republic v. Commission of the European Communities. 1989. CJEU Case 30/88, Judgment of the Court (ECLI:EU:C:1989:422), 14 November.

Kassim, Hussein, and Anand Menon. 2003. "The Principal-Agent Approach and the Study of the European Union: Promise Unfulfilled?" *Journal of European Public Policy* 10, no. 1: 121–39. https://doi.org/10.1080/1350176032000046976.

Keohane, Robert O. 1984. *After Hegemony*. Princeton: Princeton University Press.

Krajewski, Markus. 2017. "Statement on behalf of the faction Bündnis 90/Die Grünen in the German Bundestag in the proceedings concerning CETA (2 BvR 1368/16, 2 BvR 1444/16, 2 BvR 1482/16, 2 BvR 1823/16, 2 BvR 3/16) before the German Federal Constitutional Court," 124–161. Accessed 4 August 2020. https://www.mehr-demokratie.de/fileadmin/pdf/2017-09-27_Stellungnahme_von_Prof._Dr._Bernd_Grzeszick_im_Namen_der_Bundesregierung.pdf.

Kuhn, Steven. 2019. "Prisoner's Dilemma." In *The Stanford Encyclopedia of Philosophy* (Summer 2019 Edition), edited by Edward N. Zalta. Stanford: Stanford University. https://plato.stanford.edu/archives/sum2019/entries/prisoner-dilemma/.

Lavranos, Nikolaos. 2004. *Decisions of International Organizations in the European and Domestic Legal Orders of Selected EU Member States*. Groningen: Europa Law Publishing.

Luce, R. Duncan, and Howard Raiffa. 1957. *Games and Decisions: Introduction and Critical Survey*. New York: Wiley.

Majone, Giandomenico. 2001. "Two Logics of Delegation: Agency and Fiduciary Relations in EU Governance." *European Union Politics* 2, no. 1: 103–22. https://doi.org/10.1177/1465116501002001005.

Martenczuk, Bernd. 2001. "Decisions of Bodies Established by International Agreements and the Community Legal Order." In *The EU and the International Legal Order*, edited by Vincent Kronenberger, 141–63. Den Haag: T.M.C. Asser Press.

Martin, Lisa L. 1992. "Interests, Power, and Multilateralism." *International Organization* 46, no. 4: 765–92. https://www.jstor.org/stable/2706874.

McCubbins, Mathew, and Thomas Schwartz. 1984. "Congressional Oversight Overlooked: Police Patrols versus Fire Alarms." *American Journal of Political Science* 28, no. 1: 165–79. https://doi.org/10.2307/2110792.

Milgrom, Paul and John Roberts. 1990. "Bargaining Costs, Influence Costs, and the Organization of Economic Activity." In *Perspectives on Positive*

Political Economy, edited by James E. Alt and Kenneth A. Shepsle, 57–89. Cambridge: Cambridge University Press.

Mortensen, Peter B. 2016. "Agencification and Blame Shifting: Evaluating a Neglected Side of Public Sector Reforms." *Public Administration* 94, no. 3: 630–46. https://doi.org/10.1111/padm.12243.

Nettesheim, Martin. 2017. *Umfassende Freihandelsabkommen und Grundgesetz*. Berlin: Duncker & Humblot.

Nielson, Daniel L., and Michael J. Tierney. 2003. "Delegation to International Organizations: Agency Theory and World Bank Environmental Reform." *International Organization* 57, no. 2: 241–76. https://doi.org/10.1017/S0020818303572010.

Niemann, Arne, and Judith Huigens. 2011. "The European Union's Role in the G8: A Principal–Agent Perspective." *Journal of European Public Policy* 18, no. 3: 420–42. https://doi.org/10.1080/13501763.2011.551080.

North, Douglass C. 1993. "Institutions and Credible Commitment." *Journal of Institutional and Theoretical Economics* 149, no. 1: 11–23. https://www.jstor.org/stable/40751576.

Pollack, Mark A. 1997. "Delegation, Agency, and Agenda Setting in the European Community." *International Organization* 51, no. 1: 99–134. https://www.jstor.org/stable/2703953.

– 2003. *The Engines of European Integration. Delegation, Agency, and Agenda Setting in the EU*. New York: Oxford University Press.

Poundstone, William. 1992. *Prisoner's Dilemma*. New York: Doubleday/Anchor.

Ricardo, David. 1817. *On the Principles of Political Economy and Taxation*. London: John Murray.

Russell, Bertrand. 1959. *Common Sense and Nuclear Warfare*. London: George Allen and Unwin.

S. Z. Sevince v. Staatssecretaris van Justitie. 1990. ECJ Case C-192/89, Judgment of the Court (ECLI:EU:C:1990:322), 20 September.

Scholz, Rupert. 2020. "Article 23 GG." *Grundgesetz-Kommentar* (91st edition) (online edition), edited by Theodor Maunz and Günter Dürig. Munich: C.H. Beck.

Thatcher, Mark, and Alec Stone Sweet. 2002. "Theory and Practice of Delegation to Non- Majoritarian Institutions." *West European Politics* 25, no. 1: 1–22. https://doi.org/10.1080/713601583.

Treaty on the Functioning of the European Union (TFEU). 2012. Accessed 23 July 2020. https://eur-lex.europa.eu/legal-content/EN/TXT/?uri=CELEX%3A12012E%2FTXT.

von Arnauld, Andreas. 2016. "Beteiligung des Deutschen Bundestages an gemischten völkerrechtlichen Abkommen." *Archiv des öffentlichen Rechts* 141, no. 1: 268–82. https://doi.org/10.1628/000389116X14684978889262.

Weiß, Wolfgang. 2016a. "Verfassungsanforderungen und Integrationsverantwortung bei beschließenden Vertragsorganen in Freihandelsabkommen." *Europäische Zeitschrift für Wirtschaftsrecht* 27, no. 8: 286–91.

– 2016b. "Verfassungsprobleme des Abschlusses und der vorläufigen Anwendung des CETA Freihandelsabkommens mit Kanada." German Bundestag, 18. Parliamentary term, Committee for the Economy and for Energy, printed document 18(9)926. Accessed 4 August 2020. https://www.bundestag.de/resource/blob/438052/9f45bd9ca1de30f51726df5d391b8702/stgn_weiss-data.pdf.

– 2017. "Demokratische Legitimation und völkerrechtliche Governancestrukturen: Bundestagsbeteiligung bei EU-Handelsabkommen mit beschlussfassenden Gremien." In *Die Welt und Wir: Die Außenbeziehungen der Europäischen Union*, edited by Stefan Kadelbach, 151–221. Baden-Baden: Nomos.

– 2018a. "Delegation to Treaty Bodies in EU Agreements: Constitutional Constraints and Proposals for Strengthening the European Parliament." *European Constitutional Law Review* 14, no. 3: 532–66. https://doi.org/10.1017/S1574019618000305.

– 2018b. "Kann Freihandel Demokratie und Rechtsstaat gefährden?" In *Erosion von Demokratie und Rechtsstaat*, edited by Hans Herbert von Arnim, 21–70. Berlin: Doncker & Humblot.

Wessel, Ramses A., and Steven Blockmans. 2014. "The Legal Status and Influence of Decisions of International Organizations and other Bodies in the EU." Research Papers in Law 1/2014, College of Europe, Brugge, Belgium.

3

Implementing CETA in the EU: Challenges for Democracy and Executive-Legislative Balance

Wolfgang Weiß

INTRODUCTION

Implementing the Comprehensive Economic and Trade Agreement (CETA) in the European Union (EU) poses challenges for democracy and the institutional balance between the executive and the legislative in the EU which so far have escaped scholarly attention, and have not been subject of the opinions of the Court of Justice of the European Union (CJEU) on Singapore and CETA.[1] Implementing CETA is particularly problematic insofar as CETA establishes an institutional structure consisting of thirteen treaty committees whose task is to further develop, amend or implement CETA. The agreement's implementation and application shall be facilitated through this structure. These treaty bodies are decision-making bodies, usually composed of representatives of Canada and the EU Commission, whose tasks are sometimes particularly far-reaching as they are authorized to take binding decisions that go beyond the mere application of CETA provisions, but encompass decision-making on important issues or the adoption of general rules. CETA confers numerous and comprehensive powers on them. The mandate of the central CETA Joint Committee is very broad as it is "responsible for all questions concerning trade and investment between the Parties and the implementation and application of this Agreement" (CETA 2016, Art. 26.1(3)); its mandate goes beyond application and implementation (ibid., Art. 26.1(4)). The CETA Joint Committee has the most extensive powers and oversees the issue-specific committees.

This chapter analyzes the democracy and institutional balance concerns prompted by these decision-making bodies. They imply a new level of exercising public powers by executive actors without parliamentarian involvement. Thus, implementing the treaty bodies' mandates in CETA may contradict the increasingly expanded role of the European Parliament (EP) in EU legislation and conclusion of international agreements. In the development of European integration, increased parliamentary empowerment has been perceived as an important way of strengthening the legitimacy of EU decision-making (Bast 2012; Krajewski 2005; Pollack 2003, 383), also by CJEU.[2] By virtue of the Lisbon Treaty, the EP gained an equal role with the Council in ordinary legislation, and was granted the right to express consent to the conclusion of most international agreements, including international trade agreements (see TFEU 2012, Art. 218(6)(a)(v) i.c.w. Art. 207(2)), in addition to its long-established right of being informed in all stages of the treaty-making procedures (ibid., Art. 218(10)). The enhanced competences of the EP in the conclusion of treaties allowed the EP to become an active actor already in the negotiations. In effect, the Lisbon Treaty rearranged the executive-legislative relationship to the advantage of the EP in legislating and treaty-making.

In contrast to negotiation and conclusion, the role of the EP in the implementation and operation of treaties is rather low, and particularly so with regard to institutions established by free trade agreements (FTAs) such as CETA, for its application and implementation. The EP is not involved in the decision-making of treaty committees, even though they interfere with the parliamentarian task of legislating and treaty-making. The EP has no say in the decision-making of these bodies, nor is it represented there, nor does it have meaningful powers of scrutiny. The EU's position to be represented in the treaty bodies is adopted by the Council only (ibid., Art. 218(9)). In most cases, the Commission represents the EU in these bodies, and the bodies' decision-making is only steered by the Council's position on behalf of the EU. This imbalance between a strong position of the EP in legislating and treaty-making and its weak position when it comes to decision-making by treaty bodies raises concerns as to their democratic legitimacy and the respect of the institutional balance between the executive and the legislative in the EU. The balance between the executive and the legislative in trade policy is shifting back in favour of the executive branch. This chapter explores this change and proposes ways in which the EP's role in the implementation of trade agreements could be strengthened. It first compares the functions of the EP in the negotiation and conclusion of FTAs such as CETA to those in the implementation and operation of such FTAS. Then, the strong executive dimension of treaty bodies, their role, and their decision-making powers in CETA is explored, in order to demonstrate the power shift to the executive brought about. In this respect, the perspective of delegation is adopted as their exercise of public powers results from a conferral of public powers (Kuijper 2018, 225; Weiß 2018, 534–43). It will be shown that the CETA committees exercise significant public powers, by virtue of broadly drafted mandates. Their increasing use strengthens the role of the executive to the detriment of the legislative and treaty-making powers of the EP. Subsequently, the two ways of protecting the EP's prerogatives are developed, by determining the constitutional constraints to the delegation of powers, and by identifying mechanisms of strengthened parliamentary control.

COMPARING THE EP'S ROLE IN THE BIRTH AND THE IMPLEMENTATION OF CETA

Negotiation of CETA

The EP has substantial significance in the conclusion of an agreement such as CETA since the Treaty of Lisbon. The consent requirement under Art. 218(6) of the TFEU mirrors the EP's internal (legislative) decision-making powers. Accordingly, EP consent to CETA was needed as a trade agreement covers fields to which the ordinary legislative procedure applies (see TFEU 2012, Art. 207(2)). Hence, the EP and the Council "enjoy the same powers in relation to a given field, in compliance with the institutional balance provided for by the Treaties" (EP v. *Council* 2014, para. 56). During the preparations and the negotiations leading to CETA, the EP enjoyed the right to be informed (TFEU 2012, Art. 218(10)), whose details have been hammered out in the Interinstitutional Framework Agreement on relations between the EP and the Commission of 20 October 2010 (hereinafter Framework Agreement; EP and European Commission 2010) with a view to accomplish equality between the Council and the EP also with regard to access to information (Puccio and Harte 2019, 395). The right to be informed and to express its consent enables the EP to exercise control functions and to play a significant political role from the beginning (EP and European Commission 2010, Annex III, para. 1), as could be observed during the CETA negotiations.[3] The EP can respond even to the Commission's draft negotiating mandate and negotiating directives sent to the Council (ibid., para. 23),[4] which requires the EP to have access to them.[5] The EP calls for "immediate, full and accurate" (Kerremans et al.

2019, 14) information at all stages of the procedures, and to be given access to the EU negotiation texts, subject to the appropriate procedures and conditions, in order to ensure that it can take its final decision fully knowledgeable of the subject matter.[6] It postulated that its members should have access to the negotiation mandates and other relevant negotiating documents (EP 2014, para. 46). As expected (Brok 2010, 209), the EP indeed uses its position as a veto player and its information rights effectively to enter into a constant dialogue with the Commission, in particular via its Committee on International Trade (INTA), and to express its political preferences and ideas from the start, before the negotiations formally begin. One can observe that the EP adopts resolutions regarding a future agreement, communicating its red lines even before the Council adopts the negotiating directives (Kerremans et al. 2019, 11). Accordingly, the EP expects the Commission to "take Parliament's views as far as possible into account" (EP and European Commission 2010, para. 24). The Commission has to explain whether and how the views and comments were incorporated in the texts and if not why (ibid., Annex III, paras 4–5), which clearly signals that the Commission is not under a legal obligation to follow the EP's wishes. This can be seen as an imbalance of power compared to the Council's position as: (a) the Council adopts the Commission's drafts of negotiating mandates and guidelines and hence can change them, and (b) the Commission is formally obliged to consult the Trade Policy Committee, hence a Council committee, whereas there is no such formal mechanism provided for with regard to the EP (see Kerremans et al. 2019, 9). One must, however, consider that during negotiations the Council and the EP effectively appear to be in a very comparable position, as the Commission is the negotiator and hence shapes the substance of a future agreement. As a result, the EP contributes to policy formation also in informal ways (Kerremans et al. 2019, 12–14) and influences the substance of a treaty under negotiation, in particular with regard to linkage of trade with social, labour, sustainability, and environmental issues (Meissner 2016; Ott 2016; Rosén 2018, 118, 122; Schütze 2014, 385; Wessel and Takács 2017, 113). With regard to CETA, the change in the investor-state dispute settlement (ISDS) system into an investment court system (ICS) was also due to EP's calls (Kerremans et al. 2019, 18).

Thus, in preparing and concluding CETA, the EP has had a considerable political function almost equivalent to the Council. This applies also to CETA's provisional application, even though Art. 218(5) of TFEU attributes the decision to the Council. According to current political practice, the Council's decision on provisional application of CETA only entered into force after the EP had consented to CETA (on 15 February 2017) (for the practice see EP 2014; EP and European Commission 2010, Annex III, para. 7; Passos 2017, 384, 387; and van der Loo 2019, 222).

Operation and Implementation of CETA

In stark contrast to this decisive political and legal function of the EP in negotiating CETA, its part in its operational phase (based on its provisional entry into force) is very low and has hitherto not been the object of further demands by the EP,[7] even though the EP is responsible for implementing CETA in case it requires changes to or adoption of secondary EU law.[8] This is in conformity with a general observation that the EP hardly participates in the daily life application and implementation of an FTA. Basically, this does not cause concern since the EP is not an executive or administrative institution. Applying or implementing international rules is not the task of a parliament. Parliamentary function, however, pertains to controlling the executive in their implementation of agreements as legislatures want to ensure that the executive does not exceed its powers and that policies obtain their objectives and meet citizens' expectations (Puccio and Harte 2019, 390, 409).

The effective control that the EP can exercise with regard to the operation of FTAs such as CETA is very limited. As the right to information generally does not apply in the implementation phase, the EP has to use informal channels of information about the implementation of FTAs (such as exchange with stakeholders, delegations, in-house research, and workshops) (Puccio and Harte 2019, 394). In addition, the Commission's annual reports on the implementation of FTAs are also sent to the EP (for the 2018 report, see European Commission 2019). The EP expanded the task of specific monitoring groups set up for new FTAs (consisting of INTA members, EP staff, and Commission staff) also to discuss implementation (Puccio and Harte 2019, 396, 400, 408), but this merely allows for ex post control. A formal EP influence on the implementation comparable to its position during the negotiations is not foreseen. In particular with regard to the decision-making by treaty bodies, EP's control is extremely limited. As mentioned, the decision that sets the EU position in the CETA committees is adopted by the Council. The EP is not involved, nor does it directly participate in the decision-making of treaty bodies. The EP is only informed of the Council positions under Art. 218(10) of TFEU as it provides for information "at all stages of the procedure," which includes information on the positions of the Council in preparation for a treaty body decision, and might also include information on the Commission draft. Former EU primary law (Art. 300(2) of the Treaty on European Community (ECT) Amsterdam/Nice) explicitly provided for immediate disclosure of the Council's position to the EP (Martenczuk 2001, 150). In practice, this information was given to the EP mainly ex post facto (Hoffmeister 2015, 124).

In any case, the EP assigns itself a right to information already on a draft Council decision under Art. 218(9) of TFEU. Rule 109 of its Rules of Procedure (which is now Rule 115 since the EP's ninth term) provides for a right to have a debate and to issue recommendations once the Commission proposes a draft. This appears to be the EP's response to the fact that it does not have a formal say in the adoption of such Council position.

On an international level, members of the EP are not present at treaty committees, nor do they have an observer status. The Framework Agreement foresees EP members as observers at international conferences, as part of the EU delegation (EP and European Commission 2010, para. 25),[9] but neither in bilateral negotiations, nor within treaty bodies. Furthermore, even if the EP adopts recommendations to the Council, there is no right for the EP that guarantees the recommendations be considered. The Rules of Procedures, a unilateral act, are only binding for the EP. The Framework Agreement entered into between the Commission and the EP does not provide for a right of the EP to follow up on its recommendations with regard to Commission's drafts to a Council position. The Framework Agreement only provides such a right with regard to EP recommendations during the negotiating phase of an agreement (ibid., Annex III, para. 4).

The Framework Agreement also ensures that the EP is systematically kept informed about meetings of treaty bodies set up by "multilateral international agreements involving the Union," and the Commission will "facilitate access as observers for Members of the EP" as part of EU delegations to meetings of such bodies. But both participatory rights are limited to multilateral as opposed to bilateral agreements such as CETA, and only apply if the treaty bodies "are called upon to take decisions which require the consent of the EP or the implementation of which may require the adoption of legal acts in accordance with the ordinary legislative procedure" (ibid., para. 26). Hence, these participatory guarantees do not apply to treaty bodies established in a bilateral FTA such as CETA (Puccio and Harte 2019, 396), and still do not provide for any influence of the EP on the Council decision under Art. 218(9) of TFEU (2012), or any effective control.

Another simplified procedure of entering into international obligations is provided in Art. 218(7) of TFEU (2012),[10] which gives the Council the power to authorize the Commission to approve, on the EU's behalf, amendments to an agreement where it provides for their adoption in a treaty body, which was used by the Council with regard to CETA.[11] But again, the EP is not involved although it concerns change of CETA that was subject to the EP's approval. The EP is only informed before the Commission approves modifications (EP and European Commission 2010, Annex III, para. 9).

In conclusion, the EP does not enjoy formal mechanisms of effective ex ante control of implementing CETA. In international relations, ex ante control is particularly important as rules agreed with a third party cannot be changed unilaterally. The EP's position in the operation of CETA, in particular as regards the decision-making of its treaty bodies does not allow the EP to have any meaningful influence on their decisions. Effective control of the EU executive by the EP even ex post is not ensured. Whereas in the preparation and conclusion of CETA the EP was fully involved and might have been able to enforce its preferences (not least by threatening to deny consent), its operation can hardly be accompanied in a meaningful, decisive way by the EP. The EP can raise concerns as to its implementation only ex post and can take sanctions under its general accountability mechanisms (e.g. inquiries, Art. 230(2) of TFEU 2012), or the ultima ratio of a motion of censure (Art. 17(8) of TEU 2012 i.c.w. Art. 234 of TFEU 2012).

This does not cause concerns as long as the powers of treaty bodies only relate to executive implementation. Treaty bodies, however, are increasingly entrusted with rather political functions of discretionary rulemaking, treaty amendment, and decision-making on quite substantial, essential issues. This increase of executive powers, in particular by conferring competences for general rulemaking and treaty amendment, raises the required level of democratic legitimacy because the requisite level of democratic legitimation of the exercise of public powers depends on the importance, relevance, and legal effects of the specific tasks, functions, and powers transferred to an executive institution.[12]

STRENGTHENING THE EXECUTIVE BY DELEGATING POWERS TO TREATY BODIES

Implementation Powers of the Treaty Bodies: Amending and Expanding CETA's Regulatory Frame

Treaty bodies such as the CETA committees are executive institutions, established in an EU FTA or in comparable agreements such as association agreements. The establishment of treaty bodies and the scope and breadth of their competences has been increased in the new generation of EU FTAS, reflecting the international move toward delegation of authority to international actors (Bradley and Kelly 2008). Art. 26.1 of CETA (2016) provides for a CETA Joint Committee and several issue-specific committees.[13] These treaty bodies are authorized to make binding decisions on diverse, even rather fundamental, issues, going beyond merely technical-administrative implementation of CETA.

The CETA Joint Committee, for example, may terminate CETA's issue-specific committees, set up new ones and assign tasks to them (CETA 2016, Arts 26.1(5)(g) 26.1(5)(h)); thus, it can change the institutional architecture of CETA. It may also amend the CETA on specific points (ibid., Art. 26.1(5)(c), i.c.w. Arts 4.7(1), 8.1, 8.10(3), and 20.22),[14] and prescribe a binding treaty interpretation (ibid., Arts 8.31(3), 8.44(3), and 26.1(5) (e)). It may decide to amend the annexes and protocols of CETA (ibid., Art. 30.2(2)). Among the issue-specific committees, the competence of the Committee on Trade in Goods to decide on measures to implement the exchange of product warnings between the EU and Canada (ibid., Art. 21.7(5)), or the competence of the Committee on Services and Investment to amend the code of conduct of the judges of the Investment Court and the applicable procedural rules (ibid., Arts 8.44(2) and 8.44(3 (b)) should be emphasized. Rulemaking is also implied in the CETA Joint Committee's mandate to set out administrative and organizational aspects of the functioning of the appellate tribunal, including procedural issues (ibid., Art. 8.28(7)). Thus, the CETA committees are mandated to decide rather fundamental issues or issues of far-reaching significance, including the adoption of general rules possibly interfering with fundamental rights of traders. They are empowered to exercise regulatory and even legislative powers (i.e., powers to adopt general rules). For example, the Committee on Trade in Goods' endorsement of implementation measures for the mutual exchange of product warnings between EU and Canada (by virtue of Art. 21.7(5) of CETA 2016) may enable the committee to set common standards including on protecting personal data and business secrets.

The Executive Nature of CETA Committees

As mentioned earlier, CETA committees consist of representatives of the parties. For the EU, it usually is the commissioner responsible for trade (ibid., Art. 26.1). Consequently, the committees are not actors independent from the parties' will. Nevertheless, their powers lead to decisions that are binding for the parties. In general, decisions of the CETA committees instantly are binding under international law and must be implemented. Only in very few cases, due to special arrangements in CETA's text, treaty bodies' decisions must be ratified or otherwise subsequently approved by the parties in order to become binding (Appel 2016, 211; Weiß 2018, 536–39).

The rules relevant for the preparation of CETA committee decision-making within the EU are Arts 218(7) and 218(9) of TFEU (2012). These rules empower executive institutions (i.e., the Commission and the Council) with the preparation and adoption of the EU decisions preparing the decision-making of CETA committees. As shown, the EP is not involved. Hence, the decision-making competences of the treaty bodies constitute public powers transferred to the committees by the EU with the (provisional) entry into force of CETA. These powers are the result of delegation from the parties to the CETA treaty bodies as they are bestowed with powers of amending and implementing CETA that otherwise would have been the competence of domestic institutions of the parties. The inclusion of rules for decision-making in treaty bodies in Art. 218(9) of TFEU (2012), the binding effect of their decisions simply by virtue of their adoption, and the wording in Art. 218(9) (ibid.), according to which these bodies are responsible for the adoption of "acts having legal effects" (and not for the acceptance of an EU treaty offer), argue in favour of the adoption of legal acts as an expression of a genuine transfer of public powers to the treaty bodies by virtue of a delegation. Delegation in this context is understood as a transfer of decision-making powers to institutions on the basis of a legal act that forms its legal basis. The wording of Art. 218(9) entails a very broad notion of the type of powers that can be delegated to treaty bodies. Hence, Arts 218(7) and 218(9) (ibid.) constitute special regimes for the EU internal adoption of "secondary" CETA law (Alemanno 2015, 636; Appel 2016, 324; *Germany* v. *Council* 2017, paras 58, 162; von Bogdandy, Arndt, and Bast 2004, 130).

Conferral of Powers to CETA Committees: Ever More Delegation to the Executive

Transferring decision-making powers to the CETA treaty bodies represents delegation of powers from the legislative to executive institutions, as shown by the analysis of their legal effects. CETA committee decisions may, not least in the view of the CJEU, influence the content of EU legislation (*Germany* v. *Council* 2014a, para. 63); they are an integral part of the EU legal system (*Greece* v. *Commission* 1989, para. 13; Lavranos 2004, 35, 53, 93). Hence, the CETA treaty bodies, by issuing binding decisions, exercise domestically relevant public powers that have been delegated to them by the EU by way of enshrining their competences in CETA. Their powers have been transferred on them by way of treaty-making which is done by the EU legislator, as shown. The EP therefore, by virtue of its consent to CETA and the committees' mandates therein, delegates part of its powers of legislating and treaty-making to them.

The new generation of EU FTAs have expanded their traditional scope and reach. They no longer only deal with tariffs and border issues of goods and services' market access to the EU, but regulate behind-the-border issues such as professional qualifications, conditions of service provision, and manufacturing practices. Therefore, those FTAs have an impact on domestic regulation. As they place some of the implementation, but also amendment and rulemaking powers, in the hands of treaty bodies, the executive thereby gains influence, whereas the EP's influence is lost.[15] The EP's effective control powers have not expanded along with the proliferation of treaty bodies. The shift of power to executive institutions has gained momentum with the proliferation of treaty bodies in new generation FTAs and their expansion of ever more comprehensive powers, based on quite broad mandates. Thus, the establishment of a treaty body system in CETA is capable of evaporating the EP's legislative and treaty-making powers. This calls for a rebalancing of the EP's control powers. Its powers have to be strengthened again. Another way of rebalancing the power shift implied in comprehensive delegation to treaty bodies would be to limit the scope of delegation. The latter is analyzed in the following section, before proposals for increased EP involvement in treaty body decision-making are presented.

CONSTRAINING DELEGATION TO TREATY BODIES

The results of this chapter so far have shown that the EP's powers can be jeopardized by the delegation of comprehensive powers to CETA committees. As the EP's powers serve its democratic functions (also in external relations, see *EP* v. *Council* 2014, para. 81), comprehensive decision-making powers of CETA bodies that go beyond mere executive implementation may violate requirements of institutional balance and democracy set by EU constitutional laws. These constitutional requirements necessarily limit the scope of delegation available to treaty bodies. Their use must be constrained. This section explores the constraints to delegation to the executive and applies them to conferral of powers to treaty bodies such as the CETA committees.

Constraints to Delegation to the Executive in EU Law

Delegation of rulemaking to executive actors on the basis of enabling acts is explicitly regulated since Lisbon in Arts 290 and 291 of TFEU (2012), and, in both cases, it is (mainly) the Commission which is the delegate. Under Art. 290 (ibid.), legislative acts may bestow the Commission with the authority to adopt delegated acts of general application that amend legislative acts (hence are quasi-legislative; Bast 2012, 917; Craig 2013, 264), whereas under Art. 291(2) (TFEU 2012), the Commission may be entrusted with the power to adopt (also: general) implementing acts, in continuation of the comitology system (Bergström 2005; Bergström and Ritleng 2016). Besides, there exist other forms of delegation to adopt individual decisions or general rules, in particular to EU agencies (*United Kingdom* v. *Parliament and Council*, 2014). Common to these variations of internal delegation is the requirement of a basic enabling legal act that establishes the mandate of the delegate. The object of delegation is rather broad: the delegate may supplement or even amend the enabling act in its substance, or implement it by applying it to individual cases or by adopting general rules that add more detail in order to make general stipulations of the basic act applicable.

The delegation of decision-making powers to CETA committees fits to the basic structures of internal delegation: committees adopt binding acts, also of general application, to implement an agreement by specifying details or by amending its text; the competences for doing so must be provided for in the empowering legal act for CETA. In a democratic order such as the EU (TEU 2012; Art. 10), the exercise of public powers by executive institutions is legitimate only if their establishment is subject to a parliamentary decision, at least a parliamentary participation (see TFEU 2012, Art. 289(2)). This requirement is confirmed by Art. 290 (ibid.), as delegation requires a legislative basic act, even so if the delegate is an EU agency.[16] Under Art. 291 (ibid.), transferring implementing powers to the Commission involves the legislative by way of enacting control mechanisms in a legislative act (ibid., Art. 291(3)). Indeed, the EP – besides the Council – is involved in the delegation of powers to CETA committees since it gave its consent to the agreement.

As can be learned from comparative constitutionalism and from principal-agent theory, delegation never comes unlimited. Domestic orders such as US constitutional law know a non-delegation doctrine that draws red lines (Schütze 2011, 663). In Germany, the delegation of legislative powers to the executive is limited by the stipulations of Art. 80 of the

Basic Law, and by the doctrine that the legislator itself must regulate the essential aspects of a legal act. Similar limits to (internal) delegation of rulemaking to the executive exist under EU law: Art. 290(1) of TFEU (2012) provides that the essential elements of an area shall be reserved for the legislator, and not be the subject of delegation. Rulemaking by the executive on fundamental issues, i.e., the basic elements of a matter, is unconstitutional. Essential issues must be reserved to the legislature because of their political nature as they comprise political or strategic decisions on the fundamental orientation of an EU policy. Such decisions require immediate democratic legitimation as they imply wide discretion, in particular the need for political choices that weigh conflicting policy aims and interests (*EP v. Council* 2012, paras 64–67, 76, 78; *Germany v. Commission* 1992, para. 37).[17] Likewise, the objectives, content, scope and duration of the delegation shall be explicitly defined in the legislative act; hence delegation must not be unspecified but determine precisely the powers transferred (Bast 2012, 914; *United Kingdom v. EP and Council* 2005, paras 49, 62). Besides, delegation must be accompanied by control mechanisms. The EP – like the Council – is entitled to revoke the delegation or reserve a veto so that it can review the exercise of delegated powers and any discretion thereby transferred, Art. 290(2) of TFEU (2012). Such mechanisms counterbalance the derogation from the principle of separation of powers inherent in the delegation of rulemaking powers to the executive, and thus ensure observance to the requirements of democratic legitimacy (*Commission v. EP and Council* 2015, para. 45). Even the delegation of implementing powers under Art. 291 of TFEU (2012) and the Comitology regulation[18] is subject to constraints: the adoption of implementing acts underlies control mechanisms, under participation of the member states and also by the EP, according to said regulation. The conferral of implementing tasks as well requires some precision as regards the scope of the powers and the provision of specific criteria to be followed. The scope of powers and the criteria for their exercise must be set out in the enabling act with a certain degree of specificity; they must be "clearly defined" (*United Kingdom v. EP and Council* 2005, paras 48, 62, regarding pre-Lisbon delegation to the Commission). As these limitations ensure democratic legitimacy of delegated rulemaking and parliamentary control, they are also based on the constitutional principle of institutional balance of EU organs.

Constraints to delegation that result from requirements of democracy and institutional balance in the EU (initially termed as "balance of power") are also enshrined in the *Meroni* case law that restrains the delegation of discretionary powers (*Meroni* 1958). The guiding principles of *Meroni* still are pertinent (Craig 2018, 169; *United Kingdom* v. EP *and Council* 2014, para. 41). *Meroni* (1958, 133 at 152) requires the transfer of power to be limited to "clearly defined executive powers" (see also *Alliance for Natural Health and Others* 2005, para. 90). The powers transferred must be set out in precise terms, and their exercise must be carried out under strict observance of objective criteria determined by the delegator, without granting a wide margin of discretion. Discretionary powers become critical as soon as they imply a wide margin of discretion (*Meroni* 1958, 154; Schütze 2011, 674 at note 89; *United Kingdom* v. EP *and Council* 2014, para. 50). The use of the powers has to be supervised by the delegating authority, in parallel with Art. 290 (TFEU 2012). *Meroni* (1958) furthermore prohibits "an actual transfer of responsibility" by way of delegation, which would be the case if the delegate enjoyed a degree of latitude that allowed it to actually exercise the political function that the EU treaties allocate to an EU institution. Hence, delegation must not conflict with the division of powers provided for in the EU primary law.

Constraints to delegation exist also with regard to external action as changes to the institutional framework of an agreement, such as CETA, are excluded from the application of the simplified procedure, as Art. 218(9) (TFEU 2012) confirms. Consequently, such changes to CETA are subject to the normal treaty-making procedure, requiring consent of the EP (De Baere 2018, 1246). "Particularly important decisions" – such as institutional changes – were not intended to be subject to the simplified procedure, only "minor and quite technical amendments" (*Germany* v. *Council* 2017, para. 58, fn. 30). Therefore, "particularly important decisions" cannot be transferred to CETA committees (*Germany* v. *Council* 2014b, para. 75). This limitation ensures the competences of the EP and, thus, institutional balance (ibid., para. 80).

In the overall view, there are clear constraints to delegation: First, there is an EU non-delegation doctrine. The provision of the essential must not be delegated. Second, delegation presupposes control mechanisms. One can distinguish mechanisms of ex ante and of ex post control: ex ante, the transferred powers must be determined with some precision. Transfer of powers requires the provision of specific criteria to be followed by the delegate. These criteria must be set out in the empowering act with certain specificity. Ex post oversight is implemented by monitoring and sanctioning powers of the delegator, like vetoes, or by withdrawal of delegation. Delegation that allows for amending legislative acts must be subject to stricter control by the EU legislature than transferral of mere implementing powers that do not alter the substance of legislation or treaties, for reasons of balance of power. Requiring specificity and control mechanisms does not indicate clear, absolute limitations to delegation, but these constraints are interrelated – the less specific a mandate is drafted, or the more impor- tant decisions by a delegate are for the lives of people, the more control powers the delegator must have.

As these constraints to delegation are anchored in EU constitutional principles (democratic legitimacy, institutional balance), they must also be respected with regard to external delegation of decision-making in the EU treaties. This can be stipulated at least with regard to external trade relations, as a consequence of the parallelism of the E P's legislative and treaty-making powers and the symmetry of the E P's and the Council's competences as such.

Even though in traditional constitutional thinking external relations are a particular area of policy and accordingly subject to specific rules, which give a primacy to the executive (with the consequence of lower control standards for parliaments), such stance nowadays does not reflect the modern reality of international relations. The domain of contemporary international legal rules considerably expanded and pertains to regulatory issues, as can be easily determined looking at the substance of C E T A. It comprises chapters containing disciplines on regulatory barriers to trade and service provision (Chapter IV on T B T; Chapter V on S P S; Chapter VII on Subsidies; Chapter X on Entry and Stay of Natural Persons; Chapter XII on Domestic Regulation; and Chapters XXI on Regulatory Cooperation, Sustainability, and Labour and Environment Standards). Hence, parliaments cannot be excluded from having a powerful position also with regard to external action (Möllers 2015, 166).

In conclusion, constraints to delegation contain a prohibition against transferring the regulation of essential aspects of a policy on the executive and requirements of specificity of delegation and of parliamentary control. Such is confirmed by principal-agent theory: a principal will not delegate very sensitive decisions to the agent, and will exercise oversight. It will establish control mechanisms to avoid agency losses, which imply checks on the ways the agent uses its powers (Brandsma and Blom-Hansen 2017, 23; Denhousse 2017, 60 f) which may translate into ex ante guide- lines on how to exercise the mandate, and into ex post monitoring and sanctioning. Accordingly, the principal will specify the mandate given to the agent as clearly as possible and determine the decisive objectives to be followed.

Consequences for Conferring Powers to Treaty Bodies: Identifying an EU (Non-) Delegation Doctrine

The constitutional limitation to delegation flowing from non-delegation doctrine prohibits a delegation of decision-making on essential, fundamental issues to treaty bodies; the non-delegation of the essential is an "absolute limitation [following] from the constitutional frame" (Schütze 2014, 396). Such decision-making has to be reserved to treaty-making institutions (Council and the EP) which means that general-abstract, hence quasi-legislative, rulemaking on essential elements of a policy, including considerable interference with fundamental rights, cannot be transferred to decision-making by treaty bodies. Amendments can be delegated to treaty bodies only with regard to nonessential issues.

Beyond such (relatively) absolute limitation, constitutional constraints to delegation require a certain degree of specificity of the competences and the establishment of effective control mechanisms to the benefit of the EP, too. The mandates for treaty bodies must be determined as precisely as possible in the agreements, with regard to their scope and the criteria for their exercise. The delegation of rulemaking of general scope or of decision-making implying considerable discretion on part of treaty bodies presupposes control mechanisms for the EP, in order to ensure its impact on the substance of the treaty bodies' decisions. Rulemaking of general scope or decision-making powers that allow wide discretion cannot be conferred to treaty bodies without assurances for the competences of the EP such as control mechanisms that can ensure the legitimacy of the substantive content of the treaty bodies' decisions. As there are no such assurances for the EP's functions under today's rules, the current lack of involvement of the EP militates in favour of constraining the type of delegatable powers, in conformity with the type of executive powers conferred to the Council. Thus, the powers of treaty bodies must be limited to decisions of an executive type that merely implement the terms of the agreement, in conformity with a formula used by the CJEU: "applying or implementing that agreement" (*Council v. Commission* 2015a, para. 65).

In short, one can identify three principles of delegation that also prevail in EU external relations: the essential is not delegable but must be provided for in CETA itself; mandates for autonomous, binding decision-making by CETA committees must be specific; any exercise of power beyond simple implementation measures must be subject to control by the EP.

Even though the theoretical conceptions, both under a comparative constitutional viewpoint as well as under the principal-agent theory, align in comparable insights, the constitutional reality of delegation practice very often gives testimony to a loss of control standards with regard to delegation (Iancu 2012). The current EU practice of increasingly making use of treaty bodies in order to delegate decision-making to international institutions in ever more substantive issues without assuring sufficient parliamentary control may be perceived as following this unfortunate trend. An explanation for this is the presence of multiple principals in EU law as their involvement in delegation might necessarily lead to exceedingly broad and not specific delegations of regulatory power (Lindseth 2010, 254). Such a plurality of principals also exists in the case of EU FTAS.

Consequences for CETA[19]

Applying these principles to the mandates of the CETA committees enshrined in CETA yields the insight that delegation by way of using the simplified procedure of Art. 218(9) of TFEU (2012) does not raise concerns if it is applied to the conferral of precisely delineated implementation powers to CETA committees – without broad discretion and limited to a mere concretization function.

Decisions of fundamental importance, however, cannot be the subject of conferrals of power under the procedure of Art. 218(9) (ibid.), if the decision-making criteria have not been clearly set out in CETA and hence had not been specifically consented to by the EP. Therefore, the competence of the CETA Joint Committee under Art. 8.29 of CETA (2016) to transfer investment protection to a multilateral investment court is not sufficiently legitimate since CETA sets requirements neither for ethical standards nor for safeguards for the independence and impartiality of the members of this court and the applicable procedures. The decision as such is fully granted to the CETA committees without any parliamentary control and without determining its conditions.

The explicit exclusion by Art. 218(9) (TFEU 2012) of institutional changes from the powers conferrable on treaty bodies means that Arts 26.1(5)(a), 26.1(5)(g), and 26.1(5)(h) of CETA (2016) – which broadly empower the CETA Joint Committee to amend the institutional structure of CETA – cannot be conferred under the simplified procedure. Such changes to CETA must be adopted by the EU by means of the ordinary treaty-making procedure, which requires EP consent; applying Art. 218(9) of TFEU (2012) in this manner is an infringement of the EU law.

The same applies to certain rulemaking competences of CETA committees. Art. 21.7(5) of CETA (2016) allows the provision of fundamental issues to a CETA committee by which the committee is empowered to establish the conditions and criteria for the exchange of product warnings, including specification of the information to be exchanged and the modalities of exchange. These rules must respect confidentiality and protect sensitive business and personal data; they could potentially interfere with fundamental rights (*Council* v. *Commission* 2015b; *Germany* v. *Council* 2017; Mendes 2017). CETA however sets no standards in this respect, even though with regard to data protection, for example, Art. 8(3) of the EU Charter of Fundamental Rights implies an obligation by which data must be retained within the EU to enable the requisite data protection control (*Digital Rights Ireland and Others* 2014, para. 68). The implementation of a committee decision under Art. 21.7(5) of CETA (2016) might also require changes to the EU RAPEX Directive 2001/95; the EP would be bound in spite of not having participated in the committee decision-making.

Autonomous rulemaking mandates in Arts 8.28(7), 8.44(2), and 8.44(3)(b) of CETA (2016) also raise concerns with regard to the above principles. Art. 8.28(7) (ibid.) allows for the adoption of procedural rules concerning certain administrative and organizational aspects of the functioning of the appellate tribunal. Under Art. 8.28(7)(g) (ibid.), the CETA Joint Committee is given broad leeway to set out "any other elements it determines to be necessary for the effective functioning of the Appellate Tribunal." The content and substance of these rules are not pre-defined; it is up to the committee itself to determine which rules might be necessary. The committee consequently enjoys a very wide range of discretion. Likewise, the autonomous rulemaking authority of the CETA Committee on Services and Investments under Arts 8.44(2) and 8.44(3)(b) (ibid.) lacks specificity with regard to a code of conduct for tribunal members and with regard to dispute settlement and transparency rules. Due to a lack of any precise conditions for the exercise of these decision-making powers by committees combined with a lack of any effective parliamentary control over their usage, their degree of legitimacy is insufficient to allow a conferral of power under the procedure of Art. 218(9) of TFEU (2012) without the EP having a decisive say in the exercise of these mandates.

MECHANISMS TO STRENGTHEN THE ROLE OF THE EP IN THE OPERATION OF CETA COMMITTEES

An alternative, partly overlapping, way of securing the EP's prerogatives is to strengthen its effective control over CETA committees' decision-making (beyond being informed and having a debate). This is constitutionally required in case of rulemaking or the exercise of powers implying wide discretion, all the more if the committees' decisions could interfere with the EU legislation. Improved mechanisms should allow a considerable, preferably ex ante, impact of the EP on the substance of the decisions. Such ways are conceivable on the international and on the domestic level.

Internationally, it could mean a direct involvement of the EP in the decision-making of CETA committees. Members of the INTA or the responsible monitoring group could become part of the EU representative in the committees, at least as observers. As mentioned, the Framework Agreement foresees members of the EP (MEPS) as observers at international conferences, as part of the EU delegation. This could be expanded to include observer status also in bilateral FTA bodies. The EP would get direct knowledge about the processes there, which increases the effectiveness of its control due to better information and the ability to directly monitor the implementation of the EU position and EP resolutions. This would, however, mainly limit the EP to ex post control, whose effectiveness is undermined by the fact that a decision once adopted in a committee cannot be overturned, but only be replaced by a new one on whose adoption the EP does not have any influence. Hence, ex post control by the EP could only be effective if there were routes in which the effect of a committee decision could be terminated. A possible remedy would be the suspension of a committee decision, in the same way as an agreement or parts thereof may be suspended, but for other reasons (because of acting ultra vires, or of adopting illegitimate rules). Such remedy, however, would be a novel feature to CETA as it is not provided therein.

More preferable are mechanisms of ex ante control. In this respect, a suitable control mechanism could mean the introduction of (Joint) Parliamentary Assemblies with parliamentarians of the other party (as is provided, for example, in the Cotonou Agreement, but not in CETA). Such assembly could represent a forum for common discussion of democracy issues and noneconomic concerns. FTAS would have to explicitly establish such assemblies and provide for their competences, in particular with regard to treaty body decision-making. They could foresee – beyond information and comments on draft decisions – suspension or veto powers in case of rulemaking decisions.

On domestic level, ex ante control would imply involving the EP in the adoption of the EU position under Art. 218(9) of TFEU (2012). Immediate and full information must be given to the EP also with regard to envisaged treaty body decisions. The full information of the EP by the Commission before approving modifications to an agreement that are authorized by the Council under Art. 218(7) of TFEU (2012) (see EP and European Commission 2010, Annex III, para. 9) must be expanded to include Art. 218(9). Furthermore, the Commission, when drafting a Council decision, should become subject to a "comply or explain mechanism" with regard to EP resolutions.

A further step towards increased scrutiny would be a direct EP involvement in the Council decision-making under Arts 218(7) and 218(9) (TFEU 2012). If the decisions relate to rulemaking requiring – in their implementation – change of the EU legislation, the Council's decision must be subject to consent of the EP. Adding an EP consent requirement to the Council decision-making would resolve the imbalance between the EP's strong role in legislating and treaty-making compared to its negligible role in the simplified procedures that have not been amended by Lisbon to reflect the EP's strengthened role in legislating and treaty-making (Alemanno 2015, 636).

Implementing these proposals would not require reform of the EU primary law. The EP's rights could be enshrined into the Council decision concluding a FTA where one could establish a legal framework for the EP's involvement in the simplified procedures under Arts 218(7) and 218(9) (TFEU 2012). The chance to do so for CETA has not lapsed as the final ratification of it is still pending. Alternatively, a framework agreement between the Council and the EP or, preferably, by virtue of a legislative act under Art. 207(2) (ibid.), a general regulatory framework for the delegation of powers to treaty bodies could foresee an EP consent requirement for certain types of Council decisions, under Arts 218(7) and 218(9) (ibid.).

In addition to, and independently from new mechanisms, the EP's monitoring of the operation of FTAs should intensely make use of the usual monitoring instruments also with regard to CETA committees' decision-making, such as oral questions, meetings with the Commission and Council staffs, or expert and stakeholder hearings, but also meetings with representatives of Canada. In future, the EP also should make its consent to FTAS subject to a commitment by the Commission and the Council to annually report on the implementation of the FTAs also with regard to treaty bodies' decision-making activities, which would add to the overall transparency and quality of information.

CONCLUSION

As EU trade policy expands beyond border issues, EU's external trade policy becomes an area for the exercise of EU's public powers, which must become subject to the same legitimacy requirements as applicable to internal policy areas. The role of the EP has to keep pace with the topical expansion of trade policy and its interference with the formerly mainly domestic regulatory policies. This creates the need for strengthening the democratic legitimacy of delegation of powers to bodies established in EU trade treaties for the sake of its swift implementation. From an EU constitutional perspective, the expansion and extension of autonomous decision-making powers of the treaty bodies as provided for in CETA with regard to the committees established therein must be viewed critically. The resulting upgrading of executive powers in rulemaking and treaty amendment exercised by way of decision-making by CETA committees urgently needs to be balanced against requirements of democratic legitimacy and institutional balance. This pleads, as is submitted here, not only for extended supervisory mechanisms in favour of the EP in the operation phase of trade agreements. Furthermore, some decision-making mandates enshrined in CETA do not conform to the EU constitutional requirements.

NOTES

This project has received funding from the EU's Horizon 2020 program under the Marie Skłodowska-Curie grant agreement No. 721916. Parts of this chapter are based on insights previously published in Weiß (2018).

1 The Court in its Opinions 2/15 and 1/17 on the scope of the EU competences to enter into the FTA with Singapore and on the conformity of ICS established in CETA with the EU primary law, respectively, did not address the issues raised here.

2 See, for example, SA *Roquette Frères* v. *Council* (1980, para. 33) (consultation is essential formality, rooted in principle of democracy); EP v. *Council* (1990); EP v. *Council* (1994, para. 9) (extension of legal standing); EP v. *Council* (2014, paras 79, 81); EP v. *Council* (2016, paras 73, 76) (scope of information rights to include negotiation directives and provisional application, also in Common Foreign and Security Policy [CFSP]); EP v. *Council* (1992, para. 17) (participation also to amended drafts); and *France* v. *Parliament* (2018, paras 28, 32, 44). See also Terpan (2019) and Terpan and Saurugger (2019, 85).

3 See, for example, EP (2011). For an analysis of the EP's role in
   Transatlantic Trade and Investment Partnership (TTIP) negotiations
   see Jančić (2016, 899).

4 The Interinstitutional Agreement of 12 March 2014 between
   the EP and the Council, concerning the forwarding to and handling
   by the EP of classified information held by the Council on matters other
   than those in the area of CFSP (EP and Council 2014), provided details
   of the EP's access to the adopted negotiating mandates and guidelines
   (hence being Council documents, to which the EP does not have immediate
   access). As these texts are now made public, institutional practice has
   gone even further.

5 See EP v. Council (2016, para. 75), also with regard to CFSP. See also
   van der Mei (2016, 1066).

6 Members of the European Parliament (MEPs) were informed by
   Commission staff about the CETA negotiation rounds; there were
   148 parliamentary questions posed to the Commission. See for example
   Committee on International Trade (2011, 2014); and for more detail
   Kerremans et al. (2019).

7 Except for reporting requirements the Commission accepted with regard
   to implementation of specific commitments enshrined in the agreements;
   furthermore, MEPs can also attend the meetings of the Commission's
   Expert Group on the Trade and Sustainable Development (TSD) chapters,
   see Kerremans et al. (2019, 16).

8 Amending the EU legislation in course of implementing CETA could be
   necessary, for example, in the implementation of mutual recognition of
   professional qualifications (MRPQ) agreements adopted in the framework
   of Chapter 11 of CETA (2016) (for requirements for change of the EU
   Directive 2005/36 on the recognition of professional qualifications,
   see Office des professions du Québec [2018, 20]), or with regard to the
   implementation of committee decision on the procedures for the mutual
   exchange of product warnings, based on Art. 21.7(5) of CETA (2016).

9 The Framework Agreement's para. 26 provides – with regard to
   multilateral as opposed to bilateral agreements – that the Commission
   "facilitate access as observers for [MEP] forming part of Union delegations
   to meetings of bodies set up by multilateral international agreements
   involving the Union, whenever such bodies are called upon to take
   decisions which require the consent of Parliament or the implementation
   of which may require the adoption of legal acts in accordance with the
   ordinary legislative procedure."

10 Art. 218(7) (TFEU 2012) is a further simplification of Art. 218(9) (ibid.); see *Council* v. *Commission* (2015b, para. 67); *Germany* v. *Council* (2017, para. 57).

11 See, for example, Art. 2 of the Council Decision 2017/38 on the provisional application of CETA (Council 2016), according to which Art. 218(7) (TFEU 2012) applies to the adoption of the CETA Joint Committee decision under Art. 20.22 (CETA 2016) to amend Annex 20-A.

12 See with regard to delegation to the EU, Lindseth (2012, 156). See also German Federal Constitutional Court (2009, para. 262).

13 For the EU FTA with Singapore or Japan, see Art. 16.1 of the EUSFTA; Art. 22.1 of the JEFTA.

14 For further powers to amend the CETA text and its annexes see Arts 2.13(1)(b) and 23.11(5) (CETA 2016).

15 For an account of the possible impact of treaty bodies' decisions on the EU legislation, see Mendes (2017, 495, 515).

16 For the EP's involvement in setting up agencies see Jacobs (2014, 201).

17 Not entirely negligible interferences with fundamental rights amount to essential elements of a policy as well. See Curtin and Manucharyan (2015, 112); *EP* v. *Council* (2015, para. 53).

18 Regulation 182/2011 of the EP and the Council laying down the rules and general principles concerning mechanisms for control of the Commission's exercise of implementing powers by the member states.

19 See Weiß (2018, 560).

REFERENCES

Alemanno, Alberto. 2015. "The Regulatory Cooperation Chapter of the Transatlantic Trade and Investment Partnership: Institutional Structures and Democratic Consequences." *Journal of International Economic Law* 18, no. 3: 625–40. https://doi.org/10.1093/jiel/jgv026.

Alliance for Natural Health and Others v. *Secretary of State for Health and National Assembly for Wales*. 2005. CJEU Joined Cases C-154/04 and C-155/04, Judgment of the Court (Grand Chamber) (ECLI:EU:C:2005:449), 12 July.

Appel, Nicole. 2016. *Das internationale Kooperationsrecht der EU*. Berlin/Heidelberg: Springer-Verlag.

Bast, Juergen. 2012. "New Categories of Acts after the Lisbon Reform: Dynamics of Parliamentarization in EU Law." *Common Market Law Review* 49, no. 3: 885–927.

Bergström, Carl Fredrik. 2005. *Comitology: Delegation of Powers in the EU and the Committee System.* Oxford: Oxford University Press.

Bergström, Carl Fredrik, and Dominique Ritleng (eds). 2016. *Rulemaking by the European Commission: The New System for Delegation of Powers.* Oxford: Oxford University Press.

Bradley, Curtis A., and Judith G. Kelly. 2008. "The Concept of International Delegation." *Law and Contemporary Problems* 71, no. 1: 1–36. https://scholarship.law.duke.edu/lcp/vol71/iss1/2.

Brok, Elmar. 2010. "Die neue Macht des Europäischen Parlaments nach 'Lissabon' im Bereich der gemeinsamen Handelspolitik." *Integration* 3: 209–23. https://www.jstor.org/stable/24223688.

CETA (Canada-European Union Comprehensive Economic and Trade Agreement). 2016. Accessed 21 July 2020. https://www.international.gc.ca/trade-commerce/trade-agreements-accords-commerciaux/agr-acc/ceta-aecg/text-texte/toc-tdm.aspx?lang=eng.

Committee on International Trade. 2011. "Minutes: Meeting of 12 July 2011, from 15.00 to 18.00, and 13 July 2011, from 9.00 to 12.30 and from 15.00 to 18.30 Brussels (INTA_PV(2011)0712_1)." Accessed 22 July 2020. https://www.europarl.europa.eu/meetdocs/2009_2014/documents/inta/pv/873/873646/873646en.pdf.

– 2014. "Minutes: Meeting of 3 September 2014, Brussels (INTA_PV(2014)09-03-1)." On File with Author.

Council of the European Union. 2016. "Council Decision (EU) 2017/38 of 28 October 2016 on the provisional application of the Comprehensive Economic and Trade Agreement (CETA) between Canada, of the one part, and the European Union and its Member States, of the other part." Accessed 22 July 2020. https://eur-lex.europa.eu/legal-content/EN/TXT/?uri=uriserv%3AOJ.L_.2017.011.01.1080.01.ENG.

Council of the European Union v. European Commission. 2015a. CJEU Case C-73/14, Judgment of the Court (Grand Chamber) (ECLI:EU:C:2015:663), 6 October.

– 2015b. CJEU Case C-73/14, Opinion of Advocate General Sharpston (ECLI:EU:C:2015:490), 16 July.

Craig, Paul. 2013. *The Lisbon Treaty: Law, Politics, and Treaty Reform.* Oxford: Oxford University Press.

– 2018. *EU Administrative Law.* Oxford: Oxford University Press.

Curtin, Deirdre, and Tatevik Manucharyan. 2015. "Legal Acts and Hierarchy of Norms in EU Law." In *The Oxford Handbook of EU Law,* edited by Damian Chalmers and Anthony Arnull, 103–130. Oxford: Oxford University Press.

De Baere, Geert. 2018. "EU Status in Other International Organizations." In *Oxford Principles of European Union Law, Volume 1*, edited by Robert Schütze and Takis Tridimas, 1234–82. Oxford: Oxford University Press.

Digital Rights Ireland Ltd v. *Minister for Communications, Marine and Natural Resources and Others and Kärntner Landesregierung and Others.* 2014. CJEU Case C-293/12, Judgment of the Court (Grand Chamber) (ECLI:EU:C:2014:238), 8 April.

European Commission. 2019. *Report from the Commission to the European Parliament, the Council, the European Economic and Social Committee and the Committee of the Regions on Implementation of Free Trade Agreements: 1 January 2018 – 31 December 2018* (COM(2019) 455 final). Brussels: European Commission.

European Commission v. *European Parliament and Council of the European Union.* 2015. CJEU Case C-88/14, Opinion of Advocate General Mengozzi (ECLI:EU:C:2015:304), 7 May.

EP (European Parliament). 2011. "European Parliament Resolution of 8 June 2011 on EU-Canada Trade Relations." Accessed 22 July 2020. https://www.europarl.europa.eu/sides/getDoc.do?pubRef=-//EP//TEXT+TA+P7-TA-2011-0257+0+DOC+XML+V0//EN.

– 2014. "European Parliament Resolution of 13 March 2014 on the Implementation of the Treaty of Lisbon with Respect to the European Parliament (2013/2130(INI))" Accessed 22 July 2020. https://www.europarl.europa.eu/sides/getDoc.do?type=TA&reference=P7-TA-2014-0249&language=EN&ring=A7-2014-0120.

EP (European Parliament) and Council of the European Union. 2014. "Interinstitutional Agreement of 12 March 2014 between the European Parliament and the Council Concerning the Forwarding to and Handling by the European Parliament of Classified Information held by the Council on Matters Other than Those in the Area of the Common Foreign and Security Policy (OJ EU 2014/C 95/01)." Accessed 22 July 2020. https://eur-lex.europa.eu/legal-content/EN/TXT/?uri=uriserv:OJ.C_.2014.095.01.0001.01.ENG&toc=OJ:C:2014:095:TOC.

EP (European Parliament) and European Commission. 2010. "Framework Agreement on Relations between the European Parliament and the European Commission." Accessed 23 July 2020. https://eur-lex.europa.eu/LexUriServ/LexUriServ.do?uri=OJ:L:2010:304:0047:0062:EN:PDF.

European Parliament (EP) v. *Council of the European Communities.* 1990. CJEU Case 70/88, Judgment of the Court (EU:C:1990:217), 22 May.

– 1992. CJEU Case C-65/90, Judgment of the Court (ECLI:EU:C:1992:325), 16 July.

– 1994. CJEU Case C-316/91 Judgment of the Court (ECLI:EU:C:1994:76), 2 March.

– 2014. CJEU Case C-658/11, Judgment of the Court (Grand Chamber) (EU:C:2014:2025), 24 June.

– 2016. CJEU Case C-263/14, Judgment of the Court (Grand Chamber) (ECLI:EU:C:2016:435), 14 June.

European Parliament v. Council of the European Union. 2012. CJEU Case C-355/10, Judgment of the Court (Grand Chamber) (ECLI:EU:C:2012:516), 5 September.

– 2015. CJEU Case C-363/14, Judgment of the Court (Fourth Chamber) (ECLI:EU:C:2015:579), 10 September.

European Union. 2017. "Notice Concerning the Provisional Application of the Comprehensive Economic and Trade Agreement (CETA) between Canada, of the One Part, and the European Union and its Member States, of the Other Part (OJ EU 2017 L 238/9)." Accessed 22 July 2020. https://eur-lex.europa.eu/legal-content/EN/TXT/?uri=uriserv%3AOJ.L_.2017.238.01.0009.01.ENG.

France v. Parliament. 2018. CJEU Case C-73/17, Judgment of the Court (Grand Chamber) (ECLI:EU:C:2018:787), 2 October.

German Federal Constitutional Court. 2009. Case 2 BvE 2/08, Judgment (Lisbon Treaty) (ECLI:DE:BVerfG:2009:es20090630.2bve000208), 30 June.

Germany v. Commission of the European Communities. 1992. CJEU Case C-240/90, Judgment of the Court (ECLI:EU:C:1992:408), 27 October.

Germany v. Council of the European Union. 2014a. CJEU C-399/12, Judgment of the Court (Grand Chamber) (ECLI:EU:C:2014:2258), 7 October.

– 2014b. CJEU C-399/12, Opinion of Mr Advocate General Cruz Villalón (ECLI:EU:C:2014:289), 29 April.

– 2017. CJEU Case C-600/14, Opinion of Advocate General Szpunar (ECLI:EU:C:2017:296), 24 April.

Greece v. Commission of the European Communities. 1989. CJEU Case 30/88, Judgment of the Court (ECLI:EU:C:1989:422), 14 November.

Hoffmeister, Frank. 2015. "The EU in the WTO: A Model for the EU's Status in International Organizations?" In The EU in International Organisations and Global Governance, edited by Christine Kaddous, 121–37. Oxford: Hart Publishing.

Iancu, Bogdan. 2012. Legislative Delegation: The Erosion of Normative Limits in Modern Constitutionalism. Berlin/Heidelberg: Springer-Verlag.

Jacobs, Francis. 2014. "EU Agencies and the European Parliament." In European Agencies in between Institutions and Member States, edited by Michelle Everson, Cosimo Monda, and Ellen Vos, 201–26. Alphen aan den Rijn: Wolters Kluwer.

Jančić, Davor. 2016. "The Role of the European Parliament and the US Congress in Shaping Transatlantic Relations." *Journal of Common Market Studies* 54, no. 4: 896–912. https://doi.org/10.1111/jcms.12345.

Kerremans, Bart, Johan Adriaensen, Francesca Colli, and Evelyn Coremans. 2019. *Parliamentary Scrutiny of Trade Policies across the Western World.* Brussels: European Parliament. https://www.europarl.europa.eu/RegData/etudes/STUD/2019/603477/EXPO_STU(2019)603477_EN.pdf.

Krajewski, Markus. 2005. "External Trade Law and the Constitution Treaty: Towards a Federal and More Democratic Common Commercial Policy?" *Common Market Law Review* 42, no. 1: 91–127.

Kuijper, Pieter Jan. 2018. "Recent Tendencies in the Separation of Powers in EU Foreign Relations: An Essay." In *Constitutional Issues of EU External Relations Law*, edited by Eleftheria Neframi and Mauro Gatti, 199–230. Baden-Baden: Nomos.

Lavranos, Nikolaos. 2004. *Legal Interaction between Decisions of International Organisations and European Law.* Zutphen: Europa Law Publishing.

Lindseth, Peter L. 2010. *Power and Legitimacy: Reconciling Europe and the Nation-State.* Oxford: Oxford University Press.

– 2012. "Power and Legitimacy: Author's Reply: 'Outstripping of the Question of Legitimate for What?' in EU Governance." *European Constitutional Law Review* 8, no. 1: 153–64. https://doi.org/10.1017/S1574019612000107.

Martenczuk, Bernd. 2001. "Decisions of Bodies Established by International Agreements and the Community Legal Order." In *The EU and the International Legal Order*, edited by Vincent Kronenberger, 141–63. Den Haag: T.M.C. Asser Press.

Meissner, Katharina Luise. 2016. "Democratizing EU External Relations: The European Parliament's Informal Role in SWIFT, ACTA and TTIP." *European Foreign Affairs Review* 21, no. 2: 269–88.

Mendes, Joana. 2017. "The External Administrative Layer of EU Law-Making: International Decisions in EU Law and the Case of CETA." *European Papers* 2, no. 2: 489–517. https://doi.org/10.15166/2499-8249/166.

Meroni & Co., Industrie Metallurgiche, SpA v. *High Authority of the European Coal and Steel Community.* 1958. CJEU Case 9/56, Judgment of the Court (ECLI:EU:C:1958:7), 13 June.

Möllers, Christoph. 2015. *The Three Branches: A Comparative Model of Separation of Powers.* Oxford: Oxford University Press.

Office des professions du Québec. 2018. "Content of CETA and Comments on the Draft Mutual Recognition Agreement (MRA) for the Architectural Profession, April 2018." Accessed 22 July 2020. https://www.opq.gouv.qc.ca/fileadmin/documents/Commissaire/CommProjARMCanEuArch2018_va.pdf.

Ott, Andrea. 2016. "The European Parliament's Role in EU Treaty-Making."
    Maastricht Journal of European and Comparative Law 23, no. 6: 1009–39.
    https://doi.org/10.1177/1023263X1602300606.

Passos, Ricardo. 2017. "Some Issues Related to the Provisional Application
    of International Agreements and the Institutional Balance." In *The EU as a
    Global Actor: Bridging Legal Theory and Practice*, edited by Jenő Czuczai
    and Frederik Naert, 380–93. Leiden, Boston: Brill.

Pollack, Mark A. 2003. *The Engines of European Integration: Delegation,
    Agency, and Agenda Setting in the EU*. Oxford: Oxford University Press.

Puccio, Laura, and Roderick Harte. "The European Parliament's Role in
    Monitoring the Implementation of EU Trade Policy." In *The European
    Parliament in Times of EU Crises*, edited by Olivier Costa, 378–412.
    Basingstoke: Palgrave.

Rosén, Guri. 2018. "The European Parliament." In *Handbook on the EU and
    International Trade*, edited by Sangeeta Khorana and María García, 117–34.
    Cheltenham: Edward Elgar.

SA Roquette Frères v. *Council of the European Communities*. 1980. CJEU
    Case 138/79, Judgment of the Court, 29 October 1980.

Schütze, Robert. 2011. "'Delegated' Legislation in the (new) European Union:
    A Constitutional Analysis." *Modern Law Review* 74, no. 5: 661–93. https://
    www.jstor.org/stable/41302774.

– 2014. *Foreign Affairs and the EU Constitution: Selected Essays*. Cambridge:
    Cambridge University Press.

Terpan, Fabien. 2019. "The CJEU and the External Powers of the Parliament:
    Self-Restraint or Activism?" In *The Democratisation of EU International
    Relations Through EU Law*, edited by Juan Santos Vara and Soledad
    Rodríguez Sánchez-Tabernero, 39–66. London: Routledge.

Terpan, Fabien, and Sabine Saurugger. 2019. "The CJEU and the Parliament's
    External Powers Since Lisbon: Judicial Support to Representative
    Democracy?" *The European Parliament in Times of EU Crises*, edited by
    Olivier Costa, 77–98. Basingstoke: Palgrave.

TEU (Treaty on European Union). 2012. Accessed 23 July 2020. http://data.
    europa.eu/eli/treaty/teu_2012/oj.

TFEU (Treaty on the Functioning of the European Union). 2012. Accessed
    23 July 2020. https://eur-lex.europa.eu/legal-content/EN/TXT/?uri=CELEX%3
    A12012E%2FTXT.

United Kingdom v. *European Parliament and Council of the European Union*.
    2005. CJEU Case C-66/04, Judgment of the Court (Grand Chamber)
    (ECLI:EU:C:2005:743), 6 December.

– 2014. CJEU Case C-270/12. Judgment of the Court (Grand Chamber). 22 January.

van der Loo, Guillame. 2019. "National Parliaments and Mixed Agreements: Exploring the Legal Bumps in a Rocky Relationship." In *The Democratisation of EU International Relations through EU Law*, edited by Juan Santos Vara and Soledad Rodríguez Sánchez-Tabernero, 210–56. London: Routledge.

van der Mei, Anne Pieter. 2016. "EU External Relations and Internal Inter-Institutional Conflicts: The Battlefield of Article 218 TFEU." *Maastricht Journal of European and Comparative Law* 23, no. 6: 1051–76. https://doi.org/10.1177/1023263X1602300608.

von Bogdandy, Armin, Felix Arndt, and Jürgen Bast. 2004. "Legal Instruments in European Union Law and their Reform: A Systematic Approach on an Empirical Basis." *Yearbook of European Law* 23, no. 1: 91–136. https://doi-org.eres.qnl.qa/10.1093/yel/23.1.91.

Weiß, Wolfgang. 2018. "Delegation to Treaty Bodies in EU Agreements: Constitutional Constraints and Proposals for Strengthening the European Parliament." *European Constitutional Law Review* 14, no. 3: 532–66. https://doi.org/10.1017/S1574019618000305.

Wessel, Ramses A., and Tamara Takács. 2017. "Constitutional Aspects of the EU's Global Actorness: Increased Exclusivity in Trade and Investment and the Role of the European Parliament." *European Business Law Review* 28, no. 2: 103–17.

PART TWO

Regulatory Process

4

"Right to Regulate" and "Regulatory Cooperation" within CETA: Two Innovations for the Promotion of Investment Liberalization and Sustainability through a Value-Based Playing Field – A Few Remarks

Pia Acconci

INTRODUCTORY REMARKS

A discussion paper titled "CETA Implementation," published by the European Commission in 2018, underlines that "[t]he European Commission has negotiated the Comprehensive Economic and Trade Agreement (CETA) with a view to establishing a state-of-the-art, privileged, and forward-looking trade and economic relationship with Canada. To this end, the EU [European Union] and Canada have reached an ambitious agreement which offers companies new opportunities for trade and investment whilst safeguarding their respective standards of protection for the environmental, health, food, safety, labour, and consumers" (European Commission 2018, 2). This sentence highlights the propensity of the CETA contracting parties to promote trade and investment liberalization within a sustainable framework, based on the combination between economic and noneconomic interests.

In effect, at this stage of the worldwide process of liberalization and interdependence, complex policy, normative issues, and sometimes conflicts of interest have arisen because of the interaction between investment protection and heterogeneous concerns, such as water tariff regulation; waste management; prohibition of harmful substances such as pesticides, petrol, and tobacco; or the safeguard of religious sites. Such interests, concerns, and needs have been considered "public" in relation to hetero-geneous actors, i.e., local populations, nongovernmental organizations (NGOs), consumers, stakeholders, and public opinion in general.

Conflicts of interests have turned out to be a relevant investment and/or trade risk since the beginning of this millennium, when both developing and economically advanced states have been respondents before investment treaty-based arbitral tribunals, following a change in their domestic legal frameworks for reasons of public interest during the post-establishment phase of a foreign investment. Foreign investors claimed that this kind of a domestic regulatory measure amounted to an indirect expropriation, namely a regulatory taking, and compensation was to be awarded, in accordance with the applicable investment treaty.

There have been inconsistent case law and uncertainty, as traditional bilateral investment treaties (BITs) do not include provisions on the safeguard of non-investment concerns and interests. These are protected by separate instruments, whether binding or nonbinding, at the international-law level because of regulatory diversification that is typical of international law. Traditional BITs aim at investment protection, through, among others, a clause on direct arbitration mainly referring to the arbitration rules of the International Centre for the Settlement of Investment Disputes (ICSID) and/or those of the United Nations Commission on International Trade Law (UNCITRAL).

This kind of arbitration has brought about criticism, as the most common mechanism to settle disputes between a host state and a foreign investor. One such criticism is related to the alleged lack of democraticity, openness, and transparency of arbitral proceedings (Caron 2009; Nolan 2016; Van Harten 2007; Waibel et al. 2010).

On initiative of a few respondent states (particularly Argentina), international organizations, and scholars, a debate has arisen about the interpretation of international investment treaties in such proceed-ings (cf., among others, Gazzini 2016; Kurtz 2014; Roberts 2010). A specific issue has been if and how arbitrators could safeguard a host state's capacity for changing its domestic legislation against a foreign investor's interests and expectations, by taking a regulatory action for a public interest such as the protection of a non-investment concern (Giannakopoulos 2019; Hueckel 2012; Korzun 2016; Langford, Behn and Fauchald 2018; Rajput 2018; Ranjan and Anand 2016; Viñuales 2014).

As a reaction, the ICSID and UNCITRAL have adopted a few changes in their respective arbitration rules, which this chapter explores.

The chapter also illustrates that to tackle the risk arising from disputes due to the competition between heterogeneous concerns and to identify common solutions, several states have revised their model BITs and negotiated new investment treaties. Specialized international organizations have promoted the mainstreaming of sustainable development-related topics into the typical legal framework of international investment treaties, by also organizing conferences and workshops.

In addition, a number of states and the EU have included a clause on the right to regulate of a host contracting party to safeguard the exercise of its regulatory capacity in the pursuit of so-called legitimate public objectives, such as protection of the environment, public health and/or cultural heritage, and mitigating the right to protect of a home contracting party.

The relevance of some noneconomic interests has become an issue from another perspective. As this chapter clarifies, a few international agreements on trade and investment of the last decade promote "regulatory cooperation," in order to level the playing field and facilitate the liberalization process in relation to a few core topics, such as food safety, consumer protection, animal welfare, and financial stability. For instance, the Comprehensive and Progressive Agreement for Tran-Pacific Partnership (CPTPP) – concluded in 2017 – includes a chapter on regulatory coherence with the aim of covering both good regulatory practices and regulatory cooperation,[1] whereas the 2018 released text of the treaty establishing a free trade area among the United States, Mexico, and Canada (USMCA) has a chapter on "good regulatory practices."[2] Several international trade agreements of the EU also cover these issues.

The clauses on the right to regulate and the chapters on regulatory cooperation are interesting innovations of the typical drafting of international trade and investment agreements such as CETA. This chapter illustrates selected main aspects of these two innovations. A few concluding remarks show how the connection between the right to regulate and regulatory cooperation through such agreements might ease and possibly prevent conflicts between a host state and a foreign investor due to competing interests, norms, and objectives. Before so doing, two preliminary remarks are desirable, which are discussed next.

First, as mentioned, chapters or provisions on regulatory cooperation in international trade and investment treaties are related to particular policy areas and sectors of international trade, such as motor vehicles, food safety (through sanitary and phytosanitary [SPS] measures), medical devices, pharmaceutical inspections, animal welfare, cyber security, and financial services. Investment is outside the scope of application of chapters and/or provisions on regulatory cooperation. Treaty chapters and/or provisions on regulatory cooperation may have a positive impact on the international investment regulatory and policy framework, and particularly on the EU common investment policy, through the establishment of a common level of the playing field based on the effectiveness and quality of foreign direct investments (FDIs). Specifically, the EU might, through the chapters on regulatory cooperation in its international trade and investment agreements, attract foreign investments that are in line with its standards of protection, its other policies and the "EU social model" as a whole. This would contribute to the pursuit of the "Europe 2020 Strategy" that is based on the realization of a smart, inclusive, and sustainable growth. This way regulatory cooperation might facilitate the admission of qualitative foreign investments into the EU internal market and indirectly contribute to the spread of these kinds of investments worldwide.

Second, the attainment of regulatory diversification through a multilateral approach would contribute to prevent conflicts of norms and possibly of interests, as well as to enhance the predictability and acceptance of international investment law. The revision of the traditional regulatory structure of international investment treaties through the adoption of a multilateral regulatory instrument, even nonbinding, would also contribute to the predictability and acceptance of investment treaty-based arbitration proceedings and would mitigate the politicization of the relationship between host states and foreign investors. On the contrary, the lack of a multilateral comprehensive legal instrument would imply that the outcome of the settlement of investor-host state disputes is still based on a case-by-case approach, i.e., the specific circumstances of a case.

Bilateralism has been popular to preserve both state-to-state intercourse and the depoliticization of the relationship between a host state and a foreign investor in case of expropriation through clauses on direct arbitration within investment treaties. Regionalism has been used to insert liberalization into the typical design of such treaties. Multilateralism might contribute to both investment protection and liberalization from a value-based perspective, by ensuring a solution for the detrimental effects of international regulatory diversification through the uniformity both of the contracting parties and of topics, as well as interests and concerns, whether economic or not.

An international organization would be a significant framework to promote special discussions and negotiations for such a multilateral regulatory instrument. In particular, the UN Conference on Trade and Development (UNCTAD) would be able to give operational and technical support to member states this regard. This might promote negotiations for a multilateral investment treaty and/or the adoption by member states of interpretative declarations, guidelines, or model clauses for recurring issues dealt with by arbitrators, concerning the relevance of international rules on the protection of non-investment concerns within international investment law (cf. Acconci 2014, 2018).

A number of economically advanced states, such as Canada, and emerging states, such as China and India, have supported multilateralism in international economic relations through their statements and treaty practice. The EU has done the same, in accordance with Art. 21 of the Treaty on the European Union (TEU).[3]

However, a few other actors, such as the United States and the United Kingdom, have challenged this approach over the last decade. Therefore, the launch of negotiations for interpretative declarations, guidelines and/or model clauses or for a multilateral investment treaty even through an international organization has not been an effective option.

That is the main reason why one has still to refer to bilateralism and regionalism when current issues and prospects of international investment law are under discussion.

"RIGHT TO REGULATE" OF THE HOST CONTRACTING PARTY WITHIN INTERNATIONAL AND EU AGREEMENTS ON TRADE AND INVESTMENT

Over the last decades, the detrimental impact of foreign investments on the territories and human communities of host states has sometimes been evident. Environmental damages and/or changes in local health or cultural conditions have occurred in host states, both economically advanced and least developed ones. A few times such an impact has flowed from the increasing technical dimension of the economic activities related to the realization of foreign investments.

As a reaction, a few of these states have adopted domestic regulatory measures to safeguard a specific public objective, such as the protection of the environment, public health, or indigenous peoples. Several times this has occurred under pressure from representatives of local communities and/or nongovernmental organizations (NGOs). Although nondiscriminatory, this kind of a domestic regulatory measure has brought about various disputes before both domestic tribunals and treaty-based arbitral tribunals.

As to the latter, cases have arisen from the request of a foreign investor for compensation when an international investment treaty or an investment chapter of another kind of international treaty was applicable to the relationship between the host state and the foreign investor, and such a treaty included clauses on treatment standards, on compensation for any kind of taking, and on direct arbitration. More specifically, the foreign investor requested compensation for the alleged breach of the treaty clauses on the fair and equitable standard and expropriation, by claiming that the domestic regulatory measure for the safeguard of a public objective amounted to unlawful expropriation under the applicable treaty. A number of these cases were settled in favour of the respondent states. The tribunals accepted that a domestic legitimate nondiscriminatory measure aimed at safeguarding a public objective could not be considered tantamount to an expropriation. No compensation was therefore awarded to the foreign investor.[4]

In a number of such cases, the outcome was due to the respondent state's requests for an extension of the applicable rules by referring to specific international non-investment obligations on the protection of the environment, public health, and/or cultural heritage.

In *Chemtura* v. *Canada* (2010, 131, 266), the UNCITRAL tribunal admitted that the change of the respondent state's domestic law was justified by its obligations under the 1998 Aarhus Protocol on Persistent Organic Pollutants to the 1979 Convention Long-range Transboundary Air Pollution. In the "tobacco" cases[5] the respondent states relied on their obligations under the World Health Organization (WHO) Framework Convention on Tobacco Control to justify the legitimacy of their domestic regulatory measures. In *Philip Morris and Others* v. *Uruguay* (2011) the tribunal upheld this objection.[6]

The possible local detrimental impact of foreign investments has brought about another reaction. In order to render arbitral proceedings more inclusive, the ICSID (2006) revised its arbitration rules in 2006, with the inclusion of Arts 36 and 37, to enhance their openness, through the admission of amici curiae briefs.[7] In 2014, the UNCITRAL also adopted special rules to enhance the transparency of its investment treaty-based arbitral proceedings (UNCITRAL 2014). The participation of third parties in arbitral proceedings may support the least economically advanced states with technical assistance and capacity-building, as well as may highlight the relevance of a specific non-investment concern. A few NGOs have been able to request, as amici curiae, arbitral tribunals' special interpretations of the applicable international investment treaty, in accordance with relevant international instruments on the safeguard of the noneconomic concerns at stake. Some arbitral tribunals admitted reports or briefs of amici curiae, but not implemented them on the merits.[8]

On the other hand, by resorting to extensive interpretative criteria in an autonomous manner, a few arbitral tribunals acknowledged that respondent states were required to safeguard specific non-investment concerns in implementing their treaty investment obligations, as far as these states had already implemented the other international obligations at stake within their domestic legal frameworks.[9] In effect, arbitrators are entitled to attribute a specific relevance to other possible international obligations at stake, by using extensive interpretative criteria in an autonomous manner, because the applicable law in investment arbitration proceedings can include international law.[10] In a few cases, a change in the host state's domestic legal framework during the post-establishment phase – due to the need to protect a non-investment concern, such as cultural heritage, environment, and/or public health – was therefore considered a legitimate exercise of the host state's regulatory sovereignty, rather than a regulatory taking, even though the change could be a breach of the investment treaty on which the arbitral tribunal's jurisdiction was based. In light of this conclusion, host states were not required to pay compensation to the foreign investors.[11]

As mentioned, the majority of traditional international treaties applicable to foreign investment do not provide for relevant provisions this regard. However, over the last decades, several states – particularly economically advanced and emerging ones – and the EU have contributed to the revision of the typical regulatory structure of relevant international treaties, by including references, on the one hand, to a few non-investment concerns and/or, on the other, to the "right to regulate" of the host contracting party.

Under the first perspective, a number of states have revised the typical structure of their BITs to include a reference to non-investment concerns in preambles, as well as special clauses on non-precluded measures[12] and on non-relaxation commitments.[13] Some states have inserted a reference to the protection of non-investment interests as an exception to treaty obligations on the "prohibition of performance requirements."[14]

Besides, a few industrialized states have inserted specific clauses in their investment treaties to protect health, environment, and/or worker rights as a new way of promoting foreign investments. The Model BIT of the United States of 2004 and that of 2012 incorporate specific clauses related respectively to the relationships between investment and environment,[15] and between investment and labour.[16]

Under the second perspective related to the relevance of the right to regulate, the annex related to expropriation of the 2004 Canadian Model BIT has been the first important example of how a host state's regulatory capacity can be safeguarded within an international investment treaty. This annex runs as follows: "For greater certainty, except in the rare circumstance where the impact of the measure or series of measures is so severe in light of its purpose that it appears manifestly excessive, nondiscriminatory measures of a Party that are designed and applied to protect legitimate public welfare objectives, such as health, safety and the environment, do not constitute indirect expropriations" (CETA 2016, Annex 8-A).[17]

This provision is also included in annex B on expropriation of the 2012 United States Model BIT,[18] as well as in the 2018 USMCA.[19]

The annex X.11 to CETA on expropriation further distinguishes between the obligation of any contracting party to compensate in the case of a taking and the right to regulate of the same party in the public interest, by distinguishing between lawful takings (those that satisfy the requirements laid down in the treaty, including compensation) and non-compensable regulatory measures (those that are the outcome of the exercise of a host contracting party's regulatory powers in the public interest and are outside the scope of application of the treaty) (Dionysiou 2021; UNCTAD 2012, 78–90). Such a provision is typical of Canadian BITs that have been concluded in light of the 2004 Canadian Model BIT.

Other international trade agreements signed by the EU and its member states also include the annex on expropriation similar to that provided in CETA.[20]

Some investment treaties refer to a host state's right to regulate as such, by including it in preambles and/or special clauses. The preamble of the 2015 Trans-Pacific Partnership Agreement (TPP) is a relevant example. It runs as follows: "[recognize] their inherent right to regulate and resolve to preserve the flexibility of the Parties to set legislative and regulatory priorities, safeguard public welfare, and protect legitimate public welfare objectives, such as public health, safety, the environment, the conservation of living or nonliving exhaustible natural resources, the integrity and stability of the financial system and public morals" (CPTPP, Preamble).[21] Preamble and Art. 5 of the 2020 Italian Model BIT are other interesting examples.

A few treaties connect the right to regulate to host state's police powers. The 2007 Investment Agreement for the COMESA Common Investment Area is a significant example as this includes a reference to international customary law to exclude that the exercise by a host contracting party of its police powers amount to an expropriation.[22]

Recent international trade agreements of the EU – concluded after the entry into force of the Lisbon Treaty – are relevant examples as to the inclusion of specific clauses on the right to regulate. The EU has given importance to the safeguard of the right to regulate since 2010, when the EU Commission and the EU Parliament had started to deal with the exercise of the new EU competence on FDI within the common commercial policy. The European Parliament (EP) has several times high-lighted the need of reconciling the protection of investment (right to protect) and a host state's right to regulate.[23] The report on the "Future European International Investment Policy," adopted by the Committee on International Trade of the European Parliament on 22 March 2011, calls on the Commission to include in all future EU trade and investment agreements specific clauses laying down the protection of the right to regulate (Committee on International Trade 2011, para. 25), the promotion of sustainable investments in terms of the protection of the environment (ibid., paras 27–30), and of "the public intervention domain" (ibid., paras 11–12). The "Statement of the European Union and the United States on Shared Principles for International Investment" published on 10 April 2012 also includes a reference to the right to regulate (Department of State 2012).[24]

In effect, CETA and a few other post-Lisbon EU international treaties on trade and investment include relevant provisions on the safeguard of the right to regulate, sustainable development and/or some of its key principles, and/or the importance of the accountable conduct of private foreign investors. The preamble of CETA (2016) includes an express reference to the right to regulate: "[r]ecognizing that the provisions of this Agreement preserve the right to regulate within their territories and resolving to preserve their flexibility to achieve legitimate policy objectives, such as public health, safety, environment, public morals and the promotion and protection of cultural diversity." Art. 8.9 of CETA (2016) specifies, among others, that: "1. For the purpose of this Chapter, the Parties reaffirm their right to regulate within their territories to achieve legitimate policy objectives, such as the protection of public health, safety, the environment or public morals, social or consumer protection or the promotion and protection of cultural diversity. 2. For greater certainty, the mere fact that a Party regulates, including through a modification to its laws, in a manner which negatively affects an investment or interferes with an investor's expectations, including its expectations of profits, does not amount to a breach of an obligation under this Section."

Section 2 under Art. 2 of the investment chapter of the 2015 draft text of the Transatlantic Trade and Investment Partnership Agreement (TTIP) with the United States is also worth mentioning. This is related to investment and regulatory measures/objectives and connects the right to regulate to the achievement of a few legitimate public objectives. This article allows changes in domestic regulatory laws of contracting parties, even if these might be detrimental to a foreign investor's expectations.[25] Art. 13 *bis* of the free trade agreement (FTA) that the EU, its member states, and Vietnam signed on 1 February 2016, and annex 4, paragraph 4, of the 2018 EU-Vietnam Trade and Investment Agreement include a similar provision. The 2018 Trade and Investment Protection Agreement between the EU, its member states, and Singapore is also relevant in this regard.[26]

Besides, subsection II, Art. 1 of Chapter 4 of the 2020 Agreement on Investment among China, the EU, and its member states is important. This provision connects the right to regulate and sustainable development in terms of national labour and environmental protection and reads as follows: "The Parties recognise the right of each Party to determine its sustainable development policies and priorities, to establish its own levels of domestic labour and environmental protection, and to adopt or modify its relevant laws and policies accordingly, consistently with its multilateral commitments in the fields of labour and environment."

"REGULATORY COOPERATION"
THROUGH INTERNATIONAL AND EU TRADE
AND INVESTMENT AGREEMENTS

A number of recent international trade agreements provide for a few relevant provisions on "regulatory cooperation" among the contracting parties. Most international trade agreements under negotiation and/or concluded by the EU after the entry into force of the Lisbon Treaty are relevant this regard. For instance, CETA; the 2015 draft text of TTIP with the United States; and the 2018 Economic Cooperation Agreement (EPA) between the EU, its member states, and Japan include a specific chapter on such cooperation.[27] Relevant chapters and provisions are directed to mitigating differences in regulatory and technical standards, as "barriers" to the freedom of trade. These provisions aim at facilitating market access through compatibility, coordination, harmonization, and mutual recognition, as well as at preventing conflicts of norms.[28] To this end, exchange of technical information, consultations, dialogues, alignment of regulatory systems, streamlining of duplicative procedures, mutual peer-reviews of regulatory practices, and regulatory impact assessments appear to be all useful activities (cf. Parker 2015). The member states of the Organisation for Economic Co-operation and Development (OECD) have promoted these goals[29] (see also Kauffman and Saffirio 2021). The approximation of differences appears to be the desirable ultimate goal of regulatory cooperation, in order to attain regulatory quality.

Regulatory cooperation also presupposes the establishment of common committees, technical working groups, and forums, as per the CETA Regulatory Cooperation Forum established under Art. 21.6 of CETA (2016). The organization of meetings, workshops, and networks with stakeholders is also recommended. According to Art. 21, paragraph 8, of CETA (2016), Canada, the EU, and its member states have to promote the involvement of civil society and other possible stakeholders, for example through calls for proposals and their debrief after the annual meeting of the CETA Regulatory Cooperation Forum.

However, the negotiation of international trade and investment agreements including stand-alone chapters on regulatory cooperation by the EU has been debated.

According to the representatives of a few NGOs and of other groups of citizens, as well according to some scholars (e.g. Fung 2016; Meuwese 2015), treaty rules on regulatory cooperation might undermine the democratic control of the regulatory decision-making process within both the EU and its member states. International procedural and administrative mechanisms for regulatory cooperation would adopt regulations and standards, instead of the EP and national parliaments of the contracting states, thereby generating a sort of pre-emption effect. This has been a first reason for criticism on the assumption that international agreements on trade an investment are not the best regulatory means available to change the allocation of regulatory capacity at the domestic law level. Another reason for criticism has been related to the uncertain impact of the activity of international mechanisms for regulatory cooperation on the exercise of a contracting party's regulatory capacity for the pursuit of social objectives by its domestic institutions. These mechanisms might permit more efficient regulatory measures for the enhancement of transnational trade transactions, but possibly at the expense of the pursuance of those objectives. In effect, such mechanisms are designed to support national bodies for the realization of the liberalization process from an economic perspective, but not necessarily from a social one.

CONCLUDING REMARKS: A FEW REASONS
FOR TREATY CORRELATION BETWEEN THE RIGHT
TO REGULATE AND REGULATORY COOPERATION

The design of international trade and investment treaties has changed, as many states and the EU have dealt with a number of risks arising from disputes between a host state and a foreign investor. Relevant provisions have been included into several treaties, in order to acknowledge and/or safeguard non-investment concerns that are more related to public concerns, such as public health and the environment. There have also been developments in transparency and openness of investment treaty-based arbitral proceedings after the revision of the ICSID's and UNCITRAL's respective arbitration rules.

However, these developments and the increasing relevance of certain social objectives within international instruments dealing with investments have not been enough to reconcile private interests of the investors and heterogeneous public interests of host states.

Specifically, the mainstreaming of the safeguard of the right to regulate and of sustainable development-related interests into international invest-ment rules, by adding references to noneconomic interests in preambles, special clauses, and/or chapters of investment treaties, has not been enough to attain international regulatory diversification, and to ensure the effective management of the possible detrimental implications of differences in the intensity of applicable rules and of available remedies (cf. IBA Arbitration Subcommittee 2018, 12–13). This can also be maintained in relation to CETA (Sobek 2019).

Chapters and/or detailed provisions on regulatory cooperation within regional and mega-regional agreements might be used as additional tools for the enhancement of the social dimension of the current international investment regulatory and policy framework, if regulatory coordination and coherence would level the existing playing field under a value-based perspective and would hence reduce differences in relevant domestic legislations. This might ease conflicts of interests and norms and possibly disputes between a host state and a foreign investor before investment treaty-based arbitral tribunals. The EU and its member states appear to be in favour of such an objective. Other players of the international investment arena might agree on the pursuit of this, on account of the widespread acceptance of the approach based on economic liberalization and sustainability, within and outside national borders.

Coordination and coherence, through provisions on regulatory cooperation in one applicable treaty, might allow a host state to take a domestic regulatory measure for the safeguard of one pre-determined noneconomic concern with no need to make a counterclaim by availing itself of the clause on the right to regulate in the same treaty. This might be a cost-effective solution from a state's perspective. That might be a relevant reason for the correlation between a host state's treaty-based right to regulate as a deterrent, and regulatory cooperation as an implementing tool for the applicable treaty.

Without treaty regulatory coordination and coherence, and to some extent harmonization and mutual recognition, the state might be brought before an investment treaty-based arbitral tribunal and could take such a measure in accordance with its treaty-based right to regulate upon a financial burden that is a counterclaim against the claimant investor. The costs of such an action would be recovered only if its counterclaim would prevail over the investor's claim for compensation. This might render the relationships between foreign investors and host states uncertain and even more conflicting.[30]

There might be another reason for treaty combination between the right to regulate and regulatory cooperation under a value-based perspective. As things stand, to facilitate the achievement of this result, states would have to mitigate differences in their interests and concerns and thus detect common shared standards and levels of protection. During negotiations, states would have to focus on the accuracy of the language of treaty clauses mentioning legitimate public objectives in relation to the right to regulate on the one hand, and relevant policy spaces and sectors for regulatory cooperation on the other, in order to reduce possible undesirable implications of these two innovations. Such negotiations would prevent an international trade and investment agreement from limiting, or at least influencing, the exercise of a host state's regulatory powers.

NOTES

1 The CPTPP Agreement incorporates the 2016 text of the Trans-Pacific Partnership (TPP) Agreement. This latter agreement was signed by Australia, Brunei, Canada, Chile, Japan, Malaysia, Mexico, New Zealand, Peru, Singapore, the United States, and Vietnam. The United States withdrew on day one of the Trump Administration, that is on 23 January 2017. Art. 8.2 of the TPP chapter, "Technical Barriers," specifies that "[t]he objective of this Chapter is to facilitate trade, including by eliminating

unnecessary technical barriers to trade, enhancing transparency, and promoting greater regulatory cooperation and good regulatory practice." Art. 8.3 also clarifies that "1. [t]his Chapter shall apply to the preparation, adoption and application of all technical regulations, standards and conformity assessment procedures of central level of government bodies (and, where explicitly provided for, technical regulations, standards and conformity assessment procedures of government bodies at the level directly below that of the central level of government) that may affect trade in goods between the Parties, except as provided in paragraphs 4 and 5."

2 Ch. 28 of USMCA.

3 According to Art. 21, paragraph 2, "[t]he Union shall define and pursue common policies and actions, and shall work for a high degree of cooperation in all fields of international relations, in order to: (a) safeguard its values, fundamental interests, security, independence and integrity; (b) consolidate and support democracy, the rule of law, human rights and the principles of international law; (c) preserve peace, prevent conflicts and strengthen international security, in accordance with the purposes and principles of the United Nations Charter, with the principles of the Helsinki Final Act and with the aims of the Charter of Paris, including those relating to external borders; (d) foster the sustainable economic, social and environmental development of developing countries, with the primary aim of eradicating poverty; (e) encourage the integration of all countries into the world economy, including through the progressive abolition of restrictions on international trade; (f) help develop international measures to preserve and improve the quality of the environment and the sustainable management of global natural resources, in order to ensure sustainable development."

4 In particular, see *Methanex Corp.* v. *The United States* (2005) and *Chemtura* v. *Canada* (2010).

5 See *Philip Morris Asia Ltd.* v. *Australia* (2015); *Philip Morris Brands Sarl, Philip Morris Products S.A. and Abal Hermanos S.A.* v. *Uruguay* (2016).

6 *Philip Morris Brands Sarl, Philip Morris Products S.A. and Abal Hermanos S.A.* v. *Uruguay* (2016; especially 306).

7 For an overview, see Antonietti (2006).

8 See, in particular, *Bernhard von Pezold and Others* v. *The Republic of Zimbabwe* (2018); *Border Timbers Limited, Border Timbers International (Private) Limited, and Hangani Development Co. (Private) Limited* v. *The Republic of Zimbabwe* (2017), and *Glamis Gold Limited* v. *The United States* (2009).

9 In a few cases the tribunals referred to the case law of the European Court of Human Rights (ECHR) to ascertain whether or not the host state had

expropriated the claimant's property (see, in particular, *Mondev v. The United States* (2002, 143–4); *Tecmed v. Mexico* (2003, 122), *Azurix v. Argentina* (2006, 311–2); and *Saipem v. Bangladesh* (2007, 130–2). In *SPP v. Egypt* (1992, 150–4), the tribunal referred to the 1972 UNESCO Convention concerning the protection of the world cultural and natural heritage. In *Myers v. Canada* (2000, 209–17) the tribunal took into consideration the Basel Convention on the Control of Transboundary Movements of Hazardous Waste and their Disposal as a relevant reference point. In *Pope & Talbot Inc. v. Canada* (2001, 45–63) the tribunal mentioned the WTO case law in relation to the definition of the field of application of the trade regulation in the North America Free Trade Area Treaty (NAFTA). In particular, the tribunal referred to the case *European Communities – Measures Concerning Asbestos and Asbestos Containing Products* (WTIDS135/R, 18 September 2000, 58–60).

10 According to Art. 42, paragraph 1, of the ICSID Convention, "[t]he Tribunal shall decide a dispute in accordance with such rules of law as may be agreed by the parties. In the absence of such agreement, the Tribunal shall apply the law of the Contracting State party to the dispute (including its rules on the conflict of laws) and such rules of international law as may be applicable."

11 Besides *Chemtura v. Canada* (2010) mentioned earlier, see *Methanex v. The United States* (2005, part IV:15); *Parkerings v. Lithuania* (2007, 382–3); *Glamis v. The United States* (2009); and *Philip Morris v. Uruguay* (2016, 90, 197, 306). In *Saluka v. The Czech Republic* (2006, 261) the tribunal referred to international customary law to deny that the host state's regulatory actions amounted to an expropriation. In the *Urbaser v. Argentina* (2016, 1193–9) the tribunal upheld the counterclaim of Argentina which aimed at establishing human rights obligations of the claimant investor, in accordance with international legal instruments such as the 1948 Declaration of Human Rights and the 1966 UN Covenant on Economic, Social, and Cultural Rights. However, according to the tribunal, the respondent state could not demonstrate that the alleged breach of the right to water "entails a duty of reparation equally based on international law, with the effect that the individuals concerned by such an alleged harm obtain an appropriate compensation." This is due to regulatory diversification and also to "the lack of any legal ground based on international law that would entitle a group of individuals to raise a claim for performance for delivery of water and sewage services directed against a company or any other private party" (ibid., 1220).

12 Following Art. XX of the General Agreement on Tariffs and Trade (GATT), the protection of public interests, such as environment and health, is

considered a general exception to treaty obligations on the treatment of foreign investments in a number of BITs and free trade agreements (FTAS). See, among others, the 1997 Canada-Armenia BIT, Art. XVII; the 2004 Model BIT of Canada, Art. 10(1); the 1998 Switzerland-Mauritius BIT, Art. 11 (3); the 1999 New Zealand-Argentina BIT, Art. 5(3); the 2020 Italian Model BIT, Art. 5. Several Indian BITs, such as the 1995 Germany-India BIT, Art. 12; the 1995 Italy-India BIT, Art. 12; the 1996 Czech Republic-India BIT, Art. 12; and the 1999 Australia-India BIT, Art. 15, refer to "measures necessary … for the prevention of diseases or pests." For example, Art. 33 of the 2012 BIT between Canada and China is also relevant, which reads as follows: "2. [p]rovided that such measures are not applied in an arbitrary or unjustifiable manner, or do not constitute a disguised restriction on international trade or investment, nothing in this Agreement shall be construed to prevent a Contracting Party from adopting or maintaining measures, including environmental measures: (a) necessary to ensure compliance with laws and regulations that are not inconsistent with the provisions of this Agreement; (b) necessary to protect human, animal or plant life or health; or (c) relating to the conservation of living or non-living exhaustible natural resources if such measures are made effective in conjunction with restrictions on domestic production or consumption." For a reference to public health and/or national security as general exceptions, see the 1994 Bolivia-Mexico FTA, Arts 3 to 13(3). The 2003 Australia-Singapore FTA includes a reference to "the protection of national treasures of artistic, historic or archeological value" (Art. 21). In addition, see the 2007 Model BIT of Colombia, Art. VII, as regards the protection of the environment. According to Art. 9.15 of the 2015 TPP Agreement, "[n]othing in this Chapter shall be construed to prevent a Party from adopting, maintaining or enforcing any measure otherwise consistent with this Chapter that it considers appropriate to ensure that investment activity in its territory is undertaken in a manner sensitive to environmental, health or other regulatory objectives."

13 See, among others, the 2002 Netherlands-Namibia BIT; the 2002 Korea-Trinidad and Tobago BIT; the 2003 Finland-Kyrgyzistan BIT; and the 2004 Dutch Model BIT. The non-relaxation clause of the 2012 Model BIT of the United States, like that of 2004, runs as follows: "[d]esiring to achieve these objectives in a manner consistent with the protection of health, safety, and the environment, and the promotion of internationally recognized labor rights." Another example of a common non-relaxation clause specifies that "[e]ach Contracting Party recognizes that it is inappropriate to encourage investment by investors of another Contracting

Party by relaxing its environmental measures. To this effect each Contracting Party should not waive or otherwise derogate from such environmental measures as an encouragement for the establishment, acquisition or expansion of investments in its territory." See the 1995 Switzerland-Mexico BIT, Protocol to Art. 3; the 2004 Model BIT of Canada, Art.11; the 2008 Canada-Colombia FTA, Art. 815; and the 2012 trilateral investment treaty among Japan, China, and South Korea, Art. 23 concerning environmental measures. See also the 2012 TPP draft investment chapter, Art. 12.15(2).

14 See the 2003 Australia-Singapore FTA, Art. 5(3)(c); and the 2012 Model BIT of the United States, Art. 8(3)(c). Art. 9.9, para. 2(d) of the 2015 TPP Agreement runs as follows "[p]rovided that such measures are not applied in an arbitrary or unjustifiable manner, or do not constitute a disguised restriction on international trade or investment, paragraphs 1(b), 1(c), 1(f), 2(a) and 2(b) shall not be construed to prevent a Party from adopting or maintaining measures, including environmental measures: (i) necessary to secure compliance with laws and regulations that are not inconsistent with this Agreement; (ii) necessary to protect human, animal or plant life or health; or (iii) related to the conservation of living or non-living exhaustible natural resources."

15 The revised Art. 12 of the 2012 US Model BIT is longer and more complex than the 2004 text. Art. 12 of the 2012 text refers to a wide-ranging concept of the environment, as well as measures that may be adopted for its protection. These measures may be directed to preventing and controlling air pollution, the employment of hazardous and toxic substances, the conservation of "wild flora and fauna," and/or "specially protected natural areas." In addition, the revised Art. 12 establishes a clear relationship between the protection of environment and of health, by specifying that "'environmental law' means each Party's statutes or regulations, or provisions thereof, the primary purpose of which is the protection of the environment, or the prevention of a danger to human, animal, or plant life or health." The same text also accords great discretion to contracting states for the protection of the environment within the invest-ment context. According to Art. 12(3), "[t]he Parties recognize that each Party retains the right to exercise discretion with respect to regulatory, compliance, investigatory, and prosecutorial matters, and to make decisions regarding the allocation of resources to enforcement with respect to other environmental matters determined to have higher priorities." Conventions, such as the Aarhus Convention, are not mentioned, probably to avoid cross-fertilization. The importance of the environment within the

framework of the revised US Model BIT further emerges from Art. 12(7), which acknowledges that the relationship between investment and environment may concern local communities and public opinion. This paragraph states that "[t]he Parties confirm that each Party may, as appropriate, provide opportunities for public participation regarding any matter arising under this Article." It is noteworthy that Art. 12(7) does not mention the 1998 Aarhus Convention of the United Nations Economic Commission for Europe (UNECE) on "access to information, public participation in decision-making and access to justice in environmental matters," although this provision is clearly inspired by that convention.

16   The revised text of Art. 13 of the 2012 US Model BIT, on the relationship between investment and labour, is based on international standards of protection. This text, as its 2004 version, is in line with the international Conventions concluded within the framework of the International Labour Organization (ILO) to protect basic labour rights, insofar as this article mentions the ILO Declaration on Fundamental Principles and Rights at Work and its Follow-Up and refers indirectly to the standards of protection included in those Conventions. None of the ILO Conventions are, however, directly named, possibly in order to avoid treaty cross-fertilization.

17   Other treaties include the provision typical of Canadian investment treaties. See, among others, the 2005 US-Australia FTA; the 2009 ASEAN Comprehensive Investment Agreement; the 2009 Colombia-India BIT, the 2010 United Kingdom-Colombia BIT; the 2012 Indian Model BIT; the 2015 TPP Agreement; the 2015 China-Korea FTA Agreement; the 2016 Nigeria-Morocco BIT; the 2018 Armenia-Korea republic BIT, the 2019 China-Mauritius FTA, the 2019 Myanmar-Singapore BIT, the 2020 Investment Cooperation and Facilitation Treaty between Brazil and India; and the 2020 Regional Comprehensive Economic Partnership (RCEP) Agreement concluded among Australia, Brunei, Cambodia, China, Indonesia, Japan, Laos, Malaysia, Myanmar, New Zealand, the Philippines, Singapore, South Korea, Thailand and Vietnam.

18   See Art. 4(b) of the annex B to the 2012 US Model BIT.

19   See Art. 3(b) of the annex 14–B on expropriation. See also Art. 4(b) of the annex 10-B of the Trade Promotion Agreement between the United States and Panama concluded in 2007 and entered into force in 2012.

20   See also, among others, the 2008 Economic Partnership Agreement (EPA) among the member states of the Caribbean Forum (CARIFORUM), the European communities and its member states, in particular Art. 60(4) and 184; the 2010 FTA among the EU, its member states and South Korea, in particular the preamble, Arts 7.1(4) and 13.3; and the 2012 trade

agreement among the EU, its member states, Colombia and Peru, in particular Arts 107(5) and 268. For further information on the CARIFORUM group of African, Caribbean, and Pacific states, see https:/ caricom.org/cariforum-the-context.

21 See also, among others, Art. 20 of the 2012 Model BIT of the Southern African Development Community (SADC); Art. 23, para. 1, of the 2016 Nigeria-Morocco BIT; the preamble of the 2019 Australia-Uruguay BIT; the preamble and Art. 2, para. 2, of the 2019 Model BIT of the Netherlands.

22 Art. 20, para. 8, of the 2007 Investment Agreement for the Common Investment Area of the Common Market for Eastern and Southern Africa (COMESA) provides that "[c]onsistent with the right of states to regulate and the customary international law principles on police powers, bona fide regulatory measures taken by a Member State that are designed and applied to protect or enhance legitimate public welfare objectives, such as public health, safety and the environment, shall not constitute an indirect expropriation under this article." See also the preamble of the 2019 Facilitation and Cooperation Investment Agreement between Brazil and the United Arab Emirates.

23 As to the European Parliament, see, among others, Resolution 2010/2203, 6 April 2011, especially paras 15, 17, 23, 26–30; Resolution 2013/2558(RSP), 23 May 2013, especially para. 16; and Resolution 2014/2228(INI), 8 July 2015, especially paras xiii–xiv.

24 The preamble of the "shared principles" underlines that "[w]e believe that governments can fully implement these principles while still preserving the authority to adopt and maintain measures necessary to regulate in the public interest to pursue certain public policies." These "principles" were negotiated by the EU Trade Commissioner within the Framework of the Transatlantic Economic Council.

25 According to the (draft) TTIP, Art. 2 of the section 2 related to investment and regulatory measures/objectives:

1. The provisions of this section shall not affect the right of the Parties to regulate within their territories through measures necessary to achieve legitimate policy objectives, such as the protection of public health, safety, environment or public morals, social or consumer protection or promotion and protection of cultural diversity. 2. For greater certainty, the provisions of this section shall not be interpreted as a commitment from a Party that it will not change the legal and regulatory framework, including in a manner that may negatively affect the operation of cov- ered investments or the investor's expectations of profits. 3. For greater certainty and subject to paragraph 4, a Party's decision not to issue,

renew or maintain a subsidy (a) in the absence of any specific commitment under law or contract to issue, renew, or maintain that subsidy; or (b) in accordance with any terms or conditions attached to the issuance, renewal or maintenance of the subsidy, shall not constitute a breach of the provisions of this Section. 4. For greater certainty, nothing in this Section shall be construed as preventing a Party from discontinuing the granting of a subsidy and/or requesting its reimbursement, or as requiring that Party to compensate the investor therefor, where such action has been ordered by one of its competent authorities listed in Annex III.

26 See annex 1, Art. 2.

27 See Chapter 21 of CETA.

28 See, for instance, Art. 21.3 of CETA.

29 The OECD Council on Regulatory Policy and Governance adopted a significant Recommendation in 2012 (https://www.oecd.org/governance/regulatory-policy/49990817.pdf).

30 As to the possibly uncertain features of counterclaims, as separate claims, see *David Aven et al.* v. *Costa Rica* (2018, 745). As to a partly successful counterclaim, as a separate claim, see *Perenco Ecuador Ltd* v. *Ecuador* (2019, 1013).

REFERENCES

Acconci, Pia. 2014. "The Integration of Non-investment Concerns as an Opportunity for the Modernization of International Investment Law: Is a Multilateral Approach Desirable?" In *General Interests of Host States in International Investment Law*, edited by Giorgio Sacerdoti, Pia Acconci, Mara Valenti, and Anna De Luca, 165–93. Cambridge: Cambridge University Press.

– 2018. *"Sustainable Development and Investment: Trends in Law-making and Arbitration."* In *General Principles of Law and International Investment Arbitration*, edited by Andrea Gattini, Attila Tanzi, and Filippo Fontanelli, 290–319. Leiden, Boston: Brill Academic Publishers Nijhoff.

Antonietti, Aurélia. 2006. "The 2006 Amendments to the ICSID Rules and Regulations and the Additional Facility Rules." *ICSID Review* 21, no. 2: 427–48. https://doi.org/10.1093/icsidreview/21.2.427.

Azurix v. *Argentina*. 2006. ICSID Case No. ARB/01/12, Award, 14 July.

Bernhard von Pezold and Others v. *The Republic of Zimbabwe*. 2018. ICSID Case No. ARB/10/15.

Border Timbers Limited, Border Timbers International (Private) Limited, and Hangani Development Co. (Private) Limited v. *The Republic of Zimbabwe.* 2017. ICSID Case No. ARB/10/25.

Caron, David D. 2009. "Investor State Arbitration: Strategic and Tactical Perspectives on Legitimacy." *Suffolk Transnational Law Review* 32: 513–24.

CETA (Canada-European Union Comprehensive Economic and Trade Agreement). 2016. Accessed 21 July 2020. https://www.international.gc.ca/trade-commerce/trade-agreements-accords-commerciaux/agr-acc/ceta-aecg/text-texte/toc-tdm.aspx?lang=eng.

Chemtura v. *Canada.* 2010. NAFTA/UNCITRAL/PCA Arbitration, Award, 2 August.

Committee on International Trade. 2011. "Report on the Future European International Investment Policy." Accessed 22 July 2020. https://www.europarl.europa.eu/sides/getDoc.do?reference=A7-2011-0070&type=REPORT&language=EN&redirect.

CPTPP (Comprehensive and Progressive Agreement for Trans-Pacific Partnership). 2018. Accessed 21 July 2020. https://www.international.gc.ca/trade-commerce/trade-agreements-accords-commerciaux/agr-acc/tpp-ptp/text-texte/00.aspx?lang=eng.

David Aven et al. v. *Costa Rica.* 2018. UNCITRAL Case under Chapter Ten of the DR-CAFTA, Case No. UNCT/15/3, Award, 18 September.

Department of State. 2012. "Statement of the European Union and the United States on Shared Principles for International Investment." Accessed 22 July 2020. https://2009-2017.state.gov/p/eur/rls/or/2012/187618.htm.

Dionysiou, K. 2021. *CETA's Investment Chapter*, Heidelberg, New York, Springer.

European Commission. 2018. "The Economic Impact of the Comprehensive Economic and Trade Agreement: An Analysis by the European Commission's Directorate-General of Trade." Accessed 22 July 2020. https://trade.ec.europa.eu/doclib/docs/2017/september/tradoc_156043.pdf.

Fung, T. Sandra. 2014. "Negotiating Regulatory Coherence: The Costs and Consequences of Disparate Regulatory Principles in the Transatlantic Trade and Investment Partnership Agreement between the United States and the European Union." *Cornell International Law Journal* 47, no. 2: 445–71.

Gazzini, Tarcisio. 2016. *Interpretation of International Investment Treaties.* Oxford: Hart Publishing.

Giannakopoulos, Charalampos. 2019. "The Right to Regulate in International Investment Law and the Law of State Responsibility: A Hohfeldian Approach." In *Permutations of Responsibility in International Law,* edited by Photini Pazartzis and Panos Merkouris, 148–84. Leiden, Boston: Brill Academic Publishers Nijhoff.

Glamis Gold Limited v. *The United States*. 2009. NAFTA/UNCITRAL Arbitration, Award, 8 June.

Hueckel, Julia. 2012. "Rebalancing Legitimacy and Sovereignty in International Investment Agreements." *Emory Law Journal* 61, no. 3: 601–40.

IBA Arbitration Subcommittee on Investment Treaty Arbitration. 2018. *Consistency, Efficiency and Transparency in Investment Treaty Arbitration.* Accessed 4 March 2020. https://www.ibanet.org/Document/Default. aspx?DocumentUid=a8d68c6c-120b-4a6a-afd0-4397bc22b569.

International Centre for Settlement of Investment Disputes (ICSID). 2006. "ICSID Convention Arbitration Rules." Accessed 22 July 2020. https://icsid. worldbank.org/en/Pages/icsiddocs/ICSID-Convention-Arbitration-Rules.aspx.

Kauffman, Céline, and Saffirio, Camila. 2021. *Good Regulatory Practices and Cooperation in Trade Agreements: A Historical Perspective and Stocktaking.* OECD Regulatory Policy Working Papers.

Korzun, Vera. 2016. "The Right to Regulate in Investor-State Arbitration: Slicing and Dicing Regulatory Carve-Outs." SJD diss., Fordham University School of Law.

Kurtz, Jurgen. 2014. "Building Legitimacy Through Interpretation in Investor-State Arbitration: On Consistency, Coherence and the Identification of Applicable Law" In *The Foundations of International Investment Law: Bringing Theory into Practice*, edited by Zachary Douglas, Joost Pauwelyn, and Jorge E. Viñuales, 257–96. Oxford: Oxford University Press.

Langford, Malcolm, Daniel Behn, and Ole Kristian Fauchald. 2018. "Backlash and State Strategies in International Investment Law." In *The Changing Practices of International Law*, edited by Tanja Aalberts and Thomas Gammeltoft-Hansen, 70–102. Cambridge: Cambridge University Press.

Methanex Corp. v. *The United States*. 2005. NAFTA/UNCITRAL Arbitration, Final Award on jurisdiction and merits, 3 August.

Methanex v. The United States. 2005. NAFTA/UNCITRAL Arbitration, Final Award on Jurisdiction and Merits, 3 August.

Meuwese, Anne. 2015. "Constitutional Aspects of Regulatory Coherence in TTIP: An EU Perspective." *Law and Contemporary Problems* 78: 153–74. https://www.jstor.org/stable/43920635.

Mondev v. The United States. 2002. ICSID Case No. ARB(AF)/99/2, Award, 11 October.

Myers v. Canada. 2000. NAFTA/UNCITRAL Arbitration, Partial Award, 13 November.

Nolan, Michael. 2016. "Challenges to the Credibility of the Investor-State Arbitration System." *American University Business Law Review* 15, no. 3: 429–45. https://ssrn.com/abstract=3157420.

Parker, Richard W. 2015. "Four Challenges for TTIP Regulatory Cooperation." In *Columbia Journal of European Law*, 1–14.

Parkerings v. Lithuania. 2007. ICSID Case No. ARB/05/8, Award, 11 September.

Perenco Ecuador Ltd v. Ecuador. 2019. ICSID Case No. ARB/08/6, Award, 27 September.

Philip Morris Asia Ltd. v. Australia. 2015. PCA Case No. 2012-12, Award on jurisdiction and admissibility, 17 December.

Philip Morris Brands Sarl, Philip Morris Products S.A. and Abal Hermanos S.A. v. Uruguay. 2011. ICSID Case No. ARB/10/7, Memorial on Jurisdiction, 24 September.

Philip Morris v. Uruguay. 2016. ICSID Case No. ARB/10/7, Award, 8 July.

Pope & Talbot v. Canada. 2001. UNCITRAL Arbitration, Award on the Merits of Phase 2, 10 April.

Rajput, Aniruddha. 2018. *Regulatory Freedom and Indirect Expropriation in Investment Arbitration.* Alphen aan den Rijn: Kluwer Law International.

Ranjan, Prabhash, and Pushkar Anand. 2016. "Determination of Indirect Expropriation and Doctrine of Police Power in International Investment Law: A Critical Appraisal." In *Judging the State in International Trade and Investment Law: Sovereignty Modern, the Law and the Economics,* edited by Leïla Choukroune, 127–54. Heidelberg/London: Springer.

Roberts, Anthea. 2010. "Power and Persuasion in Investment Treaty Interpretation: The Dual Role of States." In *The American Journal of International Law,* 179–225.

Saipem v. Bangladesh. 2007. ICSID Case No. ARB/05/07, Decision on Jurisdiction and Recommendation on Provisional Measures, 21 March.

Saluka v. The Czech Republic. 2006. UNCITRAL Arbitration, Partial Award, 17 March.

Sobek, Antonin. 2019. "The FET Standard under CETA." In *Yearbook on International Investment Law & Policy 2017,* edited by Lisa Sachs, Lise Johnson, and Jesse Coleman, 356–88. Oxford: Oxford University Press.

SPP v. Egypt. 1992. ICSID Case No. AF/84/3, Award on the Merits, 20 May.

Tecmed v. Mexico. 2003. ICSID Case No. ARB(AF)/00/2, Award, 29 May.

United Nations Commission on International Trade Law (UNCITRAL). 2014. *Rules on Transparency in Treaty-based Investor-State Arbitration.* New York: UNCITRAL.

Urbaser S.A. et al. v. Argentina. 2016. ICSID Case No. ARB/07/26, Award, 8 December.

Van Harten, Gus. 2007. *Investment Treaty Arbitration and Public Law.* Oxford: Oxford University Press.

Viñuales, Jorge E. 2014. "Sovereignty in Foreign Investment Law." In *The Foundations of International Investment Law: Bringing Theory into Practice*, edited by Zachary Douglas, Joost Pauwelyn, and Jorge E. Viñuales, 317–62. Oxford: Oxford University Press.

Waibel, Michael, Asha Kaushal, Kyo-Hwa Chung, and Claire Balchin, eds. 2010. *The Backlash against Investment Arbitration: Perceptions and Reality.* Alphen aan den Rijn: Wolters Kluwer.

5

Regulatory Cooperation under CETA: Facing Up to the "Gorilla in the Room"

Mark A. Camilleri

Gorilla in the room *[English idiom]: a problem or difficult issue that is very obvious, but is ignored for the convenience or comfort of those involved.*[1]

INTRODUCTION

The Comprehensive Economic Trade and Investment Agreement (CETA) between Canada and the European Union (EU) represents a novel and potentially transformative trade deal for both Canada and the EU. As the international global economic order comes under strain, the importance of CETA extends beyond the Atlantic and has been referred to as a "beacon for open global trade" (Malmström 2019, 4). The key significance of CETA is its attempt to address not just tariff barriers to trade, but also non-tariff barriers (NTBs). It is largely for this reason that CETA is seen as a blueprint for the next or "second" generation of trade agreements. Among the more innovative aspects of CETA is its approach to regulatory cooperation between Canada and the EU.

With few chapters dealing with nonregulatory matters, CETA is, as some have suggested, essentially a deal about regulatory cooperation in its broadest sense (Hoekman 2018, 245; Hübner, Balik, and Deman 2016, 8). For this reason, and given the fact that tariffs were already quite low between Canada and the EU before the implementation of CETA,[2] the success of CETA largely depends on its ability to deliver on issues of regulatory cooperation (Conference Board of Canada 2014; Wolfe 2016).

International regulatory cooperation (IRC) has, for decades, been seen as both the Holy Grail and the poisoned chalice of international trade and globalization more generally. For those championing regulatory cooperation in trade agreements, differences in regulation between markets increase the costs of trade and render it inefficient and costly, especially for small- and medium-sized businesses (SMES). On the other side of the debate, some citizens, consumers, and members of civil society worry about a "race to the bottom" in a drive to harmonize regulatory standards, and the impact of such new deals on the right of a nation to regulate within their markets. With these divergent views on IRC, CETA has become a lightning rod for the issue.

Given all the political drama that involved the negotiation, conclusion, and now ongoing ratification (within the EU) of CETA, it is both understandable and surprising that the issue of regulatory cooperation under CETA has not been more publicly discussed or assessed, especially compared to the more traditional measure of trade success (for example, increased exports).[3] The effect of this relative silence is to render regulatory cooperation under CETA the "gorilla in the room."

As this chapter examines, the mechanisms of IRC under CETA are quite new and innovative and, contrary to certain public perception, do not inevitably lead to a lower degree of regulatory standards. However, as the chapter suggests, more dialogue, transparency, and ambition at this critical time is needed to face up to the gorilla and ensure CETA's success – dialogue to dispel many of the myths of IRC; transparency to help stakeholders understand the impact of proposed IRC; and an ambition to make CETA a success by addressing NTBS that are detrimental to Canada-EU trade.

REGULATION AND TRADE

Broadly, NTBS comprise all measures other than tariffs that restrict or otherwise distort international trade flows (OECD 2009). NTBS include "at-the-border" restrictions, such as restrictive licensing, permitting, and other requirements applied at the border, and "behind-the-border" restrictions, such as unjustified technical barriers to trade and sanitary and phytosanitary (SPS) measures (US Trade Representative n.d.). The reference to the latter group of regulatory barriers as "behind the border" denotes that they are a product of domestic policy as opposed to trade policy (Canadian Chamber of Commerce 2016, 4).

Regulations on products and services (for example, consumer safety or performance requirements, requirements related to the origin of inputs or raw materials used in a product sold on a domestic market, and sanitary and health regulations) can have a discriminatory effect on trade and, at worst, be used as a disguised form of protectionism (Krstic 2012, 1). At a minimum, regulatory differences give rise to potentially adverse effects on trade, particularly raising the cost for foreign suppliers seeking to access other (differently) regulated markets. These costs include information costs (i.e., the costs associated with learning regulatory details of a market), adjustment costs (i.e., the costs of redesigning and conforming goods and services to the market), and conformity assessment costs (i.e., the costs with having products and services inspected to ensure conformity to the domestic regulations of the importing market).

Of course, regulations do not exist simply to hinder trade. They seek to address important societal issues such as health, safety, and security of its inhabitants; protection and management of the environment; and proper functioning of financial markets, to name a few. Good regulation should positively affect a society's welfare or otherwise serve a social purpose. Effective regulation is necessary to address market imperfections and spillovers or failures, such as those related to negative externalities, risks for human, animal or plant health, or information asymmetries (Stone and Lejárraga 2018, 5). What is more, regulation can also be a force for competitiveness and for building trust with consumers and investors alike (Canadian Chamber of Commerce 2016, 3). As van Tongeren, Bastien, and von Lampe (2015, 1) observe, a well-designed policy can boost trade by providing further information or assurance to consumers, which may outweigh any additional costs.

Nevertheless, regulations can create barriers that otherwise hinder trade and increase costs (ibid.). Today NTBs are considered the most significant source of trade costs in the world economy with most NTBs stemming from domestic regulation (Stone and Lejárraga 2018, 5). Studies have found that NTBs restrict trade almost twice as much as tariffs (Canadian Chamber of Commerce 2016, 6).

Given the high costs of NTBs, there has been a growing push by businesses for greater cooperation in cross-border regulation. The concerns of business over regulatory divergencies has been made more pronounced not just by the success in lowering tariff barriers, but also by changes in the global economy which, in effect, have pushed regulations much closer to the border – namely with the shift to a services economy and the rise of global value chains (GVCs). Services are, in general, highly regulated with requirements often having a more local flavour. GVCs result in goods and services passing through many different jurisdictions and therefore subject to many more regulations.

Yet, even apart from trade considerations, there is a growing acceptance among regulators themselves that societal problems cannot be viewed or solved from a domestic perspective alone. In a globalized world, addressing market imperfections and other social ills (from financial market fallouts to air and water pollution and other environmental issues) requires greater international coordination of regulatory policy.

INTERNATIONAL REGULATORY COOPERATION

The Organisation for Economic Co-operation and Development (OECD) has engaged in extensive research on the subject of IRC, and has defined it as being "the range of institutional and procedural frameworks within which national governments, sub-national governments, and the wider public can work together to build more integrated systems for rule-making and implementation, subject to the constraints of democratic values, such as accountability, openness and sovereignty" (OECD 1994, 15).

The OECD has mapped out various forms of IRC mechanisms ranging from integration and harmonization through supranational institutions (e.g., the EU itself) to informal dialogue and exchanges of information (as per the US-EU relationship) before the recent establishment of the Trade and Technology Council. Between these models are other forms of IRC, ranging from specifically negotiated agreements, formal regulatory cooperation, international organizations (e.g., the OECD), regional agreements with regulatory provisions, mutual recognition agreements (MRAs) in national law, trans-governmental networks of regulators, to intergovernmental reliance on international standards and codes of conduct.

Whatever form IRC takes, there are different degrees and tools of cooperation. At the "softer" end of the cooperation spectrum are ad hoc exchanges of information; along the "harder" end is procedural and legislative harmonization (Golberg 2019, 6). Within these ranges are mechanisms such as mutual recognition of each other's laws, standards, rules, and/or processes (ibid.). In addition, jurisdictions may cooperate to pursue regulatory "equivalence," whereby the parties agree that the regulatory objectives of the parties are equivalent and accept the effectiveness of the implementation and enforcement mechanisms in the parties' respective jurisdictions (Hoekman 2015, 6). Finally, cooperation can be formal (i.e., binding) or informal (i.e., nonbinding) with arrangements established for monitoring implementation, information exchanges, consultations, and dispute resolution (Golberg 2019, 7).

The fact that IRC comes in different forms and degrees reflects the myriad of issues that can be the subject of cooperation and the variances in the legal, economic, and cultural perspectives of the parties seeking to pursue IRC. If the conditions are right, IRC can lead to regulatory harmonization, but these cases have, to date, been relatively few and specific. The point to be stressed then is that IRC does not mean an automatic harmonization in regulatory measures as some, including those engaged in the CETA debate, fear (Bull et al. 2015, 8).

PRE-CETA CANADA-EU
REGULATORY COOPERATION

Canada and the EU have a long history of carrying out regulatory dialogues, having established the Joint Cooperation Committee pursuant to the 1976 Framework Agreement for Commercial and Economic Cooperation. Since then, Canada and the EU have also engaged in more sector-specific bilateral regulatory dialogues with a view to trying to address differences in regulatory practices along sectoral lines (Krstic 2012, 2). There is limited publicly available information on the processes and outcomes of these dialogues. They have been described as executive-led informal processes of consultation, information, and best practices and it is questionable how effective they have been in terms of addressing NTBS (ibid.).

Following a failed attempt between 2004 and 2006 to negotiate a more comprehensive economic relationship between Canada and the EU, a number of studies emerged highlighting the costs and impediments to trade resulting from the divergent regulatory requirements and practices (ibid.). In 2007, Canada and the EU agreed to conduct their own joint study examining the cost and benefits of pursuing a closer economic partnership with a particular focus on the potential impact of eliminating existing barriers to trade including NTBS. The study, entitled the "Joint Study on Assessing the Cost and Benefits of a Closer EU-Canada Economic Partnership" (the Joint Study), was released in 2008 and provided a wide-ranging examination of the Canada-EU political and economic relationship to date, as well as making projections on what it could look like under a comprehensive trade agreement.

While the Joint Study was meant for illustrative purposes, it nevertheless proved very influential in the CETA talks, which formally commenced in 2009 at the Canada-EU Summit in Prague. In conducting the Joint Study, the views of the private sector were actively consulted and considered in both the EU and Canada. Business groups continued to play an influential role throughout the CETA negotiation process and, from the Canadian side, active efforts were made by the Canadian government for businesses to lobby each other with a view to helping inform the Canadian negotiating position, a process that has been described as "reverse lobbying" (Hübner, Balik, and Deman 2016, 18–19). Indeed, discussions with Canadian businesses were a critical part of the Canadian negotiations and mobilizing these views was no small achievement (particularly in Canada which is far more focused on trade with the United States). For this author, it represents one of the achievements of the CETA negotiations (Wolfe 2016, 11).

This dialogue between the governments and businesses was the subject of criticism from civil society on both sides of the Atlantic (Hübner, Balik, and Deman 2016). For many such groups, it underscored the corporate agenda of trade agreements such as CETA at the expense of regulatory autonomy in setting standards of social welfare. These views would come to a head in the Belgian region of Wallonia in October 2016 when opposition from the local government (supported by a wider anti-CETA lobby) threatened to derail the signing of CETA (see McKenna 2016 for an overview). The backlash of CETA in Wallonia was fierce and no doubt left a deep impression on both the Canadian and EU governments that arguably continues to linger (particularly in light of the fact that CETA ratification continues in many EU member states).

REGULATORY COOPERATION UNDER CETA

General

IRC takes a number of different forms within CETA, addressing a number of at-the-border and beyond-the-border matters. Table 5.1 is an overview of some of the broad IRC provisions contained within CETA.

CETA (2016) contains a number of chapters specifically addressing regulatory cooperation for certain areas, such as electronic commerce (Chapter 16), intellectual property (Chapter 20), trade and sustainable development (Chapter 22), trade and labour (Chapter 23), and trade and the environment (Chapter 24). Chapter 25 (ibid.) provides for bilateral dialogues and cooperation on issues of common interest including a dialogue on issues of biotech market access (Art. 25.2), a dialogue on forest products (Art. 25.3), a dialogue on raw materials (Art. 25.4), and enhanced cooperation on science, technology, research, and innovation (Art. 25.5).

While it is beyond the scope of this chapter to discuss each of the forms of IRC under CETA, it looks at three innovative mechanisms of IRC under CETA – the mutual recognition of professional qualifications (MRPQ; ibid., Chapter 11), the overall IRC institutional arrangement established

Table 5.1
Examples of IRC provisions in CETA

Chapter	Title	Summary
4	Technical Barriers to Trade (TBT)	Canada and the EU commit to working more closely together on technical regulations for testing and certifying products.
5	Sanitary and Phytosanitary Measures (SPS)	The parties endeavour to ensure that measures by either side to ensure food safety and animal and plant health do not create unjustified barriers to trade, but rather facilitate trade.
6	Customs and Trade Facilitation	The parties agree to streamline customs procedures and make them more efficient by ensuring (a) transparency, (b) streamlined, risk-based procedures, and (c) certainty and predictability.
25	Bilateral Dialogues	The EU and Canada agree to work more closely with each other in areas such as science and forestry and incorporates the existing agreements on dialogue and cooperation on trade and economic matters between them.
27	Regulatory Transparency	The EU and Canada agree to publish the laws, regulations, procedures, and administrative rulings on matters which CETA covers, and otherwise make them available and to promptly share information and respond to questions on measures affecting the way they implement CETA.

Source: Compiled by the author.

under CETA (ibid., Chapter 26) and the specific chapter on regulatory cooperation (ibid., Chapter 21).

Before examining these features, it is important to make two general observations. First, there is no single model of IRC under CETA. The form of IRC varies depending on the sector and the alignment of public policy goals between the parties. These varying expressions of IRC under CETA reflect not only the history of Canada-EU regulatory cooperation and the output of the Joint Study, but also the ambition of CETA in seeking to address a variety of cross-Atlantic NTBs.

Second, it is important to stress that regulatory cooperation under CETA is an exercise in positive cooperation. CETA contains numerous exceptions which give the parties a high degree of discretion to act in the public interest and pursue other societal values (apart from promoting freer trade). As de Mestral (2015) observes, these exceptions can be found in virtually every chapter of CETA, from the preamble to the definitions (CETA 2016, Chapter 2), to even the separate chapter on exceptions (ibid., Chapter 32). Moreover, in response to the civil society opposition to the conclusion of CETA (most notably in Wallonia), Canada and the EU released the Joint Instrument which further affirmed, by way of an interpretative instrument, the ability of governments to regulate in the public interest and the voluntariness of regulatory cooperation.[4] In this way, CETA makes a concerted and explicit point of preserving a high degree of regulatory space to ensure that wider values of society, such as public health, safety, and environment, are sufficiently protected.[5]

Chapter 11: Mutual Recognition of Professional Qualifications

One of the most innovative aspects of CETA is its Chapter 11 on MRPQ (CETA 2016). Professional services are part of a wider range of trade in services and include services by lawyers, accountants, auditors, engineers, architects, and medical professionals. This category of service providers is notable because these types of services are generally highly regulated in most countries. Professional service providers must obtain licences or other specific authorizations, which in turn are linked to education, qualification tests, or licensing requirements. Regulations relating to professionals aim to ensure a level of competence and that service providers adhere to rules relating to training, ethics, and consumer protection (Kerneis 2018, 245–6).

Domestic regulations governing professions represent a major obstacle for professionals seeking to provide their services in other markets as professional service providers are often required to re-qualify in the new market as a condition of providing services. MRPQ under CETA provides an avenue to overcome this hurdle by setting out guidelines on how MRAS on sector-specific professional qualifications can form part of CETA (i.e., an international binding treaty) once the MRAs have been concluded by the relevant professional licensing bodies.

Chapter 11 sets out a process for negotiating an MRA (which starts with each party encouraging its relevant authorities or professional bodies to develop and provide joint recommendations on proposed MRAs) and concluding the same. Annex 11-A of CETA provides a set of guidelines offering practical guidance to facilitate the above-mentioned negotiation of MRAS.

Chapter 11 is, like much of IRC under CETA, an "enabling tool" for the relevant professions themselves (Kerneis 2018, 254). It contains guidelines that provide both a path and legal security for an MRA. There is no requirement for those professions which do not wish to enter into an MRA or do not otherwise seek to cooperate in this way.

Chapter 26: Institutional Design

CETA creates a complex institutional architecture that aims to support and actively encourage IRC. Chapter 26, Administrative and Institutional Provisions, establishes the IRC architectural infrastructure of CETA which includes a number of specialized committees and bilateral dialogues to address specific areas of regulatory cooperation (CETA 2016). As Leblond (2016, 12) makes clear, this architecture is designed to be linked with governments in both Canada (at the federal and provincial levels) and the EU (the supranational and national levels), so as to ensure that regulatory cooperation can best be achieved generally and specifically.[6]

The joint committee established under Art. 26.1 is CETA's highest political authority (CETA 2016). It is co-chaired by the Canadian Minister for International Trade and the EU Commissioner responsible for trade, or designate, who are required to meet once a year or at the request of a party (ibid., Art. 26.1(2)). The committee is responsible for the implementation of CETA as well as all questions concerning trade and investment between the parties (ibid., Art. 26.1(3)). It has the power to, among other things, make decisions in respect of all matters when CETA provides, change, dissolve, or undertake the tasks of any specialized committee under CETA; establish specialized committees and bilateral dialogues in order to assist it in the performance of its tasks; and the power to make recommendations suitable for promoting the expansion of trade and investment (ibid.).

Assisting with the coordination of this extensive institutional system are the CETA contact points whose role, under Art. 26.5 (ibid.) includes: (a) monitoring of the work of all CETA institutional bodies, (b) coordinating the preparation for the meetings of the committees; (c) following up on any decisions made by the CETA Joint Committee; and (d) responding to any information requests of the parties.

Chapter 21: Regulatory Cooperation

While CETA provides for different expressions of IRC, the regulatory cooperation section of Chapter 21 (ibid.) is a central aspect of the IRC under CETA given its broad scope and objectives, as well as its proposed activities and structure (not to mention its name).

Art. 21.1 (ibid.) provides for a wide range of areas of regulatory cooperation within the chapter including both at-the-border and beyond-the-border regulations. This is reflective in the list of topics referenced in

Art. 21.1 – an inclusive, but not an exclusive, list. Moreover, by listing certain topics that are specifically addressed elsewhere in CETA, it is clear that regulatory issues addressed elsewhere in CETA are not excluded from the scope of Chapter 21. For example, Annex 4-A of CETA (ibid.), which deals with the cooperation in the field of motor vehicle regulations, specifically commits the parties to enhance their efforts in the area of regulatory cooperation including pursuant to Chapter 21.

Art. 21.3 (ibid.) sets out the objectives of regulatory cooperation which include building trust; facilitating bilateral trade and investment; and contributing to the protection of life (human, animal, or plant), health, and environment. It goes on set out various activities that the parties endeavour to undertake aimed at regulatory cooperation. These include: ongoing bilateral discussions on regulatory governance, consultations and information exchange, examining opportunities to minimize unnecessary divergences in regulations, cooperating on issues relating to international standards, conducting post-implementation reviews of regulations and policies, and identifying appropriate approaches to reduce adverse effects of existing regulatory differences on bilateral trade and investment, including through greater convergence, mutual recognition, and the use of international standards, including standards and guides for conformity assessment.

Art. 21.6 (ibid.) provides for a regulatory cooperation forum (RCF) to "facilitate and promote regulatory cooperation between the Parties." While technically a "specialized committee" under Art. 26.2 (ibid.), the role of the RCF is in reality quite general and designed to perform a number of tasks including provide a forum to discuss regulatory policy issues of mutual interest that the parties have identified through, among other things, consultations with stakeholders and interested parties (including representatives from academia, think tanks, nongovernmental organizations [NGOs], businesses, and consumer and other organizations); assisting individual regulators to identify potential partners for cooperation activities; reviewing regulatory initiatives, whether in progress or anticipated, that a party thinks may provide potential for cooperation; and encouraging the development of bilateral cooperation activities.

Technically, the RCF has no decision-making power and reports to, and otherwise informs the work of, the CETA Joint Committee (Meyer-Ohlendorf, Gerstetter, and Bach 2016). But given its responsibilities and composition, it wields great potential for meaningful IRC under CETA.

Importantly, the RCF is co-chaired by a senior representative of the Government of Canada at the level of deputy minister and a senior representative of the European Commission at the level of director general, or an equivalent or designate of either. The Canadian RCF co-chairs are representatives of Global Affairs Canada and the Treasury Board of Canada Secretariat and the Commission co-chairs are representative of the Directorate-General for the Internal Market, Industry, Entrepreneurship and SMES (DG GROW) and the Directorate-General for Trade (DG Trade). Given the key role that each of the Treasury Board of Canada and DG GROW plays in ensuring the proper implementation of regulations in their respective markets, this is an important step forward in terms of Canada-EU regulatory cooperation that should not be understated. What is more, the RCF has the power to invite other interested parties to participate in its meetings (including technical experts and private entities).

Reglatory cooperation envisaged under Chapter 21 is, consistent with the rest of CETA, voluntary. Art. 21.5 (CETA 2016) states that "[a] Party is not prevented from adopting different regulatory measures or pursuing different initiatives for reasons including different institutional or legislative approaches, circumstances, values or priorities that are particular to that Party." Yet, while the commitments of regulatory cooperation under CETA are not mandatory, it is evident from such objectives that the underlying intention of the IRC under CETA was comprehensive in ambition. This is very much reflected in the broader institutional design of CETA in which Chapter 21 and the RCF is at the heart.

CETA REGULATORY COOPERATION – EARLY OBSERVATIONS AND RECOMMENDATIONS

IRC is a long-term process and so it is still too early to assess whether CETA is living up to its vaunted ambitions in terms of IRC. That said, some initial observations can be noted.

For one, the institutional architecture that underpins CETA is taking shape. According to each of the Government of Canada's and the EU Commission's websites, most of the committees under CETA have, as of the date of this chapter, already formed and met (in most cases more than once) and are producing workplans and agendas and meetings with stakeholders (Government of Canada 2020). The Canadian government and the EU Commission each make available certain documentation relating to the meetings of these committees (ibid.; European Commission 2020). There is, however, a degree of inconsistency in the reporting, with some committee reports being more detailed than others, and the delayed publishing of reports of some meetings. Given the importance of transparency to promote engagement and build trust among stakeholders (which is an essential ingredient in any successful IRC effort), it is recommended that a higher degree of consistency in format, detail, and time of publication be applied to the reports of the committees, a point that is discussed further in the next paragraph.

In the case of the MRPQ Committee, they are already considering their first MRA request. In April 2018, a draft MRA was concluded by The Architects' Council of Europe (ACE) and The Canadian Architectural Licensing Authorities (CALA). At the first meeting of the MRPQ Joint Committee held on 16 April 2019, the committee accepted the submission of CALA and ACE as well as acknowledged that the requirements of Chapter 11 were met in terms of establishing the rationale and information on the envisaged economic impact and providing an indication of the capability of licensing and qualification regimes in the EU and Canada. The MRPQ Committee then agreed to further discussions in order to establish the necessary next steps in the Art. 11.3 process, in which the specific terms and conditions recommended by ACE and CALA for a future, binding MRA, will be further elaborated and developed as required (Joint Committee on Mutual Recognition of Professional Qualifications 2019).

While the architect MRA has now been approved,[7] progress was relatively slow considering that ACE and CALA had begun their work on an MRA even before the signing of CETA, giving Canada and the EU sufficient notice of the request (Kerneis 2018, 254). As one of the important early test cases of regulatory cooperation under CETA, it is important that continued and sustained efforts are made to progress this matter and ensure that any delays are not administrative in nature. In addition to the fact that other professions will be looking closely at this process as part of their own considerations of engaging in bilateral mutual recognition, it will be seen a litmus test for IRC under CETA more generally.

In addition to the above-mentioned preliminary observations, there are several more critical comments to be made regarding IRC under CETA at this relatively early stage. The first has to do with the overall management and coordination of the complex structure of IRC under CETA. With so many different specialized committees and forums, there is a real risk that CETA IRC will progress in a haphazard manner or even result in the atomization of the IRC process. Regulatory cooperation under CETA should be synchronized with the wider objective of improving overall Canada-EU trade and investment opportunities. According to the public record, there is already a discrepancy in the number of meetings that have taken place among the committees (which some committees meeting more regularly than others) and, as already noted, in the availability or quality of the information discussed at the meetings.

This chapter suggests that what is needed is the establishment of a secretariat to support the CETA Joint Committee. While the CETA Joint Committee is the ultimate supervisor of the various committees, it is arguably too senior and too political a committee to address the kind of minute but important administrative and managerial efforts needed to sustain the CETA IRC architecture. Moreover, while the CETA contact points in theory could act as CETA secretariat (Leblond 2016, 10), early indications suggest that these contact points are not sufficiently empowered with the resources to drive or supervise the IRC process. This chapter instead proposes that the RCF acts as a CETA secretariat.

A CETA secretariat is important to ensure that IRC under CETA progresses in a coordinated, efficient, and transparent manner. In the first instance, the secretariat should ensure that committee meetings are scheduled with sufficient notice to the public in a single centralized (online) location (as opposed to separate websites and databases for Canada and the EU which is currently the case).

The secretariat should also take steps to standardize the format and information that is publicly disclosed. This would involve one official source (as opposed to Canada and the EU each publishing separate reports which is currently the case), and less variance on meeting agendas and reports among the various committee and dialogue meetings. The information presented should disclose enough information about the business under consideration so that stakeholders have a better understanding of not only the subject matter of discussion, but its relevance in terms of IRC and wider trade liberalization efforts. In other words, the report should make some attempt to explain the tangible benefit of the issues under consideration. This would greatly improve the transparency of the business of the meetings and help ensure that both businesses and regulators understand the objectives of any proposed regulatory cooperation efforts.

The role of the secretariat should also involve the active monitoring of the work of the committees and even produce regular reports or scorecards on the progress made in various IRC efforts with an overall assessment of CETA IRC. The reports should be publicly available and help to inform the work and deliberations of the CETA Joint Committee. Part of this oversight should be a critical examination of the stakeholder consultations for each specialized committee and dialogue to ensure that there is a reasonable and appropriate balance and mix of views, including critical stakeholders in any particular subject matter – technical, business (including SMEs), civil society, or otherwise. This is important because, when assessing technical aspects of regulatory measures, it is important that there are a sufficient number of interests represented to identify areas of priority and concern (Hoekman and Mavroidis 2015, 5). Businesses should be properly engaged so that they can explain the implications of such measures and provide a rationale in removing them from an operational perspective. Businesses are also better suited to appreciate how regulatory and policy issues feed into supply chains (Hoekman 2015, 10). This also applies to other stakeholders potentially affected.

It must be stressed that the CETA secretariat would essentially be administrative in nature and all political decisions would remain within the realm of the CETA Joint Committee. A CETA secretariat that sits outside of the CETA Joint Committee might also help insulate regulatory cooperation from the winds of wider political pressures of government and ensure that issues relating to trade do not otherwise get swept away (Ciuriak 2003, 2). In particular, it might help make assessments more objective and even more politically feasible for the joint committee.[8]

Given such tasks, it is logical that the RCF gets to serve as the CETA secretariat. The activities of the RCF contained in CETA suggest that it should play a prominent role in all areas of IRC. This is supported by the particular composition of representatives of the RCF which allow for it to take a horizontal view of Canada-EU IRC (in terms of bilateral trade and within the respective markets of the parties). Its composition also gives it the gravitas to ensure that more specialized committees adhere to agreed procedures and decisions and otherwise drive the IRC process including taking into consideration policy objectives of the joint committee. This role would, it is suggested, be a more efficient and productive use of the time and resources of the RCF which currently focuses on specific regulatory matters that may be just as well suited to more specialized committees (RCF 2019).

In addition to the formation of a CETA secretariat, this chapter strongly advocates that a new comprehensive study of NTBs between Canada and the EU be undertaken which would further inform the wider IRC efforts under CETA. The Joint Study is now well over ten years old and in need of an update to better inform decision makers and stakeholders alike. As with the Joint Study, a new study should involve as many stakeholders as possible, especially those of industry and business who are faced with the regulatory barriers. Just as the Joint Study was able to capture significant private sector views, so should the new study aim to do the same.

The new study would also be a potentially effective tool for Canada and the EU as each seeks to address a critical challenge of trying to ensure that SMES take advantage of and enjoy the benefits of CETA. This is certainly a challenge for the Canadian government given the high lack of knowledge and awareness of CETA by Canadian SMES (Blatchford 2019). A new study would give Canada and the EU an opportunity to proactively solicit the views of SMES, while at the same time also creating a specific opportunity to promote CETA and explain in concrete terms how it works (or could work) to SMES.

The aim of the study should not be to try and resolve any issue or make any policy recommendations; rather it should be to try and identify as many NTBS as possible generally and specifically by sector. In particular, the new study should seek to categorize and measure existing NTBS between Canada and the EU as well as anticipate, as much as possible, areas of future regulatory needs.

The study would be an important tool for the RCF (and by extension the secretariat) and the CETA Joint Committee to assess the areas where regulatory cooperation should be encouraged and resources expended. It would also assist in developing a framework for determining which model of regulatory cooperation should (or can) be pursued depending on the sector or issue. The study should also be made public and updated regularly (for example, at least every five years).

CONCLUSION

This chapter has argued that, while the IRC framework within CETA provides a framework for effective and meaningful regulatory cooperation between Canada and the EU, more needs to be done to coordinate efforts to ensure successful IRC under CETA. It is argued that the best way to achieve this coordination is through oversight of the IRC architecture by a more permanent secretariat. The RCF is ideally designed and constituted to assume this role and take a more horizontal view of regulatory cooperation than it presently does. For both the EU and Canada, greater efforts and resources are needed to engage with businesses and other industry stakeholders to raise awareness of CETA and foster the type of intelligence gathering, particularly with respect to its SMES. This is something that should be undertaken through the commissioning of a new study in NTBS between Canada and the EU.

Underlying these suggestions is an assumption that more ambition is required for implementing CETA and tackling NTBS between Canada and the EU. Yet such ambition will not be realized without first having a meaningful and transparent approach to IRC with all stakeholders. This means that the parties to CETA should give more voice to the promotion of regulatory cooperation as a principal benefit of CETA and to not treat it as the gorilla in the room.

Of course, the ambitions of IRC under CETA must be matched by efforts of not just the signatories, but by all interested parties, not least the regulators, industry, civil society, and individual businesses (including SMES) on the front lines of trade. It is only through the regular and open exchange of views from these different groups that the foundation of trust can be laid and a true attempt at IRC can be realized. Such a realization is not just important for realizing the potential of CETA, but also for providing a new model of regulatory cooperation beyond Canada and the EU.

NOTES

1 This idiom is perhaps more popularly used with reference to an "elephant"; however, in the Canadian context, the role of the elephant is respectfully reserved for the United States of America (an analogy made famous by former prime minister Pierre Elliott Trudeau in remarks to the Press Club in Washington, DC, 25 March 1969).

2 CETA has been provisionally applied effective 21 September 2017. The ratification process is ongoing at the member state level for the EU. Canada ratified CETA on 17 May 2017.

3 On the first anniversary of CETA's provisional implementation, Canadian news headlines highlighted the fact that Canadian exports to the EU during this period did not perform as well as those in previous years or those of the EU during the same period. See, for example, Parkinson (2018) and McGregor (2018).

4 For example, see preamble and Chapter 3 of The Joint Interpretative Declaration on the Comprehensive Economic and Trade Agreement (CETA) between Canada and the European Union and its Member States (the Joint Instrument).

5 While this is certainly the view of the author, it should be noted that this remains a subject of considerable debate, with a number of civil society groups remaining concerned that CETA does not do enough to protect the ability of states to regulate in favour of wider societal interests.

6 See also Steger (2012).

7 Canada and the EU have recently concluded the negotiations for an MRA on the professional qualifications of architects, which will come into effect

in 2023 (https://policy.trade.ec.europa.eu/news/eu-and-canada-lay-
    foundations-free-movement-architects-2022-03-21_en).
8 See, for example, the Report of the Meeting of the Wines and Spirits
    Committee (2018).

REFERENCES

Blatchford, Andy. 2019. "Ottawa is working hard to land trade deals abroad
    that businesses at home have never heard of – and may never use." *National
    Post*, 19 July. https://financialpost.com/news/economy/firms-know-little-
    about-trade-deals-as-canada-pushes-to-diversify-federal-survey.
Bull, Reeve T., Neysun A. Mahboubi, Richard B. Stewart, and Jonathan B.
    Wiener. 2015. "New Approaches to International Regulatory Cooperation."
    Law and Contemporary Problems 78, no. 1: 1–29.
Canadian Chamber of Commerce. 2016. "Canada's Next Top Trade Barrier:
    Taking International Regulatory Cooperation Seriously." Ottawa: Canadian
    Chamber of Commerce.
CETA (Canada-European Union Comprehensive Economic and Trade
    Agreement). 2016. Accessed 21 July 2020. https://www.international.gc.ca/
    trade-commerce/trade-agreements-accords-commerciaux/agr-acc/ceta-aecg/
    text-texte/toc-tdm.aspx?lang=eng.
Ciuriak, Dan. 2003. "The Quantification and Impact of Non-Tariff Measures:
    Why do NTMs Proliferate and What Are the Consequences?" Accessed
    6 August 2020. https://papers.ssrn.com/sol3/papers.cfm?abstract_
    id=1660165.
Conference Board of Canada. 2014. "For Innovators Only: Canadian
    Companies' EU Export Experience." Ottawa: Conference Board of Canada.
de Mestral, Armand. 2015. "When Does the Exception Become the Rule?
    Conserving Regulatory Space under CETA." *Journal of International
    Economic Law* 18, no. 3: 641–54. https://doi.org/10.1093/jiel/jgv033.
European Commission. 2020. "CETA – Meetings and Documents." Accessed
    18 February 2020. http://trade.ec.europa.eu/doclib/press/index.cfm?id=1811.
Golberg, Elizabeth. 2019. "Regulatory Cooperation – A Reality Check."
    M-RCBG Associate Working Paper No. 115, Mossavar-Rahmani Center for
    Business & Government, Harvard Kennedy School, Cambridge, MA. https://
    www.hks.harvard.edu/centers/mrcbg/publications/awp/awp115.
Government of Canada. 2020. "Canada-European Union Comprehensive
    Economic and Trade Agreement (CETA) – Governance and Committees."
    Accessed 18 February 2020. https://www.international.gc.ca/trade-commerce/

trade-agreements-accords-commerciaux/agr-acc/ceta-aecg/committees-
comites.aspx?lang=eng.

Hoekman, Bernard. 2015. "International Regulatory Cooperation in a Supply
Chain World." In *Redesigning Canadian Trade Policies for New Global
Realities,* edited by Stephen Tapp, Ari Van Assche and Robert Wolfe.
Montreal: Institute for Research on Public Policy.

– 2018. "'Behind-the-Border' Regulatory Policies and Trade Agreements."
In *East Asian Economic Review* 22, no. 3 (September): 243–73.

Hoekman, Bernard, and Douglas Nelson. 2018. "21st Century Trade
Agreements and the Owl of Minerva." EUI Working Paper RSCAS 2018/04,
Robert Schuman Centre for Advanced Studies, Florence, Italy.

Hoekman, Bernard, and Petros C. Mavroidis. 2015. "Regulatory Spillovers
and the Trading System: From Coherence to Cooperation." E15 Initiative,
International Centre for Trade and Sustainable Development (ICTSD)
and World Economic Forum, Geneva, Switzerland.

Hübner, Kurt, Tugce Balik, and Anne-Sophie Deman. 2016. "CETA: The
Making of the Comprehensive Economic and Trade Agreement Between
Canada and the EU." Paris: Notes de l'Ifri.

Joint Committee on Mutual Recognition of Professional Qualifications. 2019.
"1st Meeting of the Mutual Recognition of Professional Qualifications Joint
Committee." Report of the meeting held in Brussels, 16 April. Accessed
18 February 2020. https://trade.ec.europa.eu/doclib/docs/2019/may/
tradoc_157902.pdf.

Kerneis, Pascal. 2018. "Professional Services." In *Potential Benefits of an
Australia-EU Free Trade Agreement: Key Issues and Options*, edited by Jane
Drake-Brockman and Patrick Messerlin, 245–58. Adelaide: University of
Adelaide Press.

Krstic, Stanko S. 2012. "Regulatory Cooperation to Remove Non-tariff
Barriers to Trade in Products: Key Challenges and Opportunities for the
Canada-EU Comprehensive Trade Agreement." *Legal Issues of Economic
Integration* 39, no. 1: 3–28.

Leblond, Patrick. 2016. "Making the Most of CETA: A Complete and Effective
Implementation is Key to Realizing the Agreement's Full Potential." CIGI
Papers No. 114, Centre for International Governance Innovation,
Waterloo, ON.

Malmström, Cecilia. 2019. "An Open Trading System: A Common
Responsibility." Accessed 6 August 2020. https://trade.ec.europa.eu/doclib/
docs/2019/september/tradoc_158367.pdf.

McGregor, Janyce. 2018. "Canada-EU Trade, One Year On: Canada's Imports
Are Rising Faster Than Exports." *CBC News,* 16 September. https://www.
cbc.ca/news/politics/ceta-anniversary-imports-exports-1.4823822.

McKenna, Barrie. 2016. "What's Wallonia's deal? A primer on its role in CETA's crisis." *The Globe and Mail*, 24 October. https://www.theglobe andmail.com/report-on-business/international-business/european-business/ explainer-ceta-wallonia-europe-and-canada/article32489554/.

Meyer-Ohlendorf, Nils, Christiane Gerstetter, and Inga Bach. 2016. "Regulatory Cooperation under CETA: Implications for Environmental Policies." Accessed 7 February 2020. https://www.greenpeace.de/sites/ www.greenpeace.de/files/publications/20161104_greenpeace_studie_ regulatorycooperationunderceta.pdf.

OECD (Organisation for Economic Co-operation and Development). 1994. *Regulatory Cooperation for an Interdependent World*. Paris: OECD Publishing.

– 2009. "Protectionism? Tariffs and Other Barriers to Trade." In *International Trade: Free, Fair and Open?*, 54–76. Paris: OECD Publishing.

Parkinson, David. 2018. "A Year Later, Canada has Failed to Take Advantage of Trade Deal with Europe." *The Globe and Mail*, 7 November. https:// www.theglobeandmail.com/business/commentary/article-a-year-later-canada- has-failed-to-take-advantage-of-trade-deal-with/.

RCF (Regulatory Cooperation Forum). 2019. "Comprehensive Economic and Trade Agreement Regulatory Cooperation Forum Work Plan." Accessed 15 August 2019. https://www.international.gc.ca/trade-commerce/trade- agreements-accords-commerciaux/agr-acc/CETA-aecg/2019-06-28-work- travail-plan.aspx?lang=eng.

Steger, Debra P. 2012. "Institutions for Regulatory Cooperation in 'New Generation' Economic and Trade Agreements." *Legal Issues of Economic Integration* 39, no. 1: 109–26. https://dx.doi.org/10.2139/ssrn.1947421.

Stone, Susan, and Iza Lejárraga. 2018. "Global Value Chain Policy Series: Regulatory Coherence." White Paper, World Economic Forum, Geneva, Switzerland.

US Trade Representative. n.d. "Non-Tariff Barriers and Regulatory Issues." Accessed 18 February 2020. https://ustr.gov/trade-agreements/free-trade- agreements/transatlantic-trade-and-investment-partnership-t-tip/t-tip-2.

van Tongeren, Frank, Véronique Bastien, and Martin von Lampe. 2015. "International Regulatory Cooperation: A Trade-Facilitating Mechanism." E15 Initiative, International Centre for Trade and Sustainable Development (ICTSD) and World Economic Forum, Geneva, Switzerland.

Wines and Spirits Committee. 2018. "Meeting of the Wines and Spirits Committee, Brussels, 5 July 2018," Report. Accessed 6 August 2020. https:// trade.ec.europa.eu/doclib/docs/2018/august/tradoc_157268.pdf.

Wolfe, Robert. 2016. "Canadian Trade Policy in a G-Zero World: Preferential Negotiations as a Natural Experiment." Montreal: Institute for Research on Public Policy (IRPP).

6

A Cautionary Tale of Regulatory Cooperation in CETA: Executive Expertise and the Influence of Foreign Governments in Domestic Regulatory Processes

Charell van Rooy

INTRODUCTION

In an age of ever-growing nationalism and protectionist policies regulatory cooperation is – perhaps paradoxically – aiming to shape a new world order. Regulatory cooperation is being formalized in free trade agreements (FTAS) such as the Canada-EU (European Union) Comprehensive Economic Trade Agreement (CETA). Regulatory cooperation is layered: it takes the World Trade Organization (WTO) rules as a starting point and adds another layer of (transatlantic) regulatory cooperation in FTAS.[1] And where the EU and the United States were once seen as the main protagonists in regulatory cooperation, the rest of the world is getting a part to play.[2]

The expansion of regulatory cooperation is accompanied by a shift in focus, evolving the notion into something conceivably more invasive, and creating a widening and deepening of the concept around the globe (see Aaron 2000; Ahearn 2008; Bermann, Lindseth, and Herdegen 2000; Meuwese 2015). Regulatory cooperation used to focus on cooperating politically, i.e. by annual summits or declarations. Nowadays, it attempts to establish cooperation on impact assessments, risk assessments, sharing of data, and providing access to regulatory processes, seemingly working toward a "global regulatory laboratory" (Wiener and Alemanno

2016, 130). The shift from political cooperation to providing access to respective regulatory processes brings about worrying questions (Meuwese 2011). Ultimately, this could result in co-decision-making and blur the nature of the exercised authority (ibid.; Vogel 2007). Considering how regulatory cooperation can potentially lead to co-decision-making rather than an exchange of information, it is crucial to assess its implications as pursued by recent FTAS such as CETA. A broad variety of regulatory cooperation mechanisms exist (Bull et al. 2015; OECD 2013).[3] In the broadest sense of the word, regulatory cooperation includes the EU. For the purpose of this chapter, regulatory cooperation is defined – and thus limited – as follows: regulatory cooperation is the creation of procedural mechanisms applicable to the preparatory stages of regulation, aimed at the convergence of standards, with a focus on international trade agreements.[4]

This chapter provides insight on regulatory cooperation in CETA by analyzing the institutional framework and the objectives and mechanisms of regulatory cooperation set up by the agreement. Furthermore, a comparative analysis of regulatory cooperation in Transatlantic Trade and Investment Partnership (TTIP), a negotiated but not signed FTA between the EU and the US, is done with the purpose of assessing the similarities and differences of regulatory cooperation in both FTAS (TTIP and CETA), confirming the idea of a global policy laboratory and illustrative of the fact that regulatory cooperation in CETA is plausibly a blueprint for future regulatory cooperation (Chase and Pelkmans 2015; Hoekman 2015; Trujillo 2018). The influence of foreign governments is dealt with separately in the final section of this chapter, elaborating on the changed role of the executive and the creation of a "shared regulatory space" (Trujillo 2018, 374), establishing an influence of foreign governments in regulatory processes that has not been seen before. The argument is that regulatory cooperation is potentially far-reaching and could impact domestic regulatory processes by changing the role of the executive in the regulatory process and by providing access to foreign governments before entering domestic democratic processes. The early implications of regulatory cooperation in CETA for legislation, regulation, and public policy is one that transforms the role of the executive branch of the participating governments and thereby allows foreign government participation without strong procedural and judicial constraints, or participatory rights.[5] A system developed without democratic checks and balances should be approached with caution. Not just in the case of CETA, but in governance in general.

REGULATORY COOPERATION IN CETA

Building on an existing agreement between the EU and Canada, CETA's regulatory cooperation creates an ongoing regulatory dialogue enabling cooperation in the preparatory stages of the regulatory process to facilitate trade, build trust and reduce regulatory divergence (CETA 2016, Art. 21.3). To facilitate trade and investment and to contribute to improving competitiveness, regulatory cooperation in CETA encourages the regulators to exchange experiences and information, and identify areas for cooperation. Regulatory cooperation in CETA is said to be voluntary and regulators in the EU and Canada maintain the power to adopt legislation as they see fit. The chapter on regulatory cooperation applies to the development, review, and methodological aspects of regulatory measures of the regulatory authorities (ibid., Art. 21.1).[6] The responsible regulatory departments and agencies are consulted and coordinated by the Canadian Technical Barriers and Regulations Divisions of the Department of Foreign Affairs, Trade, and Development and the EU's International Affairs Unit of the Directorate-General for Internal Market, Industry, Entrepreneurship, and SMES respectively (ibid., Art. 21.9).[7]

Regulatory cooperation in CETA has two major elements. On the one hand, an institutional framework is put in place to implement regulatory cooperation and, on the other hand, CETA provides objectives and mechanisms of regulatory cooperation. It is important to realize that outcomes of regulatory cooperation in CETA – whether by decisions taken in its context or by the processes which regulatory cooperation adheres to – may have substantive legal effects in both the EU and Canada (Mendes 2017). The following section elaborates on the CETA's institutional framework and the objectives and mechanisms of regulatory cooperation.

Institutional Framework

CETA creates an institutional framework to supervise and oversee the agreement, attempting to create a "living agreement."[8] First and foremost, a joint committee is set up, comprised of representatives of the EU and Canada respectively (CETA 2016, Art. 26.1). The joint committee meets either once a year or upon request of either the EU or Canada. The responsibility of the joint committee is to "supervise and facilitate the implementation and application of this Agreement and further its general aims" (ibid., Art. 26.1(4)(a)). Decision-making in CETA is reserved to the joint committee, which has "the power to make decisions in respect of all matters when this Agreement so provides" (ibid., Art. 26.3), by mutual consent, with the purpose of attaining the – very broad – objectives of CETA. Decisions are binding on the parties alongside an obligation to implement decisions made by the joint committee – assuring legal effect in both legal systems (ibid., Art. 26.3(2)). More so, the joint committee has been given general oversight powers to "supervise the work of all specialised committees and other bodies established under this Agreement" (ibid., Art. 26.1(4 (b)). CETA also provides a number of discretionary powers to the joint committee such as making recommendations or delegating responsibilities to the specialized committees (ibid., Arts 26.3(2), 26.1(5)).

The joint committee held its inaugural meeting on 26 September 2018 (CETA Joint Committee 2018), which provided a bit more insight on its composition and procedures, though much remains unclear.[9] On transparency, the rules of procedure stipulate that the decisions, recommendations or interpretations adopted by the CETA Joint Committee are made public by the EU and Canada respectively – while its meetings are closed to the public. This is not much, however, the fact that its decisions are made public and the negotiation papers have been publicly available does illustrate "the start of a new approach to transparency ... that is very much to be welcomed" (Cremona 2015, 361–2). On the decisions made by the joint committee, the rules of procedure repeat that decisions, recommendations, or interpretations of the joint committee are made by mutual consent. Aside from this, procedural rules are presumably to be developed.

Aside from the joint committee, CETA (2016, Art. 26.2) sets up specialized committees, required to report to the joint committee, as established in their distinctive articles, and able to develop recommendations to submit to the joint committee. Parties can also bring any matter directly to the joint committee (ibid., Art. 26.3(6)). The specialized committees of CETA can propose draft decisions to the joint committee or, when provided by CETA, take decisions (ibid., Art. 26.2(4)). As with the joint committee, the procedural rules or controls for the specialized committees are currently unknown. As Mendes (2017, 510) concludes: "The picture that emerges is clearly one where a concern for procedural constraints over the powers of those committees – those that could ground objective controls or facilitate the protection of rights and legal interests – is virtually non-existent."

On regulatory cooperation specifically, the regulatory cooperation forum (RCF) – a specialized committee dealing with regulatory cooperation directly– facilitates and promotes regulatory cooperation (CETA 2016, Arts 21.6, 26.2(h)).[10] The RCF reports "as appropriate" to the joint committee on the implementation of the regulatory cooperation chapter (ibid., Art. 21.6(4)(c)). The functions of the RCF are to: (a) provide a forum to discuss regulatory policy issues; (b) assist individual regulators to identify potential partners for cooperation activities; (c) review regulatory initiatives, whether in progress or anticipated, that may provide potential for cooperation; and (d) encourage the development of bilateral cooperation activities in accordance with the regulatory cooperation activities and review the progress, achievements, and best practices of regulatory cooperation initiatives in specific sectors (ibid., Art. 21.6(2)). Furthermore, in accordance with these functions of the RCF, Art. 21.7 (ibid.) makes way for further regulatory cooperation. To enable monitoring of upcoming regulatory projects and to identify opportunities for regulatory cooperation, the EU and Canada will periodically exchange information of ongoing or planned regulatory projects in their areas of responsibility (ibid., Art. 21.7(1)). On non-food product safety, the EU and Canada will attempt to cooperate and voluntarily share information particularly relating to, among others, scientific, technical, and regulatory matters to help improve non-food product safety and risk assessment methods and product testing (ibid., Art. 21.7(3)). The impact of the RCF is extremely hard to predict however, it has been argued that – due to the technical nature of regulatory cooperation – the discussions in the RCF may "de facto predetermine the joint committee's decision-making and shape the regulatory agendas of the Parties" (Meyer-Ohlendorf, Gerstetter, and Bach 2016, 5). While this remains to be seen, and can generally be met with skepticism, the RCF's (2019) Work Plan – a living document – was made available on 28 June 2019 and the RCF had its inaugural meeting (RCF 2018) on 14 December 2018.[11] The RCF's work plan repeats its functions as set out by CETA and clarifies its structure. Where CETA states the RCF will report to the joint committee "as appropriate" the work plan clarifies that this will take place annually. Furthermore, the RCF will post online agendas, work plans and reports, in response to the great level of public interest shown in the RCF, to promote transparency and facilitate consultations with stakeholders (ibid.). While this does not clarify much regarding the RCF's impact, this is very welcome in view of transparency.

   Though there is attention for stakeholder participation in CETA in Art. 21.8 (CETA 2016), there is no obligation or guarantee in CETA regarding participatory rights. If details on consultations are decided based on the needs of the CETA institutions, their value becomes minimal and they are in no way able to "structure or constrain" the authority of CETA's institutions (Mendes 2017, 511). A first glance on how consultations work in practice was given on 18 January 2018, when the European Commission (2018a) called for proposals for regulatory cooperation activities in the RCF under CETA. Furthermore, the work plan shows that from February to April 2018, Canada sought comments from stakeholders, received forty responses, and committed to make them public, illustrating that Canada and the EU are working to identify issues of mutual interest. So far, regulatory cooperation under CETA's RCF is taking place in several areas as published by the RCF (2018, 2019). Notably, the transparency of the RCF's work is refreshing.

The most remarkable thing about the creation of these institutional bodies is the lack of clear procedural and legal constraints on decisions made by the committees in CETA. Not only is CETA rather vague about what the participants of its institutional bodies are, the joint committee has been given powers to adopt internationally binding decisions (Mendes 2017). This could affect both Canada's and the EU's legal systems without clear procedural requirements for decisions made by the joint committee. The joint committee has a broad mandate and its decisions have legal effect without any binding procedural or judicial constraints in CETA – aside from mutual consent and the procedural constraints it decides for itself – thereby not limiting but strengthening its authority (ibid.). Clearly, this is rather worrying considering the effect the decisions could have on both the Canadian and the European legal order (ibid.).

Overall, the powers of the joint committee are quite substantive and its procedural checks and balances quite nominal. Not only is this worrying regarding their legal effect, it also adds another level of concern when considering the far-reaching objectives and mechanisms of regulatory cooperation. Furthermore, the relation between the joint committee and the RCF is not quite clear. Aside from annually reporting, it is possible that the RCF will dictate decision-making in the joint committee. On the bright side, the RCF is doing a relatively good job regarding transparency. While its procedural rules are the exact same as the joint committee's, the RCF has considered public criticism and decided to update frequently online. A lot of information on regulatory cooperation has been made available by the RCF. And while it is procedurally as weak as the joint committee, the transparency of its work counts for something. Nonetheless, CETA paints a picture of executive expertise. Regulatory cooperation and cooperation through joint committee procedures has been pushed to the limit in CETA (de Mestral 2015). This, indeed, is hard to justify "unless one is willing to accept a regression of law in the name of executive expertise" (Mendes 2017, 517).

Objectives and Mechanisms of Regulatory Cooperation in CETA

The objectives of regulatory cooperation in Art. 21.3 of CETA (2016) seem to aim beyond facilitating trade between the EU and Canada. The article gives the impression that the EU and Canada have dedicated themselves to, by means of regulatory cooperation, finding best practices and learn from each other to ideally achieve some sort of harmonization in their regulations or work toward uniform regulatory standards – despite not explicitly stating as such. As Canada and the EU intend to contribute to the protection of human life, health or safety, animal or plant life, or health and environment, they aim to share their resources and knowledge to address regulatory issues – of local, national, and international concern – and build a common base of information used by regulatory departments for matters of risk identification, assessment, and management (CETA 2016, Art. 21.3(a)).

By obtaining each other's expertise and perspectives, including the use of best practices; avoiding unnecessary regulatory differences; identifying alternative instruments; improving planning, development, implementation, and compliance; and promoting transparency and predictability in developing and establishing regulations, the EU and Canada are working to "deepen mutual understanding of regulatory governance" (ibid., Art. 21.3(b)). To facilitate trade and investment and to contribute to improving competitiveness, regulatory cooperation in CETA aims at reducing unnecessary differences in regulation and generally pursues compatibility in regulatory approaches (ibid., Arts 21.3(c) and 21.3(d) (iii)). Even though the articles of CETA address the protection of say, environment, regulatory cooperation shows bias toward the facilitation of trade, investment, and converging regulatory policies (Meyer-Ohlendorf, Gerstetter, and Bach 2016). The "promotion of convergence" is mentioned last in Art. 21.3 (CETA 2016), however the entire article dealing with the objectives of regulatory cooperation suggests that CETA aims at converging regulatory standards.

The key mechanisms used in CETA are equivalence of regulations, mutual recognition, and the use of international standards – thus moving more toward harmonization of regulatory standards than merely the sharing of data and best practices (ibid., Arts 21.2(4), 21.3(d), 21.4(g), 21.4(r); O'Brien 2016). And while CETA does not oblige regulatory authorities to cooperate or to apply the outcome of the cooperation, CETA is not as voluntary as may seem at first hand as it dictates parties to either cooperate or explain (ibid., Art. 21.2(6); Joint Interpretative Instrument 2016; Trew and Plank 2018).

However unclear how EU-Canada regulatory cooperation will take place in practice, CETA (2016, Art. 21.4) provides a long list of activities to achieve the objectives of regulatory cooperation. To establish an ongoing regulatory dialogue, the EU and Canada will have continuing bilateral discussions on regulatory governance (ibid.).[12] By providing endless activities to achieve regulatory cooperation, CETA goes beyond cooperation and toward convergence of regulatory standards and procedures. In contrast to the great detail in the regulatory cooperation activities, democratic features are notably absent in CETA aside from the non-obligatory Art. 21.8 on stakeholder consultation (O'Brien 2016, 9).

The essence of regulatory cooperation lies in the EU and Canada consulting each other "as appropriate" and exchanging information throughout the regulatory process, "as early as possible" in that process (CETA 2016, Art. 21.4(b)). Moreover, to enhance convergence and compatibility between regulatory measures, the EU and Canada have obliged themselves to, "when appropriate," consider the other's regulatory measures or initiatives when regulating on a similar or related topic (ibid., Art. 21.5). This does not prevent the EU or Canada from regulating measures differently or pursuing different initiatives – albeit with the need for an explanation when not cooperating – "for reasons including different institutional or legislative approaches, circumstances, values or priorities" (ibid., Art. 21.5). Since it is unclear what is meant with 'when appropriate,' this could be interpreted in various ways. Considering current day's risk regulation being in fact predominantly transnational, it could be deemed appropriate to consider regulatory measures of each other the majority of the time. Furthermore, it could be appropriate when concerning trade in one way or the other. This could mean that regulating any product covered by CETA – which, considering the broad application of the agreement on matters of trade, are many of them – could call in the applicability of regulatory cooperation and thus call for the EU and Canada to discuss possible regulatory measures before proposing them to their respective bodies responsible for approving draft regulatory measures. De facto – as regulatory cooperation takes place alongside domestic regulatory processes – this would lead to the responsible directorate-general (DG) of the Commission to discuss a regulatory measure with DG GROW which then has to negotiate with the Canadian Technical Barriers and Regulations Divisions of the Department of Foreign Affairs on a majority of matters considering risk regulation before the draft proposal is formally adopted and thus sent to the European Parliament and Council (O'Brien 2016, 6).

While the regulatory cooperation activities are essentially procedural and voluntary by nature, CETA could be far-reaching. By agreeing to inform each other as early as possible in the regulatory process, even regarding non-public information, CETA will effectively give another government access to information before a democratic debate can take place regarding said process. This could lead to the Commission consulting with Canada, and vice versa, on a draft proposal before the draft is adopted by the College of Commissioners and thus before Council and parliament even get word of it. From a democratic point of view, this is rather problematic, especially when regulatory cooperation is aimed at the convergence of standards considering that cooperation alone is less invasive than converging regulatory standards.

Before further elaborating on democracy issues that will likely occur, the following section discusses regulatory cooperation as proposed in TTIP, illustrating that it goes beyond the EU and Canada and confirming the idea of CETA being a blueprint for it (e.g. Chase and Pelkmans 2015; Hoekman 2015; Trujillo 2018), thereby making an assessment of CETA's regulatory cooperation all the more important. Surely, TTIP's opposition and ultimate failing illustrates that regulatory cooperation is controversial. The general critique against FTAs being undemocratic extends to regulatory cooperation and ultimately, the failing of TTIP illustrates the broader point made here in relation to the democratic issues faced when engaging in regulatory cooperation.

Proposed Regulatory Cooperation in TTIP

In TTIP, proposed regulatory cooperation takes place along the same lines as in CETA – which is not surprising since CETA is regarded as a possible blueprint for future trade deals (Chase and Pelkmans 2015). This section analyzes the similarities and differences between regulatory cooperation in CETA and proposed regulatory cooperation in TTIP with the purpose of confirming the idea of a global policy laboratory being built – often seen as an "international effort by the rich countries and their companies to control domestic regulation through international trade agreements that override domestic laws" (O'Brien 2016, 1) – and to illustrate that regulatory cooperation in CETA is most likely a blueprint for future regulatory cooperation considering its similarities to what could have been under the TTIP.

Negotiations for TTIP were stopped without conclusion at the end of 2016 (European Commission 2018b). Considering the political shift in the US and the issues surrounding Brexit in the EU – and surely the COVID-19 pandemic – it is difficult to predict what will happen in the future of EU-US transatlantic relations (Kaufmann and Lohaus 2018). As a response to the Trump administration withdrawing from the Paris Agreement and the imposed import tariffs on steel and aluminum as part of President Trump's economic policy, the Council of the EU (hereinafter the Council) declared the negotiation directives for TTIP obsolete and no longer relevant (Council 2019).[13] In 2019, the Council authorized the opening of fresh negotiations for an agreement on the elimination of tariffs for industrial goods, emphasizing that the EU seeks deep and comprehensive FTAs with parties to the Paris Agreement and acknowledging the difficulties of negotiations in TTIP to achieve mutually acceptable commitments. The Council (ibid.) therefore concludes that it is "appropriate to pursue with the United States a more limited agreement covering the elimination of tariffs on industrial products only, and excluding agricultural products." Nonetheless, the proposed regulatory cooperation in TTIP is worth analyzing because a future US administration may very well wish for a deeper and more comprehensive FTA with the EU (Latorre and Yonezawa 2018). Furthermore, current trends in regulatory cooperation through preferential trade agreements give reason to believe a continuation of these efforts is likely (Chase and Pelkmans 2015; Hoekman 2015; Trujillo 2018). While the TTIP negotiation directive is now obsolete and no longer relevant, proposed regulatory cooperation, as envisioned in the TTIP, is still relevant – as its similarities to CETA will show.

The well-known and rather controversial TTIP negotiations started in July 2013. While many economic scholars agree the TTIP could have economic benefits for consumers (e.g. de Ville and Siles-Brügge 2016, 2017; Haar 2015; Latorre and Yonezawa 2018), a wide range of criticism came from NGOs, academics, civil society, and through social movements from both the EU and US. In contrast, the adoption of CETA seems to have gone by relatively unnoticed aside from the Wallonia and Italy threatening not to ratify CETA (European Parliament 2019).[14] Called "an innovative approach to international regulatory cooperation" (Alemanno 2015, 626), the EU's regulatory cooperation proposals for TTIP set out the scope, objectives, principles, and a model for enhanced cooperation across the Atlantic (Commission 2016c). The rationale behind TTIP's regulatory cooperation chapter is that "convergence upon procedures might induce convergence upon regulatory outcomes" (Alemanno 2015, 630). Ultimately, the goal – in the words of the Commission (2013, 3) – is to move toward "a more integrated transatlantic market where goods produced and services originating in one party in accordance with its regulatory requirements could be marketed in the other without adaptations or requirements."

Similar to CETA, TTIP's regulatory cooperation was envisioned as a "living agreement" consisting of an ongoing regulatory dialogue and a series of exchanges between the regulatory authorities (Alemanno 2015, 631; Cremona 2015, 352; European Commission 2016c, Art. x2; Weiner and Alemanno 2016, 133). In the several textual proposals from the EU and leaked documents that illustrate the position of the US, the overarching idea of regulatory cooperation is essentially the same as in CETA.[15] The so-called horizontal chapters of TTIP would consist of a chapter on good regulatory practices (GRPs), regulatory cooperation, and chapters on technical barriers to trade (TBT) and sanitary and phytosanitary (SPS) measures. Aside from this, there are sector-specific chapters.[16] In contrast to CETA, the TTIP proposals dealt with GRP explicitly. The GRPs – designed to promote good governance in the EU and US alike – relate to "transparent planning, stakeholder consultation, impact assessments and retrospective evaluations of regulatory acts" (European Commission 2016b, Art. 3).[17] TTIP's GRPs focused on publishing major regulatory acts and their accompanying impact assessments "as early as possible" with an obligation to consult stakeholders (European Commission 2016b, Arts 5, 6, 7).[18] Regarding the applicability of TTIP's horizontal chapters, it seems the general idea was that when the EU and US have determined common interest in certain regulatory issues and there is or is likely to be a significant impact on trade or investment, the regulatory cooperation chapter would apply to any regulatory measure that falls within this (rather broad) description (European Commission 2016c, Art. x3), as is the case with CETA.[19]

TTIP would have created an institutional framework predominantly identical to the institutional framework of CETA (Alemanno 2015). TTIP's joint committee, envisioned to be the overarching body, supervised and facilitated the implementation and application of the agreement (European Commission 2016a, Art. xi.1, jo. xi.3).[20] In contrast to CETA, the TTIP joint committee would "guide and facilitate the implementation and application of regulatory cooperation," consider ways to further enhance regulatory cooperation, and "have a dedicated session on regulatory cooperation at its meeting, at least once a year" (ibid., Art. xi.4 jo. xi.5.b). The joint committee would review the overall process of regulatory cooperation every three years, suggest improvement where needed and present the results of this review results at the EU-US summit (ibid., Art. x1.4). It may also make recommendations on regulatory cooperation, including to the Transatlantic Regulators' Forum (the forum) (ibid., Art. x1.6.d).[21]

This forum replaced the previously established regulatory cooperation body (RCB), thus "implying a more casual and informal institution" (Garcia 2018, 232). The RCB was faced with criticism essentially saying that "it will circumvent parliaments, governments or stakeholders' roles in the regulatory process" (European Commission 2015a, 2). While it has been argued that the RCB and the forum are practically the same (Garcia 2018), the textual proposals imply a downgrade of the significance of the RCB (Fahey 2018, 12). Seeking to evolve the RCB "into a mere institutional mechanism," TTIP's institutional framework emphasized "learning processes and exchanges and extensive participation" (ibid., 12). In a strictly formalistic approach, institutionalization in TTIP became significantly weaker by 2016 (ibid.). The RCB would monitor and facilitate the implementation of regulatory cooperation in TTIP and report its findings; prepare an annual regulatory cooperation program; consider new initiatives for regulatory cooperation; prepare joint initiatives; and ensure transparency, with the power to create sectoral working groups (European Commission 2015b, 2015d). The tasks of the forum, however, are rather limited compared to the RCB, as the forum will discuss general trends in regulatory cooperation and consider regulatory cooperation activities covered by TTIP, prepare a joint overview of regulatory cooperation, and, organize public sessions involving EU and US stakeholders (European Commission 2016a, Art. x2.2). Furthermore, while unclear who would participate in the RCB, the forum will comprise senior officials.[22] The tasks of these institutions affirms that from a textual standpoint, the forum is significantly weaker than the RCB and thus the RCB was indeed downgraded. However, considering that the TTIP joint committee has the powers that the RCB used to have, this changes practically nothing. Here we find a striking difference with CETA, since the CETA Joint Committee has no specific powers relating to regulatory cooperation. The RCF in CETA has more in common with the RCB in TTIP. And where the RCB in TTIP was drastically reduced in power (on paper, that is), CETA's RCF resembles TTIP's proposed RCB more than its forum. This can be explained by the difference in attention, i.e. lack of criticism, in case of CETA.

By agreeing to inform each other "at the earliest possible stage" when there is or likely will be an impact on trade, in practice the EU would "provide cooperation opportunities before the Commission adopts a formal position" and the "US regulatory agencies shall provide cooperation opportunities before the launch of the (advanced) notice of proposed rulemaking or in a timely manner before adopting or consulting on a guidance document" (European Commission 2016c, Art. x4). While "such cooperation opportunities do not imply any commitment to share draft texts before they have been made public under the respective regulatory or administrative procedures" (ibid., Art. x4, fn), the question remains when exactly this should take place? On the EU's side, a suggestion comes from Chase and Pelkmans (2015, 15): "the Commission could accept comments on the proposals for, say 60 days; these comments would be published on the Commission website, and the Commission's analysis and response to them could then be made available to the Council and Parliament upon formal presentation of the proposals to those institutions." This rather startling suggestion brings rise to important questions such as: "Will de facto regulatory authority migrate to a transatlantic forum of executive governance?" (Meuwese 2015, 164).

Considering the possible consequences of regulatory cooperation, is important to see what the role of parliament could have been in TTIP's regulatory cooperation, since the aforementioned might "result in fundamental accountability problems" (Alemanno 2014, 56), as seems to be the case in CETA. Parliamentary ties will have to be enhanced to prevent democratic accountability issues that were likely to occur (ibid.; Haar 2015). Should the regulatory cooperation chapter in the TTIP have resulted in the Commission giving the US the possibility to comment on draft proposals before being adopted by the College of Commissioners, thus prolonging the democratic debate in parliament or Council, the level of democratic accountability in the EU might have reached a new low.

Contrastingly, the process of regulatory cooperation could also be viewed "as a collaborative effort, aimed at a greater mutual understanding of different regulatory approaches" (Cremona 2015, 353). According to Alemanno (2015, 631), TTIP was "set to create the conditions for prompting a new awareness in the minds of the respective regulators: that of the extraterritorial impact of their existing and proposed regulations." While this could be true, it is important that parliamentary ties get strengthened when engaging in regulatory cooperation. As seen from the analysis of regulatory cooperation, parliament has not been attritubuted any oversight mechanism in either of the FTAS.[23] It does stand out that the TTIP proposals mentioned certain democratic features as opposed to the lack thereof in CETA. TTIP paid some attention to political accountability, effective coordination, transparency with regards to the institutional setup for implementation, and the involvement of legislators.[24] TTIP specifically acknowledged the role of the Transatlantic Legislators Dialogue (TLD) and aimed to ensure that future implementation "is accompanied, as appropriate, by a deepening of transatlantic parliamentary cooperation" (European Commission 2016a, Art. x6).[25] Drawing upon the experiences of this dialogue, TTIP aimed to "foster the parliamentary dimension ... without prejudice to the Parliamentary sovereignty of the Parties' legislative authorities" (ibid.). In CETA, there is no mention of any parliament whatsoever and, regardless of the demise of TTIP, this is troublesome.

With regard to transparency, it is noted that the involvement of stakeholders "is critical for the success of regulatory cooperation activities."[26] It is stressed that all "natural and legal persons need to be given the opportunity to provide input to ongoing regulatory cooperation initiatives and suggest new initiatives."[27] As in Art. 22.5 (CETA 2016), TTIP intended to establish a civil society forum (European Commission 2016a, Art. x8). It is stated in both TTIP and CETA that the parties "shall promote a balanced representation of all relevant interests including independent representative organisations of employers, workers, environmental interests, business groups, consumers groups, and public health associations" (CETA 2016, Art. 22.5; European Commission 2016a, Art. x8.2). While it remains unclear how this would have been done in practice, there was an attempt to enhance the legitimacy of the agreement – albeit in very vague and non-obligatory terms.

TTIP built on past experiences in the EU-US regulatory cooperation, attempted to improve what has been done before, and ultimately aimed to be the "treaty to end trade treaties" (Chase and Pelkmans 2015; Garcia 2018, 235; Haar 2015; Wiener and Alemanno 2016, 130). Regulatory cooperation in TTIP and CETA has many similarities and it can be said that regulatory cooperation takes places along the same lines – albeit that TTIP ultimately did not come to fruition. A striking difference in CETA, however, is the complete absence of the respective parliaments. It is remarkable that democratic checks and balances have not found their way to CETA – in comparison to TTIP's intentions but also in general.

THE INFLUENCE OF FOREIGN GOVERNMENTS

Over the years, transatlantic regulatory cooperation has shifted from a focus on the rules to the procedures for making the rules, resulting in an attempt to regulate the regulatory procedures (Meuwese 2015). By creating joint procedures and institutional mechanisms, governance is no longer seen as a barrier but as a gateway to transatlantic regulatory cooperation (ibid.). And while it is not completely clear how regulatory cooperation in FTAS will take place, it is highly likely that the trend of including regulatory cooperation in future FTAS will continue (Trujillo 2018, 404). It is not surprising that the overarching idea of regulatory cooperation is the same in both TTIP and CETA. Furthermore, the institutional frameworks in TTIP and CETA are similar (Garcia 2018, 235) – both are envisioned as "living agreements," establishing an ongoing dialogue and allowing their respective joint committees to make decisions to achieve the purpose of the agreements, which enables future regulatory cooperation in ways that cannot yet be predicted (Chase and Pelkmans 2015). CETA and TTIP are the embodiment of "the institutionalization of regulatory cooperation through preferential trade agreements" (Trujillo 2018, 366).

While regulatory cooperation as envisioned in these agreements can increase efficiency and effectiveness of regulators across the Atlantic, the decision-making processes of the respective parties could potentially be limited by participating in regulatory cooperation (Chase and Pelkmans 2015; Meuwese 2015). This is where key questions on principal issues such as democratic accountability, legitimacy of decision-making, and transparency play a crucial role and are therefore unsurprisingly widely debated (see, for example, Meuwese 2015). The fact that these agreements are evolving into "living agreements," focused on learning under supervision of their institutional frameworks, could strengthen the application of GRPS and turn these FTAS into a "transatlantic policy laboratory" (Wiener and Alemanno 2016, 132–3). Rather than considering these FTAS as a potential threat or problem, they can be seen as a stepping stone toward a "global regulatory laboratory" (ibid., 130). In this view, regulatory cooperation is more than merely the reduction of trade barriers but rather cooperating to learn and decide on optimal approaches through impact assessments on regulatory variation (ibid.). Regulatory cooperation could indeed be seen an important step toward global governance (Trujillo 2018). Viewing current trends as focusing on learning through a continuous dialogue, however, requires trust in the legislators, particularly when deciding whether specific regulatory standards should be set cooperatively or not (Cremona 2015; Madner 2017). Needless to say, this is hard to do especially considering the lack of democratic checks and balances provided in CETA.

By engaging in regulatory cooperation, these FTAS create a "shared regulatory space" (Trujillo 2018, 374). This has at least two very important consequences: (1) by participating in an ongoing regulatory dialogue with foreign governments, especially when done before a draft proposal is agreed upon, the executive plays a new role in setting regulatory standards, while (2) it simultaneously allows foreign governments to influence the setting of these regulatory standards (ibid.). With this new way of working, procedural and judicial control, participation of civil society and citizens, transparency, legitimacy, and democratic accountability become extremely important – although disappointingly not acknowledged enough in these FTAS (Hoekman 2015; Mendes 2017; Trujillo 2018, 405).

The role of the executive is thus transformed (Claussen 2017; Trujillo 2018) and the creation of a shared regulatory space allows foreign government access to domestic regulatory processes. Allowing foreign government participation is not inherently negative when tackling transnational risks. Neither is building the so-called global policy laboratory. In theory, a transatlantic or even global policy laboratory sounds appealing considering transnational risks and the globalized world we are living in today. However, national structures that have been put in place to guarantee democracy and the protection of democratic principles cannot be ignored. As the EU has been struggling with this for as long as one can remember, a transnational or global policy laboratory as found in these FTAS will be subject to immense criticism by national governments and interest groups alike. The transatlantic marketplace as envisioned by CETA and TTIP will be faced with more severe criticism on principle issues of democracy than what the EU has seen to this day. Especially when considering the poor procedural and judicial constraints on decision-making in CETA, where democratic checks and balances are hard to find.

Furthermore, there is a strong bias toward trade and investment facilitation rather than protecting citizens or the environment (Meyer-Ohlendorf, Gerstetter, and Bach 2016, 5). Regulatory cooperation has been said to be – disappointingly – industry- and commerce-focused (Trew and Plank 2018). That the industry and its lobbying groups have an influence on regulatory processes is a well-known fact. However, this influence is twofold in matters of regulatory cooperation. On the one hand, big business exerts an influence on regulatory cooperation. On the other hand, by gaining access to the early stages of regulatory processes via regulatory cooperation, businesses are given another way to exert their influence. Thus, the industry can both implicitly and explicitly exert their influence on regulatory cooperation. Explicitly, by exerting influence over regulatory cooperation. Implicitly, by exerting influence over national policymakers that trickle down to regulatory cooperation between governments. The bias toward trade facilitation can result in a focus on trade at the expense of other considerations (Meyer-Ohlendorf, Gerstetter, and Bach 2016, 5).

While regulatory cooperation does not necessarily alter domestic processes, regulatory cooperation creates another layer of governance that is deserving of its own checks and balances. Perhaps this problem is currently theoretical, however, it is important to tread with caution. Regulatory convergence, building a global policy laboratory and cooperating in regulatory processes before national democratic processes is a step that should not be taken lightly (Pitschas 2016). Regulating the regulatory procedures in view of a shared regulatory space inevitably allows foreign governments access to regulatory procedures. While this is not inherently a bad thing, it has consequences that affect the democratic process.[28] And, considering the influence of business, there is a great risk for behind-the-door deals. Regulatory cooperation facilitates trade, but basic democratic features need to find their way into CETA and other FTAs dealing with regulatory cooperation – such as oversight mechanisms for parliaments and participatory rights supported by procedural rules aiming to prevent bias toward business and behind-the-door deals. In general, it is wise to tread with caution when engaging in regulatory cooperation and to keep in mind that democratic checks and balances exist for a reason and should not be ignored, not in national processes and certainly not in transnational governance.

NOTES

1 Regulatory cooperation in the WTO takes place using international standards, good regulatory practices, equivalence, mutual recognition, and working towards harmonization. The TBT and SPS committees deal directly with the impact of regulation on trade and promote regulatory cooperation through using and disseminating good regulatory practices. See Mavroidis (2016, 6); OECD (2013, 31); WTO (2012, 177).

2 E.g., Bermann, Lindseth, and Herdegen (2000) on the EU and the US specifically. Regulatory cooperation chapters are increasingly found in FTAS, for example the new North American FTA (NAFTA) and other FTAS done by the EU with, for example, Singapore or Japan.

3 Regulatory cooperation mechanisms vary from building trust by using good regulatory practices to harmonization through equivalence provision, international standards, and mutual recognition.

4 Providing an exhaustive overview of regulatory cooperation mechanism is – however interesting it might be – beyond the scope of this chapter. For a thorough study on the wide range of regulatory cooperation mechanisms, see OECD (2013, 23).

5 On the lack of procedural and judicial constraints on decisions made by the bodies specifically in CETA, see Mendes (2017).

6 What we see here is a confirmation of the WTO often serving as a starting point for regulatory cooperation, as can be seen in CETA and also in other FTAS dealing with regulatory cooperation.

7 As CETA is only provisionally in force at the time of writing this, the way in which consulting and coordinating will take place remains unclear.

8 The same goes for TTIP. Both FTAS aim to create a "living agreement" in the sense that the agreement will keep evolving over time using committees. However, one might wonder what exactly would be a non-living agreement. See Alemanno (2015, 631); Cremona (2015, 352); European Commission (2016c, Art. x2); and Weiner and Alemanno (2016, 133).

9 The inaugural meeting was co-chaired by the Canadian minister for international trade diversification, James Carr, and the European commissioner for trade, Cecilia Malmström. The representatives seem to consist of – based on the participants of the inaugural meeting of the joint committee – representatives of the government of Canada, the EU Trade commissioner and representatives of DG Trade, senior officials of the provincial governments of Canadian, as well as officials of the embassies or consulate-generals of EU member states and/or the Canadian provinces. The participants of the inaugural meeting of the joint committee can be found at CETA Joint Committee (2018).

10 The RCF is co-chaired by a senior representative of the Government of Canada at the level of a deputy minister and a senior representative of the European Commission at the level of a director general, and the RCF is comprised of officials of the EU and Canada respectively. By mutual consent, other interested parties may be invited to participate in the meetings of the RCF, following Art. 21.6(3) of CETA (2016). The RCF meets annually and will adopt a term of reference, procedure, and work plan at the first meeting after CETA enters into force, following Arts 21.6(4)(a) and 21.6(4)(b) of CETA (2016).

11 The co-chairs of the RCF were director Ignacio Garcia-Bercero of DG Trade, director Eric Mamer of DG GROW, Jeannine Ritchot of the Treasury Board of Canada Secretariat, and Dough Forsyth of Global Affairs Canada. Aside from these co-chairs, participants of the first meeting of the RCF were officials and stakeholders from the EU and Canada respectively.

12 This includes but is not limited to: regulatory reforms and its effect; lessons learned; exploring alternatives approaches to regulation; and exchanging experiences with regulatory tools and instruments, including regulatory

impact assessments, risk assessment, and compliance and enforcement
strategies. Other activities of regulatory cooperation include, amongst
others: sharing non-public information; sharing – proposed – regulations to
allow sufficient time for interested parties to provide comments; exchange
information regarding contemplated regulatory actions, measures, or
amendments at the earliest stage possible; assessing opportunities to
minimize regulatory divergence; examining possibilities on using the same
methodologies and date; and conducting cooperative research agendas to
possibly establish a common scientific basis.

13 For an analysis, see Schlesinger, Nicholas, and Radnofsky (2018);
 Widmer (2018).

14 It has been said that "public opposition to CETA has piggybacked upon
 TTIP opposition" (Fahey 2017, 301).

15 There is a certain information asymmetry regarding TTIP, as US positions
 remain rather confidential except for when Greenpeace leaked restricted
 documents on TTIP – see Alemanno (2016); European Commission
 (2015b, 2015c, 2016c); and "Leaked" (2016).

16 These chapters include industries such as chemicals, cosmetics,
 engineering products, information and communication technologies,
 medical devices, pesticides, pharmaceuticals, textiles, and vehicles
 (European Commission 2015d).

17 Also see Pitschas (2016, 331).

18 What this basically comes down to is that planned regulatory acts,
 accompanied by an impact assessment, should include a consideration of
 both parties' regulatory approaches and the impact on trade, alongside the
 exchange of information on evidence and data, practices, methodology,
 and economic assumptions.

19 The logical conclusion seems to be that "purely domestic rules" will not
 fall under the scope of either of the FTAs; see Alemanno (2015, 629).

20 The joint committee would consist of representatives of the EU and the US,
 co-chaired by the US Trade Representative and the EU's Trade Commissioner.

21 Art. x2 (European Commission 2016a) establishes the Transatlantic
 Regulators' Forum.

22 Senior officials responsible for cross-cutting issues of regulatory policy
 and good regulatory practices, senior officials responsible for international
 trade, and senior regulators for the areas they are respectively responsible
 for (European Commission 2016a, Art. x.2.1).

23 One could argue that democratic checks and balances can be found – i.e.
 parliament gets a say at the signing of the FTA and subsequently after the
 adoption of the draft proposal. This, however, leads to parliament merely

getting to nod in agreement or shake their head in disagreement at the outcome of regulatory cooperation. The question then becomes if it is legitimate in a democracy for parliament to do nothing more but approve or disprove legislative proposals.

24 See European Commission (2016c) in the Annex: Institutional Set Up for Implementation.

25 The TLD is a transatlantic dialogue aiming to strengthen and enhance the level of political discourse between European and American legislators.

26 See European Commission (2016c) in the Annex: Institutional Set Up for Implementation.

27 See European Commission (2016c) in the Annex: Institutional Set Up for Implementation.

28 A more detailed description of the problems that occur as a result of regulatory cooperation can be found in my thesis and has been left out considering the scope of this chapter, which is based on the research done for the thesis.

REFERENCES

Aaron, David L. 2000. "The United States and Europe: Seeking Common Ground." In *Transatlantic Regulatory Cooperation: Legal Problems and Political Prospects*, edited by George A. Bermann, Peter L. Lindseth, and Matthias Herdegen, 25–8. Oxford: Oxford University Press.

Ahearn, Raymond J. 2018. "Transatlantic Regulatory Cooperation: Background and Analysis." Report for Congress, Congressional Research Service, Washington, DC.

Alemanno, Alberto. 2014. "The Transatlantic Trade and Investment Partnership and the Parliamentary Dimension of Regulatory Cooperation." Directorate-General for External Policies of The Union, Policy Department Study.

– 2015. "The Regulatory Cooperation Chapter of the Transatlantic Trade and– Investment Partnership: Institutional Structures and Democratic Consequences." *Journal of International Economic Law* 18, no. 3: 625–40. https://doi.org/10.1093/jiel/jgv026.

– 2016. "What the TTIP Leaks Mean for the On-going Negotiations and Future Agreement?" *European Journal of Risk Regulation* 7, no. 2: 237–41. https://doi.org/10.1017/S1867299X00005602.

Bermann, George A., Peter L. Lindseth, and Matthias Herdegen, eds. 2000. *Transatlantic Regulatory Cooperation: Legal Problems and Political Prospects*. Oxford: Oxford University Press.

Bull, Reeve T., Neysun A. Mahboubi, Richard B. Stewart, and Jonathan B. Wiener. 2015. "New Approaches to International Regulatory Cooperation." *Law and Contemporary Problems* 78, no. 1: 1–29.

CETA (Canada-European Union Comprehensive Economic and Trade Agreement). 2016. Accessed 21 July 2020. https://www.international.gc.ca/ trade-commerce/trade-agreements-accords-commerciaux/agr-acc/CETA-aecg/ text-texte/toc-tdm.aspx?lang=eng.

CETA Joint Committee. 2018. "CETA Joint Committee Meeting September 26, 2018: Summary Report." Accessed 15 August 2019. https://www. international.gc.ca/trade-commerce/trade-agreements-accords-commerciaux/ agr-acc/CETA-aecg/2018-09-26-summary_report-rapport_sommaire. aspx?lang=eng.

Chase, Peter, and Jacques Pelkmans. 2015. "This Time It's Different: Turbo-Charging Regulatory Cooperation in TTIP." IDEAS Working Paper Series from Research Papers in Economics.

Claussen, K. 2017. "Trading Spaces: The Changing Role of the Executive in US Trade Lawmaking." *Indiana Journal of Global Legal Studies*, 24: 345–68.

Council of the European Union. 2019. "Council Decision Authorising the Opening of Negotiations with the United States of America for an Agreement on the Elimination of Tariffs for Industrial Goods (No. 6052/19)." Accessed 5 August 2020. https://www.consilium.europa.eu/media/39180/st06052-en19.pdf.

Cremona, Marise. 2015. "Negotiating the Transatlantic Trade and Investment Partnership (TTIP)." *Common Market Law Review* 52, no. 2: 351–62.

de Mestral, Armand. 2015. "When Does the Exception Become the Rule? Conserving Regulatory Space under CETA." *Journal of International Economic Law* 18, no. 3: 641–54. https://doi.org/10.1093/jiel/jgv033.

de Ville, Ferdi, and Gabriel Siles-Brügge. 2016. *TTIP: The Truth About the Transatlantic Trade and Investment Partnership*. Cambridge: Polity Press.

– 2017. "Why TTIP Is a Game-Changer and Its Critics Have a Point." *Journal of European Public Policy* 24, no. 10: 1491–505. https://doi.org/10.1080/ 13501763.2016.1254273.

European Commission. 2013. "EU-US Transatlantic Trade and Investment Partnership: Trade Cross-Cutting Disciplines and Institutional Provisions." Initial EU Position Paper. http://trade.ec.europa.eu/doclib/docs/2013/july/ tradoc_151622.pdf.

– 2015a. "Factsheet on Regulatory Cooperation." Accessed 17 August 2020. https://trade.ec.europa.eu/doclib/docs/2015/january/tradoc_153002. 1%20RegCo.pdf.

- 2015b. "Initial Provisions for Chapter [ ] Regulatory Cooperation, 10 February 2015." Accessed 15 August 2019. http://trade.ec.europa.eu/doclib/docs/2015/february/tradoc_153120.pdf.
- 2015c. "TTIP: Initial Provisions for Chapter [ ] Regulatory Cooperation, 4 May 2015." Accessed 15 August 2019. http://Trade.Ec.Europa.Eu/Doclib/Docs/2015/April/Tradoc_153403.pdf.
- 2015d. "TTIP and Regulation: An Overview, 10 February 2015." Accessed 15 August 2019. https://Trade.Ec.Europa.Eu/Doclib/Docs/2015/February/Tradoc_153121.pdf.
- 2016a. "EU Proposal for Institutional, General and Final Provisions, 14 July 2016." Accessed 15 August 2019. https://trade.ec.europa.eu/doclib/docs/2016/july/tradoc_154802.pdf.
- 2016b. "TTIP – EU Proposal for Chapter: Good Regulatory Practices, 21 March 2016." Accessed 15 August 2019. http://trade.ec.europa.eu/doclib/docs/2016/march/tradoc_154380.pdf.
- 2016c. "TTIP - EU Proposal for Chapter: Regulatory Cooperation, 21 March 2016." Accessed 15 August 2019. https://Trade.Ec.Europa.Eu/Doclib/Docs/2016/March/Tradoc_154377.pdf.
- 2018a. "Call for Proposals for Regulatory Cooperation Activities in the Regulatory Cooperation Forum (RCF) under CETA." Accessed 5 August 2020. http://trade.ec.europa.eu/doclib/press/index.cfm?id=1781.
- 2018b. "United States." Accessed 5 May 2018. https://ec.europa.eu/trade/policy/countries-and-regions/countries/united-states/.
European Parliament. 2019. "A Balanced and Progressive Trade Policy to Harness Globalisation: CETA." Accessed 16 August 2019. https://www.europarl.europa.eu/legislative-train/theme-a-balanced-and-progressive-trade-policy-to-harness-globalisation/file-CETA.
Fahey, Elaine. 2017. "CETA and Global Governance Law: What Kind of Model Agreement Is It Really in Law?" *European Papers* 2, no. 1: 293–302. https://doi.org/10.15166/2499-8249/119.
- 2018. "Introduction: Institutionalisation Beyond the Nation State: New Paradigms? Transatlantic Relations: Data, Privacy and Trade Law." In *Institutionalisation Beyond the Nation State: Transatlantic Relations: Data, Privacy and Trade Law*, edited by Elaine Fahey, 1–27. Cham: Springer Law.
Garcia, Maria. 2018. "Building Global Governance One Treaty at a Time? A Comparison of the US and EE Approaches to Preferential Trade Agreements and the Challenge of TTIP." In *Institutionalisation Beyond the Nation State: Transatlantic Relations: Data, Privacy and Trade Law*, edited by Elaine Fahey, 213–42. Cham: Springer Law.

Haar, Kenneth. 2015. "Cooperating to Deregulate." Accessed 5 August 2020. https://corporateeurope.org/en/international-trade/2015/11/cooperating-deregulate.

Hoekman, Bernard. 2015. "Fostering Transatlantic Regulatory Cooperation and Gradual Multilateralization." *Journal of International Economic Law* 18, no. 3: 609–24. https://doi.org/10.1093/jiel/jgv028.

Joint Interpretative Instrument on the Comprehensive Economic and Trade Agreement (CETA) between Canada & the European Union and its Member States. 2016. Accessed 21 July 2020. https://www.international.gc.ca/trade-commerce/trade-agreements-accords-commerciaux/agr-acc/CETA-aecg/jii-iic.aspx?lang=eng.

Kaufmann, Sonja, and Mathis Lohaus. 2018. "Ever Closer or Lost at Sea? Scenarios for the Future of Transatlantic Relations." *Futures* 97: 18–25. https://doi.org/10.1016/j.futures.2017.04.007.

Latorre, María C., and Hidemichi Yonezawa. 2018. "Stopped TTIP? Its Potential Impact on the World and the Role of Neglected FDI." *Economic Modelling* 71: 99–120. https://doi.org/10.1016/j.econmod.2017.12.006.

"Leaked. Consolidated TTIP Chapter: Initial Provisions for Chapter [Eu: Regulatory Cooperation] [US: Regulatory Coherence, Transparency, and Other Good Regulatory Practices]." 2016. Accessed 5 May 2018. https://trade-leaks.org/.

Madner, Verena. 2017. "A New Generation of Trade Agreements: An Opportunity Not to Be Missed?" In *Mega-Regional Trade Agreements: CETA, TTIP and TISA: New Orientations for EU External Economic Relations*, edited by Stefan Griller, Walter Obwexer, and Erich Vranes, 307–13. Oxford: Oxford University Press.

Mavroidis, Petros C. 2016. "Regulatory Cooperation: Lessons from the WTO and the World Trade Regime." E15 Task Force on Regulatory Systems Coherence – Policy Options Paper, Geneva, International Centre for Trade and Sustainable Development (ICTSD) and World Economic Forum.

Mendes, Joana. 2017. "The External Administrative Layer of EU Law-Making: International Decisions in EU Law and the Case of CETA." *European Papers* 2, no. 2: 489–517. http://doi.org/10.15166/2499-8249/166.

Meuwese, Anne. 2011. "EU-US Horizontal Regulatory Cooperation: Mutual Recognition of Impact Assessment?" In *Transatlantic Regulatory Cooperation: The Shifting Roles of the EU, the US and California*, edited by David Vogel and Johan Swinnen, 249–69. Cheltenham: Edward Elgar.

– 2015. "Constitutional Aspects of Regulatory Cooperation in TTIP: An EU Perspective." *Law and Contemporary Problems* 78, 4: 153–74. https://www.jstor.org/stable/43920635.

Meyer-Ohlendorf, Nils, Christiane Gerstetter, and Inga Bach. 2016. *Regulatory Cooperation under CETA: Implications for Environmental Policies*. Berlin: Ecologic Institute.

O'Brien, Ronan. 2016. "Moving Regulation out of Democratic Reach: Regulatory Cooperation in CETA and Its Implications." Working Paper Reihe der AK Wien – Materialien zu Wirtschaft und Gesellschaft 158, Kammer für Arbeiter und Angestellte für Wien, Abteilung Wirtschaftswissenschaft und Statistik.

OECD (Organisation for Economic Co-operation and Development). 2013. International Regulatory Co-operation: Addressing Global Challenges. Paris: OECD.

Pitschas, Christian. 2016. "Transatlantic Trade and Investment Partnership (TTIP): The Devil in Disguise or a Golden Opportunity to Build a Transatlantic Marketplace?" *British Journal of American Legal Studies* 5, no. 2: 315–40. https://doi.org/10.1515/bjals-2016-0011

RCF (Regulatory Cooperation Forum). 2018. "1st Meeting of the CETA Regulatory Cooperation Forum." Accessed 15 August 2019. https://www.international.gc.ca/trade-commerce/trade-agreements-accords-commerciaux/agr-acc/CETA-aecg/2018-12-14_rcf_report-rapport_fcr.aspx?lang=eng.

– 2019. "Comprehensive Economic and Trade Agreement Regulatory Cooperation Forum Work Plan." Accessed 15 August 2019. https://www.international.gc.ca/trade-commerce/trade-agreements-accords-commerciaux/agr-acc/CETA-aecg/2019-06-28-work-travail-plan.aspx?lang=eng.

Schlesinger, Jacob, Peter Nicholas, and Louise Radnofsky. 2018. "Trump to Impose Steep Aluminum and Steel Tariffs; President Plans Next Week to Approve 25% Duties on Steel Imports and 10% on Aluminum over the Objection of Allies and Some Advisers." *Wall Street Journal*, 2 March. https://www.wsj.com/articles/trump-wont-quickly-announce-new-tariffs-on-aluminum-steel-1519921704.

Trew, Stuart, and Max Plank. 2018. "Regulatory cooperation in CETA: Exporting the NAFTA model or something more?" Paper presented at CETA Implementation Workshop, Dalhousie University, 18 May 2018.

Trujillo, Elizabeth. 2018. "Regulatory Cooperation in International Trade and Its Transformative Effects on Executive Power." *Indiana Journal of Global Legal Studies* 25, no. 1: 365–412.

Vogel, David. 2007. "Can It Be Done? Suggestions for Better Regulatory Cooperation between the US and Europe." Transatlantic Thinkers No. 7, Bertelsmann Stiftung, Gütersloh.

Widmer, Lori. 2018. "The Business Impact of Trump Tariffs." *Risk Management* 65, no. 6: 18–22. http://www.rmmagazine.com/2018/06/01/the-business-impact-of-trump-tariffs.

Wiener, Jonathan B., and Alberto Alemanno. 2016. "The Future of International Regulatory Cooperation: TTIP as a Learning Process toward a Global Policy Laboratory." *Law & Contemporary Problems* 78, no. 4: 103–36.

WTO (World Trade Organization). 2012. *World Trade Report 2012: Trade and Public Policies: A Closer Look at Non-Tariff Measures in the 21st Century.* Geneva: WTO.

PART THREE

Public Procurement

7

Public Procurement under CETA Chapter 19

Agnès Ruffat and Patrick Leblond

INTRODUCTION

Since the Comprehensive Economic and Trade Agreement (CETA) between Canada and the European Union (EU) provisionally entered into force in late September 2017, many barriers to access public procurement contracts remain in both the EU and Canada despite Chapter 19, whereby Canada and the EU have both committed to open up their government procurement markets to each other. Why is it so difficult to remove these barriers? What are those obstacles and what could be done to remove them? These are the questions that this chapter addresses.

It is important for Canadian firms to be able to take advantage of the opportunities offered by the EU's government procurement markets and vice versa for EU firms. After all, this is why Canada and the EU agreed to Chapter 19 of CETA (D'Erman 2020). But as with many other aspects of third-generation free trade agreements (FTAS),[1] a lot of work has to be done once the agreement is in force in order for its provisions to be effective (Leblond 2016). For public procurement, this includes ensuring that all levels of government have changed their administrative proced-ures and even laws or regulations, so that there is no discrimination against EU firms in Canada and Canadian firms in the EU in deciding on which bidders to choose from or even in inviting into a bidding process (Lusenko, Schwartz, and Schwartz 2020). It also includes making sure that firms, especially small- and medium-sized enterprises (SMES), have easy access to the necessary information in order to bid on projects. For example, as part of its CETA commitments, Canada undertook to develop a common online platform for all government (municipal, provincial, and federal) contracts on offer, in order to make it easy for EU firms to have access to the Canadian market. At the time of writing, however, the platform is nowhere to be seen. Finally, Canadian and EU firms must first and foremost be made aware of the fact that CETA allows them access to government procurement contracts on the other side of the Atlantic. This can only be done through the active promotion of the agreement to businesses.

After describing CETA Chapter 19 and explaining how it applies, we examine what barriers to access government procurement markets on both sides of the Atlantic remain two years after the agreement has entered into force and why it is so. Finally, we propose solutions to remove these obstacles.

CETA AND PUBLIC PROCUREMENT

After eight years of negotiations, CETA entered into force on a provisional basis on 21 September 2017.[2] Chapter 19 (CETA 2016) defines the rules of public procurement between the EU and Canada at federal and sub-federal levels. Accessing provincial and municipal government procurement markets in Canada was one of the EU's major goals in negotiating CETA (D'Erman 2020; Leblond 2010; Paquin 2020). According to D'Erman (2020, 4), government procurement markets accounted for 13 per cent and 18 per cent of Canadian and EU GDP, respectively. At the time the CETA negotiations began (2008–09), the World Trade Organization's (WTO's) Agreement on Government Procurement (GPA) did not include Canadian provinces and municipalities. It covered only federal government procurement contracts.[3]

In Canada, the federal government is ultimately legally responsible for negotiating and signing international trade agreements, even in areas that fall under provincial jurisdiction (Fafard and Leblond 2012; Kukucha 2008; Paquin 2020). "Generally, the federal government will not ratify a treaty until it is confident that Canada's domestic law is consistent with the treaty and that there are sufficient legal powers in place to comply with its obligations. If legislation is necessary, it is usually passed before the treaty is ratified. The same considerations apply when a treaty relates to matters falling within both federal and provincial jurisdiction, and a fortiori when the treaty relates to matters exclusively within provincial jurisdiction." (de Mestral and Fox-Decent 2008, 624, quoted in Paquin 2020, 42). As a pre-condition for launching the negotiations, the EU wanted provincial governments to be present at the CETA negotiating table(s), following the failed attempt to negotiate a Trade and Investment Enhancement Agreement between Canada and the EU in the mid-2000s (Woolcock 2011, 27). The EU's goal was to get political buy-in from Canadian provinces and territories with respect to implementing the agreement's provisions that would fall under their competences. As such, it would then make it politically difficult for the provincial and territorial governments to say that they did not know about or never agreed to such provisions. By the same token, the EU also wanted Canada to make deeper commitments within the GPA, notably with respect to provinces and municipalities (D'Erman 2020, 15).

Chapter 19 (CETA 2016) gives firms access, with no discrimination or unfair competition (above-value thresholds), to public markets in the EU and all its member states as well as in Canada and its provinces, territories, and municipalities. The goal is to liberalize government procurement in order to increase business between the two jurisdictions, enhance economic growth, and, ultimately, create new jobs.

Chapter 19 first defines what is public procurement and related terms (ibid.). It then defines its scope and coverage. Then, it names what it covers and what is excluded, states the general principles, gives information on the procurement system, and presents the notices and conditions of participation. In addition, it presents the criteria for supplier qualification as well as the technical specifications and tender documentation time periods. It gives all the information for the tendering process and how it should be publicized online, including transparency and disclosing obligations, review and modification processes, and the committee in charge.

The specific commitments in terms of entities, goods, and services covered by Chapter 19 are found in the annexes. Annex 19-A (CETA 2016) contains Canada's market access schedule while Annex 19-B (ibid.) contains that of the EU's.[4] In Canada's case, the annexes are as follows:

- Annex 19-1, the central government entities whose procurement is covered by this chapter;
- Annex 19-2, the sub-central government entities whose procurement is covered by this chapter;
- Annex 19-3, all other entities whose procurement is covered by this chapter;
- Annex 19-4, the goods covered by this chapter;
- Annex 19-5, the services, other than construction services, covered by this chapter;

- Annex 19-6, the construction services covered by this chapter;
- Annex 19-7, any general notes; and
- Annex 19-8, the means of publication used for this chapter.

The annexes also indicate the thresholds over which the chapter applies. For example, in the case of the Canadian federal government, the thresholds are:[5]

- Goods: SDR 130,000
- Services: SDR 130,000
- Construction Services: SDR 5,000,000

This means that federal government entities do not have to concern themselves with the provisions in Chapter 19 for contracts whose value fall under these thresholds. In other words, they can choose to discriminate against EU-based firms in their procurement process for tenders below the thresholds. However, they cannot break down contracts into smaller values in order to avoid the thresholds. For Canadian provinces, the thresholds for goods and services are SDR 200,000. Another example of the kinds of details found in Chapter 19's annexes is the following: "Procuring entities in the provinces of Ontario and Quebec, when purchasing mass transit vehicles, may, in accordance with the terms of this Chapter, require that the successful bidder contracts up to 25 per cent of the contract value in Canada" (CETA 2016, Notes to Canada's Annex 19-4, 1.a).

According to Casier (2019, 13), Chapter 19 goes beyond Canada's commitments under the GPA: "CETA covers more entities, and the thresholds for goods and services procurement by sub-central entities is also lower than under the WTO GPA. CETA includes roughly twenty more central government entities and significantly more subnational entities, including most regional, local, district or other forms of municipal government, as well as all publicly funded academic, health and social-service entities." In exchange, the EU agreed to open its access "to most of the utility sectors that it withholds under the GPA, namely: drinking water; electricity; transport by urban railways; automated systems; tramways; trolley bus, bus or cable; and transport by railways" (Grier 2020, 202).

In sum, Chapter 19 (CETA 2016) sets the bases for the greater liberalization of public procurement markets between Canada and the EU.

OTHER CHALLENGES FOR FIRMS TO ACCESS PUBLIC PROCUREMENT MARKETS

Although CETA facilitates access to government procurement markets in Canada for EU-based firms and vice versa for Canadian firms in the EU, it remains a challenge for SMEs to be competitive in such markets. For instance, they have to understand how Chapter 19 applies to their business. They need to figure out which entities they could sell their goods or services to. Then they have to monitor tenders that are issued by such entities (all tenders are made public in Canada and the EU). They also have to consider the value of tenders – if it is below the threshold, it may not be worth submitting a bid since the contracting entities are likely to favour local or domestic firms. Researching all government tenders available online can be difficult and time consuming if there is no single and easily searchable platform that contains these tenders for all levels of government. If public procurement tenders are scattered across different platforms and websites, then the majority of SMEs cannot afford the resources for conducting an effective and comprehensive research and monitoring. Big corporations, on the other hand, have specialists (lawyers, business developers, and other employees) to support their government market development. Hence, they have a competitive advantage over SMEs. And by winning public procurement contracts, they also solidify their competitive position as they gain experience, knowledge, and financial resources through the process.

In order to make it easier for SMEs to find out about available tenders, there should be a single platform where the tenders are found. Such a platform should also be easy to use and search based on relevant criteria (e.g., tender value). In Canada, there is currently no such single platform for public procurement tenders. The federal government has one and provinces, territories and, in some cases, municipalities have their own as well. In Canada, there is a federal platform that offers the same kind of services: it is provided by Public Procurement Canada on their website buyandsell.ca. However, sub-federal bids currently still need to be accessed locally. These multiple platforms are one of the main barriers to access the Canadian public procurement market, both for Canadians as well as foreign firms.[6] In the EU, a single electronic platform (Tenders Electronic Daily – https://ted.europa.eu) gives access to all the public procurement contracts on offer from the EU and its member states. It is accessible and easy to use for all companies, big and small.

As part of its CETA commitments, Canada undertook to create a single platform (the "single point of access" [SPA]) for all public procurement by 2022. By then, all tenders would be accessible online, which would make it easy for the firms to monitor and access them. The creation of such a platform requires negotiations and coordination between provincial, territorial, municipal, and federal governments in terms of the technology that will underpin the platform and the organization that will manage it. Once there is an intergovernmental agreement, a public bidding process has to take place to identify the provider that will design, build, and test the SPA. This is a multi-year endeavour. At the time of writing, it was unclear how much progress had been made on the SPA, since CETA's Committee on Government Procurement does not provide information on the SPA's progress (it simply says that a progress report was provided). In private, EU officials expressed concerns about Canada's ability to deliver the SPA on schedule. It would appear that their concerns were well-founded, since, by the end of the summer 2021, the platform's principles were set but had not yet been finalized, making it unlikely that the platform would be operational in 2022.

Another challenge for new entrants is the competition with established players. Local corporations are more familiar with local public services, and there is oftentimes a temptation by local officials to protect or promote local interests at the expense of new entrants. CETA prohibits discrimination based on the origin of products, services, and suppliers. There are, however, exceptions. For example, in Canada's Annex 19-7 ("General Notes") (CETA 2016), CETA's provisions do not apply to cultural industries in Quebec, aboriginal people and businesses, or the promotion of regional economic development (below a certain threshold).[7] The EU, for its part, lists fewer exceptions in the notes to its annexes. In addition to the exceptions to Chapter 19 commitments by both Canada and the EU, CETA's nondiscrimination provisions only apply above certain thresholds, which are set out in the annexes (ibid.). For instance, the thresholds for procurement contracts by central government entities in both Canada and the EU are: SDR 130,000 for goods and services and SDR 5,000,000 for construction services and works concessions. This means that central government entities on both sides of the Atlantic are entitled to ignore the provisions and commitments under Chapter 19 for contracts whose value falls below these thresholds, as long as they do not purposefully slice up contracts to keep them under the thresholds. Under the reasonable assumption that SMEs are likely to offer their goods and/or services for lower-value contracts, given their limited production capacities, these thresholds imply that outsider-SMEs stand to be at a disadvantage against local competitors, which may be preferred to stimulate the local economy's development. Only if they offer significantly lower prices are non-local suppliers likely to be competitive in contracts below the thresholds. However, in such a case, it is probable that it is larger non-local firms that may have the upper hand, in light of the economies of scale and scope that their production process makes possible.[8]

Official language requirements are an additional challenge that put SMEs at a competitive disadvantage vis-à-vis their larger brethren. Canada has only two official languages but the EU has twenty-four. If a bid has to be made in a particular language (or in more than one) that is not the bidding firm's language, then this means that the latter will face additional translation costs, which local firms do not have to incur. It also means that business managers will need time and resources – something they have in short supply – to familiarize themselves with a particular culture in order to understand the local peculiarities that may be associated with a given government's needs and expectations beyond what is on the procurement notice. Large multinational firms, for their part, are used to dealing in multilingual and multicultural environments, which gives them a competitive advantage over SMEs. For Canadian SMEs wanting to take advantage of the EU's government procurement market, the different languages found across the EU represent a potential barrier to selling their goods and services to government entities there.

A final possible challenge associated with Chapter 19 (CETA 2016) is the fact that it is excluded from the agreement's investor-state dispute settlement (ISDS) mechanism, which is found in Chapter 8 (ibid.).[9] This means that firms from the other party cannot launch a dispute directly against a government through the CETA in the case where they deem themselves discriminated against. Their only recourse in such a case is to use the domestic court system or some other judicial or administrative review process set up for this purpose, as per Art. 19.17 (ibid.).[10] It is therefore possible that firms may decide not to enter the other party's procurement market for fear of not being adequately protected in case of discrimination (at any stage of the procurement process). However, Art. 19.17 clearly stipulates that a party's domestic judicial or administrative system has to effectively protect the interests of suppliers from the other party. The only issue of concern for firms would be the time it takes for such review systems to produce judgments and corrective actions, if applicable. Art. 19.17 (ibid.) does not impose time limits on procedures, it simply states, in paragraph 7, that "Each Party shall adopt

or maintain procedures that provide for: rapid interim measures to preserve the supplier's opportunity to participate in the procurement. Such
interim measures may result in suspension of the procurement process."
Finally, it is not clear how expensive such legal/administrative challenges
will be for firms, depending on the mechanism in place.[11] If the costs are
high because of the length and technical nature of the procedures, then
SMES could decide not to undertake such challenges to save time and
money, which might ultimately lead them to avoid competing in the other
CETA party's public procurement market or potentially be more easily
discriminated against. Again, larger firms would benefit from this reduced
competition, because they have the financial and legal resources to take
on such legal/administrative challenges and defend their interests.

In any case, relying on a domestic review process has the benefit to
put Canadian and EU firms involved in government procurement markets
in Canada and the EU on an equal legal footing. As such, it avoids the
traditional discrimination associated with ISDS whereby domestic firms
have to use the domestic judicial or administrative system while foreign
firms can use an agreement's ISDS mechanism, which has been criticized
for often being partial to investors (for a review, see VanDuzer and
Dumberry 2020). Furthermore, relying on ISDS to address situations
where a government procurement process discriminates against a foreign
supplier would make it easier for provincial and municipal governments
in Canada to avoid their obligations under Chapter 19 (CETA 2016). This
is due to the fact that under an ISDS mechanism solely signed by the
Canadian federal government, either through a bilateral investment treaty
or an FTA, only the latter is legally bound by the agreement to pay damages
to the investor in case an arbitration panel rules in the investor's favour.
In such cases, the federal government has little to no effective recourse
against the provincial/municipal governments, either for recovering the
damages paid to the plaintiff investor or to obtain corrective action
(for details, see Fafard and Leblond 2012).

In the case of discriminatory behaviour on the part of a government
entity against a firm from the other CETA party in the course of a
procurement process, the state-to-state dispute-settlement mechanism
under Chapter 29 (CETA 2016) could be an alternative solution to
domestic courts. In such case, the federal government in Canada and the
European Commission in the EU would be responsible to cover the costs
of the dispute, unlike in the case of domestic courts, where firms are
responsible for legal and administrative costs. However, unless there is
egregious and sustained discriminatory behaviour by one of the parties,

it is highly unlikely that that a full-fledged dispute would be undertaken under Chapter 29 (ibid.). Moreover, the only remedy in case of dispute settlement success is the imposition of compensatory duties on the other party's goods, which would neither help the aggrieved firm nor punish the discriminating government entity.

POTENTIAL SOLUTIONS FOR MAKING CETA CHAPTER 19 MORE EFFECTIVE

Public procurement markets present the same kind of dilemma for governments that trade does in general: promote economic development through protection of (or discrimination in favour of) domestic firms or through competition and open markets. With the first approach, the rationale is that domestic firms cannot compete successfully against foreign firms. With the second approach, the rationale is that competition leads to greater innovation and efficiency, which increase productivity and economic growth. In the case of public procurement, it also means lower costs for taxpayers. In general, governments resolve this dilemma by compromising (or finding a balance) between these two approaches to economic development. Chapter 19 (CETA 2016) is a good example of this compromise with its provisions to give nondiscriminatory access to firms from the other party (EU firms in the Canadian market and Canadian firms in the EU market) but only above certain thresholds, which allow governments to discriminate in favour of local (or domestic) firms as a way promote local jobs and investment.

But competition above the thresholds can also be limited, as discussed in the previous section. When it comes to accessing government procurement markets, both at home and abroad, SMEs are at a disadvantage to larger, multinational firms because of so-called transaction costs, from monitoring tenders to launching a review process against a government in the case of suspected discrimination. If governments want to promote innovation and competition rather than protectionism and discrimination, then they must develop solutions that give SMEs easier access to public procurement markets, both at home and abroad (in the other CETA party, in the present case).

As mentioned above, the most important solution to making the public procurement market in Canada more accessible to EU firms as well as Canadian firms, especially SMEs, is the creation on a single platform where firms can easily find and monitor tenders for all levels of government and their procuring entities. It falls to the federal government to take the lead on a single platform for tenders in Canada. It is the only institution that has the necessary coordinating capacity to get all the required stakeholders involved across the country. Moreover, it is also the only actor that has the ability, if necessary, to impose a carrots-and-sticks policy on provincial governments in order to get them to cooperate on such an endeavour. Leaving it to the provincial governments to coordinate among themselves to set up such a single platform is likely to be a recipe for failure, as their limited ability to implement their commitments under the Canadian Free Trade Agreement (CFTA) demonstrates (see Hederer and Leblond 2020).

Another solution is for the principles and rules that surround government procurement markets to be more standardized, including review processes. As mentioned earlier, the EU has taken steps in this direction with a number of legislations (i.e. directives) in place. There is nothing similar in Canada, except for the four western provinces, which have adopted a common bid-protest mechanism based on arbitration. Perhaps this system could be extended to the rest of Canada in order to provide a common procurement review process that could make it cheaper for SMEs to contest tenders when they deem that discrimination is taking place or has taken place. This would require all the Canadian provinces to first agree on such a common system with each other, which the CFTA should, in principle, make easier. They could then negotiate with the federal government to extend their system to all levels of government in the country. For EU firms looking to enter the Canadian government procurement market, a common review process would give them greater certainty with regards to the available recourse mechanism if they feel discriminated against.

In addition, the Canadian federal and provincial governments could agree to create an intergovernmental committee or agency responsible for monitoring public procurement markets in order to make sure that they operate as effectively as possible, following some common principles and standards, at all levels of government in Canada. For example, it could look at the procurement rules and procedures in place, the decisions that have been made and the types of firm that have responded to tenders and those that have won contracts. Such a body would not have sanctioning powers but it could "name and shame" as well as issue recommendations for improvements to procurement procedures.[12] Such an approach would relieve the burden that is currently put on procurement suppliers (i.e., firms) to launch a review or bid-protest process if they think that procurement procedures are not being conducted in a fair and nondiscriminatory manner. Such an intergovernmental body could eventually help push for more harmonization of government procurement rules and procedures across Canada. It could also collaborate closely with CETA's Committee on Government Procurement, which currently meets about once a year. As such, it would ensure more effective coordination and action between Canada and the EU in terms of resolving problems that firms face when accessing the other party's public procurement markets.

A third solution to make government procurement more effective and accessible is to integrate public procurement in support programs for SMES, whether the latter access government procurement markets at home or abroad. For instance, Export Development Canada (EDC) has launched programs to support SMES that want to export to the EU while France and Canada have created a common investment fund to encourage exports on both sides of the Atlantic. There are also programs, such as Innovations for Defence Excellence and Security (IDEAS) in Canada or the EU's Horizon 2020, that encourage innovative SMES to develop their products and export them. These programs are only stronger and more effective when they include access to government procurement markets.

In 2017, the EU Commission launched a procurement package to encourage the transition toward a strategic public procurement. The objective was to improve European SMES' access to government procurement markets in the EU as well as stimulate innovation through procurement processes and methods. In addition, through the EU's innovation funds, such as Horizon 2020, public agencies can apply for financial support to implement some aspects of the procurement package.

Canada could follow a similar model, using Greening Government Fund, Innovative Solutions Canada, IDEAS, and Build in Canada Innovation Program. For example, IDEAS set up a platform with calls for proposals on various subjects. The intent is to have anyone (a single person, a group or an SME that has a minimum of 50 per cent local participants) applying to a bid whether they have already launched or not their project. If their proposal is selected, IDEAS will provide financial support to research and develop the product or service offered. The goal is to enable new entrants to develop innovative products or services that will serve Defence Canada.

Trade promotion agencies or organizations should not only work to help SMES enter the government procurement market directly, by submitting bids, but also to enter it indirectly, by being part of the value chain of larger firms bidding on public procurement contracts: as suppliers or subcontractors. For example, they could introduce Canadian SMES to European firms looking to enter the government procurement in Canada and vice versa for European SMES and Canadian firms entering the EU market. Once a Canadian SME has become part of a European firm's value chain (or a European SME becomes part of the Canadian value chain), then it can also become part of this larger firm's offering in third (i.e. beyond Canada and the EU) markets. Large multinational firms interested in responding to a government procurement contract in a foreign market will be looking for local suppliers or subcontractors, either to lower their costs or because a minimum level of local content is required by the tender process. Allowing foreign firms to bid on public procurement contracts thus offers local/domestic firms an opportunity to showcase their products and services to such firms, in the hope not only to be part of procurement contracts with these firms at home but also abroad afterwards.

Finally, to support the above solutions, government authorities must also educate the public on the benefits of greater competition in government procurement markets, as made possible by trade agreements such as CETA. It is not enough to advertise CETA with the business community and encourage larger or smaller businesses to participate in public tenders. The general public has to be told how making it easier for Canadian (European) firms to compete on an equal basis with local/domestic firms in European (Canadian) government procurement markets can be good for the local economy. For instance, greater competition can lead to lower costs, which ultimately mean a lower tax burden on the population. It can also lead to better products or services on offer, which increase the value for money that governments receive from their tenders, again benefiting taxpayers. As mentioned earlier, allowing foreign firms to compete for local government procurement contracts provides opportunities for local enterprises to enter these foreign firms' value chains, not only at home but also abroad. Lastly, allowing foreign firms to compete on an equal footing with local/domestic firms for public procurement tenders as a result of agreements such as CETA means that local/domestic firms can also compete in the other party's markets in a fair and equitable way, reciprocity being the basis for international trade agreements. If these benefits are clearly explained to the population, then the latter's reluctance to having foreign firms bid on local/domestic government procurement contracts should decrease. This then makes it easier for governments to resolve the public procurement dilemma described at the beginning of this section and improve the effectiveness of CETA Chapter 19.

CONCLUSION

With CETA, through Chapter 19, Canada and the EU agreed to create a level-playing field for their firms, given certain thresholds and exceptions, when it comes to accessing their respective government procurement markets. However, a number of barriers remain to taking full advantage of Chapter 19. Most of these barriers relate to the higher transaction costs that SMEs face relative to larger, multinational firms as pertains monitoring the issuance of tenders and putting together competitive bids. Governments at various levels on both sides of the Atlantic need to adopt measures to overcome these barriers in order for Chapter 19 to effectively achieve its desired outcome of fully opening up these governments' public procurement markets to Canadian and European firms.

NOTES

1 First generation trade agreements are limited to addressing at-the-border obstacles such as tariffs and quotas (e.g., various negotiation rounds under the General Agreement on Tariffs and Trade [GATT]). In addition to dealing with tariffs and quotas, second-generation agreements also seek to remove or reduce some beyond-the-border obstacles to trade such as differing regulations and standards (e.g., North American Free Trade Agreement [NAFTA]). Third-generation trade agreements build on second-generation ones by expanding the range of regulatory issues addressed and making regulatory cooperation a core element of the agreement.

2 The agreement is in force on a provisional basis until the EU member states' national (and, in some cases, regional) parliaments have all ratified it.

3 This situation changed with the revised GPA, which entered into force on 6 April 2014. In this revised agreement, the provinces accepted to be part of Canada's schedule.

4 The annexes use the positive-list approach (i.e., only what is specified is covered, as opposed to a negative-list approach where everything is covered unless it is specifically excluded).

5 These thresholds are derived from the WTO's GPA. SDR means special drawing rights, which are a synthetic unit of measure, derived from a basket of currencies, used by the International Monetary Fund (IMF) for its financing and operations.

6 To get a sense of the challenge faced by business in monitoring and accessing government procurement notices in Canada, see Canada's Annex 19-8,

Section B. In the EU's Annex 19-8, Section B, notices are published in one place for all member states: the Official Journal of the European Union.

7 The notes to Canada's Annexes 19-3, 19-4, 19-5, and 19-6 also include exclusions.

8 In their study of CETA's likely impact on municipal procurement markets in Canada, Lyzenko et al. (2020, 274) "do not find that [CETA] will significantly change local practices or policies." This is because the procurement markets in the four major cities that they studied were "already largely open" (ibid.). The authors found only weak evidence that foreign firms had a lower probability of winning a contract than Canadian firms, mostly because bids with the lowest price won the large majority of tenders (above 85 per cent in Ottawa and Edmonton; 100 per cent in Hamilton and Vancouver).

9 CETA's ISDS provisions are suspended while the agreement is provisionally in force (i.e. until CETA is ratified by all EU member-state parliaments).

10 Art. 19.17, paragraph 1 states: "Each Party shall provide a timely, effective, transparent and nondiscriminatory administrative or judicial review procedure through which a supplier may challenge: 1. a breach of the Chapter; or 2. if the supplier does not have a right to challenge directly a breach of the Chapter under the domestic law of a Party, a failure to comply with a Party's measures implementing this Chapter, arising in the context of a covered procurement, in which the supplier has, or has had, an interest. The procedural rules for all challenges shall be in writing and made generally available." For its part, paragraph 4 states: "Each Party shall establish or designate at least one impartial administrative or judicial authority that is independent of its procuring entities to receive and review a challenge by a supplier arising in the context of a covered procurement."

11 In the EU, national courts or specific administrative review bodies are responsible for examining requests for reviewing public procurement procedure; however, they follow the same standards and principles, which are set by a number of EU directives (European Union 2020). There is no such harmonization in Canada. The federal and provincial governments each set their own principles, rules and mechanisms. For instance, the federal government relies on federal courts to deal with review requests while the four western provinces (British Columbia, Alberta, Saskatchewan, and Manitoba) have set up a specific arbitration-based bid-protest mechanism (New West Partnership 2019).

12 In the EU, the European Commission has, in principle, such monitoring powers in light of existing directives, although they tend to be limited to ensuring that member states have transposed the directives into their

national laws and regulations. Nevertheless, given its overall role as guar-
antor of the single market, it is ultimately responsible for making sure that
national and local government procurement markets are equally and fairly
accessible to firms from other EU member states.

REFERENCES

Casier, Liesbeth. 2019. "Canada's International Trade Obligations: Barrier or
Opportunity for Sustainable Public Procurement? Unpacking Canada's WTO
GPA and CETA Commitments in Relation to Sustainable Procurement."
IISD Report, International Institute for Sustainable Development. Accessed
23 February 2022. https://www.iisd.org/sites/default/files/publications/
canada-international-trade-spp.pdf.
CETA (Canada-European Union Comprehensive Economic and Trade
Agreement). 2016. Accessed 21 July 2020. https://www.international.gc.ca/
trade-commerce/trade-agreements-accords-commerciaux/agr-acc/ceta-aecg/
text-texte/toc-tdm.aspx?lang=eng.
de Mestral, Armand, and Evan Fox-Decent. 2008. "Rethinking the
Relationship between International and Domestic Law." *McGill Law
Journal* 53, no. 4: 573–648. Accessed 22 February 2022. https://lawjournal.
mcgill.ca/article/rethinking-the-relationship-between-international-and-
domestic-law/.
D'Erman, Valerie J. 2020. "The EU's Realist Power: Public Procurement
and CETA Negotiations with Canada." *Journal of International Relations and
Development* 23, no. 1: 1–23. https://doi.org/10.1057/s41268-018-0135-3.
European Union. 2020. "Public Tendering Rules." Accessed 5 August 2020.
https://europa.eu/youreurope/business/selling-in-eu/public-contracts/public-
tendering-rules/index_en.htm.
Fafard, Patrick, and Patrick Leblond. 2012. "Twenty-First Century Trade
Agreements: Challenges for Canadian Federalism." The Federal Idea,
Montreal. Accessed 23 February 2022. https://thetyee.ca/News/2014/08/13/
CETA-challenges.pdf.
Grier, Jean Heilman. 2020. "Growing Significance of Regional Trade
Agreements in Opening Public Procurement." In *The Challenges of Public
Procurement Reforms*, edited by Annalisa Castelli, Gustavo Piga, Stéphane
Saussier, and Tünde Tátrai, 184–218. New York: Routledge.
Hederer, Christian, and Patrick Leblond. 2020. "Implementation of Twenty-
First-Century Trade Agreements in Canada: CETA and Intergovernmental
Cooperation." In *The Multilevel Politics of Trade*, edited by Jörg Broschek,
and Patricia Goff, 56–80. Toronto: University of Toronto Press.

Kukucha, Christopher J. 2008. *The Provinces and Canadian Foreign Trade Policy*. Vancouver: UBC Press.

Leblond, Patrick. 2016. "Making the Most of CETA: A Complete and Effective Implementation is Key to Realizing the Agreement's Full Potential." CIGI Papers No. 114. Waterloo, ON: Centre for International Governance Innovation. Accessed 23 February 2022. https://www.cigionline.org/publications/making-most-ceta-complete-and-effective-implementation-key-realizing-agreements-full-0/.

– 2010. "The Canada-EU Comprehensive Economic and Trade Agreement: More to it than meets the Eye." *Policy Options*, 1 July 2010. Accessed 23 February 2022. https://policyoptions.irpp.org/magazines/immigration-jobs-and-canadas-future/the-canada-eu-comprehensive-economic-trade-agreement-more-to-it-than-meets-the-eye/.

Lusenko, Dmitry, Elizabeth Schwartz, and Saul Schwartz. 2020. "Short-Term Effects of the Comprehensive Economic and Trade Agreement on Municipal Procurement in Canada." *Canadian Public Policy* 46, no. 2: 264–78. https://doi.org/10.3138/cpp.2019-042.

New West Partnership. 2019. "Part I: Bid Protest Mechanism." Accessed 5 August 2020. http://www.newwestpartnership.ca/Bid-Protest-Mechanism pdf.

Paquin, Stéphane. 2020. "Federalism and Trade Negotiations in Canada: CUSFTA, CETA and TPP Compared." In *The Multilevel Politics of Trade*, edited by Jörg Broschek, and Patricia Goff, 35–55. Toronto: University of Toronto Press.

VanDuzer, J. Anthony, and Patrick Dumberry. 2020. "Investor–State Dispute Settlement." In *Promoting and Managing International Investment: Towards an Integrated Policy Approach*, edited by J. Anthony VanDuzer and Patrick Leblond, 223–46. New York: Routledge.

Woolcock, Stephen B. 2011. "European Union Trade Policy: The Canada-EU Comprehensive Economic and Trade Agreement (CETA) Towards A New Generation of FTAS?" In *Europe, Canada and the Comprehensive Economic and Trade Agreement*, edited by Kurt Hübner, 21–40. New York: Routledge.

8

Is CETA a Major Threat to Municipal Autonomy?

Elizabeth Schwartz and Saul Schwartz

INTRODUCTION

Early on in the negotiations for the Comprehensive Economic and Trade Agreement (CETA) between Canada and the European Union (EU), Canadian municipalities were clearly concerned their inclusion in the agreement would jeopardize their ability to use procurement to promote local employment, to favour local businesses, and to otherwise privilege local interests. In the early 2010s, a number of municipalities passed resolutions asking the federal government to exempt cities from CETA. Two influential think tanks – the Council of Canadians (Council of Canadians 2014) and the Canadian Centre for Policy Alternatives (Trew and Sinclair 2014) – emphasized threats to municipal autonomy as part of their critiques of the proposed agreement.

Those concerns now seem to have vanished. In this chapter, we discuss the two major threats to municipal autonomy that were raised early on and suggest that, as implemented, CETA (2016) is unlikely to affect what little autonomy Canadian municipalities have. One threat is the commitment by Canada to have municipal governments treat EU suppliers in the same way as they treat domestic suppliers, reducing the scope for favouring local firms. A second threat arises from the prohibition of "offsets."[1] In this context, offsets would include municipal policies that require the hiring of local workers or the use of local firms as part of the fulfilment of a contract.[2]

Overall, we conclude that neither of these two features of CETA seriously limits municipal autonomy. Our previous empirical work (Lysenko, Schwartz, and Schwartz 2020) suggests that municipalities do not heavily discriminate against foreign-controlled suppliers. The prohibition of offsets might limit the ability of municipalities to include domestic content requirements as part of contracts. But given the broad support of such provisions within the EU and the limited scope of enforcement outlined in the procurement chapter of CETA, we doubt that such requirements, whether as part of social procurement policies or as part of community benefit agreements (CBAs), will be challenged, at least not in the short term.

AN OVERVIEW OF CETA
AND LOCAL GOVERNMENT PROCUREMENT

Although Canada has been party to other international trade agreements that include chapters on government procurement, CETA is the first that applies to procurement by municipalities and other institutions in the "municipal, academic, schools, and hospitals" (MASH) sector.[3]

Commitments related to public procurement are set out in Chapter 19 of the agreement.[4] In that chapter, Canada agreed: (1) to treat suppliers from the EU in the same way as they do suppliers from Canada, even if the firm does not have a Canadian presence; (2) to increase the transparency with which procurement notices are made available, primarily by creating a single point of access (SPA), a website on which all public procurement notices would appear;[5] and (3) to increase accountability by setting up or designating at least one independent appeals body that would hear appeals from suppliers who feel that they have been treated unfairly or that procuring entities have violated provisions of the treaty.

Beyond these commitments, Art. 19.4(6) of CETA (2016) prohibits offsets – a condition, often related to domestic economic development, imposed on all potential suppliers as part of the bidding process.[6] A clear example involving offsets is the Government of Canada's Industrial and Technological Benefits (ITB) policy, under which "companies awarded defence procurement contracts are required to undertake business activities in Canada, equal to the value of the contract" (Innovation, Science and Economic Development Canada 2019).[7] The "business activities" can take a variety of forms, including the purchase of local content or the employment of local workers. In the context of municipal procurement, "local" would mean workers living in the city or in nearby areas. To be an offset, the commitment of the bidder to meet the condition must be explicitly stated in both the bid and any resulting contract. Art. 19.4(6) (CETA 2016) reads: "With regard to covered procurement, a Party, including its procuring entities, shall not seek, take account of, impose or enforce any offset."

While CETA extends coverage to the MASH sector, and thus potentially represents a major expansion of access for the EU, not all procurement is covered. In the procurement chapter, only entities listed in the annexes to Chapter 19 are subject to its procurement provisions (ibid.). Specifically, in the annexes to Chapter 19, Canada lists the public organizations whose procurement is covered by the agreement. Organizations as well as specific goods and services that are not listed in the Chapter 19 annexes are not covered (ibid.). For example: (1) Canadian subnational governments are covered in the agreement because they are listed in Annex 19-2; and (2) social service and health services provided by municipal governments and hospitals are not listed in Annex 19-5 and are therefore not subject to CETA's government procurement provisions.[8]

Additionally, regardless of their nature, contracts with values below specified thresholds are not covered. There are different monetary thresholds for the federal government and for provincial and MASH sector contracts, with the latter having higher thresholds below which their contracts are exempt from CETA provisions (including both nondiscrimination and the prohibition of offsets). The threshold values are shown in table 8.1. The rationale for having higher thresholds for lower levels of government is to reduce the administrative burden on the smaller units of government. The thresholds for construction, however, are the same for all entities. While many municipal procurement contracts are valued well below these thresholds, a large proportion of the dollar value of procurement is in contracts above the thresholds.

WHAT IS LOCAL AUTONOMY?

In our opinion, a number of CETA provisions, aside from those in Chapter 19, may threaten municipal autonomy. In this chapter, however, we consider only the threats that might arise from the inclusion of municipal procurement in a major trade agreement.[9] Before discussing the relevant threats, we outline what we mean by "municipal autonomy." Smith and Spicer (2018, 20) adopt a fairly simple and straightforward definition of municipal autonomy: "the ability to develop and implement policies at the local level, free from provincial institutional constraints." They go on to measure autonomy along three dimensions: legal, fiscal, and political.

From a legal perspective, Canadian municipalities are often considered to be "creatures of the province" because Section 92 of the Canadian constitution gives the provinces exclusive jurisdiction over the "Municipal

Table 8.1
Government procurement threshold values in CETA

Sector	Special drawing rights (SDR)[1]	Value in Canadian dollars[2]
Federal government		
Goods	130,000	238,000
Services	130,000	238,000
Construction	5,000,000	9,100,000
Provincial government, municipalities, and MASH		
Goods	200,000	366,200
Services	200,000	366,200
Construction	5,000,000	9,100,000
Federal or provincial crown corporations and government-owned enterprises		
Goods	355,000	650,000
Services	355,000	650,000
Construction	5,000,000	9,100,000

Notes:

1 In CETA as well as in other international trade agreements, threshold values are specified in terms of SDRS. SDRS represent the value of a basket of major currencies expressed in US dollars. Further information about SDRS is available at https://www.imf.org/en/About/Factsheets/Sheets/2016/08/01/14/51/Special-Drawing-Right-SDR.

2 The CAD values shown were in force until 21 December 2021.

Sources: SDRS: https://www.tradecommissioner.gc.ca/guides/eu_procurement-guide-marches_publics_ue.aspx?lang=eng#a2_3. Value in CAD: https://trade.ec.europa.eu/doclib/docs/2020/february/tradoc_158655.pdf.

Institutions in the Province" (Constitution Act 1867).[10] As a result, "the incorporation of municipalities and the design of municipal systems are left to the provinces to establish through legislation" (Good 2019, 3). Courts seem to have generally supported this view. When, in the late 1990s, several cities in what was then Metro Toronto fought the efforts of the provincial government to force their amalgamation, the Ontario Superior Court of Justice ruled in the province's favour, clearly stating that provinces have legal control over most aspects of municipal action (Milroy 2002). Another high-profile dispute about the authority of provinces to impose their will on municipalities was the Government of Ontario's unilateral decision in 2018 to reduce the size of Toronto's city council from forty-seven to twenty-five members under its Better Local Government Act. When the City of Toronto argued in court that the decision interfered with candidates' right to freedom of expression under the Charter of Rights and Freedoms, the Ontario Superior Court of Justice rejected the City's argument in a 3–2 decision.[11]

Good (2019, 2) argues, however, that the idea that municipalities are merely creatures of the province "is neither historically accurate, since some communities had a long history of municipal incorporation before Confederation (and the establishment of provinces), nor an objective assessment of their democratic importance." She goes on to argue that municipalities have a legitimate role to play as an expression of the democratic will of local residents and to suggest various ways in which that role could be constitutionally strengthened. Additionally, all Canadian provinces have created municipal acts, which outline the responsibilities and authority of municipalities within the province. Some cities have been granted specific city charters that grant them greater legal authority than other municipalities in the province. Examples include the Winnipeg Charter, the City of Toronto Act, and the Vancouver Charter. Smith and Spicer (2018), however, find that these charters do not lead to significantly higher levels of overall autonomy, perhaps because they have not been accompanied by greater fiscal autonomy.

Fiscal autonomy relates to the money available to cities, independent of the provincial government. Cities generally collect and spend local property taxes but do not have city-specific sales taxes, income taxes, or fuel taxes. The majority of their funds come from provincial sources. While cities have long called for greater fiscal independence, "any new taxes at the local level would require provincial approval and the provinces would likely want a good reason for granting this authority" (Kitchen and Slack 2016, 2). Moreover, Canadian municipal governments have limited borrowing capacity relative to other levels of government. For instance, they can borrow money only to pay for capital expenses, not operational expenses. Additionally, municipal governments are not permitted to run budget deficits, which limits their ability to hire staff and engage in ambitious new policies.

For Smith and Spicer (2018, 5), the political dimension of municipal autonomy refers to "the extent to which local governments can access and influence the decision-making process at the national level." They measure political autonomy using indicators such as provincial restrictions on financial contributions to mayoral campaigns, strength of associations representing municipal interests at the provincial level, and the extent to which officials have held office in both municipal and provincial governments.

The definition of municipal autonomy explored by Schwartz (2019) is a different interpretation of this political dimension. She argues that municipalities are autonomous to the extent that they set their own policy goals and achieve them within the context of the legal framework provided by provincial governments. In other words, while municipalities are constrained by provincial legislation, there remains substantial leeway for local policy action. Local governments and politicians can find ways around restrictions, petition provincial governments for exceptions or legislative changes, and otherwise achieve their own goals within the constraints of provincial law. Municipalities are autonomous to the extent that they exercise the authority granted to them in order to achieve political and policy goals not explicitly mandated by the provincial government.

Smith and Spicer (2018, 17) find that, using their definitions and measures, "no city in Canada ... has achieved a significant amount of autonomy from its provincial government." Nonetheless, they note variation among the municipalities. On a scale of 1 to 6, where lower numbers indicate less autonomy, they assess the City of Saskatoon's autonomy measures as 1; Toronto, Halifax, Montreal, and Winnipeg as 2; and Vancouver as 3. According to Smith and Spicer, Vancouver is therefore the most autonomous of Canadian cities.

In this chapter, we are not focused on measuring current levels of autonomy in Canadian cities, or the precise impact of CETA Chapter 19 on the autonomy of particular municipalities. Rather, we begin from the premise that municipal autonomy in Canada is relatively weak.

Next, we explore whether and how CETA Chapter 19 might further reduce that autonomy as posited by the Council of Canadians and the Canadian Centre for Policy Alternatives in 2014.

TWO THREATS TO MUNICIPAL AUTONOMY

CETA's procurement rules potentially threaten two areas in which Canadian municipalities currently have a measure of autonomy: one, their ability to favour local businesses, an ability that would conflict with the CETA commitment to nondiscrimination. Two, their ability to implement social policies aimed at improving the economic fortunes of disadvantaged groups, including low-income families, recent immigrants, and young people out of school and out of work.

Eliminating Home Bias

"Home bias" in government procurement means that governments favour local firms when deciding who wins government contracts, perhaps awarding the contract to a local firm even when there is a better offer from a foreign firm.[12] This sort of bias is thought to be pervasive (Brülhart and Trionfetti 2005; Rickard and Kono 2014). Nonetheless, demonstrating the existence of home bias is not easy. It is true that the vast majority of Canadian municipal contracts are awarded to companies based in or near the municipality in question. Does this mean that municipal procurement entities are biased in favour of local companies or simply that local firms are able to offer the required goods and services on better terms?[13]

In a previous work (Lysenko, Schwartz, and Schwartz 2020), we collected and analyzed data on bids submitted for municipal contracts. In that analysis, we focused on four large municipalities in three provinces – Edmonton, Alberta; Hamilton and Ottawa, Ontario; and Vancouver, British Columbia.[14] Across the four municipalities, we collected data on approximately 17,000 bids on 6,000 contracts. To get a sense of the extent of foreign participation, we examined the "country of control" of each bidder as documented in Statistics Canada's Inter-corporate Ownership (ICO) tables.[15] We then used those data to explore the relationship between the probability of winning a contract and the nationality of bidders.

Our analysis revealed only weak indications that foreign-controlled firms had a lower probability of winning a contract. For tenders – proposals to supply standardized products – our results suggested little scope for discrimination. In Vancouver and Hamilton, the lowest price won almost every time; in Ottawa and Edmonton, the lowest price won 83 per cent of the time. For requests for proposal (RFPS) – proposals for goods or services that can be provided in many different ways – there is weak evidence of a difference in the probability of winning a contract based on country of control: the coefficient capturing this difference was statistically significant in the regressions for one of the three cities for which we had data on requests for proposals (Ottawa) in that analysis.[16] Given these econometric results, our judgment was that the quantitative evidence is not strong enough to assert that there is any significant home bias. If there is no home bias, Chapter 19 provisions (CETA 2016) designed to eliminate it will have no effect.[17]

We also interviewed managers of procurement in six large Canadian municipalities, asking them what effect CETA might have on their operations.[18] Overall, their view was that municipalities were already largely compliant with the rules that CETA has set out. Most importantly, the managers did not seem to believe that there is any widespread discrimination against EU firms in their current procurement policies or procedures. These interviews, as well as our review of CETA and Canadian interprovincial trade agreements, indicate that one reason for this compliance is that previous interprovincial trade agreements have required that municipalities treat bids from firms located in other provinces in nondiscriminatory and transparent ways. CETA simply extends that commitment to EU firms without requiring any material change in current procurement practices.

CETA's Threat to Municipal Efforts to Help Disadvantaged Groups

The second reason why Chapter 19 of CETA may threaten municipal autonomy is because it prohibits offsets. Recall that offsets are conditions in a contract that require that the firm winning a government contract meet certain conditions such as ensuring that a certain proportion of workers on a project are drawn from disadvantaged groups in the local area. Offsets are not necessarily discriminatory; when allowed, they are demanded of all bidders on a public contract. Each bid on a contract must describe how it will meet the offset and the proposal of the winning bidder becomes part of the contractual agreement.[19] If there are no requirements in the bid documents, however, and the winning bidder instead agrees to provide benefits to local workers or communities after a contract is signed, such benefits would not be defined as offsets.

The prohibition of offsets could limit the ability of municipalities to use procurement as they have used it historically – as a way to encourage both local economic development and the employment of local workers. Public purchasing and expenditure have long been used as social policy tools (McCrudden 2004). Beginning in the nineteenth century, governments in Britain, France, and the United States used public contracts – particularly for infrastructure construction – to reduce unemployment and ensure fair wages and working conditions. In the first half of the twentieth century, government contracts were the first to include mandatory minimum wages and were used to promote the employment of some marginalized groups, including veterans and people with disabilities. This use of public procurement to promote equity and other social policy goals is often called "social procurement."

Clearly, there is a direct conflict between (a) requirements in government procurement contracts to employ local workers or to buy from local businesses and (b) the prohibition of exactly those requirements in trade treaties such as CETA. How, then, can municipal governments (as well as hospitals and universities and school districts) establish social procurement policies that are aligned with municipal goals but do not violate these trade agreements?

A number of avenues are open:

1 Attach social procurement conditions only to contracts whose value is below the CETA thresholds.
2 Make the conditions aspirational rather than mandatory. To be an offset, a condition must be a requirement to be met by the winning bidder; simply promising to consider hiring local workers or trying to buy from local businesses is not an offset.
3 Apply social procurement conditions only in areas exempted from coverage of the treaties. CETA has a number of exemptions from its prohibition of offsets. Among them are support for Aboriginal groups and a limited set of economic development projects. In addition, CETA does not cover social or health services so that social procurement can be used for contracts in those areas.
4 Apply social procurement conditions regardless of CETA and hope that no firm will complain about it. The provisions for enforcing the procurement rules in CETA's Chapter 19 are not particularly strong. Furthermore, very few cases involving the violation of the offset rules in the closely related Agreement on Government Procurement have been brought forward and, given the prevalence of social procurement policies in the European Union, it seems unlikely that many complaints will be brought against Canadian cities (Semple 2017, 304). And, even if complaints are brought forward and even if compensation is awarded, it will be the federal or provincial governments that pay, not the municipalities involved.

In our review of social procurement policies and in our qualitative interviews, we saw each of these methods being used. When we asked procurement staff in Toronto about tensions between Toronto's Social Procurement Policy and CETA, their response was that "[w]e don't see these efforts as being in conflict." The Toronto Social Procurement Policy certainly encourages workforce development (i.e., local employment and training) and supplier diversity (i.e., awarding contracts to local minority-owned businesses). None of its provisions, however, actually *require* increased local employment or increased use of minority-owned businesses.

Instead the requirements are that bidders must have a workforce development plan and that departments seek minority-owned bidders. By not having "hard targets" in the bidding documents, the city avoids conflict with the prohibition of offsets.

That same careful dance around offsets can be seen in CBAS, particularly in the context of the procurement of large infrastructure projects. CBAS, "formal contractual agreements between developers and community groups representing those who will be affected by a given project" (van Ymeren and Ditta 2017, 5), aim to provide jobs and training for particular groups in the geographic area surrounding a project.

Advocates for CBAS see the agreements as a tool that municipal governments and other agencies can use to achieve social policy goals, both within and outside government procurement processes. For example, outside any procurement process, the City of Toronto concluded a CBA with the operators of the Woodbine Casino as part of the process for approving the expansion of the casino's operations (City of Toronto 2019). In addition to promoting their use, advocates of CBAS push for wording that ensures accountability. Like all legal agreements, the precise language used determines the degree to which the provisions are enforceable. In most of the CBAS concluded in Canada as part of government procurement processes, parties agree to language that commits developers to create plans, identify employment targets, and meet other "soft" goals. None of these legally bind the parties to specific outcomes. Proponents of CBAS have thus far been unsuccessful in pushing governments to include "hard" targets and requirements that are legally enforceable (Nugent 2017).

While all governments and government agencies can engage in CBAS, some Canadian local governments have created explicit policies to promote their use. Two prominent examples are the City of Vancouver's Community Benefit Agreement Policy (2018) and the City of Toronto's Community Benefits Framework (2019). Both policies bring consistency and coordination to processes that had largely been carried out in an ad hoc manner. Although the City of Vancouver policy requires the negotiation of CBAS that impose a set of minimum standards, it applies only to real estate development projects, not to government procurement. Moreover, it includes an explicit exemption for developers that are public sector entities and subject to internal or international treaties prohibiting "local preference procurements" (City of Vancouver 2018, 2.6). In contrast, the City of Toronto's policy applies *only* to government procurement, but is set up as a supportive, coordinating mechanism (City of Toronto 2019). Entities within the municipal government will continue to negotiate and implement CBAS as they see fit – the policy neither requires agreements nor sets minimum standards. Instead, it proposes a set of principles (e.g., social and economic inclusion, community engagement and involvement, and accountability) and provides material supports to promote the negotiation of CBAS. The material supports include a new community benefits coordinator, a data tracking system, a multi-stakeholder advisory group, and programs to promote the capacity of equity-seeking groups to participate in the workforce by "enhanc[ing] and optimiz[ing] community benefits hiring pathways" (ibid., 14).

These policies, therefore, are unlikely to conflict with CETA's prohibition of offsets. They do not impose strict requirements for workforce inclusion or community benefits within the public procurement process and are therefore unlikely to be challenged under CETA. Should advocates be successful in convincing governments to require more legally enforceable provisions, however, CBAS may yet run up against CETA.

To provide concrete examples of how CBAS can be compatible with CETA, we now briefly describe two examples of large infrastructure projects in Ontario: the procurement of a light rail transit (LRT) project in Toronto, which was negotiated prior to CETA coming into effect, and a 2018 agreement to build a bridge linking Windsor, Ontario and Detroit, Michigan.

EGLINTON CROSSTOWN LRT

Metrolinx, the Ontario provincial body that manages several large provincial transit projects, agreed to include a CBA in the request for proposals associated with the Eglinton Crosstown, a 19 km LRT line running down a major Toronto thoroughfare.[20] Negotiations between Metrolinx and the Toronto Community Benefits Network (TCBN) had resulted in a 2014 agreement on the CBA (Metrolinx 2014a).[21] In summarizing that agreement, Metrolinx (2014b) wrote: "[a]s part of their bid proposals, qualified consortia must include *plans* for increasing apprenticeship training on the Crosstown, providing significant opportunities for local companies, and ensuring design excellence and community benefits" (emphasis added).

The contract was awarded in July 2015 to the international consortium known as Crosslinx Transit Solutions (CTS). Section 20.14(a) of the Eglinton Crosstown project agreement (Infrastructure Ontario 2020) lists six items that the Apprenticeship Plan and Program developed by CTS must include. Five are couched in terms of "objectives" and "opportunities." The sixth requires "a focused apprenticeship program for youth-at-risk, historically disadvantaged groups in local communities including low-income, racialized and immigrant populations, and military veterans" (ibid., 68).

In the CBA between Metrolinx and CTS, the authors wrote that "[t]he Crosstown is also unique because it is Ontario's first large-scale public infrastructure project to contractually require the developer, CTS, to ensure that local communities and historically disadvantaged and equity-seeking groups directly benefit from the province's investment" (Crosslinx Transit Solution 2016, 1). The actual project agreement, however, is couched in terms of plans rather than hard targets. For example, the agreement includes a "declaration re. apprentices" that declares that CTS "aspire[s] to achiev[e]" a target of 10 per cent for the proportion of workers from historically disadvantaged communities and equity-seeking groups (Metrolinx 2016). Note that this secondary agreement contains no hard commitment to hire local people.

The Eglinton Crosstown CBA demonstrates that there can be room within the procurement process to incorporate social policy goals. However, it also demonstrates that the language used in the RFPs and in the agreements matters. Nugent (2017) presents a detailed case study of the evolution of the CBA in the Eglinton Crosstown LRT project. While he lauds the success of TCBN in successfully negotiating with Metrolinx and, through those negotiations, securing the 2014 agreement for a CBA to be included in the project RFP, he emphasizes that the eventual CBA lacks legally enforceable specifications for exactly how many people from historically disadvantaged communities and equity-seeking groups must be hired (ibid.).

While the contract between CTS and Metrolinx predates CETA, the language in the contract does not impose mandatory requirements to hire local apprentices or any other conditions that might have been deemed to be offsets, even if the contract had been covered by CETA.

GORDIE HOWE BRIDGE

The CAD 5.7 billion Gordie Howe Bridge, expected to be completed by 2024 (Windsor-Detroit Bridge Authority 2021), is another example of governments using CBAS in the context of the procurement of large infrastructure projects. The bridge will create a new road link between Detroit, Michigan and Windsor, Ontario; the project has been undertaken under the direction of the Windsor-Detroit Bridge Authority (WDBA), a Canadian crown corporation.[22] A request for qualifications (RFQ) was issued in July 2015. Three consortia were selected to respond to the November 2016 RFP. The winning bidder was international consortium known as Bridging North America, which includes several firms headquartered in the EU. The WDBA and Bridging North America signed the project agreement in September 2018, after CETA had come into effect.[23]

In the "Community Benefits" section (Schedule 36) of the project agreement (Windsor-Detroit Bridge Authority 2018), the requirements of a workforce development plan are set out. This section lays out a series of commitments to establish plans for workforce development, to consult with communities and to keep track of how local workers and firms are involved in the project. There are no mandates as to the exact numbers of local workers to be hired or the amount to be spent on goods and services obtained from local business. Specifically, Schedule 36 established a "Local Canadian Workforce Goal" which it defined as "the goal that at least $[REDACTED] of the total value of the DB [Design Build] Work in Canada will be performed by, contracted to, or supplied by the Local Canadian Workforce" (ibid.). This is a goal, not an explicit requirement.

These "soft" commitments requiring planning, consultations, and monitoring are consistent with the language of the RFQ, in which the WDBA wrote that the winning bidder "must not discriminate based on nationality in its hiring decisions or anything else" (Windsor-Detroit Bridge Authority 2015, 22) suggesting that the hiring of local workers would not be required (even if it were strongly encouraged) in the eventual contract.[24]

In both the Crosstown LRT and the Gordie Howe Bridge projects, the winning consortium was required only to propose a community benefits plan involving workforce development, along with other community benefits, and to commit themselves to working with the communities to implement the plan.

This is not to say that the winning consortia have failed to deliver some of the desired community benefits; however, to be considered an offset, the relevant conditions must be a required part of the contract. In consultation with community groups – notably TCBN and the construction unions – CTS has hired apprentices from the local community and successfully developed a number of community projects. As for the Gordie Howe Bridge project, in a March 2020 "fact sheet," the WDBA outlined a CAD 20 million fund to implement a series of projects to improve the communities on both sides of the bridge between 2019 and 2025 (Windsor-Detroit Bridge Authority 2020).

Overall, the routine inclusion of CBAs in municipal procurement projects would be a positive development for community development.

And, as currently formulated, they are not threatened by Chapter 19 of CETA. In the future, municipalities can continue to promote CBAs through their procurement processes by adopting the same careful language from the Crosstown LRT and Gordie Howe Bridge projects and thereby avoid the violation of CETA prohibitions.

What would happen if a CBA were challenged as a violation of CETA's prohibition of offsets?

One of the features of Chapter 19 (CETA 2016) and of the closely related Agreement on Government Procurement (GPA) is that the mechanisms for enforcing the agreements are weak. In general, if no one complains about the violation, nothing will be done about it. Because hiring local workers or using local firms is likely to happen in any major project, complaints may be unlikely to arise, especially after the winning bidders have given "soft" commitments in pre- or post-contract agreements.

If a firm wants to complain about either the process or the result of a procurement, it has two options to pursue: the first is the WTO dispute settlement process, initiated by the firm's national government. That process is particularly troublesome in the context of public procurement. As Lester and Bacchus (2019, 1) point out, the process is now so slow that "governments can have a three-year or longer 'free pass' to implement illegal protectionist measures while litigation drags on." In a procurement, there is an obvious need for urgency because the signing of a contract and delivery on its provisions usually occurs fairly rapidly.

The second option is to use the independent appeals body that both Art. 19.17 of CETA (2016) and Art. VIII of GPA establish. The text of these two sections is almost identical. Such an appeals body would "provide a timely, effective, transparent and non-discriminatory administrative or judicial review procedure" (CETA 2016, Art. 19.17) that could rule on the complaint and provide a remedy if the complaint is justified. The affected firm would be encouraged to negotiate directly with the procuring entity. Failing that, CETA envisions ways to stop the procurement from proceeding until the complaint can be heard. While most Canadian cities have a procedure that firms can use when they have a complaint, these are rarely used and there is no national body in place. To our knowledge, there has been no movement toward establishing "at least one impartial administrative or judicial authority" to review complaints (CETA 2016, 19.17(4)). This second option appears to have been little used under the GPA. Semple reviewed the case law databases in the United Kingdom,

Ireland, Canada, and the United States, and found few cases involving the GPA. She reports being "of the view that the domestic remedies provided for under the GPA have to date been little invoked" (Semple 2017, 304).

In sum, there seems to be little reason to fear that CETA's prohibition of offsets will affect how municipalities currently use procurement to encourage local employment or to direct project business to local firms. Being careful about how the relevant conditions are phrased in the contract – as goals rather than hard targets – might keep them from being characterized as offsets. And even if hard targets are included in the contracts, thus creating offsets, the weak Chapter 19 enforcement provisions, combined with the lack of any strong opposition to such efforts either in Canada or in the EU, suggest that they will not be challenged.

CONCLUSION

For the EU, one of the major outcomes of CETA was the provision that, in evaluating bids on contracts, Canadian cities, hospitals, and academic institutions must treat EU firms in the same way as they treat domestic bidders. Moreover, contract provisions that require the winning bidder to hire local workers or to buy products from local firms are prohibited. Together, these two features of CETA provide "unconditional access" to EU firms.[25]

Canadian cities have shown themselves to be adept at achieving their policy goals, as is evident in the social procurement and CBA policies adopted by the City of Toronto and the City of Vancouver. Their autonomy is significantly constrained, however, by legal, fiscal, and political factors (Smith and Spicer 2018). In this chapter, we ask whether the provisions of Chapter 19 of CETA further limit their ability to use their procurement powers to achieve their economic development and social policy objectives.

In previous work, we showed that EU firms already have access to Canadian municipal procurement markets, at least in large cities. We found only weak evidence of discrimination. Nonetheless, the prohibition of offsets could conflict with the common desire of cities to promote local economic and social development by requiring that firms that win government contract hire local workers or buy products from local suppliers. Our analysis here suggests that this prohibition will not affect current practices. Thus far, cities have managed to balance an increased emphasis on CBAS and social procurement policies with the obligations created by trade agreements.

NOTES

1 "Offsets" are defined in the next section, along with the reasons for their prohibition.

2 Chapter 19 of CETA applies only to contracts valued above specified thresholds. For contracts below the threshold, discrimination in favour of local firms would be allowed.

3 In addition to municipalities, the MASH sector includes public school boards, health authorities, and post-secondary institutions.

4 The text of Chapter 19 of CETA draws very heavily from the text of the revised Agreement on Government Procurement (GPA) which was negotiated under the auspices of the World Trade Organization (WTO) and came into force in 2014. Both Canada and the EU are GPA signatories.

5 In July 2018, the Canadian federal government awarded a CAD 80 million contract to Infosys Public Services, the large Indian technology firm, to build the SPA website for use by 2022 (Cision 2018). Art. 19.17(4) (CETA 2016) mandates enhanced accountability by requiring that Canada "establish or designate at least one impartial administrative or judicial authority that is independent of its procuring entities to receive and review a challenge by a supplier arising in the context of a covered procurement." The current situation is that each Canadian municipality has its own system of handling complaints by bidders.

6 Art. 19.1 (CETA 2016) defines as offset as follows: "offset means any condition or undertaking that encourages local development or improves a Party's balance-of-payments accounts, such as the use of domestic content, the licensing of technology, investment, counter-trade and similar action or requirement." This definition is identical to that in Art. 1 of the GPA.

7 The ITB requirement is a 100 per cent offset (i.e., the relevant business activities must be equal to the value of the contract) and the proposed offset is considered as part of the bid evaluation process. Despite CETA's general prohibition of offsets, the ITB arrangement is allowed because defence procurement is excluded from coverage in Art. 19.3 of CETA. In the ITB context, the range of business activities required is quite broad and often unrelated to the goods or services being provided. The range includes foreign direct investment (FDI), the import by foreign bidders of Canadian goods or services or the purchase of parts made in Canada. See Innovation, Science and Economic Development Canada (2019).

8 See BoardVoice (2019) for the comments of Scott Sinclair and Gus van Harten on the coverage of social services. Annexes 19-2 and 19-5 use a "positive list" to define which organizations are covered: those listed are

covered, those not listed are not covered. Annex 19-4, on the other hand, is a "negative list": all goods are covered except those listed.

9   "Other threats," beyond the scope of this chapter, come from provisions in the investment chapter and the trade in services chapter. For an elaboration on those threats, see Sinclair and Trew (2019).

10 Section 92 stipulates all areas of provincial jurisdiction, including health care and education.

11 The freedom of expression argument was an attempt to use the Canadian Charter of Rights and Freedoms to overcome the view that the province could cut the size of the city council because cities were "creatures of the province." The charter includes freedom of expression as a fundamental freedom. More importantly, this strategy shows that the City of Toronto seems to have accepted the Section 92 authority of provincial governments, as they chose to present an argument based on different grounds.

12 Despite the negative connotation of the word "bias," conditions that favour local economic development may be an efficient way to foster such development.

13 We thank an anonymous referee for suggesting that there might be a concern that foreign firms will take initial losses in order to establish themselves in a local market.

14 The choice of these four cities was driven by a number of practical considerations, namely, data availability and the effort needed to process the data. Moreover, these cities are of similar size which facilitates comparison.

15 For a description of these tables, see Statistics Canada (2020).

16 We did not include the City of Hamilton in our econometric analysis, as the data for that city were insufficient.

17 Because our data covered only a limited number of large cities, it is of course possible that home bias exists in other large cities or in smaller municipalities.

18 Between December 2016 and May 2019, we spoke in person or by telephone with ten current and former municipal staff with specific procurement responsibilities in Edmonton, Ottawa, Thunder Bay, Toronto, Vancouver, and Winnipeg. Many of our interviewees were directors or managers of procurement, some were city legal counsel involved in procurement activities, and others were specifically responsible for sustainable procurement activities. Many of the more senior procurement officials managed procurement processes and procurement staff, drafted and revised procurement policies, and met with provincial officials regarding municipal procurement guidelines and the potential impacts of trade agreements such as CETA. We asked our respondents to describe how

procurement fit within the administrative structure of their respective cities, and to comment on the overall goals of procurement activities in their city and the degree to which these goals are impeded or threatened by CETA. We further asked them to comment on the extent to which previous trade agreements, such as the Agreement on Internal Trade, have affected procurement processes and whether they anticipated future changes in response to CETA's entry into force. Finally, we asked about their perceptions of barriers facing foreign firms that seek to bid on contracts in their municipalities.

19 In defence-related contracts, such as the ITB program described earlier, there is often a main contract and a separate offset contract. See ICC (2019, 5). Defence-related contracts are exempt from CETA.

20 See Infrastructure Ontario (2020) for copies of the project agreement and the RFP.

21 TCBN is a coalition of community organizations and labour organizations that seeks to extend access to employment opportunities resulting from increased transit and other infrastructure development. Its website lists five primary objectives of the organization: "1. Provide equitable economic opportunities that promote economic inclusion for all Toronto residents; 2. Contribute to the development of a system of training and workforce development programs that can enable economic inclusion; 3.Support social enterprises and other related vehicles to economic inclusion through commitments to social procurement; 4. Contribute to sustainable communities with neighbourhood and environmental improvements built through new transit infrastructure; 5. Ensure clear commitments and accountability from all parties to deliver on Community Benefits" (TCBN n.d.).

22 Although the WBDA is a crown corporation which would normally be covered by CETA's government procurement rules, Annex 19-7 exempts procurement "in relation to an international crossing between Canada and another country, including the design, construction, operation and maintenance of the crossing as well as any related infrastructure" (CETA 2016, Annex 19-7(1)(d)). As a result, WBDA is not subject to the government procurement provisions of CETA (WBDA 2020, personal correspondence).

23 All three of the documents referenced in this paragraph are available at Windsor-Detroit Bridge Authority (n.d.).

24 See page 22 of the RFQ, referenced in the previous note.

25 Cecilia Malmström, the EU commissioner on trade, wrote in 2015 that the CETA's provision of unconditional access to public procurement, was second only to the tariff reductions as an achievement for the EU in the agreement. See Malmström (2015).

REFERENCES

BoardVoice. 2019. "Social Services Exempt from Trade Agreements." Blog Post. Accessed 2 February 2022. https://boardvoice.ca/2019/10/04/.

Brülhart, Marius, and Federico Trionfetti. 2005. "A Test of Trade Theories When Expenditure Is Home Biased." SSRN Scholarly Paper ID 779124. Rochester, NY: Social Science Research Network. https://papers.ssrn.com/abstract=779124.

CETA (Canada-European Union Comprehensive Economic and Trade Agreement). 2016. Accessed 21 July 2020. https://www.international.gc.ca/trade-commerce/trade-agreements-accords-commerciaux/agr-acc/ceta-aecg/text-texte/toc-tdm.aspx?lang=eng.

City of Toronto. 2019. "Community Benefits Framework." Accessed 2 February 2022. https://www.toronto.ca/legdocs/mmis/2019/ec/bgrd/backgroundfile-134595.pdf.

City of Vancouver. 2018. "Community Benefit Agreements." Accessed 2 February 2022. https://council.vancouver.ca/20180918/documents/rr2.pdf.

Council of Canadians. 2014. "Canada-EU CETA." Accessed 2 February 2022. https://canadians.org/ceta.

Good, Kristin R. 2019. "The Fallacy of the 'Creatures of the Provinces' Doctrine: Recognizing and Protecting Municipalities' Constitutional Status." IMFG Papers on Municipal Finance and Governance No. 42, Institute on Municipal Finance and Governance, Toronto, ON.

Infrastructure Ontario. 2020. "Eglinton Crosstown LRT." Accessed 2 February 2022. https://www.infrastructureontario.ca/Eglinton-Crosstown-LRT.

Innovation, Science and Economic Development Canada. 2019. "Industrial and Technological Benefits." Accessed 2 February 2022. https://www.ic.gc.ca/eic/site/086.nsf/eng/home.

International Chamber of Commerce. 2019. "ICC-ECCO Guide to International Offset Contracts." Accessed 2 February 2022. https://iccwbo.org/publication/icc-ecco-guide-international-offset-contracts-2019/.

Kitchen, Harry, and Enid Slack. 2016. "More Tax Sources for Canada's Largest Cities: Why, What, and How?" IMFG Papers on Municipal Finance and Governance, no. 27.

Lester, Simon, and James Bacchus. 2019. "Trade Justice Delayed Is Trade Justice Denied." Accessed 2 February 2022. https://papers.ssrn.com/sol3/papers.cfm?abstract_id=3490661.

Lysenko, Dmitry, Elizabeth Schwartz, and Saul Schwartz. 2020. "Short-Term Effects of the Comprehensive Economic and Trade Agreement on Municipal

Procurement in Canada." *Canadian Public Policy* 46, no. 2: 264–78. https://doi.org/10.3138/cpp.2019-042.

Malmström, Cecilia. 2015. "CETA: Europe's Next Trade Step." Speech to the Workshop on the EU-Canada Comprehensive Economic and Trade Agreement (CETA), 9 December. https://trade.ec.europa.eu/doclib/html/154022.htm.

McCrudden, Christopher. 2004. "Using Public Procurement to Achieve Social Outcomes." In *Natural Resources Forum*, 28: 257–67. Wiley Online Library. http://onlinelibrary.wiley.com/doi/10.1111/j.1477-8947.2004.00099.x/abstract.

Nugent, James. 2017. "The Right to Build the City: Can Community Benefits Agreements Bring Employment Equity to the Construction Sector?" *Labour / Le Travail* 80: 81–114.

Rickard, Stephanie J., and Daniel Y. Kono. 2014. "Think Globally, Buy Locally: International Agreements and Government Procurement." *The Review of International Organizations* 9, no. 3: 333–52. https://doi.org/10.1007/s11558-013-9177-x.

Schwartz, Elizabeth. 2019. "Autonomous Local Climate Change Policy: An Analysis of the Effect of Intergovernmental Relations Among Subnational Governments." *Review of Policy Research* 36, no. 1: 50–74. https://doi.org/10.1111/ropr.12320.

Semple, Abby. 2017. "Socially Responsible Public Procurement (SRPP) under EU Law and International Agreements." *European Procurement & Public Private Partnership Law Review* 12: 293–309.

Sinclair, Scott, and Stuart Trew. 2019. "Taking Stock of CETA: Early Impacts of the EU–Canada Comprehensive Economic and Trade Agreement." Friedrich-Ebert-Stiftung, September.

Smith, Alison, and Zachary Spicer. 2018. "The Local Autonomy of Canada's Largest Cities." *Urban Affairs Review* 54, no. 5: 931–61. https://doi.org/10.1177/1078087416684380.

Statistics Canada. 2021. "Inter-Corporate Ownership." 17 June. https://www150.statcan.gc.ca/n1/en/catalogue/61-517-X.

Toronto Community Benefits Network. n.d. "Who We Are." Toronto Community Benefits Network. Accessed 18 February 2022. https://www.communitybenefits.ca/about.

Trew, Stuart and Scott Sinclair. 2014. "Public Procurement: Provincial and Municipal Coverage." In *Making Sense of the CETA: An Analysis of the Final Text of the Canada–European Union Comprehensive Economic and Trade Agreement*, edited by Scott Sinclair, Stuart Trew, and Hadrian Mertins-Kirkwood. 1st Edition. Canadian Centre for Policy Alternatives.

Van Ymeren, Jamie, and Sara Ditta. 2017. "Delivering Benefit: Achieving Community Benefits in Ontario." Mowat Centre. Accessed 18 February 2022. https://ccednet-rcdec.ca/sites/ccednet-rcdec.ca/files/delivering_ benefit_-_achieving_community_benefits_in_ontario.pdf.

Windsor-Detroit Bridge Authority. 2015. "Request for Qualifications: Gordie Howe International Bridge." Request for Qualifications. Accessed 18 February 2022. https://www.gordiehoweinternationalbridge.com/u/files/ Procurement/Documents/wDBA%20RFQ.pdf.

– 2018. "Gordie Howe International Bridge Execution Version Project Agreement for Gordie Howe International Bridge between Windsor-Detroit Bridge Authority and Bridging North America Partnership." Project Agreement. Accessed 18 February 2022. https://www.gordiehowe internationalbridge.com/u/files/Procurement/Documents/103646563_v(5)_ Gordie%20Howe%20International%20Bridge%20-%20Public%20 Project%20Agreement%20and%20Schedules%20-%20Consolida,._.pdf.

– 2020. "9 Things to Know About … Neighbourhood Infrastructure Strategy." Fact Sheet. Accessed 18 February 2022. https://www.gordiehoweinter nationalbridge.com/en/9-things-to-know-about-neighbourhood-infrastructure-strategy-fact-sheet.

– 2021. "Significant Progress Made on Gordie Howe International Bridge Project in First Thousand Days | News Releases | Gordie Howe International Bridge." News Release. Accessed 18 February 2022. https://www. gordiehoweinternationalbridge.com/en/significant-progress-made-on-gordie-howe-international-bridge-project-in-first-thousand-days.

– n.d. "P3 Procurement." Fact Sheet. Accessed 3 June 2020. https://www. gordiehoweinternationalbridge.com/en/p3-procurement.

PART FOUR

Investment Disputes

9

Canada's Approaches to Investor-State Dispute Settlement: Addressing Divergencies among CETA, USMCA, CPTPP, and the Canada-China FIPA

David A. Gantz

Investment is a key driving force for economic growth and competitiveness in Canada. It spurs innovation, creates jobs and connects Canada to global value chains. Canada has a clear interest in ensuring that Canadian individuals and companies are well protected when they invest abroad, and the CPTPP *[Comprehensive and Progressive Agreement for Trans-Pacific Partnership] provides a strong, rules-based framework through which to grow our investment relationship with key Asia-Pacific economies.*
(Government of Canada 2018a, para. 9)

INTRODUCTION

In recent years, Canada has concluded four major trade agreements incorporating investment protection, the Comprehensive Economic and Trade Agreement (CETA 2016) between Canada the European Union (EU);[1] the CPTPP (2018);[2] the United States–Mexico–Canada Agreement (USMCA 2018; alternatively known as the Canada–United States–Mexico Agreement, or CUSMA); and the Canada-China Foreign Investment Protection Agreement (Canada-China FIPA 2012). The first three are comprehensive free trade agreements (FTAs) with investment chapters; the fourth is a stand-alone bilateral investment agreement. These agreements reflect somewhat and in some instances significantly different approaches to protection of foreign investment, commonly known as investor-state dispute settlement, or ISDS, and are the principal subject of this analysis.

USMCA has been approved by the US Congress and the Canadian Parliament and took effect on 1 July 2020, defying predictions that it would be delayed because of political factors in the United States. CETA has been in provisional force since September 2017, albeit without the investment protection provisions.[3] CPTPP entered into force for Canada and five other signatories (Australia, Japan, Mexico, New Zealand, Singapore) on 30 December 2018 and for an additional signatory (Vietnam) a month later (with the investment provisions more or less intact). Canada-China FIPA has been in force since 2014.[4]

These agreements are potentially significant for several reasons, particularly because all except USMCA represent a major effort by Canada to diversify its trade away from its traditional heavy dependence on the United States for some 76 per cent of total goods exports (Trading Economics 2017). However, for those interested in ISDS and broader issues of foreign investment, the agreements represent a divergence (some would say "inconsistency") in Canada's investment policies, although as discussed herein there are rational reasons for the divergence. Moreover, recent developments such as the issuance of the 2021 Model FIPA in May 2021, which incorporates more traditional ISDS, suggest that Canadian acceptance of the EU's investment court mechanism (ICM) in CETA is an exception to, rather than a departure from, Canadas's now-traditional approach to investment protection. CPTPP incorporates in its Chapter 9 a more-or-less traditional ISDS using ad hoc arbitration under International Centre for Settlement of Investment Disputes (ICSID) or United Nations Commission on International Trade Law (UNCITRAL) rules. It is noted in this respect that in the past Canada's approach to ISDS has reflected the traditional (non-Trumpian) United States' approach, as evidenced by their respective model bilateral investment treaties (BITS), now including the 2021 Model BIT[5] (see Titi 2013; US Department of State 2012).

Canada-China FIPA (2012) reflects a compromise between a traditional Canadian approach to investment protection and a much more cautious Chinese approach. CETA, in its Chapter 8, embodies the first effort by the EU to promulgate its appellate body system or ICM (now followed by similar language in investment agreements parallel to the EU-Vietnam and EU-Singapore FTAS). The EU ICM would substitute a standing investment court and an appellate body for more traditional arbitration. Those provisions will not enter into force unless and until they are ratified by the parliaments of all EU states; as of March 2021, twelve EU member states have not ratified CETA, including France, the Netherlands, and Germany,[6] ratifications are also lacking for the Vietnam and Japan foreign investment agreements, and the Japanese agreement has not been approved by Japan. Given the recalcitrance of many EU members to accept the ICM (a recalcitrance that almost certainly would have applied to the ISDS mechanism in the first public draft of CETA), it will likely be some years before any of the ICMs will be in force and able to accept complaints.

In USMCA, in contrast, the United States and Canada have agreed to eliminate ISDS entirely after a three-year transition period. The USMCA investment chapter (USMCA 2018, Chapter 14, Annex 14-E) incorporates most of the traditional protections relating to national treatment, fair and equitable treatment (FET), and expropriation, but ISDS obligations apply only between the United States and Mexico, and then only to a more limited degree than under North American Free Trade Agreement (NAFTA) 1994, Chapter 11. Among other innovations, as far as I am aware, this is the first time that the investment protection provisions in a regional trade agreement have treated the developed country (Canada) differently than the developing country (Mexico). Table 9.1 lists the various ISDS types in the Canadian agreements.

As is perhaps self-evident, a major if not controlling factor when discussing Canada's varying approaches to ISDS in recent trade and investment agreements is that in most instances, Canada is the weaker negotiating party. This is true of the agreements with the EU (CETA 2016), the United States (USMCA 2018 and Trans-Pacific Partnership (TPP) 2016, with Japan being a powerful player in the latter along with the United States) and in the Canada-China FIPA (2012). Canada's gross GDP in 2018 was US$1.7 trillion; Japan's, US$4.97 trillion; China's, US$13.5, trillion; EU's, US$18.7 trillion; and the United States', US$20.5 trillion (IMF 2019). In other words when Canada is negotiating with these major players in the world economy it is with a GDP one-third of Japan's, one-eleventh of China's, one-twelfth of the EU's and one-thirteenth of that of the United States. Among other factors, this disparity suggests that Canadian negotiators need to have a very clear idea of their priorities in each of their negotiations since more tradeoffs may be required than on the part of the negotiators sitting across the table.

If one considers these economic disparities, the accomplishments of Global Trade Canada in the four negotiations seem impressive indeed. Moreover, broad differences among these various negotiating partners' approaches to investment issues has allowed Canada to consider such agreements to some extent on case-by-case basis, possibly giving Canadian negotiators more flexibility in fashioning favourable provisions than might otherwise be the case, or obtaining other treaty benefits in exchange for

Table 9.1
Canada's investment agreements

Agreement	In force from	Type of ISDS included
CETA	21 September 2017[1]	Investment court/appellate body mechanism
USMCA	1 July 2020	None for Canada and the US; missed for US-Mexico
CPTPP	30 December 2018	Traditional ISDS with some additions and limitations
Canada-China FIPA	1 October 14	Traditional ISDS with some additions and limitations
2021 Model FIPA	13 May 2021	Traditional ISDS with some additions and limitations

Notes: "Traditional ISDS" as used herein is defined in the next section, when discussing TPP/CPTPP.
1 Excluding the investment provisions.
Source: Compiled by the author.

concessions on investment protection that ultimately risk little harm to Canadian interests. Such an approach may permit Canada to assure flexibility for national and provincial governments to pursue important environmental goals. For example, Canada was able to secure the inclusion of language designed to protect indigenous rights,[7] in case of USMCA, and to exclude ISDS coverage for investment agreements and investment authorizations in CPTPP (2018, Annex, para. 2), both included in the original TPP (TPP 2016, Chapter 9; USMCA 2018, Chapter 14). Still, the 2021 Model FIPA suggests that Canada, in future agreements, intends to revert to a modified version of its traditional ISDS mechanism, rather than adopting either the EU's ICM or to eschew ISDS entirely, as in the USMCA (Government of Canada 2021).

Canada's differentiated treatment of ISDS raises issues that go well beyond its own approach to investment. Which of the recent models, along with the 2021 Model BIT, is likely to dominate investor protection chapters (if any) in future trade agreements concluded by Canada, along with the United States, China, and the EU? Do the divergent CETA and USMCA mechanisms suggest the possibility of a broader departure from the NAFTA/CPTPP models, and if so, is the EU (investment court/appellate body) or the United States (no ISDS with Canada and reduced scope with Mexico) likely to ultimately prevail in agreements with other countries in future trade agreements? What are the prospects for the EU's efforts to conclude a broad-based multilateral agreement embodying the ICM/appellate body system, perhaps with Canada's support? Will the United States' apparent rejection or limitation of ISDS in its newest agreements, such as the one signed with Japan in October (US-Japan Trade Agreement 2019) and in the USMCA as noted above, convince other developed countries to act in a similar manner? Or will new proposals arising out of the UNCITRAL (2018) Working Groups provide yet a different approach?

Further, given Canada's highly regarded domestic court system, to what extent will potential foreign investors in Canada be seriously concerned whether ISDS is incorporated in Canada's future trade agreements? Even though Canadian law has no direct equivalent to the Fifth Amendment to the US Constitution, providing that "no person ... [shall] be deprived of life, liberty or property, without due process of law, nor shall private property be taken for public use, without just compensation." Some potential agreement parties may not care.

Nor does Canadian national or provincial law necessarily include many of the investment protections of NAFTA (1994) Chapter 11 (de Mestral and Morgan 2016). Canada has been sued under NAFTA Chapter 11 (ibid.) more often than either the United States or Mexico, and has lost multiple cases, most of which have involved alleged indirect takings by provincial governments.[8] But one must ask whether the absence of functioning investor protections in CETA and in USMCA for the US and Canada in future investment disputes in Canada, risks exposing the Canadian federal government to diplomatic pressures from the investors' home governments, particularly the United States? These are among the issues that will be discussed after comparing the investment protection alternatives supported by Canada.

In the balance of this chapter, four key agreements or investment chapters are discussed. The second section addresses CPTPP; the third addresses CETA; the fourth addresses USMCA; and the fifth, the Canada-China FIPA. References are also made to the 2021 Model FIPA where appropriate. The last section provides a brief summary and conclusion.

INVESTMENT PROTECTION UNDER TPP AND CPTPP

TPP (2016) and to a great extent the successor CPTPP (2018) remain wedded to the traditional ISDS provisions included in FTA investment chapters that have evolved over the past several decades from NAFTA (1994). As many are aware, these chapters contain in Part A broad definitions of "investment" protections for foreign investors (and in some cases definitions of the scope of coverage), the most important of which are guarantees of national treatment; most favoured nation (MFN) treatment; FET; protection against performance requirements; control over senior management and boards of directors; freedom for financial transfers; and protection from direct and indirect expropriation (NAFTA 1994, Arts 1101–10; TPP 2016, Arts 9.1–9.11). TPP Chapter 9 (section B) and NAFTA Chapter 11 (section B) also provide for negotiations, mediation, and ultimately arbitration, under the rules of ICSID or UNICTRAL. There, the investor and government each choose an arbitrator on an ad hoc basis, agree on a chair, and proceed to arbitration, normally with no right to an appeal. (See, e.g., CPTPP 2018, Chapter 9; NAFTA 1994, Chapter 11.)[9]

The evolution of Canadian investment protection agreements since NAFTA entered into force in 1994, which in most respects is parallel to what occurred in the United States, has been summarized elsewhere (e.g. Gantz 2017a). Among the most important changes compared to NAFTA are a recommendation for preliminary consideration of procedural issues by the tribunal; transparency in arbitral proceedings including open hearings; the tribunal's authority to accept amicus curiae submissions; definitions for customary international law intending to narrow the scope; broader definitions of what constitutes FET, and, perhaps most important, specifying that "[n]on-discriminatory regulatory actions by a Party that are designed and applied to protect legitimate public welfare objectives, such as public health, safety, and the environment, do not constitute indirect expropriations, except in rare circumstances" (CPTPP 2018, Chapter 9; Gantz 2017a, 254). The 2021 Model FIPA continues the evolution in several respects, including inter alia an exclusion of ISDS for any intellectual property rights that are consistent with the WTO's TRIPS Agreement (Agreement on Trade-Related Aspects of Intellectual Property Rights) (TRIPS 1995, Art. 9.6), sustainable development, corporate social responsibility, human rights, indigenous rights, and the right to regulate.[10]

TPP and now CPTPP also go further in their language seeking to preserve the governments' regulatory flexibility, limiting the scope of investors' "reasonable expectations," restricting damages in pre-investment violations to incurred expenses; allowing counterclaims in disputes over investment authorizations or investment agreements (now superseded by CPTPP); and permitting governments to exclude tobacco-based claims from ISDS (Gantz 2017b, 254–7; TPP 2016, Chapter 9).

CPTPP makes one significant change compared to the original TPP investment provisions by deleting (at the insistence of Canada) coverage of investment agreements and investment authorizations (CPTPP 2018,

Annex; TPP 2016, Art. 8.18). As Global Affairs Canada (2019) has noted, the modification received strong support from Canada: "Following the United States' departure from the Trans-Pacific Partnership (TPP), Canada and the other CPTPP members agreed to suspend certain TPP obligations that would have expanded the scope of ISDS beyond Canada's past approach. These suspensions bring the CPTPP in line with Canada's preferred approach to ISDS in FTAs, which balances clear and enforceable rights for investors with flexibility for governments to regulate in important areas" (Government of Canada 2018b). It may be that for some parties concerns existed that an investment authorization initially issued by a party but later rescinded because of subsequently discovered information could become the subject of a demand for arbitration by the person to whom the original authorization had been issued.

Within the CPTPP negotiations there is little public history of Canadian discussion of investment issues. Still, Canadian investments in the territories of some parties – Australia in the case of natural resources, Vietnam more generally – may raise concerns, suggesting that traditional ISDS is probably popular with Canadian investors at least in the extractive industries. Chile among CPTPP parties already has an FTA with Canada (Canada-Chile FTA 1996), with then standard investment protection provisions, which was modernized in 2019 (Government of Canada 2019), although Chile had not ratified the CPTTP as of August 2021. A 2009 FTA with Peru, with investment provisions also evolving from NAFTA, remains in force (Canada-Peru FTA 2009); Peru was a ratification hold-out among the CPTPP signatories until September 2021. Negotiations between Canada and Singapore, Japan, and Malaysia were undertaken in the past (Government of Canada 2020), but presumably have been abandoned given that all three of those countries are CPTPP signatories or parties.

Since the powerhouses in the original TPP negotiations were the US and Japan, Canada was once again in a disadvantaged negotiating position. However, as the opening quotation to this chapter indicates as well, as Canada's history in negotiating investment provisions in agreements such as the FTAs with Chile and Peru, there does not appear to have been any Canadian objection to the revised standard ISDS provisions in TPP previously favoured for FTAs by both the United States and Canada. Moreover, the TPP provisions seem to be generally consistent with Canada's 2004 Model FIPA (Italaw 2004), as periodically modified, and, except as noted herein, with the 2021 Model FIPA.

With TPP (2016) Chapter 9, a major question for Canada and for the other CPTPP parties is whether this arguably most balanced of all ISDS chapters will be extended when new investment chapters in trade agreements are negotiated, or whether the parties will seek different approaches. In my view it is very unlikely that the TPP parties would retreat from the greater regulatory flexibility embodied in TPP compared to earlier investment chapters, whether concluded by Canada or by other nations that are likely to continue to favour the traditional ISDS approach. In several recent investment agreements, Canada incorporated its traditional ad hoc arbitration form of ISDS, as in the recent investment promotion agreement with Moldova (Canada-Moldova FIPA 2018, section C).[11] This preference has been clarified beyond much doubt in the 2021 Model FIPA with its mostly traditional approach to ISDS. Some may consider it significant that this represents an implicit rejection of the EU/CETA model incorporating the ICM.

INVESTMENT PROTECTION UNDER CETA

It is unclear whether existing and potential Canadian investors in the EU believe that ISDS along the traditional lines, as incorporated in the TPP (and discussed in that section) and CPTPP, is essential to their future welfare or is likely to impact Canadian foreign investment in the EU member nations. Many who value investment protection may not find any particular approach critical, and in any event the investment court ultimately incorporated in CETA was substituted for the prior ISDS provisions in secret negotiations concluded in October 2015, without any public consultation as far as the public record indicates, well after a traditional ISDS mechanism had been included in the initial public version of CETA (Gantz 2017b).

The EU ICM/appellate body mechanism has been discussed in detail elsewhere and is only be summarized here. In CETA, the traditional ad hoc arbitration is to be replaced by a standing investment "court" (actually a group of fifteen part-time tribunal members), five each from Canada and the EU and five citizens of neutral countries, all subject to various qualifications and conflict of interest requirements, appointed for five-year renewable terms by the two parties without any direct role for disputing investors (CETA 2016, Art. 8.27). A separate appellate tribunal is also contemplated to review not only errors of law but "manifest errors in the appreciation of the facts, including the appreciation of relevant domestic law" (ibid., Art. 8.28). While the appellate tribunal is to sit in panels of three, the precise number of tribunal members to be appointed and many other procedural details are left for future discussion by the CETA Joint Committee, presumably when, and if, all of the EU member state parliaments have approved CETA, including its investment provisions. Since no EU invest-ment tribunal/appellate body mechanism has entered into force anywhere to date,[12] many of the operational details remain to be discussed and decided among the parties to agreements which incorporate the mechanism.[13]

Still, the investment court/appellate body approach if and when it enters into force is likely to be generally satisfactory to most Canadian investors even if they might have preferred more traditional ISDS. Canada has only half a dozen foreign investment agreements with Eastern Europe EU members (UNCTAD 2018),[14] which will remain in force unless and until the investment provisions of CETA enter into force. However, investments elsewhere in Eastern Europe currently have no ISDS protection for Canadian investors. Some Canadian investors may well be nervous about the investment climate and safety of their activities in some Eastern Europe EU member countries and perhaps Greece and Italy, given that they all rank relatively poorly in Transparency International (2018) Corruptions Perceptions Index.[15] In retrospect, some Canadian stakeholders are likely to live to regret that CETA contains an ICM that remains not in force for an extended period, in comparison to the more traditional ISDS mechanism contained in the CETA as originally agreed upon by the EU and Canada. (Realistically, similar ratification delays might well have occurred had the original CETA ISDS provisions been finalized and submitted to the EU member states for approval.) In any event these stakeholders now have considerably less reason for concern that Canada will seek the ICM in future trade and investment agreements.

Presumably, Canada was willing for political as well as economic reasons to accommodate the desires of the EU Commission and EU Parliament, which designed the investment court/appellate body primarily for inclusion in the Transatlantic Trade and Investment Partnership (TTIP) negotiations and thought (erroneously in retrospect) that the mechanism would discourage widespread European opposition to ISDS and more broadly to trade agreements in general (European Commission 2015; European Parliament 2015).[16] The Commission probably believed it would have been impractical to offer traditional ISDS in CETA Canada simultaneously while advocating the ICM/appellate mechanism in the then-ongoing TTIP negotiations. Because of the late timing of the modification of CETA investment provisions Canada does not appear to have received any new concessions from the EU in return. Still, it was clearly beneficial to Canada for CETA to go into force even if only provisionally without any further delays resulting from disagreements among the EU members, particularly at a time when the future of NAFTA was in doubt.[17]

For reasons noted further in regard to USMCA, Global Trade Canada and the Joint Legal Team (lawyers from Global Trade and the Justice ministry) that defends ISDS cases against Canada (overwhelmingly brought under NAFTA), may well have seen the EU mechanism, under which the judges/arbitrators are all chosen in advance by the two governments and providing for a full appeal before another panel chosen entirely by the two governments (CETA 2016), as more friendly to respondent governments than traditional ISDS (where one of the arbitrators is chosen by the claimant and the claimant and respondent jointly choose the chair of the tribunal).

It would be tempting to try to compare the efficacy of the EU ICM with the only mechanism with which Canada has any significant experience, but this is impossible because neither the CETA nor any similar ICMs in other EU trade agreements are currently in force. As noted earlier, a dozen EU members have refrained from ratifying CETA, primarily because of the investment protection provisions. The international investment community (governments and investors) has also not shown any significant interest in a multilateral version of the investment court (MIC). Among the apparent opponents to this mechanism was the Trump Administration, and there is no reason to believe that current Democratic Party leaders, who have opposed NAFTA (1994) Chapter 11 and other ISDS mechanisms for decades, would be more forthcoming.[18] Thus, any actual comparisons between traditional ISDS and the ICM, whether bilateral or multilateral, and beyond the speculation in this chapter, remain for a later analysis.

ELIMINATION OF NAFTA'S ISDS UNDER USMCA

In its USMCA (2018) trade negotiations, the Trump Administration departed from policies favoured by other US administrations since Ronald Reagan that advocated robust investor protections in FTAs, where government actions allegedly violated basic principles protecting foreign investment under international law were subject to ISDS. The former president and his then US trade representative and chief USMCA negotiator, Robert Lighthizer, appeared to be convinced that ISDS infringes US sovereignty and may encourage American enterprises to move the facilities to lower-wage countries such as Mexico (Lester 2018). These views are not confined to the Trump Administration. For example, law professor Jason Yackee (2015) has long argued that the inclusion of ISDS in treaties such as TPP (or, by extension, USMCA) is "unlikely to provide significant benefits" and that because of ISDS "costs" the "rational way to proceed" is to exclude ISDS.

For Canadian investors in Mexico and the United States, and Mexican and American investors in Canada, the elimination of ISDS protections to enforce claims by one investor against the other state will apply after a three-year transition period beginning 1 July 2020; during that period NAFTA "legacy" investment claims and pending claims remain subject to NAFTA Chapter 11 (USMCA 2018, annex 14-C). The absence of ISDS after the USMCA has been in force for three years affects most significantly US investors in Canada and Canadian investors in the United States (since there have been no claims between Canada and Mexico). Both US and Canadian investors will be required to rely on the other's national courts for their disputes, courts which with a few exceptions are generally considered to be competent, unbiased and free of corruption with rare exceptions (e.g., *Loewen Group, Inc. and Raymond L. Loewen* v. *United States of America* 2005).[19] Still, there is no equivalent of the prohibition of takings without just compensation under the Fifth Amendment to the US Constitution in Canada, although takings are prohibited in some instances by statute. One study concludes that of thirty-five Chapter 11 claims against Canada, awards would have been equivalent in only four cases had they been adjudicated by Canadian federal courts (de Mestral and Morgan 2016, 11).[20] Also, as with the US states, Canadian provinces, which in some areas have more autonomy than US states, are responsible for most of the claims filed under Chapter 11 (Global Affairs Canada 2019). Many of the claims against the United States – none of which were resolved in favour of the investor – were also based on alleged state violations, including *Loewen* v. *United States* 2002 (Louisiana) covered ahead and *Methanex* v. *United States* 2005 (California).

Canada has paid claims of some US$220 million in at least half a dozen cases brought by US claimants while Canadians have won none against the US (although the US prevailed in one, *Loewen*, in the author's view only by suborning one of the tribunal members). Global Trade Canada officials (like some of their US State Department counterparts) may well be weary of defending (and losing) such cases and can argue that both countries have robust legal systems to protect foreigners, although its provinces, like the US states, have a mixed record on treatment of foreign investors. Some of these have been politically sensitive, as in *Clayton/Bilcon* v. *Canada* (2019), where a majority of a tribunal has directed Canada to pay damages as a result of the cancellation allegedly on environmental grounds of a licence to undertaking certain mining and quarrying operations in Nova Scotia. While the claimant originally sought US$188 million (*Clayton/Bilcon* v. *Canada* 2008), the actual award was only US$7 million.

Some Canadian government officials as well as those from the United States government may for similar reasons have welcomed the elimination of ISDS from USMCA. The change according to one official "strengthened the Canadian government's right to regulate in the public interest" (Munson 2019). This comment likely reflected the public as well as governmental concerns noted earlier. However, it is not evident that US concerns that ISDS encourages domestic businesses to export jobs, or functions as a subsidy for such businesses, was a significant factor in the negotiation. Given the weaker ISDS provisions offered in the USMCA negotiations and accepted by Mexico, Canadian negotiators may well have concluded that having no ISDS provisions applicable to Canada was preferable for precedential purposes in future trade negotiations with third countries to accepting to what many believed was a flawed system.[21]

One may also speculate that additional factors led the Canadian negotiators to agree to US requests to eliminate ISDS from USMCA, and the willingness to do so could have been related to one or more of Canada's major objectives in the negotiations. It can be speculated that the most likely factor was Canada's "redline" demand to retain in USMCA the NAFTA Chapter 19, binational panel mechanism, that substitutes binational arbitral panels for the federal courts of the NAFTA countries in reviewing antidumping and countervailing duty administrative decisions that are issued by agencies such as the US Department of Commerce and the US International Trade Commission (NAFTA 1994, Chap. 19; USMCA 2019, Chap. 10, Sec. D, Art. 4). Chapter 19 was critical to the Canadian acceptance of the US-Canada FTA in 1987 and Canadian policy does not appear to have changed in the ensuing thirty-plus years.[22] However, ISDS may have been used as a bargaining chip for some of the other successful Canadian demands in the USMCA negotiations, such as maintenance of the "cultural industries" exemption originally a carry-over into NAFTA from the US-Canada FTA,[23] or limiting Canada's opening of its milk solids market to only 3.6 per cent of total consumption (USMCA 2019, annex 3-B, sec. C).

The alternatives for Canada had the negotiators sought to preserve ISDS in one form or another seem limited indeed. Presumably, Canada could not have achieved greater investor protection in USMCA than Mexico. There NAFTA's Chapter 11-like traditional ISDS prevails only for a few sectors: hydrocarbons, power, some transportation and other infrastructure, and telecommunications (ibid., annex 14-E, para. 6(b)). In other sectors FET and indirect expropriation as a basis for dispute settlement disappear, and national treatment is not required for pre-investment activities (ibid., annex 14-D, Art. 14.D.3). Also, claimants seeking ISDS against Mexico under USMCA in the less-favoured sectors must demonstrate that they have first pursued proceedings before national courts or administrative tribunals and have either received a final decision or thirty months have elapsed from the date national judicial proceedings were initiated (ibid., annex 14-D, Art. 14.D.5).

Still, in my view, it could have been beneficial for US investors in Canada (and vice versa) if they had been afforded ISDS treatment comparable to Mexico's. Moreover, such provisions would probably have worked better, with the obligatory requirement of exhausting local remedies likely eliminating many if not most of the disputes given the competence of Canadian courts and the prospect of binding international arbitration, a result that would have benefited both the foreign investor and the Canadian government. The more difficult question is whether the United States would have been prepared to afford reciprocal treatment to Canadian investors in the United States. Without such reciprocity it would have been politically impossible for the Trudeau government to take this approach; in the end, the actual result, i.e., no ISDS between Canada and the United States, may have been the only feasible solution, particularly for those in the government who felt that signing on to a deficient dispute settlement system, such as the one between the United States and Mexico in USMCA, would be an unfortunate precedent to be avoided. As discussed in the CPTPP/TPP section, CPTPP (2018) Chapter 9, as modified from the TPP, governs ISDS as between Mexico and Canada as well as among the other CPTPP parties.

One obvious question in the absence of the NAFTA-Chapter-11 ISDS mechanism that has governed investor-state disputes between Canada and the United States for over twenty-five years is: what happens if in the future disputes arise, particularly those between US investors in Canada and the federal or provincial governments? Will US investors simply proceed to bringing actions in Canadian courts, or will they seek the assistance of the US government or their members of Congress to pressure the Canadian government to resolve the cases in their favour? One may perhaps pardon my skepticism that political or other extra-judicial pressures will *not* be applied in such circumstances. Avoiding such political pressures was after all one of the principal reasons for designing the ISDS system almost forty years ago, by transferring investment disputes "from the political bilateral arena to a judicial forum especially charged with the settlement of mixed investor-State disputes. The dispute settlement process is depoliticized and subjected to objective legal criteria. The investor's home State is absolved of the inconvenience of having to represent its nation and is able to conduct its foreign policy free from the embarrassment and obstruction caused by investment disputes" (Schreuer 2007, 347). Here again, the unequal economic power of Canada and the United States suggests that in a serious political dispute between the US and Canada, Canada is unlikely to prevail.

Conversely, for the same reason this may not be a problem for the United States since it has the power to resist pressures from Canada and its officials and members of Congress are not likely to be embarrassed by doing so.

INVESTMENT PROTECTION AND FACILITATION UNDER CANADA-CHINA FIPA

Canada and China in recent years (but not in the past several years) have had significant reciprocal levels of investment, although the differing sizes of the economy suggest that it will remain unbalanced. In the ten-year period between 2003 and 2013, Canadian investment in China grew from US$838 million to US$4.9 billion, while Chinese investment in Canada increased from US$216 million to US$16.7 billion (Tremblay 2014). Awareness of such increases and the potential for further Chinese investment in Canada was undoubtedly a major driving force for the negotiations on the part of Canada (Gange 2019, 365). This remains a reasonable objective even if at the time of this writing relations between Canada and China have become increasingly strained as a result of Canada's arrest of Huawei official Meng Wanzhou on a US warrant and the resulting Chinese campaign of an escalating series of "insults and snubs" including a partial trade blockade.[24]

The Canada-China FIPA (signed in 2012 after twenty years of negotiations and in force 2014) is advanced by Chinese standards, particularly as it relates to ISDS. However, compared to CPTPP and CETA it is effectively "ISDS-lite" in that it fails to provide pre-establishment national treatment or any right of establishment (Canada-China FIPA 2012, Art. 6), in contrast with most other Canadian FIPAs. Post-investment national treatment *is* generally protected, unusual in prior Chinese BITs.[25] National treatment is also somewhat circumscribed, by limiting coverage for "expansion" of existing investments. Expansion rights apply only to "sectors not subject to a prior approval process under the relevant sectoral guidelines and applicable laws, regulations and rules in force at the time of expansion" (ibid., Art. 6.3). Interestingly, Canada extends MFN treatment to the pre-establishment phase of investment in Canada, while

China does not provide reciprocal benefits (ibid.,Art. 5). This occurs through the MFN clause because Canada has granted such rights in other FIPAS, although the applicability of Canada's Foreign Investment Review Act may significantly restrict the scope of this benefit (Gagne 2019, 368). The coverage of performance requirements, which is detailed in the invest-ment provisions of the three other agreements discussed in this chapter, is far more circumscribed in the Canada-China FIPA (2012, Art. 9), limited to reiterating the parties' WTO obligations under TRIMS. Canada-China FIPA (2012, Art. 10) also provides protection against direct or indirect expropriation similar to that in NAFTA (1994, Art. 1110).

Dispute resolution is provided in the Canada-China FIPA, similar to that found in the ISDS provisions of NAFTA (1994), Chapter 11, but not as advanced as in CPTPP. Among the departures is an exhaustion of local remedies clause, in which use of China's administrative reconsideration procedure must be exhausted (or four months elapsed) and any domestic court proceedings must have been withdrawn (Canada-China FIPA 2012, annex C.21). This does not seem as abnormal as it may have when the agreement was concluded. As noted in Part IV, above, in USMCA for most disputes between the United States and Mexico an exhaustion of local remedies condition precedent exists. (USMCA 2019, Arts 14.D.5:1(a) and 14.D.5:1(b)) Surprisingly, exhaustion rules do not apply on a reciprocal basis to Chinese investors seeking ISDS against Canada.

Among the differences compared to other FIPAS as well as CPTPP and other post-NAFTA Canadian ISDS provisions are reduced transparency requirements. While under CPTPP (2018, Art. 9.24), virtually all case documents are to be made publicly available, under Canada-China FIPA (2012, Art. 28) only the award is subject to that requirement; other documents and the hearings are to be made public only if the disputing contracting party decides that it is in the public interest to do so. In other words, should China decide that when it is the responding party in an investment dispute it wishes to keep the proceeding secret, it may do so. Given that this lack of a transparency requirement departs from most other Canadian FIRAS and investment chapters, its inclusion presumably reflects the unequal bargaining power of the parties despite the relatively advanced nature of the FIPA by Chinese standards. Presumably, in these negotiations China was also concerned with setting precedents for its future BITs.

Criticisms of Canada's decision to conclude the Canada-China FIPA were common at the time the agreement was concluded and made public. Some called it a "lopsided deal," while others have objected to the lack of transparency compared with other Canadian investment agreements (CBC News 2012). Some also expressed concerns with the departures from then-contemporary Canadian investment agreements as noted before.

Given the size differences and the relative ease of investment in Canada compared to China there may eventually be more Chinese investment in Canada than vice versa. Also, investing in Canada is relatively straight-forward even in the absence of any treaty obligations even with the FIRA and other restrictions designed to protect national security. In China in contrast there are many more substantive restrictions and bureaucratic hurdles for foreign investors from Canada or elsewhere. Thus, lack of national treatment for establishment is a much more serious potential defi-ciency for Canadian investors in China than for Chinese investors in Canada.

In my view, those who are critical of the Canada-China FIPA would do well to consider the unsuccessful US efforts over more than a decade to conclude a BIT with China. Even before the current trade war between the United States and China made the conclusion of a BIT impossible, progress on the discussions, which were launched in June 2008 (Congyan 2009), had stalled in 2016 after twenty-four rounds of negotiations. The challenges from the US side included restricted market access, performance require-ments, discrimination against foreign investors, and an opaque national security review mechanism (Gantz 2014; Gloudeman and Salidjanova 2016, 3). These, along with broader economic and political differences between the US and China, suggest than conclusion of an investment agreement is at best a remote possibility in the foreseeable future.

CONCLUDING OBSERVATIONS

Canada is in a consistently difficult position when its government finds it necessary to negotiate trade agreements with much larger economies such as the EU, United States, Japan, and China. The challenges of such negotiations, as reflected in the four agreements discussed in this chapter, suggest that the level of success that has been achieved is influenced by several key factors which may not be shared by large economies when they are negotiating investment and trade agreements. In my view they include the following:

1 Effective preparation, including a careful ordering of priorities,
   as with the USMCA negotiations, where ISDS may have been
   relinquished at least in part in favour of achieving other perceived
   benefits such as maintaining the Chapter 19 review of unfair trade

actions intact and the conclusion of a revised NAFTA (in contrast to its termination), both of which were rightly considered essential to Canada's national interest;

2 Strong awareness of which other negotiating parties are taking certain positions (as with the EU's insistence on the inclusion of ICM/appellate body mechanism in CETA, at least partially in the realization that it was in Canada's interest to see the CETA enter into force, even provisionally, as promptly as possible;

3 Using changes in the nature of the negotiations to secure strategic advantages that may not have been achievable before, as with the elimination of coverage of investment agreements and investment authorizations after the United States had withdrawn from TPP (in a context where the US absence may have made it easier for Canada to promote its views);

4 A willingness to take risks that other nations might not accept, as with the Canada-China FIPA's lack of full reciprocity (rejected by the United States), in the hope (perhaps naïve in retrospect) that early conclusion of a FIRA with China would give Canadian enterprises in China a competitive advantage and encourage desired Chinese investment in Canada; and

5 Continuing to seek traditional ad hoc arbitration provisions in agreements where Canada has the upper hand, such as the recent investment agreements with Moldova and Mongolia, as noted earlier, and more broadly as reflected in the 2021 Model FIPA.

Despite these considerations, the results of these negotiations for Canada are in my view mixed for Canada and for Canadian enterprises operating internationally. My assessment in each of the four agreements is as follows:

1 In CPTPP and TPP, the parties have adopted investment provisions that follow most closely Canada's earlier model FIPA and do not depart significantly from the 2021 Model FIPA. Whether the removal of coverage from TPP's Chapter 9 for investment authorizations and investment agreements is beneficial to Canada's interests will not be clear for some years. It is notable, however, that several of the parties, including Malaysia and Vietnam, could present problems for Canadian investors under some circumstances. In any event, most traditional investment disputes are encompassed by the CPTPP provisions.

2 It is impossible at this time of writing to assess the efficacy of the highly innovative ICM/appellate body mechanism originally incorporated in CETA, since the mechanism is not in force in any of the EU trade agreements. The procedural aspects of the ICM, including the choosing and compensation of arbitrators; compensation for part-time members who may be precluded from accepting other service as arbitrators or counsel; limiting costs and over-reaching by the appellate body; increasing the costs of ISDS through incorporation of an appellate mechanism; and avoiding an unacceptable bias or appearance of bias against private investors through the appointment of panel members, none of which are chosen by the investors and who are beholden to the EU and Canada for reappointment, raise difficult questions in practice, with the answers likely to be widely criticized by potential litigants and their counsel even if welcomed by the many opponents of ISDS. Those provisions in CETA will not go into effect unless and until they are unanimously approved by approximately thirty-seven national and regional EU parliaments, a process that could take many years (with five years having elapsed since the CETA's signing on 30 October 2016) or may never occur. Since the EU approach has not entered into force in any other agreement, any accurate assessments must necessarily await practical implementation experience.

3 The absence of ISDS or the ICM could be a significant disadvantage for some Canadian enterprises investing in certain EU nations where the rule of law, within the national court systems, particularly for treatment of foreigners, is suspect. This group includes Hungary, Poland, the Czech Republic, Slovakia, Slovenia, Bulgaria, Romania, Greece, Spain and Italy, none of which rank well on the World Justice Project's Open Governance Index.[26] Canada in the past has concluded half a dozen BITs with Eastern European EU members, which fortunately will remain in force for those countries until the CETA investment provisions become effective.[27] This discussion begs the broader question of whether investment arbitration in the EU will be blocked entirely by the Court of Justice of the European Union (CJEU). It is already prohibited in intra-EU disputes.[28]

4 I am aware that some of the other authors of chapters in this book are much more optimistic about the future of the ICM, both bilaterally and multilaterally, than I am at the present time. I hope that I am being unduly pessimistic, but I am also aware of ICSID deputy director Tony Parra's efforts in 2004 to float the idea of an

appellate body for investment disputes, which is an integral part
of the EU's ICM – a very wise idea in my view – which was quickly
rejected by all of ICSID's then members (Gantz 2006).

5 USMCA (2018) is the agreement where Canada has taken the
greatest medium- and longer-term risk, by agreeing with the Trump
administration to eliminate ISDS completely after a three-year
phase-out period for "legacy" investments under NAFTA. As the US
Trade Representatives' Industry Trade Advisory Committee Report
on Services (2018) observed, "The Committee rejects this view
[that ISDS is not needed for US investments in Canada because of
Canada's dependable court system]" in part because "U.S. investors
will have to rely on the U.S. government to enforce the Trade
Agreement's investment protections not subject to ISDS, which will
politicize the process, as well as prevent investors from 'being made
whole.'" The issue for Canada is the likelihood that disputes over
billions of dollars' worth of cross-border investment will have no
effective remedy except a political one. Without ISDS, if a major US
investor in Canada, who is also a major campaign contributor and
employer, becomes involved in an investment dispute with the
Canadian federal government or a provincial government, it likely
will become one of the major issues in US-Canada relations, with
the State Department, the US Embassy in Ottawa, and members
of the Senate and Congress pressuring Canada to accede to the
demands of the enterprise. In this respect, the United States is in
a much better position politically and economically to pursue its
demands than is Canada against the United States on behalf of
Canadian investors. On the positive side, Canada will no longer
have to defend against multiple investment claims brought on
behalf of US nationals. While Canadian investors in the United
States are somewhat better off because of the existence of the Fifth
Amendment to the US Constitution, the assumption that American
courts will always render a fair and just decision is as indicated
earlier potentially in doubt in at least a small number of cases. In
any event, reverting to customary international law principles of
espousal (Irwin Law 2019), formal or informal, puts investors at
risk. Either they will become the focus of bitter intergovernmental
disputes that could poison their futures, or the enterprise will be
unable to convince its home government to take up the matter, and
thus be left without out the more convenient and effective, if costly,
remedy of ISDS. Still, as noted earlier, without US willingness for

reciprocity it was likely politically impracticable for Canada to agree to any approach other than the one ultimately chosen.

6   With the Canada-China FIPA, it is difficult to see how Global Affairs Canada could have done much better in their negotiations. It convinced China to accept most of the provisions of its Model BIT and other contemporary investment agreements or chapters, even though, as noted earlier in some instances, Canada was forced to compromise. How the agreement's ISDS provisions will work in practice remains uncertain, since it appears that to date no cases have been brought on either side.

NOTES

1   All provisions of CETA except those relating to investment entered into provisional force 21 September 2017. For a discussion of the complex political issues surrounding CETA ratification, see Gantz (2017b).

2   The CPTPP, which incorporates almost all of the Trans-Pacific Partnership (TPP) Agreement countries (Australia, Brunei, Canada, Chile, Japan, Malaysia, Mexico, New Zealand, Peru, Singapore, the United States, and Vietnam), as of August 2019, entered into force for six parties on 30 December 2018 and 19 January 2019 for Vietnam. Parties Brunei, Chile, Malaysia, and Peru ratified CPTPP on 19 September 2021. A consolidated text is available at Government of Canada (2016).

3   CETA will not enter into full force unless and until it has been ratified by all EU member states (including several regional parliaments). The primary hang-up has been the investment provisions. See European Commission (2017); Gantz (2017b).

4   Canada-China FIPA entered into force 10 January 2014.

5   See Government of Canada (2021).

6   See Foodwatch (2021).

7   See, e.g., O'Callaghan, Bundock, and Grist (2018).

8   See Global Affairs Canada (2019).

9   An excellent source of information on ISDS is UNCTAD's Investment Policy Hub.

10   See Prokic and Gore (2021).

11   See also Canada-Mongolia FIPA (2016, sec. C).

12   The EU-Vietnam FTA (2019), which contains a similar ICM, entered into force 1 August 2020, but without the ICM. The EU Commission noted that the (separate) investment protection agreement "will enter into force after ratification by all EU member states." European Commission (n.d.). A

similar situation apparently exists with the separate investment
agreement – also incorporating the ICM.

13 A similar mechanism has been incorporated into Chapter 8 the
. EU-Vietnam FTA (2019). Here, the investment provisions have been
designated for a separate agreement, to be concluded and submitted to
the EU member parliaments later. The remaining text is subject to approval
by the EU Parliament. See European Commission (2019).

14 BITs are in force with Slovakia, the Czech Republic, Latvia, Croatia,
Romania, Hungary, and Poland.

15 None of the Eastern European EU members rank above 36 (Poland)
and several including Malta, Mauritius, Bulgaria, Romania, Hungary,
and Croatia, as well as Italy and Greece, rank below 50.

16 The European Parliament (2015) notes: "The EP recommendations
adopted in July 2015 called for ISDS to be abandoned and replaced by
a proper tribunal. The proposal issued by the Commission in September
2015, and then fine-tuned in November 2015 proposed the creation of
an investor-state court system."

17 See Gillespie (2016) who notes that at the "Top of Trump's wish list
is to renegotiate or 'terminate' NAFTA – the North American Free
Trade Agreement."

18 See Investment Treaty News (2019).

19 See *Loewen Group, Inc. and Raymond L. Loewen v. United States of
America* (2005), where what some believe was a gross miscarriage of justice
by the Mississippi state courts was effectively upheld by the Chapter 11
tribunal, with the tribunal noting, inter alia, "A reader following our account
of the injustices which were suffered by Loewen and Mr. Raymond Loewen in
the Courts of Mississippi could well be troubled to find that they emerge from
the present long and costly proceedings with no remedy at all" (para. 241).

20 Others would have received only administrative remedies and no
monetary damages.

21 "Chamber [of Commerce] members believe strongly that the USMCA outcomes on investment protection … must not be viewed as precedents for
future trade agreements" (World Trade Online 2018).

22 For example, "It was Canada's ultimate prize in the original free-trade deal
with the U.S.: a third-party arbitration system to judge whether punitive
duties were being applied unfairly" (Panetta 2018).

23 See CUSFTA (1987), USMCA (2019, Art. 32.6), and NAFTA (1994,
Annex 2106) – incorporating relevant provisions of the US-Canada FTA.

24 See Kirby (2019), detailing the diplomatic "spat" between Canada and
China and criticizing Prime Minister Trudeau's handling of it.

25 Canada-China FIPA (Art. 6) applies to the "expansion, management, conduct, operation and sale or other disposition" of investments.

26 See World Justice Project (2019). In the rankings, Poland, the Czech Republic, Spain, and Italy are ranked in the twenties; Slovakia and Greece in the thirties, and Bulgaria, Romania, and Hungary from 49 to 56.

27 Canada's Eastern European BITs include the Czech Republic, Hungary, Lithuania, Poland, Romania, and the Slovak Republic (SICE 2019).

28 See Risse and Oehm (2018).

REFERENCES

Canada-Chile FTA. 1996. Canada-Chile Free Trade Agreement Accessed 4 August 2019. https://www.international.gc.ca/trade-commerce/trade-agreements-accords-commerciaux/agr-acc/chile-chili/fta-ale/03g.aspx.

Canada-China FIPA. 2012. Agreement between the Government of Canada and the Government of the People's Republic of China for the Promotion and Reciprocal Protection of Investments. Accessed 4 August 2020. https://www.international.gc.ca/trade-commerce/trade-agreements-accords-commerciaux/agr-acc/china-chine/fipa-apie/index.aspx.

Canada-Moldova FIPA. 2018. Agreement between the Government of Canada and the Government of the Republic of Moldova for the Promotion and Protection of Investments. Accessed 24 November 2019. https://www.international.gc.ca/trade-commerce/trade-agreements-accords-commerciaux/agr-acc/moldova/fipa-apie/text-texte.aspx.

Canada-Mongolia FIPA. 2016. Agreement between Canada and Mongolia for the Promotion and Protection of Investments. Accessed 24 November 2019. https://www.international.gc.ca/trade-commerce/trade-agreements-accords-commerciaux/agr-acc/mongolia-mongolie/fipa-apie/text-texte/canada_mongolia-mongolie.aspx.

Canada-Peru Free Trade Agreement (FTA). 2009. Accessed 4 August 2019. https://www.international.gc.ca/trade-commerce/trade-agreements-accords-commerciaux/agr-acc/peru-perou/fta-ale/08.aspx.

CBC News. 2012. "5 Things to Know about the Canada-China Investment Treaty." 27 October. https://www.cbc.ca/news/politics/5-things-to-know-about-the-canada-china-investment-treaty-1.1183343.

CETA (Canada-European Union Comprehensive Economic and Trade Agreement). 2016. Accessed 4 August 2020. https://www.international.gc.ca/trade-commerce/trade-agreements-accords-commerciaux/agr-acc/ceta-aecg/text-texte/toc-tdm.aspx.

Clayton, Bilcon of Delaware Inc. v. Government of Canada. 2008. PCA Case No. 2009-04, Notice of Intent, 5 February 2008.

– 2019. PCA Case No. 2009-04, Award on Damages, 10 January 2019.

Congyan, Cai. 2009. "China-US BIT Negotiations and the Future of the Investment Treaty Regime: A Grand Bargain with Multilateral Implications." *Journal of International Economic Law* 12, no. 2: 457–506. https://doi.org/10.1093/jiel/jgp020.

CPTPP (Comprehensive and Progressive Agreement for Trans-Pacific Partnership). 2018. Accessed 4 August 2019. https://www.international.gc.ca/trade-commerce/trade-agreements-accords-commerciaux/agr-acc/cptpp-ptpgp/text-texte/index.aspx.

CUSFTA (Canada-United States Free Trade Agreement). 1987. Accessed 5 August 2019. https://www.international.gc.ca/trade-commerce/assets/pdfs/agreements-accords/cusfta-e.pdf.

CUSMA (Canada–United States–Mexico Agreement). 2018. Accessed 4 August 2020. https://www.international.gc.ca/trade-commerce/trade-agreements-accords-commerciaux/agr-acc/cusma-aceum/text-texte/toc-tdm.aspx.

de Mestral, Armand, and Robin Morgan. 2016. "Does Canadian Law Provide Remedies Equivalent to NAFTA Chapter 11 Arbitration?" Investor-State Arbitration Series, Paper No. 4, Center for International Governance and Innovation, Waterloo, ON. https://www.cigionline.org/publications/does-canadian-law-provide-remedies-equivalent-nafta-chapter-11-arbitration.

EU-Vietnam Free Trade Agreement. 2019. Accessed 4 August 2019. http://trade.ec.europa.eu/doclib/press/index.cfm?id=1437.

European Commission. n.d. Countries and Regions: Vietnam. Accessed 22 July 2021. https://ec.europa.eu/trade/policy/countries-and-regions/countries/vietnam/.

– 2015. "Transatlantic Trade and Investment Partnership: Trade in Services, Investment and E-Commerce, Chapter II-Investment." Accessed 4 August 2019. http://trade.ec.europa.eu/doclib/docs/2015/september/tradoc_153807.pdf.

– 2017. "EU-Canada trade agreement enters into force." Accessed 4 August 2019. https://ec.europa.eu/commission/presscorner/detail/en/IP_17_3121.

– 2019. "EU-Viet Nam free trade agreement - Joint press statement by Commissioner Malmström and Minister Tran Tuan Anh." Accessed 4 August 2019. http://trade.ec.europa.eu/doclib/press/index.cfm?id=2041.

European Parliament. 2015. "The Negotiations on Investment Court System for TTIP." Accessed 4 August 2019. http://www.europarl.europa.eu/

legislative-train/theme-reasonable-and-balanced-trade-agreement-with-the-united-states/file-ttip-investment-court-system-for-ttip.

Foodwatch. 2021. "12 EU Member States Can Still Stop CETA." 16 March. Accessed 22 July 2021. https://www.foodwatch.org/en/campaigns/ceta/12-eu-member-states-can-still-stop-ceta/.

Gagne, Gilbert. 2019. "The Canadian Policy on the Protection of Foreign Investment and the Canada-China Bilateral Investment Treaty." *Beijing Law Review* 10, no. 3: 361–77. http://doi.org/10.4236/blr.2019.103021.

Gantz, David A. 2006. "An Appellate Mechanism for Review of Arbitral Decisions in Investor-State Disputes: Prospects and Challenges." *Vanderbilt J. Transnat'l L.* 39, no. 1: 39

– 2014. "Challenges for the United States in Negotiating a BIT with China: Reconciling Reciprocal Investment Protection with Policy Concerns." *Arizona Journal of International & Comparative Law* 31, no. 2: 203–50.

– 2017a. "Increasing Host State Regulatory Flexibility in Defending Investor-State Disputes: The Evolution of US Approaches from NAFTA to the TPP." *The International Lawyer* 50, no. 2: 231–60.

– 2017b. "The CETA Ratification Saga: The Demise of ISDS in EU Trade Agreements?" *Loyola University Chicago Law Journal* 49: 361–85. http://dx.doi.org/10.2139/ssrn.2974439.

Gillespie, Patrick. 2016. "NAFTA: What it is, and Why Trump Hates." *CNN Business*, 15 November. https://money.cnn.com/2016/11/15/news/economy/trump-what-is-nafta/index.html.

Global Affairs Canada. 2019. "NAFTA – Chapter 11 – Investment: Cases Filed against the Government of Canada." Accessed 5 August 2019 and 22 July 2021. https://www.international.gc.ca/trade-agreements-accords-commerciaux/topics-domaines/disp-diff/gov.aspx.

Gloudeman, Lauren, and Nargiza Salidjanova. 2016. "Policy Considerations for Negotiating a U.S.-China Bilateral Investment Treaty." Accessed 5 August 2019. https://www.uscc.gov/sites/default/files/Research/Staff%20Report_Policy%20Considerations%20for%20Negotiating%20a%20U.S.-China%20Bilateral%20Investment%20Treaty080116.pdf.

Government of Canada. 2016. "Consolidated TPP Text." Accessed 4 August 2019. https://www.international.gc.ca/trade-commerce/trade-agreements-accords-commerciaux/agr-acc/tpp-ptp/text-texte/toc-tdm.aspx.

– 2018a. "How to read the Comprehensive and Progressive Agreement for Trans-Pacific Partnership (CPTPP)." Accessed 4 August 2019. https://www.international.gc.ca/trade-commerce/trade-agreements-accords-commerciaux/agr-acc/cptpp-ptpgp/chapter_summaries-sommaires_chapitres.aspx.

– 2018b. "What Does the CPTPP Mean for Investment?" Accessed 4 August 2019. https://www.international.gc.ca/trade-commerce/trade-agreements-accords-commerciaux/agr-acc/cptpp-ptpgp/sectors-secteurs/investment-investissement.aspx.

– 2019. "About the Canada-Chile Free Trade Agreement (CCFTA)." Accessed 4 August 2019. https://www.international.gc.ca/trade-commerce/trade-agreements-accords-commerciaux/agr-acc/chile-chili/about_a-propos.aspx.

– 2020. "Map of Canada's Trade and Investment Agreement." Accessed 8 August 2020. https://www.international.gc.ca/trade-commerce/trade-agreements-accords-commerciaux/agr-acc/index.aspx.

– 2021. "Model FIPA, Section E: Investor-State Dispute Settlement." Accessed 22 July 2021. https://www.international.gc.ca/trade-commerce/trade-agreements-accords-commerciaux/agr-acc/fipa-apie/2021_model_fipa-2021_modele_apie.aspx.

IMF (International Monetary Fund). 2019. "World Economic Outlook Database." Accessed 4 August 2019. https://www.imf.org/external/pubs/ft/weo/2019/01/weodata/index.aspx.

Industry Trade Advisory Committee. 2018. "Report of the Industry Trade Advisory Committee on Services." Accessed 12 September 2019. https://ustr.gov/trade-agreements/free-trade-agreements/united-states-mexico-canada-agreement/advisory-committee.

Investment Treaty News. 2019. "US Officials Raise Concerns Over Proposed MIC in Talks with the United Kingdom, Documents Say." 17 December. Accessed 22 July 2021. https://www.iisd.org/itn/en/2019/12/17/u-s-officials-raise-concerns-over-proposed-mic-in-talks-with-the-united-kingdom-documents-say/.

Irwin Law. 2019. "Espousal of Claim." Accessed 12 September 2019. https://irwinlaw.com/cold/espousal-of-claim/.

Italaw. 2004. "Agreement between Canada and _____ for the Promotion and Protection of Investments, 2004." Accessed 12 September 2019. https://www.italaw.com/documents/Canadian2004-FIPA-model-en.pdf.

Kirby, Jason. 2019. "Trudeau Muddles His Message in Huawei Spat with China." *Financial Times*, 4 August. https://www.ft.com/content/43d19dba-c776-11e9-af46-b09e8bfe60c0.

Lester, Simon. 2018. "Brady-Lighthizer ISDS Exchange." *International Economic Law and Policy Blog*, 21 March 2018. https://worldtradelaw.typepad.com/ielpblog/2018/03/brady-lighthizer-isds-exchange.html.

Loewen Group, Inc. and Raymond L. Loewen v. United States of America. 2005. ICSID Case No. ARB(AFT)/98/3, https://www.italaw.com/cases/632.

Munson, James. 2019. "Canada Told to Pay $7 million in NAFTA Quarry
    Case." *Bloomberg Law*, 26 February 2019. https://news.bloomberglaw.com/
    international-trade/canada-told-to-pay-7-million-in-nafta-quarry-case-2.
NAFTA (North American Free Trade Agreement). 1994. Accessed 4Irwin Law.
    2019. "EspousalAugustIrwin Law. 2019. "Espousal2019. https://www.
    international.gc.ca/trade-commerce/trade-agreements-accords-commerciaux/
    agr-acc/nafta-alena/fta-ale/index.aspx.
O'Callaghan, Kevin, Emilie Bundock, and Madison Grist. 2018. "USMCA
    Aims to Protect the Interests of Indigenous Peoples in International Trade,"
    Fasken Indigenous Bulletin, 22 October. Accessed 10 February 2022. https://
    www.fasken.com/en/ knowledge/2018/10/van-usmca-aimsto-protect-the-
    interests-of-indigenouspeoples-in-international-trade.
Panetta, Alexander. 2018. "NAFTA's Third-Party Arbitration System was
    Canada's Big Prize ... Is It Worth Fighting For?" *The Star,* 23 August. https://
    www.thestar.com/news/canada/2017/08/23/naftas-chapter-19-was-canadas-
    big-prize-but-is-it-still-worth-fighting-for.html.
Prokic, Dina, and Kiran Nasir Gore. 2021. "Release of the New Canadian
    FIPA Model: Reflections on International Investment and ISDS at
    CrossRoads." *Kluwer Arbitration Blog*, 31 May. Accessed 22 July 2021.
    http://arbitrationblog.kluwerarbitration.com/2021/05/31/release-of-the-
    new-canadian-fipa-model-reflections-on-international-investment-and-isds-
    at-a-crossroads/.
Risse, Joerg, and Max Oehm. 2018. "European Court of Justice Stops
    Investment Arbitration in Intra-EU Disputes." 7 March. Accessed
    27 July 2021. https://globalarbitrationnews.com/ecj-stops-investment-
    arbitration-intra-eu/.
Schreuer, Christoph. 2007. "Investment Protection and International
    Relations." In *The Law of International Relations: Liber Amicorum
    Hanspeter Neuhold,* edited by August Reinisch and Ursula Kriebaum,
    345-58. The Hague: Elven International Publishing.
SICE. 2019. "Information on Canada." Accessed 12 September 2019. http://
    www.sice.oas.org/ctyindex/CAN/CANBITS_e.asp.
Titi, Catharine. 2013. "The Evolving BIT: A Commentary on Canada's Model
    Agreement." Accessed 10 September 2019. https://www.iisd.org/itn/2013/
    06/26/the-evolving-bit-a-commentary-on-canadas-model-agreement/.
TPP (Trans-Pacific Partnership Agreement). 2016. Accessed 4 August 2019.
    https://ustr.gov/trade-agreements/free-trade-agreements/trans-pacific-
    partnership/tpp-full-text.
Trading Economics. 2017. "Canadian Exports by Country." Accessed
    4 August 2019. https://tradingeconomics.com/canada/exports-by-country.

Transparency International. 2018. "Corruptions Perception Index 2018."
 Accessed 4 August 2019. https://www.transparency.org/cpi2018.

Tremblay, Pascal. 2014. "Canada-China: Foreign Investment Promotion and
 Protection Agreement Comes into Force." *HillNotes,* 30 September 2014.
 https://hillnotes.ca/2014/09/30/canada-china-foreign-investment-
 promotion-and-protection-agreement-comes-into-force/.

UNCTAD (United Nations Conference on Trade and Development). 2018.
 "Investment Policy Hub: Canada." Accessed 4 August 2019. https://
 investmentpolicy.unctad.org/international-investment-agreements/
 countries/35/canada?type=bits.

UNICTRAL (United Nations Commission on International Trade Law). 2018.
 "Working Group III." Accessed 4 August 2019. http://www.uncitral.org/
 uncitral/en/commission/working_groups/3Investor_State.html.

US Department of State. 2012. "United States Concludes Review of Model
 Bilateral Investment Treaty." Accessed 10 September 2019. https://2009-
 2017.state.gov/r/pa/prs/ps/2012/04/188198.htm.

US-Japan Trade Agreement. 2019. Accessed 7 August 2020. https://ustr.gov/
 countries-regions/japan-korea-apec/japan/us-japan-trade-agreement-
 negotiations/us-japan-trade-agreement-text.

USMCA (United States–Mexico–Canada Agreement). 2019 (2018). Agreement
 between the United States of America, the United Mexican States, and
 Canada. Accessed 9 August 2020. https://ustr.gov/trade-agreements/
 free-trade-agreements/united-states-mexico-canada-agreement/
 agreement-between.

World Justice Project. 2019. "Global Scores and Rankings." Accessed
 12 September 2019. https://worldjusticeproject.org/our-work/wjp-rule-
 law-index/wjp-open-government-index/global-scores-rankings.

World Trade Online. 2018. "Chamber: Elements of USMCA Should not be
 Seen as Model for New FTAS." *World Trade Online,* 8 November 2018.
 https://insidetrade.com/inside-us-trade/chamber-elements-usmca-should-
 not-be-seen-model-new-ftas.

Yackee, Jason. 2015. "New Trade Agreements Don't Need ISDS." Accessed
 4 August 2019. https://www.cato-unbound.org/2015/05/19/jason-yackee/
 new-trade-agreements-dont-need-isds.

10

Innovations in CETA's Investment Chapter: Will Reform Enhance Legitimacy?

Elizabeth Whitsitt

INTRODUCTION

Investor-state dispute settlement (ISDS) has been a contentious element of international investment law for decades. Debates surrounding ISDS often centre around two broad issues: the first has to do with whether a foreign investor should even have the right to seek compensation for an alleged violation of investment treaty obligations. For some, this "private right of action" raises concerns that ISDS empowers multinational corporations to the detriment of less economically developed states (Sornarajah 2016). Others contend that ISDS is an essential feature of the international investment law regime because it ensures that foreign investors are not left vulnerable to the political interests of home and host states (ECIPE 2014). ISDS has been at the centre of a second set of concerns about the institutions and rules underpinning international investment law disputes. Such concerns include skepticism about the transparency of arbitral proceedings, the legal correctness of arbitral decisions, the consistency of arbitral decisions, and conflicts of interest (Osmanski 2018).

A movement to reform ISDS considering these (and other) concerns took shape in the European Union (EU) in 2014, when it was negotiating the Transatlantic Trade and Investment Partnership (TTIP) with the United States (US) (Titi 2016). In 2014, the EU Commission (the Commission) launched a public consultation process on ISDS and received over 150,000 submissions (EC 2015). Responses were submitted by individuals, nongovernmental organizations (NGOs), trade unions, government organizations, consumers, business associations, companies, and academics. According to the Commission, most responses were collective submissions coordinated by several NGOs in online platforms with pre-defined answers that made it possible to submit significant number of replies in a limited time (ibid.). Nonetheless, the Commission considered that its consultation process engaged a wide diversity of interests within the EU (ibid.). According to the Commission, consultation submissions on ISDS generated divergent views, with a large majority of NGOs expressing opposition to ISDS while business associations and companies supported ISDS in the TTIP (ibid.).

The EU Commission subsequently proposed the establishment of an investment court system (ICS) (EU 2015).[1] So far, Canada and Vietnam have accepted the creation of a permanent investment court in recent treaties concluded with the EU. For Canada, this institutional shift comes at a time of transition in its investment protection policies. After renegotiating the North American Free Trade Agreement (NAFTA) 1994, American and Canadian investors will no longer have access to ISDS as a way of redressing their rights. For some, who have been skeptical of NAFTA's Chapter 11 dispute settlement mechanism, this change comes as a welcome development (Canadian Centre for Policy Alternatives 2021). Moreover, Canada's public consultations considering efforts to modernize its model foreign investment protection agreement (FIPA) have illuminated concerns with ISDS (Canadian Government 2019). As in the EU, the Canadian government reports a divide between NGOs and the civil society who are critical of ISDS and business/investor groups who support the mechanism (ibid.). Canada reports criticisms similar to those about which we so often hear: ISDS gives investors a private right of action to challenge government measures, it lacks transparency, leads to legal and ethical conflicts, and results in decisions that are incorrect and inconsistent (ibid.).

Proponents of ICS believe that this institutional innovation will solve the legitimacy problems that have plagued traditional ad hoc investor-state arbitration. Advocates of ICS envisage, for example, that introduction of an appeal mechanism similar to the World Trade Organization's (WTO) appellate body will enhance predictability of treaty interpretation, improve consistency in decisions, and ultimately contribute to greater legitimacy of ISDS. In so doing, some suggest that ICS will do a better job of attaining the ever elusive "balance" between investor protection and sovereign interests. But will this actually happen? Will the investment court established pursuant to the Canada-EU Comprehensive Economic and Trade Agreement (CETA) 2016 really resolve ISDS legitimacy concerns?

The answer to those questions is necessarily speculative, given that ratification of CETA is pending and its implementation is still in early stages.

CETA entered into force provisionally on 21 September 2017 (Global Affairs Canada 2017). As a result, although the vast majority of its provisions, including those pertaining to procurement, tariff reductions and elimination, and trade and the environment, are applicable between the parties (CETA 2016, Art. 30.7(3)), most of the investment provisions in CETA Chapter 8, including those pertaining to the resolution of disputes between investors and states, will not come into force until CETA is ratified by all EU member states. CETA's investment chapter, including its proposed ICS mechanism, has been controversial within the EU, particularly in Belgium and Cyprus (Charalambous 2020; Hazou 2020; McKenna 2016).

Nonetheless, some preliminary observations about CETA's ICS may help to inform future legitimacy discourse in the context of CETA and international investment law more generally. Since 2017, the United Nations Commission on International Trade Law (UNCITRAL 2017a, 42–7) has been considering reform of ISDS. This work is being carried out by Working Group III (WG III). In the fall of 2019 and early 2020, WG III discussed a variety of possible reform options, including the development of an appellate and/or standing court mechanism, in order to address concerns raised regarding ISDS. In light of ongoing conversations about ISDS reform, consideration of CETA's ICS mechanism, particularly as it relates to legitimacy, is timely.

This chapter explores this theme by first considering what legitimacy means in the context of international dispute settlement. This portion of the chapter examines legitimacy as understood in normative and sociological terms. Having outlined some of the key theories on the concept of legitimacy, the third section takes up the foundational question of this chapter –whether CETA's ICS mechanism will alleviate legitimacy concerns so often launched against ISDS. This section pays particular attention the various features of CETA's ICS mechanism and assesses whether those provisions do indeed address ISDS legitimacy concerns. This section also examines CETA's underlying normative framework, and the final section provides some concluding remarks.

DISENTANGLING LEGITIMACY
AND APPLYING IT TO ISDS

Legitimacy plays a crucial role in helping us to understand and evaluate systems of law. We often hear it mentioned in concert with other foundational concepts such as the rule of law, justice, and equality. Yet, the notion of legitimacy is notoriously difficult to define. It means different things to different people across a spectrum of disciplines. In broad terms, legitimacy presents us with a theoretical frame of reference that seeks to explain why we are compelled to follow the mandates of those in authoritative positions and who is a *proper* authority in any given circumstance (Buchanan and Keohane 2006). Applied to international adjudicative bodies, the concept of legitimacy seeks to explain why different subjects (e.g. states, foreign investors, and NGOs) participate in, abide by, support, and/or disparage the processes and decisions of such bodies. Those questions may be examined by thinking about legitimacy in both normative and sociological terms.

Normative Legitimacy

The normative legitimacy of authority – or the "right to rule" – can be examined with reference to standards established in a variety of disciplines. Normative legitimacy of international adjudicative bodies may be assessed by considering legal principles such as consent, the procedural fairness guarantees afforded participants in the adjudicative process, and whether an institution is effective at achieving its objectives (Grossman 2013; Shany 2014). Given CETA's nascent ICS mechanism, the following discussion focuses on consent and procedural fairness.

Those who have studied the normative legitimacy of international adjudicative bodies with reference to state consent focus on the source of authority. In such instances the authority of an international adjudicative body is justified if states consent to that authority (Grossman 2013; Meyer and Sanklecha 2009). Where states provide such consent, the international adjudicative body has legitimate authority to issue judgments, decisions, opinions, or orders that are binding on those states or litigants to which such documents are addressed (Bodansky 1999). By the same token, the legitimacy of international adjudicative bodies may be lessened if they make decisions that fall outside the scope of authority granted (i.e. consented) to them by states. For example, Art. 42 of the Convention on the Settlement of Investment Disputes between States and Nationals of Other States outlines the laws that an arbitral tribunal under the International Centre for Settlement of Investment Disputes (ICSID) is required to apply in any given dispute. First and foremost, ICSID tribunals are required to apply the rules agreed to by the parties to the dispute (i.e. investment treaty). Where those rules to do not address a particular issue, ICSID tribunals must apply the law of the respondent state to the dispute and any applicable rules of international law.[2] If a tribunal were to deviate from this directive in coming to a decision, its normative legitimacy could be called into question.

An international adjudicative body's normative legitimacy may also be established by considering the fairness and adequacy of the process that leads to a judgment, decision, opinion, or order (Grossman 2013). Processes that help to establish normative legitimacy include those which ensure that disputing parties (e.g. investors and states) are provided with equal opportunity to be heard and that adjudicators make decisions in an unbiased manner, on the basis of the evidence and argument provided by the parties to a dispute. In short, disputing parties will be more likely to comply with decisions reached through fair and impartial proceedings and by fair and impartial adjudicators (ibid.). As I highlight in later sections of this chapter, some have criticized the legitimacy of ad hoc investment arbitration on procedural fairness grounds. Those criticisms have prompted some states, including Canada and the EU, to make changes to the ISDS mechanism in their investment treaties. The implications of these changes are covered in later discussions of this chapter.

Sociological Legitimacy

In contrast to normative legitimacy, which is evaluated with reference to pre-determined benchmarks, sociological legitimacy is grounded in *perceptions* or *beliefs* that an institution has the right to rule or that one should comply with a system of law (Buchanan and Keohane 2006). Sociological legitimacy is achieved where a decision from an international adjudicative body (or any other institution for that matter) secures acceptance from the relevant players within the international community (e.g. states, individuals, institutions). As a result, it is possible that an institution may enjoy a degree of support from some constituencies and not others (Grossman 2009; Weiler 2001). Moreover, such support may wax and wane throughout the lifespan of the institution (Shany 2014).

Thomas Franck (1995) outlined a series of factors to consider when thinking about the perceived legitimacy of international law more generally. According to Franck, without clarity and consistency of both the rules of law and their application, those governed by those rules lose their ability and desire to adhere to such rules, which can undermine the legitimacy of any legal order. Conversely, a belief in the law's legitimacy re-enforces the perception of its fairness and encourages compliance (ibid.). According to Franck, each rule is likely to be perceived as more or less legitimate as evidenced by certain indicia, including: (i) determinacy, (ii) symbolic validation, (iii) coherence, and (iv) adherence (ibid., 30–46).

More recent scholarship suggests that other factors may impact perceptions of justified authority in the context of international adjudicative bodies (Grossman 2009). According to Grossman, actors within the global order are unlikely to *view/perceive* an adjudicative body as legitimate unless it is governed by rules that ensure fair process, including a commitment to independent and impartial adjudicators. International adjudicative bodies also have greater likelihood of being perceived as legitimate if an international actor perceives that the underlying normative regime is consistent with its view of what the law is or should be. Said another way, the underlying normative regime must have "currency" for an international actor (ibid., 143). Currency is not a static idea; it is something that can evolve (as do normative regimes) over time. According to Grossman, the currency of an underlying regime is impacted by an international actor's interests and values and the legal soundness of an adjudicative body's decisions. Finally, Grossman points out that transparency has direct and indirect consequences for the legitimacy of international adjudicative bodies. Indirectly, greater transparency leads to more information about the adjudicative process, which permits international actors the opportunity to understand and evaluate how such a body functions and makes decisions. More directly, increased transparency facilitates accountability by providing global actors the information to evaluate their own relationship with the international adjudicative body, the participants within the adjudicative process, and the governments that consent to such processes (ibid.).

Franck and Grossman agree that the underlying normative framework of a regime as well as the quality of an international adjudicative body's decisions interpreting and applying those norms impact perceptions about the legitimacy of that body. But Grossman advocates for a conception of legitimacy that considers whether international adjudicative bodies provide stakeholders (beyond the litigants in any given case) participatory rights (Grossman 2013). The crux of her claim relies on democratic theory. In short, Grossman argues that evaluating the legitimating the power of international adjudicative bodies in democratic terms is necessary given the fact that such bodies make policy decisions that affect a variety of stakeholders within the world order. The authority of international adjudicative bodies is, therefore, strengthened when processes are transparent and facilitate relevant stakeholder participation (ibid.).

Here, Grossman's work intermingles with notions of normative legitimacy. Recall that procedural fairness is also one of the traditional yardsticks used to evaluate the legitimacy of international institutions. One could, therefore, argue that transparency and expanded participatory

rights are features that objectively demonstrate the legitimacy of an international adjudicative body regardless of whether a decision from such a
body secures acceptance from various constituencies within the world
order. It is true that in making this observation some might accuse me of
proverbially splitting hairs. After all, it stands to reason that increased
transparency and participatory rights would also positively impact
perceptions about the legitimacy of an international adjudicative body – at
least in the eyes of some constituencies. My primary point is that it is
difficult to disentangle normative and sociological forms of legitimacy
from each other when talking about the legitimacy of international
institutions, including international adjudicative bodies. As a result, it is
difficult and potentially obfuscating to make conclusive statements such
as whether one particular aspect in the operation of international
adjudication by itself creates legitimacy and whether one form of
international dispute settlement is more legitimate than another.
Imprecision in the way in which we speak about legitimacy also impacts
debates surrounding various international institutions, including those
within the international investment law regime (Bjorklund 2018).

DOES CETA ADDRESS ISDS
LEGITIMACY CONCERNS?

With that in mind, the normative and the sociological constructions of
legitimacy are still helpful lenses through which to assess CETA's ICS mechanism, provided that the overlaps are acknowledged, and legitimacy typologies
are not slavishly applied as mutually exclusive. The legitimacy (or illegitimacy) of investment treaty arbitration, and the institutions that facilitate
such proceedings, have garnered considerable attention since the early 2000s
(e.g. Balchin et al. 2010; Franck 2005; Sornarajah 2008). Debates about
the normative legitimacy of ISDS centre around private-public dynamic of
ISDS. Tensions between the private rights of investors, state consent,
sovereign interests, procedural fairness versus public interest concerns,
potential for regulatory chill, identity of decision makers, and the substantive
correctness of decisions generate concerns about the normative legitimacy
of ISDS (Bjorklund 2018; Behn 2015; Brunné and Toope 2010; Grossman
2013; Roberts 2013). From a sociological perspective investor-state
arbitration raises legitimacy concerns because investment treaties and the
substantive obligations therein are indeterminate, inconsistent, and therefore
lead to unpredictable results (Bjorklund 2018; Franck 2005). In the following discussion, I consider whether CETA addresses these concerns by

assessing a number of key features of its investment chapter: standing tribunals, committees responsible for investment policy governance among other things, transparency rules, and clarified drafting of CETA's normative framework (fair and equitable treatment [FET] and exceptions).

Standing Dispute and Appellate Tribunals

One of the most significant procedural concerns encapsulated by both normative and sociological ideals of legitimacy, pertains to those who resolve investment treaty disputes and the host of concerns raised about the system of party appointments as well as conflicts of interest or ethical conflicts (Bjorklund 2018; Eberhardt and Olivet 2012). These concerns have found voice as disputing parties have launched an increasing number of challenges to arbitral appointments across various arbitral institutions (Vasani and Palmer 2015). Concerns about the independence and impartiality of arbitrators were also specifically raised during the EU TTIP consultations in 2014 (EC 2015). Similar sentiments were also expressed on the heels of CETA's provisional implementation in 2018 when Canada launched public consultations launched as part of its effort to modernize its model FIPA (Canadian Government 2019).

The investment chapter of CETA (2016, Art. 8.27(1)) establishes a standing tribunal of first instance whose fifteen members are appointed by a joint committee (discussed in greater detail further). Nationality of the appointed members is evenly split into thirds between nationals of the EU, Canada, and third countries (ibid.).[3] Members of the tribunal are appointed for a five-year term, renewable once. Initially seven members' terms will be extended to six years, presumably to help stagger the time-frames for renewal and appointment to avoid complete replacement of the tribunal at one time and ensure continuity of the tribunal's functioning (ibid., Arts 8.27(2), 8.27(5)). People appointed as members of this tribunal must possess qualifications required of judicial appointments in each party's respective jurisdiction and have expertise in public international law. Expertise in international trade and international investment law is desirable (ibid., Art. 8.27(4)).[4]

An appointed president of CETA's first instance tribunal, who is neither a national of either Canada nor an EU member state, is responsible for deciding which members hear which disputes.[5] As a general rule, disputes will be heard by a division of three tribunal members chosen to hear cases on a rotating basis to ensure all tribunal members have equal opportunity to serve.[6] The division of three chosen to hear a case will comprise a

Canadian national, an EU national, and chaired by a member who is the national of a third country (Art. 8.27(6)).[7]

Similar to the continued evolution occurring in ad hoc arbitral institution rules directed at enhancing principles of fair process,[8] CETA (2016, Art. 8.30) requires that members of the tribunal be independent and impartial. Under CETA, tribunal members must not receive instruction from any organization or government regarding matters related to the dispute (ibid.) People so appointed are also not to be affiliated with any government, although remuneration alone is not enough to establish a government "affiliation" and thereby preclude a person from being appointed to the tribunal (ibid., Art. 8.30, fn 8). Additionally, CETA precludes tribunal members from considering *any* disputes that would create a *direct* or *indirect* conflict of interest and makes compliance with the International Bar Association Guidelines on Conflicts of Interest in International Arbitration (IBA Guidelines) mandatory or any supplemental rules adopted by CETA's Committee on Services and Investment (CSI) (ibid., Arts 8.30, 8.44(2)).[9]

The IBA Guidelines outline a set of general principles to which arbitrators should adhere in order to avoid a material conflict of interest. In addition, they outline a particularized list of circumstances in which: (i) an arbitrator cannot act (non-waivable red list); (ii) an arbitrator may act subject to disclosure and consent requirements (waivable red list); (iii) an arbitrator can act subject to disclosure requirements and as long as parties do not object (orange list); and (iv) an arbitrator is not subject to disclosure requirements (green list). Inclusion of the IBA Guidelines as compulsory is a notable development under CETA as it reflects the widespread support the guidelines have received in the international arbitration community. Even more importantly, the inclusion of these guidelines along with the criteria for appointment to CETA's dispute settlement mechanism provides objective evidence that investment disputes under CETA will be resolved by adjudicators who are committed to principles of independence and impartiality. These procedural modifications and appointment requirements facilitate the normative legitimacy of CETA's ICS mechanism as they help to ensure that disputes are resolved in accordance with fair processes.

The foregoing requirements also apply to members appointed to CETA's appellate tribunal (CETA 2016, Art. 8.28(4)).[10] The appellate tribunal contemplated in CETA is somewhat different than that which was first proposed by the EU and then subsequently established in the EU-Vietnam Bilateral Investment Treaty (BIT).[11] CETA's appellate tribunal will comprise six members appointed by the CETA Joint Committee with a view to principles of diversity and gender equality (CETA 2016, Art. 2(1); CETA Joint Committee 2021). Two members will be selected from nominations proposed by Canada, two from nominations proposed by the EU, and two from nominations by Canada or the EU (CETA 2016, Art. 2(1)(a–c)). In the latter instance, the nominees cannot be nationals of either Canada or an EU member state (ibid, Art. 2(1)(c)). Members are appointed for a nine-year non-renewable term (ibid., Art. 2(3)). However, three of the first six members appointed to the appellate tribunal will serve for a more limited six-year term (ibid., Art. 2(3)). Appeals will be heard by three members, a member from each of the three nominating criteria outlined in above represented (ibid., Art. 2(5)). A disputing party may appeal a decision of the tribunal of first instance within ninety days of the issuance of an award. In so doing, the disputing party is obliged to refrain from pursuing other appellate processes or remedies such as annulment or revision (ibid., Art. 8.28(9)(a–b)). Most importantly for our purposes, the appellate tribunal has powers to uphold, modify, or reverse an award where the award is based on errors in the application or interpretation of applicable law or manifest errors in the appreciation of the facts, including the appreciation of relevant domestic law. Appeal proceedings can also be grounded on the same basis as those for annulment outlined in Art. 52(1) of the ICSID Convention, but only insofar as they are not covered by paragraphs (a) and (b) of CETA Art. 8.28 (ibid., Art. 8.28(2)). Where the appellate tribunal upholds the appeal in whole or in part, it must specify how it has modified or reversed the relevant findings and conclusions of the tribunal (CETA 2016, Art. 3(2); CETA Joint Committee 2021).

Perhaps the most significant institutional change introduced in CETA is the shift from ad hoc investment treaty arbitration to a dispute settlement process that is more reminiscent of a court process in which disputes are resolved by adjudicators who are appointed to standing rosters for fixed terms. In ad hoc investment treaty arbitration, where disputes are usually heard by a three-member arbitral tribunal, each of the disputing parties appoint one arbitrator and agree on a third arbitral appointment. Supplemental procedures exist if there are delays constituting the arbitral tribunal or if the parties cannot agree on the appointment of a third member. However, one would expect disputing parties (foreign investors and states) in an investment treaty arbitration to take full advantage of the strategic opportunity they have to choose an arbitrator they feel is best positioned to understand their perspective for that particular dispute. The same strategic opportunity is not part of the CETA's ICS model. Instead, delegates of Canada and the EU choose adjudicators for the first instance and appellate tribunals to standing rosters prior to the commencement of a dispute. Further, selection of each adjudicator to hear a particular dispute is delegated to the tribunal president and subject to nationality requirements as well as a commitment to ensure that all those appointed to the roster have an equal opportunity to hear cases. While the process of selection for hearing appeals has yet to be firmly outlined, there is a requirement that three-member appeals tribunals be selected randomly.

Whether stakeholders perceive the change from ad hoc to an ICS model in CETA as an increase or decrease in the legitimacy of ISDS will depend upon their respective interests and perspectives represented. One hesitates to say too much without having undertaken a more rigorous sociological research methodology (e.g. survey) of the various constituencies that may be impacted by CETA's ISDS mechanism. Nonetheless, it seems plausible to expect that the question will most likely be debated at least until we have more experience and jurisprudence relating to CETA.

For those who have expressed legitimacy concerns about the procedural aspects of investment treaty arbitration, establishment of the earlier-described process may be perceived as a welcome development that more firmly cements the authority of adjudicators to resolve disputes under CETA's investment chapter. Further, fixed-term tenure adjudicative appointments, as well as CETA's appointment requirements and the adoption of the IBA code of conduct, all help distance adjudicators from political constraints and pressure, thus mitigating some perceptions that CETA's dispute settlement mechanism will only serve the interests of its consenting states.

For others these developments may be concerning and diminish sociological legitimacy. Foreign investors and those who represent them may perceive CETA's standing roster and appointment process as a modification that shifts power to CETA's state parties. Where ad hoc investment treaty arbitration provides both claimant investors and a respondent state a strategic opportunity to appoint an arbitrator, CETA's dispute settlement mechanism takes that opportunity away for foreign investors while retaining that option for Canada and the EU. As a result, some may be concerned that prospective decisions emanating from CETA's first instance and appeals tribunals will favour the respondent states on which they rely for appointment. The dismantling of the WTO's appellate body reminds us of the delicate balance between state power, adjudication, and legitimacy in the context of a standing dispute resolution body. As a result, investor-side stakeholders may claim that CETA's contracting parties have simply replaced one set of legitimacy problems for another (Whitsitt and Weiler 2019).

Turning now to the introduction of CETA's appellate tribunal, some critics of ISDS have pointed to illegitimacy concerns related to decision quality, correctness, consistency, and coherence (e.g. Franck 2005; Kurtz 2014). Not all agree with such concerns. Indeed, some contend that themes of decision inconsistency and incoherence are over blown and argue that such occurrences are a natural part of the development of any legal system (e.g. Gill 2005). In the midst of this debate members of various constituencies in the international investment law regime have examined whether establishment of an appellate mechanism could help alleviate legitimacy concerns tied to decision quality, correctness, consistency, and coherence. Those in favour of establishing such a mechanism often highlight the importance of investment treaty arbitration in the development of international law citing its engagement with general international law rules regarding the interpretation of treaties and the law of state responsibility as well as customary international law (e.g. Reinisch 2012; Steger 2012). Others are skeptical that the introduction of an appeals mechanism can help to legitimate investment treaty arbitration through enhanced decision quality, correctness, consistency, and/or coherence. Some of this skepticism is rooted in the structure of international investment law's normative framework. Commentators point out that where open-textured rules are housed in thousands of investment treaty instruments, it seems unlikely that an appellate mechanism will be able to address concerns of inconsistency and incoherence (e.g. Kaufmann-Kohler 2004; Paulsson 2008).

Scholars and practitioners have identified other challenges associated with the establishment of an appellate mechanism.[12] I do not canvass all of those concerns here. I raise this only to say that establishment of an appellate mechanism within international investment law involves variables that extend beyond issues of decision correctness, consistency, and coherence. For a time, the multiplicity of issues associated with such a mechanism seemed insurmountable. ICSID (2004) proposed establishment of such a mechanism in 2004, but state parties were not receptive to the idea. However, attitudes of some constituencies in the international investment law regime have since changed. More recently, the work of UNCITRAL WG III reveals a shift in political will of various players in international investment law to reconsider ISDS reforms, including establishment an appellate mechanism (UNCITRAL 2020).

CETA's establishment of a standing appeals tribunal is also evidence of this evolution insofar as Canada and the EU are concerned. Many of the details about the working procedures of CETA's appellate mechanism, including procedures to initiate disputes and the conduct of appeals, remain unknown and subject to decision by the CETA Joint Committee. Still some preliminary observations about the potential legitimacy implications of CETA's appeals mechanism are warranted. As a starting point, it seems fair to say that the decision to include an appeals mechanism as part of CETA's ISDS mechanism signals a shift in the mandate of dispute settlement under CETA. In contrast to the ICSID Convention's preference for finality, CETA's negotiating parties have opted for process that prioritizes the substantive correctness of the decision.[13] As a result, those who questioned the legitimacy of ISDS, because of concerns about the correctness of arbitral decisions, are likely to perceive establishment of an appeals mechanism as a step in the right direction. Building legitimacy on the basis of decision quality, coherence, and consistency will take time and may even present some challenges along the way (Weiler 2001). As we have seen in the WTO context, establishing legitimate dispute settlement institutions in the eyes of various stakeholders is at times a tenuous process (Whitsitt and Weiler 2019). Nonetheless, one would expect that a standing body of adjudicators, such as those who will serve on the appellate tribunal and concerned about their own legitimacy, will want to ensure that CETA's normative framework is interpreted and applied in a coherent and consistent manner.

The Joint Committee and the Committee on Services and Investment

In addition to dispute settlement mechanisms, functioning of CETA's investment chapter is overseen by the CETA Joint Committee and the more specialized CSI. CETA's Joint Committee is responsible for all trade and investment policy issues between the parties (CETA 2016, Art. 26.1). Chaired by government officials who are responsible for trade, the joint committee comprises representatives from both Canada and the EU (ibid.). Under the terms of its mandate, the joint committee exercises both a supervisory and a facilitative function.[14] Among its many roles, the joint committee may consider or agree on amendments to CETA (ibid., Art. 26.1(5)(c)). It can also adopt interpretations of CETA provisions, and, in doing so, bind tribunals established under the CETA's investment chapter (ibid., Art. 26.1(5)(e)).

The CSI is intended to facilitate consultation of the parties on issues pertaining to the CETA's investment chapter (ibid., Art. 26.2(c)). More particularly, this committee can make recommendations to the joint committee about: (i) the adoption of interpretations under the investment chapter; (ii) the adoption of dispute settlement and transparency rules; (iii) the adoption of mediation rules; (iv) further elements of the FET obligation; and (v) the functioning of the appellate tribunal (ibid., Art. 8.44(3)). The inaugural meeting of the CSI took place on 18 September 2018 with sessions dedicated to outstanding issues about dispute settlement, including rules on the functioning of the appellate tribunal and development of a code of conduct (CETA Joint Committee 2018).

The notion that Canada and the EU have reserved for themselves – as a state and a conglomeration of states, respectively – sovereign authority over matters of treaty interpretation or amendment, as well as administrative and organizational matters may be troubling to some, especially those committed to traditional models of investment arbitration designed to depoliticize dispute settlement. Perceptions that CETA's ICS model permits too much state intrusion may well be amplified when one considers that the trajectory of governance of foreign direct investment (FDI) has been trending toward increased state discretion for some time. In this context, the powers of the joint and specialized committees (both of which comprise state delegates) to impact interpretations of CETA's investment chapter may be seen as an institutional development that swings the pendulum too far in the direction of sovereign interests.

But administrative committees with similar powers to the joint and specialized committees are not a new invention and may facilitate both normative and sociological legitimacy (Whitsitt and Weiler 2019). NAFTA's Free Trade Commission (FTC) is one such example. In 2001, the FTC issued an interpretive statement that connected the minimum standard of treatment to customary international law and limited FET obligation to the customary international law minimum standard of treatment (Global Affairs Canada 2001). The interpretive note also increased transparency of NAFTA Chapter 11 proceedings by permitting, under certain restrictions, access to documents submitted to, or issued by, NAFTA Chapter 11 tribunals (ibid.). FTC's interpretive statement generated an abundance of commentary debating the statement's status as lawful interpretation or unlawful amendment of NAFTA (e.g. Brower 2006). NAFTA's tribunals subsequently engaged in a careful and nuanced consideration of FTC's interpretive statement (ibid.). Most tribunals accepted that the FTC statement excluded independent treaty obligations from the minimum standard. However, NAFTA's tribunals largely rejected the idea that general principles of international law are excluded from the scope of NAFTA Art. 1105 (ADF Group 2003; Loewen Group 2002; *Merrill & Ring Forestry* 2010; Mondev 2003).

The termination of ISDS in NAFTA's successor, the Canada–United States–Mexico Agreement (CUSMA), makes it challenging to draw firm conclusions about the legitimizing (or de-legitimizing) impact of the FTC statement on NAFTA's ISDS mechanism. In my view, however, the NAFTA experience with the FTC statement is an important one to consider when thinking about the legitimacy implications of CETA's joint and specialized committees. As in the case of NAFTA's FTC, any interpretation rendered by CETA's joint and/or specialized committees will be closely scrutinized. One would anticipate that the committees would exercise their powers cautiously. This will be particularly important given the need for CETA's institutions, including the ICS, to establish legitimacy (normatively and sociologically).

Transparency Rules

Consistent with progressive developments in many arbitral institutions, dispute settlement processes under CETA are to be carried out transparently. In dispute settlement, transparency often refers to access to information about disputes, nondisputing party participation, and public access to hearings. Transparency in each of these areas is addressed in the CETA investment chapter by making the UNCITRAL Transparency Rules, albeit with some modifications, binding (CETA 2016, Art. 8.36(1)).

The public will have access to information about disputes promptly after they are initiated (ibid., Art. 8.36(4); UNCITRAL 2014, 2017b). The public will also have access to pleadings (i.e. written submissions from the disputing parties and nondisputing parties), hearing transcripts, orders, decisions, and awards rendered under CETA's investment chapter (CETA 2016, Art. 8.36). In addition, CETA requires that exhibits be made available to the public – an obligation that goes beyond what is provided for in the UNCITRAL Transparency Rules (ibid., Art. 8.36(3)).[15] However, these publication requirements do not apply absolutely. Where information is "confidential" or "protected," there is no publication obligation.[16] Subject to the same restrictions about confidential or protected information, all hearings that take place under CETA's investment chapter will be open to the public with logistics of those arrangements left to the determination by the tribunal and disputing parties (ibid., Art. 8.36(5)). CETA also permits the tribunal to consider and accept the application by interested parties to participate as amici curiae.

As noted earlier, increased transparency in arbitration proceedings may have legitimacy implications in normative and sociological terms. Consistent with evolutions toward greater transparency in investment arbitration,

CETA's ICS mechanism will operate in a manner that facilitates public access to the dispute settlement process. As Grossman (2009) acknowledges, this type of transparency imbues an international adjudicative body – CETA's ICS mechanism in this case – with normative legitimacy by permitting various international actors the opportunity to evaluate how the international body functions. Furthermore, the resulting accountability should help guarantee fairness in the adjudicative process. Consideration of the relationship between CETA's transparency provisions and sociological legitimacy is more complicated as it depends upon the perceptions of various actors. I do not purport to address all of those intricacies here. Suffice it to say that there may be some who disagree that transparency enhances legitimacy. Those committed to arbitration may believe that confidentiality – rather than transparency – helps to legitimize dispute settlement processes in the international investment law regime. It is true that CETA's publication and hearing requirements attempt to balance these interests by creating exceptions for confidential and protected information. Nonetheless, in the eyes of some constituencies, this accommodation may not do enough to alleviate concerns about the increasingly public nature of what they believe should be a private dispute settlement process. At this stage in CETA's evolution, it is difficult to say much else on this point except that perceptions about the legitimacy of the ICS mechanism will depend, in part, on how CETA's adjudicators interpret and apply the transparency provisions.

CETA's Normative Framework

In addition to its institutional (standing tribunals and committees) and procedural (transparency rules) features, CETA's investment chapter makes alterations to a number of the normative obligations, the interpretation and application of which has previously led to concerns about consistency, predictability and determinacy in other investment treaties (Banifatemi 2009; Bjorklund 2008; Dumberry 2013; Mortenson 2010). It is important to remember that decision quality, correctness, coherence, and consistency will be primarily shaped by CETA's underlying normative framework. Changes to standards of investor protections and corresponding exceptions reflected in CETA's are relevant because they reveal a desire to address concerns about normative ambiguity (or "indeterminacy" as Franck [1995] might say) in the construction of investment treaty standards of protection. With more definitive textual guidance about the parameters of investor rights and host state obligations, adjudicators under CETA's investment chapter have less room to adopt interpretations that may be considered incorrect, inconsistent or incoherent (Pauwelyn and Elsig 2013). This is particularly true where changes to CETA's normative framework are responsive to interpretive controversies that have arisen with respect to investment treaty standards. Given space constraints the following discussion focuses on two evolutions in CETA's underlying normative framework: (1) FET and (2) exceptions.

FAIR AND EQUITABLE TREATMENT

The FET standard plays a central role in many investor-state disputes making it one of the most powerful tools an investor has against host states – it has been applied by investment tribunals in a wide range of cases involving a variety of government measures.[17] The frequency with which this obligation is raised in investment disputes may well be related to the vagueness of its textual contours and uncertainty about whether the standard is tied to the minimum standard of treatment (MST) in international law.[18] The lack of definition historically given to FET clauses in investment treaties makes it ripe for creative argumentation about its definition and the factors that adjudicators should consider when determining whether a state has violated this commitment. Arbitral tribunals and commentators generally agree that transparency, stability, and an investor's legitimate expectations play a key role in defining FET standard (Dolzer and Schreuer 2012). However, application of these factors in determining whether a host state has violated its FET commitments has been controversial. Critics have expressed concern that any regulatory change which negatively impacts a foreign investor will lead to state liability under the FET doctrine.[19]

The parties to CETA attempt to address this concern by departing from historical investment treaty language and instead define the FET standard by expressly drafting in six exclusive enumerated grounds: denial of justice, breach of due process, manifest arbitrariness, targeted discrimination, abusive treatment, or any other elements as adopted by CETA's state parties (CETA 2016, Art. 8.10(2)).[20] In addition to being a closed list of grounds for violation, language such as "manifest," "targeted," and "abusive" suggests that Canada and the EU intended to circumscribe the FET obligation so that it captures state behaviour that violates a foreign investor's rights only in the clearest (and most extreme) circumstances. For example, the idea of targeted discrimination seems to imply that a foreign investor is going to need to show that Canada or the EU (and one of its member states) *intended* to treat it differently than other investors. Similarly, the ground of manifest arbitrariness suggests that a foreign investor operating within Canada and the EU should expect a certain amount of uncertainty and that they will only be able to show violation of the FET obligation where government measures very clearly lead to arbitrary treatment. How a tribunal will interpret and apply each of these grounds remains an open question. Nonetheless, inclusion of this exclusive list defining FET violations reveals a clear intention of the CETA parties to reimagine the FET obligation in the wake of criticisms about the breadth of its application and resultant liability risk to host states.

Further support for this observation is seen when we consider how CETA's FET clause addresses the concept of legitimate expectations. As I note before, the notion of legitimate expectations plays a key role in FET jurisprudence. However, in CETA, Canada and the EU have empowered tribunals considering violations of FET to ignore the idea of legitimate expectations altogether.[21] Whether the tribunals continue to use legitimate expectations as a means to define CETA's FET standard is uncertain. Nevertheless, CETA's FET clause opens the door for the tribunals to adopt an interpretive approach to the FET obligation that minimizes the impact of the investor's expectations about the outcome of their investment activities in either Canada or the EU. One can surmise that this provision was included in CETA as a way of recalibrating its FET obligation so that Canada and the EU (along with its member states) have greater space to regulate for public purposes. This is also supported by other treaty language reaffirming the parties' right to regulate and clarifying that regulations, or modifications to regulations, which negatively impact a foreign investor or interferes with their expectations, will not substantiate claims of FET violation (CETA 2016, Arts 8.9(1), 8.9(2)). As a final point of clarification, the CETA parties confirm that a breach of domestic law, another provision in the treaty, or separate treaty obligation will not establish a breach of the FET clause (ibid., Arts 8.10(6), 8.10(7)).

EXCEPTIONS

In addition to the host state obligations noted earlier, investment treaties often include exceptions which permit host states to derogate from their commitments in certain circumstances. Investment treaties have a diverse catalogue of exceptions. For example, in their investment treaties, Canada and the United States outline a core list of reservations that exclude any claims of noncompliance for specified existing and future measures (Government of Canada 2013, Art. 9; United States Government 2013, Art. 14).[22] Both countries also seek to make exemptions for "prudential measures" so that a host state can maintain the integrity of its financial institutions and ensure the stability of its financial system (Government of Canada 2013, Art. 10(2); United States Government 2013, Art. 20(1)). Some countries include exceptions in their investment treaties for emergencies by virtue of so-called non-precluded measures clauses.[23] Others exempt cultural policy measures from the oversight of an investment treaty (see, generally, Burke-White and von Staden 2008). Still others, such as China, very often stay silent on the issue.[24]

CETA includes a diverse suite of exceptions, including carve-outs for existing nonconforming measures and certain industry sectors (e.g. CETA 2016, Art. 8.15). Here, I do not discuss all of these exceptions. Rather, I focus on CETA's general exceptions clause (ibid., Art. 28.3). Consistent with the evolution of treaty language in US Model BITs and modelled on exceptions in the international trade law context, CETA permits Canada, the EU, and EU's member states to violate their market access and nondiscrimination obligations where necessary to: protect public morals, maintain public order, protect human, plant or animal health, and or secure compliance domestic laws or regulations (ibid.). Presumably, Canada and the EU included these provisions as a way to better balance investor rights with a state's regulatory autonomy and avoid regulatory "chill" (Henckels 2013; Rogers 2013; Tienhaara 2011). And, perhaps more importantly, Canada and the EU arguably included these familiar WTO law exceptions with the aim of increasing legal certainty about the parameters of investor protection and state liability. Whether or not inclusion of these exceptions will achieve that objective is still unknown. Nonetheless explicit delineation of grounds pursuant to which a host state may deviate from its investment law commitments provides CETA tribunals with a textual basis for balancing a state's obligations with its sovereign regulatory autonomy.

Consequences of CETA's Normative Framework for Legitimacy

Each of the examples discussed here is illustrative of a normative framework intended to resolve criticisms about the appropriate interpretation and application of various investment treaty standards. This may impact perceptions about the currency of CETA's underlying normative regime (Grossman 2009). To the extent that criticisms levelled at ISDS and the international investment law regime more generally are addressed in CETA's FET and exceptions provisions, international actors will be more likely to perceive CETA's underlying normative regime as a legitimate reflection of their interests and values. In that same vein, the perceived legitimacy of CETA – both its institutions and normative framework – will be intimately tied to the decisions of its international adjudicative bodies.

Where CETA's underlying normative framework resolves interpretive challenges, controversies, or ambiguities, there is greater determinacy of the rights and obligations governing investor-state relations between the EU and Canada. It therefore seems fair to say that clarifications in treaty text may have a positive impact on CETA's legitimacy. In some cases, interpretive controversies about the scope and application of investment treaty standards are diminished through inclusion of language that more clearly outlines parameters for treaty obligations resulting in a more predictable set of rules for foreign investors and CETA state parties. This is the case, for example, with CETA's FET clause. In other instances, criticisms – whether interpretation of investment treaty protections properly balance the rights of foreign investors and host states – are addressed through inclusion of treaty language that will require adjudicators to address this concern as they interpret CETA's treaty rights and obligations. Such language is found in many of CETA's provisions, including its FET obligations as well as its general exceptions provision. This is not to say that CETA's normative framework is perfectly determinative. On the contrary, its provisions contain textual ambiguities that adjudicators will need to interpret and apply. Nonetheless, inclusion of treaty language which expressly recognizes regulatory autonomy and permits derogation from treaty obligations provides a textual reference point with which an adjudicator may need to deal when determining liabilities under CETA's investment chapter.

All this to say that CETA's underlying normative framework has import-ant consequences for adjudication of investor-state rights and obligations. Increased determinacy of treaty language affects the space an adjudicator has to adopt interpretations that are perceived as activist or beyond the scope of the CETA parties' consent (see generally Pauwelyn and Elsig 2013). Where ambiguity in CETA's norms exists – and I have already intimated that it does – one should expect that adjudicators have greater room to adopt varied interpretations of the rights and obligations underpinning investor-state relations (ibid.). In such circumstances, jurisprudence under CETA's investment chapter may be scrutinized. One should, therefore, anticipate that it will take time for jurisprudence considering such ambigu-ities to develop and that legitimacy concerns may arise as a result of those uncertainties. This last point is particularly prescient for our purposes. As is true of other international dispute settlement institutions (e.g. the WTO appellate body), legitimacy (particularly sociological legitimacy) takes time to establish, and even then, perceptions about CETA as an institution and the decisions of its adjudicative bodies will change over time.

CONCLUDING REMARKS

International investment law is in the midst of a reformation brought on by pervasive challenges to the regime's legitimacy. Many, but not all, of those concerns are tied to ISDS. Calls for reform have culminated in proposals to establish an ICS mechanism. Canada and the EU have taken up this call, leading to questions about whether this new dispute settlement model addresses those legitimacy criticisms.

Whether CETA's investment court will resolve the legitimacy criticisms launched at ISDS remains, however, an open question. This chapter demonstrates that questions of legitimacy are multivariate. Numerous elements (e.g. adjudicator qualifications, provisions on conflict of interest, tenure and reappointment, and transparency) of a dispute settlement model, including CETA's ICS, may be said to enhance its normative legitimacy. Those same elements may impact the sociological legitimacy of an adjudicative body in different ways. Future work on the legitimacy of CETA's investment court will need to be cautious in its definition of legitimacy and design methodologies that acknowledge and measure the perceptions of the diverse constituencies involved in CETA's investment chapter. Because legitimacy is multivariate, one should also exercise caution when drawing conclusions about whether one variable (e.g. establishment of an appellate mechanism) resolves (or not) legitimacy concerns. CETA's investment chapter has numerous variables, including its institutional features and a normative framework that will impact legitimacy should its investment court become operational. As a result, any future work on CETA's legitimacy must account for the challenges associated with trying to isolate and measure the impact of certain variables on its legitimacy.

This same caution applies to comparative studies that ask whether CETA's investment court is the solution to the ISDS legitimacy crisis. Should CETA's investment court secure acceptance from relevant constituencies in a manner that has eluded investment treaty arbitration, it may be tempting to conclude that this new-found legitimacy is due to certain institutional features such as tenure of appointment and establishment of an appeals process. However, in my view, such a conclusion fails to recognize the importance of CETA's normative framework. In contrast to many of investment treaties, CETA's normative framework more definitively outlines the contours of certain treaty rights and obligations. This reality alters an adjudicator's interpretive task and, in my view, has the greatest potential to enhance CETA's legitimacy.

NOTES

1 Hereinafter, the EU proposal.
2 ICSID Convention (2006), Art. 42(1) reads, "The Tribunal shall decide a dispute in accordance with such rules of law as may be agreed by the parties. In the absence of such agreement, the Tribunal shall apply the law of the Contracting State party to the dispute (including its rules on the conflict of laws) and such rules of international law as may be applicable."
3 See also footnote 7, which permits either Canada or the EU to opt to appoint five tribunal members of any nationality should they chose to do so. If either party opts to do this, the appointed tribunal members will be considered nationals of the party that proposed the appointment.
4 CETA's appointment requirements are somewhat more prescriptive than the requirements for panelists appointed pursuant to ICSID Arbitration Rules and UNCITRAL Arbitration Rules. Art. 14 of the ICSID Convention requires panel members to be of high moral character with recognized competence in the fields of law, commerce, industry, or finance. Panelists must also be relied upon to exercise independent judgment. Additional criteria are "highly desirable," including knowledge of and experience with international investment law, public international law, and international arbitration (https://icsid.worldbank.org/sites/default/files/Considerations_for_States_on_Panel_Designations.pdf). The UNCITRAL Arbitration Rules are even less prescriptive requiring that arbitrators remain independent and impartial throughout the proceedings (Art. 11) but leaving more particular criteria to be decided by the parties. Where selection of an arbitrator falls to the Secretary-General of ICSID, consideration will be given to criteria such as availability, expertise, and nationality. In trying to remedy concerns associated with traditional ISDS, the more prescriptive requirements in CETA may raise a new set of legitimacy concerns worthy of consideration. I do not analyze that hypothesis in these pages as it is outside the scope of this chapter. Nonetheless, it may merit further inquiry and analysis.
5 See CETA (2016), Art. 8.27(6). Terms of reference for appointment as president and vice president of the tribunal are outlined in Art. 8.27(8) (ibid.).
6 See CETA (2016), Art. 8.27(7). It is possible for disputes to be heard by a sole tribunal member should the disputing parties agree (ibid., Art. 8.27(9)).
7 Nationality of arbitrators is also a concern in ICSID arbitrations. Where a dispute is heard by a three-member arbitration panel and the disputing parties cannot agree on the appointment of arbitrators, the majority of

arbitrators must be nationals of states other than the respondent state and the home state of the claimant investor (Art. 39, ICSID Convention 2006). The UNICTRAL Arbitration Rules do not set out any specific nationality requirements, although other applicable instruments may do so. Nationality is also one of the factors that the ICSID secretary-general will consider where they must select an arbitrator (https://icsid.worldbank.org/ services/arbitration/uncitral/selection-appointment-arbitrators).

8   For example, a series of changes were made to ICSID's arbitration rules in April 2006 after a lengthy review and consultation process. Those changes strengthened many aspects of ICSID proceedings, including delineation of more robust disclosure requirements for arbitrators. More recently, ICSID and UNCITRAL have joined forces to develop a draft code of conduct for adjudicators in ISDS (the draft code). The draft code outlines that all adjudicators participating in the settlement of investor-state disputes must, among other things, "[b]e independent and impartial, and [sic] avoid any indirect or direct conflicts of interest, impropriety, bias and appearance of bias." In furtherance of these principles the draft code requires broad disclosure by adjudicators to ensure that disputing parties have as much information as possible in order to make informed decisions about the independence and impartiality of adjudicators. Moreover, the draft code precludes adjudicators from having a business, financial, or personal relationship with any party to an investment arbitration proceedings. From a normative perspective, inclusion and revision of rules as well as the eventual adoption of the draft code, which is aimed at ensuring arbitrator independence and impartiality, should help ensure that parties comply with decisions reached through arbitral institutions such as ICSID and UNCITRAL. Whether adoption of a draft code will overcome concerns about the party appointments and related perceptions about ethical conflicts remains an open question. What we do know is that adjustments to rules at arbitral institutions, include those made to ICSID's arbitration rules in 2006, did not stave off the most recent onslaught of legitimacy criticisms against investment treaty arbitration and the institutions that facilitate those processes. See also ICSID (2006); LCIA (2017, section 2; 2020, Art. 5.4); SCC (2017, Art. 18).

9   The IBA Guidelines have not been adopted by ICSID or UNCITRAL, but both institutions are collaborating on the draft code of conduct for adjudicators in international investment disputes (https://icsid.worldbank. org/resources/code-of-conduct). Consideration of the intricacies of the draft code with the IBA Guidelines, while useful, falls outside the parameters of this examination.

10 People appointed to the appellate tribunal must also satisfy the same qualifications as those appointed to CETA's first instance tribunal.

11 The appeals mechanism contemplated by the EU and incorporated into its FTA with Vietnam establishes a tribunal composed of six members, with two members being EU nationals, two nationals of the other treaty party and two nationals of third countries. As with the first instance tribunal, members of the appeal tribunal are appointed for a six-year term, subject to renewal for one additional term. However, three of the six members appointed immediately after the entry into force of the agreement have terms that extend to nine years. Selection of those three members is determined by lot. Provisions on the required qualifications, nomination of members and constitution of tribunal divisions hearing appeal proceedings are similar to first instance tribunals.

12 See, e.g., Steger (2012, 254) on issues of costs and delays. See also Calamita (2017).

13 Under the ICSID.

14 See Art. 26.1(4)(a) (CETA 2016), which states: "The CETA Joint Committee shall supervise and facilitate the implementation and application of this Agreement and further general aims."

15 UNCITRAL Rules, Art. 3(1) only requires publication of a list of exhibits.

16 Confidential and protected information is broadly defined in UNCITRAL Rules, Art. 7(2) as: (a) confidential business information; (b) information that is protected against being made available to the public under the treaty; (c) information that is protected against being made available to the public, in the case of the information of the respondent state, under the law of the respondent state, and in the case of other information, under any law or rules determined by the arbitral tribunal to be applicable to the disclosure of such information; or (d) information, the disclosure of which would impede law enforcement. See also CETA (2016, Art. 8.36(6)), which clarifies that where Canada and the EU are by law required to disclose information, that obligation should be interpreted in a manner sensitive to tribunal determinations about whether information is "confidential" and/or "protected."

17 See, e.g., *Petrobart Limited* v. *The Kyrgyz Republic* (2005, 75–82), where the investor had obtained a judgment from a Kyrgyz court against a state-owned gas company for amounts owed to Petrobart under a delivery and supply contract. At the request of the political authorities in the Kyrgyz Republic, the court postponed the execution of that judgment for a few months. During this period, pursuant to a presidential decree, the state-owned gas company was restructured and declared bankrupt,

resulting in Petrobart's inability to collect on its debt judgment or obtain any proceeds from the sale of assets. The tribunal found a violation of the FET standard articulated in Art. 10(1) of the Energy Charter Treaty (ECT) as a result of the host states interference with Petrobart's due process rights. See also *Ioannis Kardassopoulos and Ron Fuchs* v. *The Republic of Georgia* (2010, paras 409–52), where the tribunal found that assurances of compensation made to the claimants after their concession over Georgia's main oil pipeline was terminated could ground a successful FET claim under the ECT.

18 Some investment treaties explicitly tie FET to the MST, but even where this connection is expressly confirmed, arbitral tribunals have recognized that MST can evolve with investors bearing the onus of proof to show those shifts in customary international law (see, e.g., *Glamis Gold Limited*. v. *The United States* 2009).

19 For incisive discussion of these issues and developments under more recent FTAS, see Henckels (2016).

20 In an attempt to lessen the impact of the concept of legitimate expectations as a predominant factor in FET jurisprudence, Art. 8.10(4) (CETA 2016) provides that "the Tribunal *may [or may not]* take into account whether a Party made a specific representation to an investor to induce a covered investment, that created a legitimate expectation, and upon which the investor relied in deciding to make or maintain the covered investment, but that the Party subsequently frustrated" (emphasis added).

21 See Note 20.

22 See also NAFTA (1994, Art. 1108) and *Mobil Investments* v. *Canada* (2012, supra note 990), where the arbitral tribunal's disagreement about the proper construction of NAFTA Art. 1108 raises questions about a host state's ability to adopt new regulations, guidelines and policies under its reserved powers).

23 Canada is one such country that includes cultural exemptions in its trade and investment agreement (see, e.g., CUSMA 2018).

24 For an overview of Chinese BIT practice, see Shan and Gallagher (2013).

REFERENCES

ADF Group Inc. v. *United States of America*. 2003. ICSID Case No. ARB/ (AF)/oo/1, Award, 9 January.

Balchin, Claire, Chung, Kyo-Hwa, Kaushal, Asha, and Waibel, Michael, 2010. *The Backlash Against Investment Arbitration: Perceptions and Reality.* Alphen aan den Rijn: Kluwer Law International.

Banifatemi, Yas. 2009. "The Emerging Jurisprudence on Most-Favoured-Nation Treatment in Investment Arbitration." In *Investment Treaty Law: Current Issues III*, edited by Andrea K. Bjorklund, Ian A. Laird, and Sergey Ripinsky, 239–72. London: British Institute of International and Comparative Law.

Behn, Daniel. 2015. "Legitimacy, Evolution and Growth in Investment Treaty Arbitration: Empirically Evaluating the State-of-the-Art." *Georgetown Journal of International Law* 46, no. 2: 363–414.

Bjorklund, Andrea K. 2008. "Investment Treaty Arbitral Awards as *Jurisprudence Constante*." In *International Economic Law: The State and Future of the Discipline*, edited by Colin Picker, Isabella D. Bunn, and Douglas Arner, 265–80. Oxford: Hart Publishing.

– 2018. "The Legitimacy of the International Centre for Settlement of Disputes." In *Legitimacy and International Courts*, edited by Nienke Grossman, Harlan Grant Cohen, Andreas Follesdal, and Geir Ulfstein, 243–83. Cambridge: Cambridge University Press.

Bodansky, Daniel M. 1999. "The Legitimacy of International Governance: A Coming Challenge for International Environmental Law?" *American Journal of International Law* 93, No. 3: 596–624.

Brower, Charles H., II. 2006. "Why the FTC Notes of Interpretation Constitute a Partial Amendment of NAFTA Article 1105." *Virginia Journal of International Law* 46, no. 2: 347–63. https://doi.org/10.1111/j.1747-7093.2006.00043.x.

Brunné, Jutta, and Stephen J. Toope. 2010. *Legitimacy and Legality in International Law: An International Account*. Cambridge: Cambridge University Press.

Buchanan, Allen, and Robert O. Keohane. 2006. "The Legitimacy of Global Governance Institutions." *Ethics and International Affairs* 20, no. 4: 405–37. https://doi.org/10.1111/j.1747-7093.2006.00043.x.

Burke-White, William W. and Andreas von Staden. 2008. "Investment Protection in Extraordinary Times: The Interpretation and Application of Non-Precluded Measures Provisions in Bilateral Investment Treaties." *Virginia Journal of International Law* 48, no. 2: 307–410.

Calamita, N. Jansen. 2017. "The Challenge of Establishing a Multilateral Investment Tribunal at ICSID." *ICSID Review – Foreign Investment Law Journal* 32, no. 3: 611–24.

Canadian Centre for Policy Alternatives. 2021. "The Rise and Demise of NAFTA Chapter 11." Accessed 15 September 2021. https://www.policyalternatives.ca/sites/default/files/uploads/publications/National%20Office/2021/04/The_Rise_and_Demise_of_NAFTA_Chapter_11.pdf.

Canadian Government. 2019. "Consultation report and FIPA review."
     Accessed 15 September 2021. https://www.international.gc.ca/trade-
     commerce/consultations/fipa-apie/report-rapport.aspx.

CETA (Comprehensive Economic and Trade Agreement). 2016. Accessed
     21 July 2020. https://www.international.gc.ca/trade-commerce/trade-
     agreements-accords-commerciaux/agr-acc/ceta-aecg/text-texte/toc-tdm.aspx.

CETA Joint Committee. 2018. "CETA Joint Committee Meeting September 26,
     2018: Summary Report." Accessed 15 August 2019. https://www.inter-
     national.gc.ca/trade-commerce/trade-agreements-accords-commerciaux/
     agr-acc/CETA-aecg/2018-09-26-summary_report-rapport_sommaire.aspx.

– 2021. "Decision No 001/2021 of the CETA Joint Committee of
     January 29, 2021 setting out the administrative and organisational matters
     regarding the functioning of the Appellate Tribunal." Accessed 15 September
     2021. https://www.international.gc.ca/trade-commerce/trade-agreements-
     accords-commerciaux/agr-acc/ceta-aecg/appellate-tribunal-dappel.aspx.

Charalambous, Annie. 2020. "Cyprus House Plenum Refuses to ratify
     EU-Canada Trade Agreement." In-Cyprus, 1 August. https://in-cyprus.
     philenews.com/cyprus-house-plenum-refuses-to-ratify-eu-canada-
     trade-agreement/.

CUSMA (Canada–United States–Mexico Agreement). 2018. Accessed
     4 August 2020. https://www.international.gc.ca/trade-commerce/trade-
     agreements-accords-commerciaux/agr-acc/cusma-aceum/text-texte/toc-
     tdm.aspx.

Dolzer, Rudolf, and Christoph Schreuer. 2012. *Principles of International
     Investment Law* (second edition). Oxford: Oxford University Press.

Dumberry, Patrick. 2013. *The Fair and Equitable Treatment Standard: A Guide
     to NAFTA Case Law on Article 1105.* London: Kluwer Law International.

Eberhardt, Pia, and Cecilia Olivet. 2012. *Profiting from Injustice: How Law
     Firms, Arbitrators, and Financiers are Fuelling an Investment Arbitration
     Boom.* Brussels: Corporate Europe Observatory and Transnational Institute.

EC (European Commission). 2015. "Report: Online Public Consultation on
     Investment Protection and Investor-To-State Dispute Settlement (ISDS) in
     the Transatlantic Trade and Investment Partnership Agreement (TTIP)."
     https://trade.ec.europa.eu/doclib/docs/2015/january/tradoc_153044.pdf.

ECIPE (European Center for International Political Economy). 2014. "The
     'Repsol Case' Against Argentina: Lessons for Investment Protection Policy."
     Accessed 15 August 2021. https://ecipe.org/publications/repsol-case-against-
     argentina-lessons-investment-protection-policy/.

EU (European Union). 2015. "Proposal of the European Union for
     Investment Protection and Resolution of Investment Disputes." Accessed

25 November 2020. http://trade.ec.europa.eu/doclib/docs/2015/november/ tradoc_153955.pdf.

Franck, Susan D. 2005. "The Legitimacy Crisis in Investment Treaty Arbitration: Privatizing Public International Law Through Inconsistent Decisions." *Fordham Law Review* 73, no. 4: 1521–625.

Franck, Thomas M. 1995. *Fairness in International Law and Institutions.* Oxford: Oxford University Press.

Gill, Judith. 2005. "Inconsistent Decisions: An Issue to be Addressed or a Fact of Life." *Transnational Dispute Management* 2. https://www.transnational-dispute-management.com/article.asp?key=404.

Glamis Gold Limited v. *The United States.* 2009. NAFTA/UNCITRAL Arbitration, Award, 8 June.

Global Affairs Canada. 2001. "Notes of Interpretation of Certain Chapter 11 Provisions (NAFTA Free Trade Commission, July 31, 2001)." Accessed 25 November 2020. https://www.international.gc.ca/trade-agreements-accords-commerciaux/topics-domaines/disp-diff/NAFTA-Interpr.aspx.

– 2017. "Provisional application of CETA – The Honourable François-Philippe Champagne, Minister of International Trade." Accessed 25 November 2020. https://www.canada.ca/en/global-affairs/news/2017/09/provisional_applicationofceta-thehonourablefrancois-philippecham.html.

Government of Canada. 2013. "2004 Canada Model BIT." In *Commentaries on Selected Model Investment Treaties*, edited by Chester Brown, 85–7. Oxford: Oxford University Press.

Grossman, Nienke. 2009. "Legitimacy and International Adjudicative Bodies." *George Washington International Law Review* 41: 107–80.

– 2013. "The Normative Legitimacy of International Courts." *Temple Law Review* 86: 61–106.

Hazou, Elias. 2020. "Talks to begin with parties after rejection of CETA." *CyprusMail*, 4 August. https://cyprus-mail.com/2020/08/04/talks-to-begin-with-parties-after-rejection-of-ceta/.

Henckels, Caroline. 2013. "Balancing Investment Protection and The Public Interest: The Role of the Standard of Review and the Importance of Deference in Investor-State Arbitration." *Journal of International Dispute Settlement* 4, no. 1: 197–215. https://doi.org/10.1093/jnlids/ids027.

– 2016. "Protecting Regulatory Autonomy through Greater Precision in Investment Treaties: The TPP, CETA and TTIP." *Journal of International Economic Law* 19, no. 1: 27–50. https://doi.org/10.1093/jiel/jgw001.

ICSID (International Centre for Settlement of Investment Disputes). 2004. "Possible Improvements of the Framework for ICSID Arbitration." Accessed 25 November 2020. https://icsid.worldbank.org/sites/default/files/

Possible%20Improvements%20of%20the%20Framework%20of%20ICSID%20Arbitration.pdf.

– 2006. "ICSID Convention Arbitration Rules." Accessed 22 July 2020. https://icsid.worldbank.org/en/Pages/icsiddocs/ICSID-Convention-Arbitration-Rules.aspx.

Ioannis Kardassopoulos and Ron Fuchs v. The Republic of Georgia. 2010. ICSID Case No. ARB/07/15, Award, 3 March.

Kaufmann-Kohler, Gabrielle. 2004. "Annulment of ICSID Awards I Contract and Treaty Arbitrations: Are There Differences?" In *Annulment of ICSID Awards*, edited by Emmanuel Gaillard and Yas Banifatemi, 189–211. New York: Juris Publishing.

Kurtz, Jurgen. 2014. "Building Legitimacy Through Interpretation in Investor-State Arbitration: On Consistency, Coherence and the Identification of Applicable Law." In *The Foundations of International Investment Law*, edited by Zachary Douglas, Joost Pauwelyn, and Jorge E. Vinuales, 257–96. Oxford: Oxford University Press.

LCIA (London Court of International Arbitration). 2017. "LCIA Notes for Arbitrators." Accessed 25 November 2020. https://www.lcia.org/adr-services/lcia-notes-for-arbitrators.aspx.

– 2020. "London Court of International Arbitration Rules." Accessed 25 November 2020. https://www.lcia.org/Dispute_Resolution_Services/lcia-arbitration-rules-2020.aspx.

Loewen Group, Inc. and Raymond L. Loewen v. United States of America. 2002. ICSID Case No. ARB/(AF)/98/3, Award 26 June.

McKenna, Barrie. 2016. "What's Wallonia's deal? A primer on its role in CETA's crisis." *The Globe and Mail*, 24 October. https://www.theglobeandmail.com/report-on-business/international-business/european-business/explainer-ceta-wallonia-europe-and-canada/article32489554/.

Merrill & Ring Forestry LP v. Government of Canada. 2010. UNCITRAL (NAFTA), Award, 31 March.

Meyer, Lukas H., and Pranay Sanklecha. 2009. "Introduction." In *Legitimacy, Justice and Public International Law*, edited by Lukas H. Meyer, 1–28. Cambridge: Cambridge University Press.

Mobil Investments v. Canada. 2012. ICSID Case No. ARB(AF)/07/4, Decision on Liability and Principles of Quantum, 22 May.

Mortenson, Julian Davis. 2010. "The Meaning of 'Investment': ICSID's Travaux and the Domain of International Investment Law." *Harvard International Law Journal* 51, no. 1: 257–318.

NAFTA (North American Free Trade Agreement). 1994. Accessed 24 July 2020. https://www.international.gc.ca/trade-commerce/trade-agreements-accords-commerciaux/agr-acc/nafta-alena/fta-ale/index.aspx.

Osmanski, Emily. 2018. "Investor-State Dispute Settlement: Is There a Better Alternative?" *Brooklyn Journal of International Law* 43, no. 2: 639–64.

Paulsson, Jan. 2008. "Avoiding Unintended Consequences." In *Appeals Mechanisms in International Investment Disputes,* edited by Karl P. Sauvant. Oxford: Oxford University Press.

Pauwelyn, Joost, and Manfred Elsig. 2013. "The Politics of Treaty Interpretation: Variations and Explanations across International Tribunals." In *Interdisciplinary Perspectives on International Law and International Relations: The State of the Art,* edited by Jeffrey L. Dunoff and Mark A. Pollack, 445–76. Cambridge: Cambridge University Press.

Petrobart Limited v. *The Kyrgyz Republic.* 2005. SCC Case No. 126/2003, Award, 29 March.

Roberts, Anthea. 2013. "Clash of Paradigms: Actors and Analogies Shaping the Investment Treaty System." *American Journal of International Law* 107, no. 1: 45–94. https://doi.org/10.5305/amerjintelaw.107.1.0045.

Rogers, Catherine A. 2013. "The Politics of International Investment Arbitrators." *Santa Clara Journal of International Law* 12, no. 1: 223–62.

SCC (Stockholm Chamber of Commerce). 2017. "Stockholm Chamber of Commerce (SCC) Arbitration Rules." Accessed 25 November 2020. https://sccinstitute.com/media/1407444/arbitrationrules_eng_2020.pdf.

Shan, Wenhua, and Norah Gallagher. 2013. "China." In *Commentaries on Selected Model Investment Treaties,* edited by Chester Brown, Chapter 5. Oxford: Oxford University Press.

Shany, Yuval. 2014. *Assessing the Effectiveness of International Courts.* Oxford: Oxford University Press.

Sornarajah, M. 2008. "A Coming Crisis: Expansionary Trends in Investment Treaty Arbitration." In *Appeals Mechanisms in International Investment Disputes,* edited by Karl P. Sauvant, Chapter 4. Oxford: Oxford University Press.

– 2016. "International Investment Law as Development Law: The Obsolescence of a Fraudulent System." In *European Yearbook of International Economic Law,* edited by Marc Bungenberg, Christoph Herrmann, Markus Krajewksi, and Jörg Philipp Terhechte. Springer, Cham.

Steger, Debra P. 2012. "Enhancing the Legitimacy of International Investment Law by Establishing an Appellate Mechanism." In *Improving International Investment Agreements,* edited by Armand de Mestral and Celine Levesque, Chapter 14. London: Routledge.

Tienhaara, Kyle. 2011. "Regulatory Chill and the Threat of Arbitration: A View from Political Science." In *Evolution in Investment Treaty Law and Arbitration,* edited by Chester Brown and Kate Miles, 606–28. Cambridge: Cambridge University Press.

Titi, Catharine. 2017. "The European Union's Proposal for an International Investment Court: Significance, Innovations and Challenges Ahead." *Transnational Dispute Management* 1. http://dx.doi.org/10.2139/ssrn.2711943.

UNCITRAL (United Nations Commission on International Trade Law). 2014. "UNCITRAL Rules on Transparency in Treaty-based Investor-State Arbitration." Accessed 13 June 2020. https://uncitral.un.org/en/texts/arbitration/contractualtexts/transparency.

– 2017a. "Report of the United Nations Commission on International Trade Law, UN Doc A/72/17, Fiftieth Session (3–21 July 2017)." New York: UNCITRAL.

– 2017b. "United Nations Convention on Transparency in Treaty-based Investor-State Arbitration ('Mauritius Convention on Transparency.'")" Accessed 13 June 2020. https://uncitral.un.org/en/texts/arbitration/conventions/transparency.

– 2020. "Working Group III: Investor-State Dispute Settlement Reform." Accessed 25 November 2020. https://uncitral.un.org/en/working_groups/3/investor-state.

UNCTAD (United Nations Conference on Trade and Development). 2012. "Expropriation, UNCTAD Series on Issues in International Investment Agreements II." Accessed 25 November 2020. http://unctad.org/en/Docs/unctaddiaeia2011d7_en.pdf.

United States Government. 2013. "2012 US Model BIT." In *Commentaries on Selected Model Investment Treaties*, edited by Chester Brown, 807–10. Oxford: Oxford University Press.

Vasani, Baiju S., and Shaun A. Palmer. 2015. "Challenge and Disqualification of Arbitrators at ICSID: A New Dawn?" *ICSID Review – Foreign Investment Law Journal* 30, no. 1: 194–216. https://doi.org/10.1093/icsidreview/siu021.

Weiler, Joseph. 2001. "The Rule of Lawyers and the Ethos of Diplomats: Reflections on the Internal and External Legitimacy of WTO Dispute Settlement." *Journal of World Trade* 35, no. 2: 191–207.

Whitsitt, Elizabeth, and Todd Weiler. 2019. "WTO Dispute Settlement, Investor-State Arbitration and Investment Courts: Exploring Themes of State Power, Adjudication and Legitimacy." *Dispute Resolution International* 13, no. 2. https://dx.doi.org/10.2139/ssrn.3391894.

PART FIVE

Environment, Energy, and Labour

Collaborative Governance for Addressing Climate Change: Evaluating CETA's Scope

Aakriti Bhardwaj

INTRODUCTION

The implementation of the Comprehensive Economic and Trade Agreement (CETA 2016), signed between the European Union (EU) and Canada (European Commission 2017a), confounding as it is (Finbow 2019), also has implications for the progress on climate-resilient trade. The EU, motivated by its constitutional mandate to contribute to and promote measures to combat climate change at the international level (TFEU 2016, Art. 191), refers to environmental protection and sustainable development as one of the primary objectives of its trade policy (European Commission 2019a; TEU 2016, Art. 3(5), 21). The European Commission (2018a, 7) contended that "there might still be margin for improvements in the integration of [climate] adaptation in some EU common policies, such as trade." Additionally, the Commission prioritized the signing of the Paris Agreement on Climate Change (Paris Agreement 2015) by a partner country as a condition for concluding free trade agreements (FTAS) (Mathiesen 2018).

The Paris Agreement, which was adopted on 12 December 2015 and entered into force on 4 November 2016,[1] is the latest international legal instrument to redefine targets for climate action.[2] The agreement does not refer to trade policy as an instrument for climate action as such, but countries may direct trade instruments in this direction. The potential of trade agreements to advance climate action is untapped (Morin and Jinnah 2018) and there is a demand that international agreements should address climate change effectively (Weiss 2008).

The EU and Canada expressed their willingness to build further linkages between trade and climate action by adopting a recommendation to this effect under CETA's Trade and Sustainable Development (TSD) chapters (CETA Joint Committee 2018). The implementation of the TSD chapters of CETA depends inter alia on dialogue and cooperation between the EU and Canada to ensure free, open and transparent trade relations that is aided by businesses, civil society organizations, and citizens for the achievement of sustainable development goals (SDGs) (CETA 2016, Arts 22.1(3)(b), 22.1(3)(d)). Public consultations and participation in the discussion of sustainable development issues are intended to shape the relevant laws and policies (ibid., Art. 22.1(3)(e)). These provisions entail the engagement of collaborative governance, a theory and practice in the field of public management,[3] which is defined as *"the processes and structures of public policy decision making and management that engage people constructively across the boundaries of public agencies, levels of government, and/or the public, private and civic spheres in order to carry out a public purpose"* (Emerson, Nabatchi, and Balogh 2011, 2; emphasis in original). Collaborative governance has three key objectives: (i) fostering public engagement on complex policy problems, (ii) furthering the legitimacy of public actions (Hysing 2020), and (iii) resolving differences between the interests represented by various actors (Silvia 2011, 69). The CETA provisions highlighted above demonstrate that the agreement provides the "legal infrastructure for collaborative governance" (Bingham 2010, 297, 333) by seeking to foster participation of private actors and transparency in the agreement's implementation. State actors remain central to the process (Keohane and Victor 2011, 8) but it is intended to steer public-private, public-civic, and public-private-civic coordination in the rulemaking process (Albareda 2008, 431; Levi-Faur 2011, 3).

COLLABORATIVE GOVERNANCE AS NECESSITATED BY INTERNATIONAL COMMITMENTS ON CLIMATE CHANGE

Collaborative governance emerged in the fields of education and health care as a framework on the ways in which public administration engaged with private and civic actors (Emerson, Nabatchi, and Balogh 2011). By underscoring "the importance of the engagements of all levels of government and various actors" the Paris Agreement (United Nations Climate Change 2020) incorporates the need for fostering communication between state and non-state actors on climate change mitigation and adaptation.[4] Collaborative governance has become increasingly relevant for consideration by governmental bodies that seek to achieve sustainable development (Florini and Pauli 2018, 583). Since climate action is one of the SDGs (United Nations 2015, Goal 13), the application of collaborative governance in this context has gathered momentum (Brink and Wamsler 2017; Emerson and Murchie 2011; Hamilton and Lubell 2017; Kalesnikaite 2018). Initially, the 1972 Stockholm Declaration stipulated that states must be held responsible for causing transboundary environmental damage on account of resource use in their jurisdictions (United Nations 1973, principle 21). However, the 1992 Earth Summit was "about governments calling non-state actors to act" (Bendell 2011, 37) in partnership.

Sustainable development, which emerged as an environmental objective from within the international community based on the link between economic activity and negative environmental externalities, depends on the principle of integration which requires that environmental considerations are assimilated in economic policies (Birnie, Boyle, and Redgwell 2009, 116; Sands 1995, 324; Schrijver and Weiss 2004, 7). Integration is thus a key technique to direct state action for achieving sustainable development (Barral 2012) and *building a nexus* between distinct regimes such as international trade law and international environmental law (French 2006, 104–106, 109). The EU has a constitutional mandate in this direction (TEU 2016, Art. 11) while the response in Canada has been driven by policy initiatives (Wood, Tanner, and Richardson 2010, 1002–3). The United Nations Framework Convention on Climate Change (UNFCCC 1992, Art. 3(4)), an outcome of the Earth Summit, also refers to integration for the purpose of adopting national policies directed at combating climate change.

CETA PROVISIONS FOR PROMOTING COLLABORATIVE GOVERNANCE

The overlap between the fields of climate action and trade policy deals with the conflict in their priorities that are in need of reconciliation. Climate policies (such as border tax adjustments and subsidies) within a host country produce competitive pressure on companies operating in carbon-intensive industries. They are likely to incur associated compliance costs along with constraints on production compared to companies in other jurisdictions that do not implement such policy responses (Marceau 2016, 4–5). Competitiveness-related aspects may be analyzed in the light of the agreements of the World Trade Organization (WTO) but "on a systemic level, the answer ... lies in deepening international cooperation and understanding of [trade and climate] regimes and the way they interact in this context" (Marceau 2016, 31). CETA seems to have taken a step in this direction by seeking to understand "the trade impact of environmental regulations and standards as well as the environmental impact of trade and investment rules including on the development of environmental regulations and policies" (CETA 2016, Art. 24.12(1)(d)). Collaborative governance for climate change under CETA can thus be utilized under two sets of provisions: the first concerns regulatory cooperation, wherein the parties seek to reduce divergences in the methods of shaping regulatory measures such as impact assessments, risk assessment, and compliance and enforcement strategies (ibid., Art. 21.4(a)(iv)). The second concerns the substantive type of provisions on environmental and climate protection (ibid., Chapter 24). These two sets of provisions are interlinked because regulatory cooperation under CETA is meant to support EU-Canada cooperation on sustainable development (ibid., Art. 21.1).

Regulatory Cooperation

CETA incorporates the intergovernmental process of regulatory cooperation wherein state actors and institutions are meant to undertake policy coordination to (i) reduce barriers to trade, (ii) stimulate competitiveness and innovation, and (iii) "promote transparent ... regulatory processes that support public policy objectives" (ibid., Art. 21.2(4)). In the context of climate change, the provision that is of particular importance directs the parties to address "important regulatory issues of local, national and international concern" in the area of inter alia the environment (ibid., Art. 21.3(a)(1)). In this respect, the EU and Canada aim to improve understanding of each other's approaches to promoting transparency (ibid., Art. 21.3(b)(ii)), recognizing the associated impacts of regulations (ibid, Art. 21.3(b)(v)); regulatory differences (ibid., Art. 21.3(b)(vi)); and regulatory implementation and compliance (ibid., Art. 21.3(vii)). Based on a nonmandatory provision, the process of regulatory cooperation may be opened to private entities "in order to gain non-governmental perspectives" (ibid., Art. 21.8). The process of regulatory cooperation is overseen by the regulatory cooperation forum (RCF).

The Sustainable Development and Environment Chapters

The TSD chapter of CETA (2016, Chapter 22) provides for transparency "as a necessary element to promote public participation" in the context of the environment (ibid., Arts 22.2 and 24.7). The Trade and Environment chapter (ibid., Chapter 24) reiterates the parties' commitments to the multilateral environmental agreements (MEAs) which they are party to (ibid., Art. 24.4),[5] and seek "exchange of views on the relationship between multilateral environmental agreements and international trade rules" (ibid., Art. 24.12(1)(j)). A reference to climate change is implied by a clause on cooperation to promote energy efficiency, and to develop and deploy low-carbon and other climate-friendly technologies (ibid., Art. 24.12.1(e)). However, it is the recommendation adopted by the EU and Canada that refers to the Paris Agreement as an MEA (CETA Joint Committee 2018, paragraph 2), incorporating it as part of the obligations falling under the TSD chapter. Under a cooperative framework, CETA encourages voluntary schemes such as eco-labelling (CETA 2016; Art. 22.3(2)(a)); corporate social responsibility (ibid., Art. 24.12(1)(c)); and best practices on product life-cycle management (ibid., Art. 24.12(1)(h)).

A governmental framework for engagement on trade-related environmental issues to develop a *global approach* to TSD (ibid., Art. 22.1(2))[6] entails the establishment of a TSD committee comprising governmental representatives. It is responsible for conducting public sessions on aspects related to the implementation of CETA's environmental provisions (ibid., Art. 22.4(3)) and promoting transparency and public participation (ibid., Art. 22.4). The EU and Canada are under the obligation to report to a civil society forum (CSF) comprising representatives from environmental groups (ibid., Art. 22.5). The TSD committee has the additional responsibility of reporting to the CSF (ibid., Art. 22.4.4(b)) as well. The civil society actors that participate in the CSF are arranged within domestic advisory groups (DAGs) on the EU and Canadian sides (ibid., Art. 24.13(5); European Economic and Social Committee 2020a). Continued collaborative governance on climate protection is plausible as the EU and Canada may involve stakeholders (CETA 2016, Art. 24.12(1)(3)) in the implementation of identified activities.

PROGRESS ON ENGAGEMENTS SO FAR AND THE IMPEDIMENTS TO COLLABORATION

Collaborative governance concerns consensus building in the decision-making process (Emerson and Murchie, 2011, 142). This section utilizes a framework, adapted by the author, on principled engagements conceived to analyze the progress in this direction (Emerson and Nabatchi 2015, 191) to assess the extent to which the actors involved in the implementation of CETA's TSD provisions have interacted on climate-related issues while participating through the various institutional mechanisms set up under the agreement. Table 11.1 covers the CETA Joint Committee, RCF, CSF, and the TSD committee against the parameters of identification, deliberation, and decision[7] as required for collaborative governance. In this manner, we are able to ascertain whether climate change has been identified, discussed, and sought to be addressed as an issue under CETA.

The CETA Joint Committee identified climate change as a concern and recognized climate action as a shared goal. As the sole committee that can take decisions concerning *all* matters covered by CETA (2016, Art. 26.3(1); emphasis added), it adopted the recommendation on Trade, Climate Action and the Paris Agreement (CETA Joint Committee 2018) reaffirming the parties' international commitments. The committee informed the CSF about the progress made in respect of the climate recommendation which concerns bringing the EU and the Canadian Small and Medium Enterprises (SMEs) together for a "*collaboration* promoting the trade and climate dimension in WTO" (European Commission 2020a, 3; emphasis added). The EU and Canadian DAGs consulted with governmental representatives on the EU's carbon border measures and Canada's interest in exploring their potential (Joint Report 2020). The CSF works in a consultative and advisory capacity and as such does not have the authority to undertake decisions pertaining to climate-related issues. At the time of writing, the RCF has not engaged with climate change along any of the parameters mentioned before. It has convened thrice and taken a sectoral approach to addressing regulatory issues.[8] As a specialized committee established for addressing all matters concerning sustainable development in the context of CETA, the TSD committee identifies its agendas and engagements with other actors and may propose draft decisions for adoption by the CETA Joint Committee or take decisions on its own accord (CETA 2016, Art. 26.2(4)). On climate change, the TSD committee developed a work plan to engage with the WTO's Committee on Trade and Environment (CTE) (European Commission 2019b, 3).

In the current format, collaborative governance under CETA is embedded in policy and soft law[9] rationale to build consensus after engaging in "collective deliberation" (Terpan 2015, 84, 88). Whether collaboration will facilitate or discourage cooperation among stakeholders is dependent upon their "*shared vision* for what they would like to achieve through collaboration and *a history of past cooperation*" (Ansell and Gash 2007, 550; emphasis added). Based on this observation, some impediments to collaborative governance arise under CETA. This is also to say

Table 11.1
Principled engagement on climate change under CETA

	Identification	Deliberation	Decision
CETA Joint Committee	✓	✓	✓
RCF	×	×	×
CSF	✓	✓	×
TSD committee	✓	✓	✓

Source: Author's adaptation of the table in Emerson and Nabatchi (2015, 192).

that collaborative governance under CETA operates in a wider context of the EU-Canada climate partnership which is framed as a commitment to international cooperation on climate action but is marked by an undercurrent of divergent regulatory approaches in this area. Some examples are discussed in the following paragraphs.

CETA's economic dimension is extended by the incorporation of the investment chapter. However, its incorporation is opposed by environmental interest groups on the ground that investment provisions favour the interests of foreign investors over environmental and climate imperatives (Corporate Europe Observatory 2016). By utilizing the investor-state dispute settlement (ISDS) mechanism, foreign investors may challenge host state regulations on the pretext that they result in the expropriation and/or unfair and inequitable treatment of their investments. There are other systemic issues with the ISDS such as: (i) granting investors the right to appoint arbitrators, and (ii) facilitating ad hoc arbitrations that generally lack transparency. The EU has sought to address these drawbacks through an investment court system (ICS) that has been incorporated in CETA. The ICS may be a reform of the ISDS process, but it maintains the right of a foreign investor to submit claims against governmental regulations. Therefore, environmental actors argue that the ICS is still effectively "an ISDS system, just institutionalized" (Riffel 2019, 2). In comparison, the dispute settlement process on environmental and climate issues makes use of soft law for resolving matters through governmental consultations and nonbinding recommendations (CETA 2016, Arts 24.14–24.16). The EU contends that it is an effective mechanism for promoting environmental protection and climate action, with no intention to introduce sanctions for the violation of the sustainable development and environment chapters of CETA (European Commission 2018b). Actors representing environmental and climate interests advocate a sanctions-based approach whereas economic actors extend their support to the cooperation-based dispute settlement mechanism on sustainable development (BusinessEurope 2017, 3). CETA's investment chapter is not in force at the time of writing this chapter. However, once it enters into force, it will trigger a power asymmetry that collaborative governance has found difficult to overcome (Ansell and Gash 2007, 550).

The resort to soft law for settling climate-related disputes under CETA may well be based on its potential to bring about a gradual change in the future conduct of the parties (Chinkin 1989, 859; Guzman and Meyer 2010, 174). However, it is the lack of enforceability of soft law that undermines the certainty with which the parties undertake their commitments under a given agreement (Schwarcz 2020, 2473). Given that the ISDS is found to have decelerated environmental regulation in host states facing rising investment claims (Berge and Berger 2021, 24) CETA may attenuate the negative correlation between investment law and sustainable development.

The EU and Canada may be "like-minded" partners in the sphere of international environmental cooperation (European Commission 2020b), but as seen in *EC-Hormones* (1998) and *EC-Biotech* (2006) cases at the WTO, the EU and Canada have divergent approaches to the "trade and environment" linkage. This is evident from their divergent interpretation of the precaution principle[10] that guides regulatory imperatives and risk assessments in the field of environment (Wiener and Rogers 2002). There is no universally accepted definition of the precautionary principle (Mead 2004) but considering that the EU has adopted the principle as a constitutional mandate in the area of environmental policy under Art. 191(2) of the Treaty on the Functioning of the European Union (TFEU 2016) which is also the foundation of its climate policy (Stoczkiewicz 2018, 47), divergences between the EU and Canada are more than likely to continue in the respect of risk regulation targeting climate mitigation and adaptation.

The EU and Canada were opposing parties in *Canada – Feed in Tariff (FIT)* (2013). The WTO's decision in this case could have strengthened the trade-climate linkage at the multilateral level had its panel and the appellate body been able to decide whether the FIT program constituted a subsidy under the Agreement on Subsidies and Countervailing Measures (SCM Agreement 1994). The indecisiveness of the panel and the appellate body has the effect of "condoning renewable energy subsidies" (Genest 2014, 240, 251). Better decision-making at the WTO level would have created an exemption for such subsidies under the SCM Agreement and bolstered the trade-climate linkage at the international level, aiding future developments under CETA.

Possibly in response to the *EC-Hormones* (1998) and *EC-Biotech* (2006) cases, CETA carries provisions on bilateral cooperation on animal welfare and biotechnology products, respectively (CETA 2016, Arts 21.4(s) and 25.2). The inclination toward soft, cooperative mechanisms is present in the respect of climate protection as well. For instance, CETA provisions direct the parties to cooperate within the international climate change regime as well as on domestic climate policies on issues such as energy efficiency, climate-friendly technologies, and renewable energy (ibid., Arts 24.12(1)(e), 24.12(1)(f)). These provisions revive the role of collaborative governance as a channel to facilitate the development of soft law. In the light of the existing imbalances between the economic provisions of CETA on the one hand and its climate goals on the other, the inclusion of non-state actors and the quality of the deliberative process should be made as intrinsic as possible in the process of implementation (Pickering et al. 2019, 28). In case of a failure in this respect, CETA may fall short on creating the required incentives to collaborate (Emerson and Nabatchi 2015, 46). Furthermore, the process outcomes (such as decisions made jointly by diverse actors on climate action) and social outcomes (such as the "creation of shared meaning, increased trust among participant" [Rogers and Weber 2010, 2]) that collaborative governance is directed at may not be achieved.

The role of governmental institutions is to bring about behavioural change in the conduct of corporate entities and investors operating in climate-sensitive industries. This is easier said than done. Negative application of power by governmental actors can thus result in "tokenistic behaviour and non-decision-making" (Morrison et al. 2019, 3). In some instances, governments may collude with economic actors as seen in Canada wherein collaborative governance in the energy industry has been unsuccessful because of the selective enforcement of rules to the benefit of industry actors (Brisbois, Morris, and de Loë 2019, 161, 166). At other times, governments may simply question the climate impacts of an FTA as the Netherlands did in the case of CETA (Klok 2020) prior to its ratification. Furthermore, the developments under RCF as discussed earlier demonstrate that climate change has not yet been considered under CETA's regulatory agenda.

THE WAY FORWARD

The hurdles in the way of collaborative governance under CETA should in no way lead to the abandonment of its "trade and climate" agenda. One of the primary arguments to support this contention is that the environmental regime depends on trade agreements such as CETA to promote environmental governance because MEAs have found it difficult to enhance the effectiveness of the environmental regime on their own (Jinnah 2011, 191).

International environmental law has utilized soft law and collaborative mechanisms since the 1992 Rio Declaration, with the objective of integrating trade, investment, and sustainable development (Segger 2021, 100, 103). Collaborative governance may be overshadowed by the outcomes of the dispute settlement process *if* and *when* they materialize. Collaborative governance remains relevant otherwise, particularly for driving sectoral policies such as those directed at fisheries and forests management.[11] Based on this premise, collaborative governance is an ongoing process aimed at "promoting collective action in a power-shared world by improving problem definitions, stimulating mutual learning and spurring innovation, facilitating coordination, and generating joint ownership of solutions that enables their implementation" (Sørensen and Torfing 2021, 2). Law faces methodological problems in assessing progress along these objectives.

Analysis from a legal perspective questions the challenges that arise in the context of accountability when there is collaboration in governance and suggest strengthening the rule of law to better define the roles and responsibilities of the participants (Qi 2019, 7, 8; Zouridis and Leijtens 2021, 126). This is also because collaborative governance overlaps with law but it is not a legal framework as such. It originated in the field of public management, as explained earlier in this chapter, which tends to either omit law and legal frameworks when administering collaborative governance (Amsler 2016), or expresses frustration with its interactions with the "legalities associated with statutory, goal-based compliance ... tied to a fragmented, siloed system of agencies" (Rogers and Weber 2010, 2). It is public management, however, that chooses to operate in silos and this is reflected from the observation that "there have been relatively few studies of climate change governance in public management literature. In contrast, environmental governance literature has provided rich insights on this topic" (McQuaid, Rhodes, and Ortega 2021, 164). Legal scholarship that engages with environmental and climate governance recognizes climate change as a very real problem with profound consequences that need collective action (Kotzé 2014). It is often stated that governments must have the political will to implement climate policies (Biesbroek, Peters, and Tosun 2018, 786), but when governmental policies express political will, it is law that "binds" political will (Zouridis and Leijtens 2021, 119). Consequently, the question that needs to be addressed is what insights law can provide to better support collaborative governance on climate.

In this context, an examination of the policy frameworks that are directed at (i) improving regulatory processes within public institutions and agencies, and (ii) strengthening corporate social responsibility (CSR) frameworks on climate change is helpful. CETA is capable of facilitating "top-down" approaches to collaborative governance. The agreement states that "The Parties shall take into account the activities of relevant multilateral environmental organisations or bodies so as to promote greater cooperation and coherence between the work of the Parties and these organisations or bodies" (CETA 2016, Art. 24.13(4)). Since the international frameworks on collaborative governance for climate have been discussed earlier in this chapter, let us not delve into them further here. The EU's own experience, however, may stimulate "bottom-up" approaches to collaborative governance.

In the process of economic integration, the regulation of the EU's internal market has necessitated innovations that operate between the field of public management and law. Better regulation is one way in which the EU manages the involvement of citizens, businesses, and other stakeholders in the decision-making process (Radaelli and Meuwese 2009). It began as a reform based on economic policy reasons, i.e., seeking growth and competitiveness of the EU internal market but came to acquire a public management function over time (Radaelli and Meuwese 2009, 646), and is now one of the primary instruments through which the EU aims to integrate sustainable development across all its policies (European Commission 2021b, 1). As a principle for better self- and co-regulation, "open governance" established under better regulation seeks *collaborative* open exchange between interested parties (European Commission 2017b, 119). In monitoring and evaluating existing legislation, the EU may require reporting from private actors and particularly in the area of trade concerning developing countries, better regulation aims to regulate the behaviour of transnational corporations (ibid., 265, 310). The better regulation "toolbox" comprises regulatory impact assessment, risk-based approaches to regulation, and ex post evaluation of regulations (European Commission 2019c). These elements are reflected in the regulatory cooperation chapter of CETA highlighted earlier, particularly Art. 21.4(a), on which the parties can engage further.

Additionally, the EU has applied collaborative governance in the field of EU environmental law and defined it as "the provision of a forum in which a range of public and private actors, from different levels of governance (local, regional, national, EU) are able to work closely and intensively on solving or even identifying, a common problem. Collaborative governance implies something more than consultation, in the potential for deliberation and interaction; and less than public participation, given that there will be restrictions on who can participate" (Lee 2014, 89). However, participation may be expanded as is being done by the EU through the introduction of a complaints mechanism for the TSD chapter of its FTAS (European Commission 2020d, 2021c). This mechanism is accessible to citizens and nongovernmental organizations (NGOS) representing environmental and climate-related interests. Although the promotion of collaborative governance under this mechanism may be along the parameter of identification alone. This is because in recognizing that "Implementing EU trade agreements is clearly a collective effort" (European Commission 2020d, 5), the Commission seeks cooperation primarily from member states. This means that citizens may help identify and inform about the infringement of TSD provisions but the participation in deliberation and decision-making remains within the domain of public authorities.

CONCLUSIONS

While collaborative governance is a means to an end, it also has inherent value as a process. This chapter sought to highlight its relevance in both these respects by discussing it as method for implementing the climate-related commitments made by the EU and Canada under CETA and then enumerating the factors that will promote or hamper its employment. This chapter showed that the implementation of CETA sits squarely between the fields of law and public management. The two are distinct and in need of better linkage for the purpose of ensuring effective execution of policy objectives in a partnership such as CETA that has been undertaken primarily to serve economic objectives. International legal developments on climate change have predominantly led to the establishment of objectives by governmental actors. However, climate action can no longer be considered without the role played by economic and social actors. In this connection, the provisions of CETA provide sufficient scope for the EU and Canada to utilize the agreement as a platform to promote collaborative governance based on the insights provided by international frameworks and independent learnings derived from managing internal affairs concerning the overlap between economic and climate objectives.

NOTES

1 All EU member states as well as Canada have ratified the Paris Agreement (United Nations Climate Change 2020).
2 The central obligations of the parties to the Paris Agreement is to keep global temperature rise in this century well below 2 degrees Celsius above

pre-industrial levels and to pursue efforts to limit the temperature increase even further to 1.5 degrees Celsius. Furthermore, the parties aim to increase the ability to deal with the impacts of climate change, and make finance flows consistent with a low greenhouse gas (GHG) emissions and climate-resilient pathway. See Paris Agreement (2020).

3 In its narrowest sense, public management is broadly defined "as encompassing the organizational structures, managerial practices, and institutionalized values by which officials enact the will of sovereign authority"; see Lynn (2005, 28). It is stated that "Public management, while about accomplishing the objectives of government, has recognized that these objectives are not solely accomplished through public organizations or even single organizational actors," highlighting the role of "other players and stakeholders in the administration of government policies and goals" (Sowa and Lu 2016).

4 Adaptation tackles the adverse effects of climate change and is concerned with taking appropriate action to prevent or minimize it. Mitigation means making the impacts of climate change less severe by preventing or reducing the emission of GHGs into the atmosphere (see European Environment Agency 2021).

5 This provision has been utilized to adopt the recommendation on Trade, Climate Action and the Paris Agreement; see para. 8 of CETA Joint Committee (2018).

6 This must also be understood in the light of the EU's objective to pursue environmental objectives through trade. See Art. 21 of the Treaty on the European Union (TEU 2016).

7 "Identification" is defined as the "[e]xtent to which participants reveal interests, concerns, and values; recognize shared goals; recognize how their own interests are served by participation in group; identify, share, and analyze relevant information"; "Deliberation" is defined as the "[e]xtent to which participants engage in fair and civil discourse"; and "Decisions" is defined as the "[e]xplicit agreement on common purpose, target goals" that can take the form of agendas and policy-related decisions (see Emerson and Nabatchi 2015, 192).

8 Under the sectoral approach, the RCF under CETA is in the process of addressing regulatory issues around cybersecurity, animal welfare, cosmetics-like drug products, pharmaceutical inspections, consumer product safety, paediatric medicines, electrical engineering, and wood pellet boilers. See European Commission (2018c, 2020c, 2021a).

9 For the purpose of this chapter, the definition of soft law is "legal or non-legal obligations which create the expectation that they will be used to

avoid or resolve disputes. They are not subject to effective third party interpretation, and their subject matter and formation are international in nature. The five main elements of this definition will be examined in detail: A) the international nature of the subject matter and means of formation; B) the inclusion of both legal and non-legal instruments; C) the creation of expectations; D) the purpose of avoiding or resolving disputes; and E) the difficulty of effective third party interpretation" (Gruchalla-Wesierski 1984, 44).

10 The precautionary principle is derived from principle 15 of the Rio Declaration which states: "In order to protect the environment, the precautionary approach shall be widely applied by States according to their capabilities. Where there are threats of serious or irreversible damage, lack of full scientific certainty shall not be used as a reason for postponing cost-effective measures to prevent environmental degradation."

11 Art. 24.10 of CETA (2016) carries the obligation of cooperating on sustainable forest management and conservation. Art. 24.11 (ibid.) states that the parties cooperate to combat illegal, unreported, and unregulated fishing as well as in the area of regional fisheries management. The EU and Canada have developed collaborative governance frameworks in the area of forest management. On fisheries management, however, Canadian approaches are considered as more effective. On the forest management approaches, see Johansson (2018) and Böhling (2019). See Birnbaum (2016) on the assessment on Canadian and EU approaches to fisheries management.

REFERENCES

Albareda, Laura. 2008. "Corporate Responsibility, Governance and Accountability: From Self-Regulation to Co-Regulation." *Corporate Governance: The International Journal of Business in Society* 8, no. 4: 430–39. https://doi.org/10.1108/14720700810899176.

Amsler, Lisa Blomgren. 2016. "Collaborative Governance: Integrating Management, Politics, and Law." *Public Administrative Review* 76, no. 5: 700–11. https://doi.org/10.1111/puar.12605.

Ansell, Chris, and Alison Gash. 2008. "Collaborative Governance in Theory and Practice." *Journal of Public Administration Research and Theory* 18, no. 4: 543–71. https://doi.org/10.1093/jopart/mum032.

Barral, Virginie. 2012. "Sustainable Development in International Law: Nature and Operation of an Evolutive Legal Norm." *European Journal of International Law* 23, no. 2: 377–400. https://doi.org/10.1093/ejil/chs016.

Bendell, Jem. 2011. "Towards Rio 2012 and Collaborative Governance for Sustainable Development." *Social Space* 36–41. Accessed 2 February 2022. https://ink.library.smu.edu.sg/lien_research/72/.

Berge, Tarald Laudal, and Axel Berger. 2021. "Do Investor-State Dispute Settlement Cases Influence Domestic Environmental Regulation? The Role of Respondent State Bureaucratic Capacity." *Journal of International Dispute Settlement* 12, no. 1: 1–41. https://doi.org/10.1093/jnlids/idaa027.

Biesbroek, Robbert, B., Guy Peters, and Jale Tosun. 2018. "Public Bureaucracy and Climate Change Adaptation." *Review of Policy Research* 35, no. 6: 776–91. https://doi.org/10.1111/ropr.12316.

Bingham, Lisa Blomgren. 2010. "The Next Generation of Administrative Law: Building the Legal Infrastructure for Collaborative Governance." *Wisconsin Law Review* 2: 297–356.

Birnbaum, Simon. 2016. "Environmental Co-governance, Legitimacy, and the Quest for Compliance: When and Why Is Stakeholder Participation Desirable?" *Journal of Environmental Policy and Planning* 18, no. 3: 306–23. https://doi.org/10.1080/1523908X.2015.1077440.

Birnie, Patricia, Alan Boyle, and Catherine Redgwell. 2009. *International Law & the Environment* (3rd Edition). Oxford: Oxford University Press.

Böhling, Kathrin. 2019. "Collaborative Governance in the Making: Implementation of a New Forest Management Regime in an Old-Growth Conflict Region of British Columbia, Canada." *Land Use Policy* 86: 43–53. https://doi.org/10.1016/j.landusepol.2019.04.019.

Brink, Ebba, and Christine Wamsler. 2017. "Collaborative Governance for Climate Change Adaptation: Mapping Citizen–Municipality Interactions." *Environmental Policy and Governance* 2: 82–97. https://doi.org/10.1002/eet.1795.

Brisbois, Marie Claire, Michelle Morris, and Rob de Loë. 2019. "Augmenting the IAD Framework to Reveal Power in Collaborative Governance – An Illustrative Application to Resource Industry Dominated Processes." *World Development* 120: 159–68. https://doi.org/10.1016/j.worlddev.2018.02.017.

BusinessEurope. 2017. "Trade and Sustainable Development Chapters in EU FTAS." 6 November. Accessed 15 August 2021. https://www.businesseurope.eu/sites/buseur/files/media/position_papers/rex/2017-11-06_sustainability_and_ftas.pdf.

Canada – Feed in Tariff (FIT) (Canada – Certain Measures Affecting the Renewable Energy Generation Sector and Canada – Measures Relating to the Feed-in Tariff Program). 2013. WT/DS412/AB/R and WT/DS426/AB/R. 24 May.

CETA (Comprehensive Economic and Trade Agreement). 2016. Accessed
    23 July 2020. https://www.international.gc.ca/trade-commerce/trade-
    agreements-accords-commerciaux/agr-acc/ceta-aecg/text-texte/toc-tdm.aspx.
CETA Joint Committee. 2018. "Recommendation 001/2018 of
    26 September 2018 of the CETA Joint Committee on Trade, Climate
    Action and Paris Agreement." Accessed 23 July 2020. http://trade.ec.europa.
    eu/doclib/docs/2018/september/tradoc_157415.pdf.
Chinkin, C.M. 1989. "The Challenge of Soft Law: Development and Change
    in International Law." *International and Comparative Law Quarterly* 38:
    850–66. https://www.jstor.org/stable/759917.
Corporate Europe Observatory. 2016. "European and Canadian Civil
    Society Groups Call for Rejection of CETA." 28 November. Accessed
    8 February 2020. https://corporateeurope.org/en/international-trade/2016/11/
    european-and-canadian-civil-society-groups-call-rejection-ceta.
Emerson, Kirk, and Peter Murchie. 2011. "Collaborative Governance and
    Climate Change: Opportunities for Public Administration." In *The Future
    of Public Administration around the World: The Minnowbrook Perspective*,
    edited by Rosemary O'Leary, David M. Van Slyke, and Soonhee Kim,
    141–54. Washington, DC: Georgetown University Press.
Emerson, Kirk, and Tina Nabatchi. 2015. *Collaborative Governance Regimes*.
    Washington, DC: Georgetown University Press.
Emerson, Kirk, Tina Nabatchi, and Stephen Balogh. 2011. "An Integrative
    Framework for Collaborative Governance." *Journal of Public Administration
    Research and Theory* 22, no. 1: 1–29. https://doi.org/10.1093/jopart/muro11.
European Commission. 2017a. "EU-Canada Trade Agreement Enters into
    Force." Accessed 23 July 2020. https://ec.europa.eu/commission/presscorner/
    detail/en/IP_17_3121.
– 2017b. "Better Regulation Toolbox." Accessed 15 August 2021. https://
    ec.europa.eu/info/sites/default/files/better-regulation-toolbox_2.pdf.
– 2018a. *Report from the Commission to the European Parliament and the
    Council on the Implementation of the EU Strategy on Adaptation to
    Climate Change*. COM(2018) 738 (final). Brussels: European Commission.
– 2018b. "Non Paper of the Commission Services: Feedback and Way
    Forward on Improving the Implementation and Enforcement of Trade and
    Sustainable Development Chapters in EU Free Trade Agreements." Accessed
    25 February 2019. http://trade.ec.europa.eu/doclib/docs/2018/february/
    tradoc_156618.pdf.
– 2018c. "1st Meeting of the CETA Regulatory Cooperation Forum." Accessed
    15 August 2021. https://trade.ec.europa.eu/doclib/docs/2018/november/
    tradoc_157552.pdf.

– 2019a. *Report from the Commission to the European Parliament, the Council, the European Economic and Social Committee and the Committee of the Regions on Implementation of Free Trade Agreements: 1 January 2018 – 31 December 2018.* COM(2019) 455 (final). Brussels: European Commission.

– 2019b. "Meeting of the Committee on Trade and Sustainable Development." Accessed 15 August 2021. https://trade.ec.europa.eu/doclib/docs/2020/january/tradoc_158604.pdf.

– 2019c. *Better Regulation: Taking Stock and Sustaining Our Commitment.* COM(2019) 178 (final). Brussels: European Commission.

– 2020a. "Meeting of the Civil Society Forum." Accessed 15 August 2021. https://trade.ec.europa.eu/doclib/docs/2021/march/tradoc_159494.pdf.

– 2020b. "Bilateral and Regional Cooperation." Accessed 15 August 2021. https://ec.europa.eu/environment/international_issues/relations_canada_en.htm.

– 2020c. "2nd Meeting of the CETA Regulatory Cooperation Forum." Accessed 15 August 2021. https://trade.ec.europa.eu/doclib/docs/2020/january/tradoc_158565.pdf.

– 2020d. "Working Approaches to the Enforcement and Implementation Work of DG TRADE." 16 November. Accessed 15 August 2021. https://trade.ec.europa.eu/doclib/docs/2020/november/tradoc_159075.pdf.

– 2021a. "3rd Meeting of the CETA Regulatory Cooperation Forum." Accessed 15 August 2021. https://trade.ec.europa.eu/doclib/docs/2021/january/tradoc_159275.pdf.

– 2021b. "Better Regulation: Joining Forces to Make Better Laws." Accessed 15 August 2021. https://ec.europa.eu/info/sites/default/files/better_regulation_joining_forces_to_make_better_laws_en_0.pdf.

– 2021c. "Operating Guidelines for the Single Entry Point and Complaints Mechanism for the Enforcement of EU Trade Agreements and Arrangements." 23 June. Accessed 15 August 2021. https://trade.ec.europa.eu/access-to-markets/en/form-assets/operational_guidelines.pdf.

EC-Biotech. 2006. *European Communities – Measures Affecting the Approval and Marketing of Biotech Products,* WT/DS291/R, WT/DS292/R, WT/DS293/R, 29 September.

EC-Hormones. 1998. *European Communities – Measures Concerning Meat and Meat Products.* WT/DS26/AB/R, WT/DS48/AB/R. World Trade Organization Appellate Body, 16 January.

European Economic and Social Committee. 2020. "The EU-Canada Domestic Advisory Group." Accessed 15 August 2021. https://www.eesc.europa.eu/en/sections-other-bodies/other/eu-canada-domestic-advisory-group.

European Environment Agency. 2021. "What is the difference between adaptation and mitigation?" Accessed 15 August 2021. https://www.eea. europa.eu/help/faq/what-is-the-difference-between.

Finbow, Robert. 2019. Welcome Address. CETA Implications Conference, 28 September, Dalhousie University, Halifax.

Florini, Ann, and Markus Pauli. 2018. "Collaborative Governance for the Sustainable Development Goals." *Asia & the Pacific Policy Studies* 5, no. 3: 583–98. https://doi.org/10.1002/app5.252.

French, Duncan. 2006. "Supporting the Principle of Integration in the Furtherance of Sustainable Development: A Sideways Glance." *Environmental Law and Management* 18: 103–17.

Genest, Alexandre. 2014. "The Canada—FIT Case and the WTO Subsidies Agreement: Failed Fact-Finding, Needless Complexity, and Missed Judicial Economy." *The McGill International Journal of Sustainable Development Law and Policy* 10, no. 2: 237–58.

Gruchalla-Wesierski, Tadeusz. 1984. "A Framework for Understanding 'Soft Law.'" *McGill Law Journal* 30, no. 1: 37–88.

Guzman, Andrew T., and Timothy L. Meyer. 2010. "International Soft Law." *Journal of Legal Analysis* 2, no. 1: 171–225. https://doi.org/10.1093/jla/2.1.171.

Hamilton, Matthew, and Mark Lubell. 2017. "Collaborative Governance of Climate Change Adaptation Across Spatial and Institutional Scales." *Policy Studies Journal* 46, no. 2: 222–47. https://doi.org/10.1111/psj.12224.

Hysing, Erik. 2020. "Designing Collaborative Governance That Is Fit for Purpose: Theorising Policy Support and Voluntary Action for Road Safety in Sweden." *Journal of Public Policy*, 1–23. https://doi.org/10.1017/S0143814X2000029X.

Jinnah, Sikina. 2011. "Strategic Linkages: The Evolving Role of Trade Agreements in Global Environmental Governance." *The Journal of Environment & Development* 20, no. 2: 191–215. https://doi.org/10.1177/1070496511405152.

Johansson, Johanna. 2018. "Collaborative Governance for Sustainable Forestry in the Emerging Bio-Based Economy in Europe." *Current Opinion in Environmental Sustainability* 32: 9–16. https://doi.org/10.1016/j.cosust.2018.01.009.

Joint Interpretative Instrument. 2017. Joint Interpretative Instrument on the Comprehensive Economic and Trade Agreement (CETA) between Canada and the European Union and its Member States. Accessed 15 August 2021. https://eur-lex.europa.eu/legal-content/EN/TXT/PDF/?uri=CELEX:22017X0114(01)&from=EN.

Kalesnikaite, Vaiva. 2018. "Keeping Cities Afloat: Climate Change Adaptation and Collaborative Governance at the Local Level." *Public Performance & Management Review* 42, no. 4: 864–88. https://doi.org/10.1080/15309576.2018.1526091.

Keohane, Robert O., and David G. Victor. 2011. "The Regime Complex for Climate Change." *Perspectives on Politics* 9, no. 1: 7–23. https://doi.org/10.1017/S1537592710004068.

Klok, Marcel. 2020. "Dutch Give Initial Approval to EU-Canada Trade Deal." *Ing*, 18 February. https://think.ing.com/snaps/the-netherlands-a-first-yes-to-ceta/.

Kotzé, Louis J. 2014. "Rethinking Global Environmental Law and Governance in the Anthropocene." *Journal of Energy & Natural Resources Law* 32, no. 2: 121–56. https://doi.org/10.1080/02646811.2014.11435355.

Lee, Maria. 2014. *EU Environmental Law, Governance and Decision-Making*. Oxford: Hart.

Levi-Faur, David (ed.). 2011. *Handbook on the Politics of Regulation*. Cheltenham: Edward Elgar.

Lynn, Laurence E. 2005. "Public Management: A Concise History of the Field." In *The Oxford Handbook of Public Management*, edited by Ewan Ferlie, Laurence E. Lynn, Jr., and Christopher Pollitt, 27–50. Oxford/New York: Oxford University Press.

Marceau, Gabrielle. 2016. "The Interface Between the Trade Rules and Climate Change Actions." In *Legal Issues on Climate Change and International Trade Law*, edited by Deok-Young Park, 3–39. Switzerland: Springer International Publishing.

Mathiesen, Karl. 2018. "EU Says No New Trade Deals With Countries Not In Paris Agreement." *Climate Home News*, 2 February. https://www.climatechangenews.com/2018/02/02/eu-difficult-imagine-trade-deals-countries-not-paris-agreement/.

McQuaid, Siobhan, Mary Lee Rhodes, and Aitzibe Egusquiza Ortega. 2021. "A Key Actors Governance Framework (KAGF) for Nature-Based Solutions to Societal Challenges." In *Handbook of Collaborative Public Management*, edited by Jack W. Meek, 164–78. Cheltenham: Edward Elgar.

Mead, Stephanie Joan. 2004. "The Precautionary Principle: A Discussion of the Principle's Meaning and Status in an Attempt to Further Define and Understand the Principle." *New Zealand Journal of Environmental Law* 8, no. 8: 137–76.

Morin, Jean-Frédéric, and Sikina Jinnah. 2018. "The Untapped Potential of Preferential Trade Agreements for Climate Governance." *Environmental Politics* 27, no. 3: 541–65. https://doi.org/10.1080/09644016.2017.1421399.

Morrison, T.H., W.N. Adger, K. Brown, M.C. Lemos, D. Huitema, J. Phelps, L. Evans, et al. 2019. "The Black Box of Power in Polycentric Environmental Governance." *Global Environmental Change* 57: 1–8. https://doi.org/ 10.1016/j.gloenvcha.2019.101934.

Paris Agreement. 2015. Accessed 1 February 2020. https://unfccc.int/ process-and-meetings/the-paris-agreement/d2hhdC1pcy.

Pickering, Jonathan, Jeffrey S. McGee, Sylvia I Karlsson-Vinkhuyzen, and Joseph Wenta. 2019. "Global Climate Governance Between Hard and Soft Law: Can the Paris Agreement's 'Crème Brûlée' Approach Enhance Ecological Reflexivity?" *Journal of Environmental Law* 31, no. 1: 1–28. https://doi.org/10.1093/jel/eqyo18.

Qi, Huiting. 2019. "Strengthening the Rule of Law in Collaborative Governance." *Journal of Chinese Governance* 4, no. 4: 52–70. https://doi.org /10.1080/23812346.2019.1565852.

Radaelli, Claudio M., and Anne C.M. Meuwese. 2009. "Better Regulation in Europe: Between Public Management and Regulatory Reform." *Public Administration* 87, no. 3: 639–54. https://doi.org/10.1111/j.1467-9299. 2009.01771.x.

Riffel, Christian. 2019. "The CETA Opinion of The European Court of Justice and Its Implications: Not That Selfish After All." *Journal of International Economic Law* 22, no. 3: 503–21. https://doi.org/10.1093/jiel/jgz021.

Rio Declaration on Environment and Development. 1992. UN Doc. A/ CONF.151/26 (vol. I), 31 ILM 874.

Rogers, Ellen, and Edward P. Weber. 2010. "Thinking Harder about Outcomes for Collaborative Governance Arrangements." *The American Review of Public Administration* 40, no. 5: 546–67. https://doi.org/10.1177/ 0275074009359024.

Sands, Philippe. 1995. "International Law in the Field of Sustainable Development." *British Yearbook of International Law* 65, no. 1: 303–81. https://doi.org/10.1093/bybil/65.1.303.

SCM Agreement (Agreement on Subsidies and Countervailing Measures). 1994. Marrakesh Agreement Establishing the World Trade Organization, Annex 1A. 1869 UNTS 14.

Schrijver, Nico, and Friedl Weiss, eds. 2004. *International Law and Sustainable Development*. Leiden: Martinus Nijhoff Publishers.

Schwarcz, Steven L. 2020. "Soft Law as Governing Law." *Minnesota Law Review* 104, no. 5: 2471–514. http://dx.doi.org/10.2139/ssrn.3307418.

Segger, Marie-Claire Cordonier. 2021. *Crafting Trade and Investment Accords for Sustainable Development: Athena's Treaties*. Oxford: Oxford University Press.

Silvia, Chris. 2011. "Collaborative Governance Concepts for Successful Network Leadership." *State and Local Government Review* 43, no. 1: 66–71. https://doi.org/10.1177/0160323X11400211.

Sørensen, Eva, and Jacob Torfing. 2021. "Radical and Disruptive Answers to Downstream Problems in Collaborative Governance?" *Public Management Review*: 1–22. https://doi.org/10.1080/14719037.2021.1879914.

Sowa, Jessica E., and Jiahuan Lu. 2016. "Considering Public Management and Its Relationship to Policy Studies." *Policy Studies Journal* 45, no. 1: 74–100. https://doi.org/10.1111/psj.12193.

Stoczkiewicz, Marcin. 2018. "The Climate Policy of the European Union from the Framework Convention to the Paris Agreement." *Journal for European Environmental & Planning Law* 15, no. 1: 42–68.

Terpan, Fabien. 2015. "Soft Law in the European Union – The Changing Nature of EU Law." *European Law Journal* 21, no. 1: 68–96. https://doi.org/10.1111/eulj.12090.

TEU (Treaty on European Union). 2016. Accessed 15 August 2021. https://eur-lex.europa.eu/legal-content/EN/TXT/PDF/?uri=CELEX:12016M/TXT&from=EN.

TFEU (Treaty on the Functioning of the European Union). 2016. Accessed 15 August 2021. https://eur-lex.europa.eu/legal-content/EN/TXT/PDF/?uri=CELEX:12016M/TXT&from=EN.

United Nations Climate Change. 2020. "Paris Agreement - Status of Ratification." Accessed 15 August 2021. https://unfccc.int/process/the-paris-agreement/status-of-ratification.

United Nations Framework Convention on Climate Change (UNFCCC). 1992. Accessed 23 July 2020. https://unfccc.int/resource/docs/convkp/conveng.pdf.

United Nations. 1973. "Declaration of the United Nations Conference on the Human Environment (U.N. Doc. A/Conf.48/14/Rev.1)." Accessed 23 July 2020. https://undocs.org/en/A/CONF.48/14/Rev.1.

– 2015. "Transforming our World: The 2030 Agenda for Sustainable Development." Accessed 23 July 2020. https://sustainabledevelopment.un.org/post2015/transformingourworld/publication.

Weiss, Edith Brown. 2008. "Climate Change, Intergenerational Equity, and International Law." *Vermont Journal of Environmental Law* 9, no. 3: 615. https://doi.org/10.2307/vermjenvilaw.9.3.615.

Wiener, Jonathan B., and Michael D. Rogers. 2002. "Comparing precaution in the United States and Europe" *Journal of Risk Research* 5, no. 4: 317–49. https://doi.org/10.1080/1366987021015 3684.

Wood, Stepan, Georgia Tanner, and Benjamin J. Richardson. 2010. "What Ever Happened to Canadian Environmental Law?" *Ecology Law Quarterly* 37: 981–1040. https://doi.org/10.15779/Z389P0Q.

Zouridis, Stavros, and Vera Leijtens. 2021. "Bringing the Law Back In: The Law-Government Nexus in an Era of Network Governance." *Perspectives on Public Management and Governance* 4, no. 2: 118–29. https://doi.org/10.1093/ppmgov/gvaa022.

12

The Implications of CETA on Energy Systems in Canada: An Integrated Geographical View

Emmanuelle Santoire

This chapter focuses on energy trade in the Comprehensive Economic and Trade Agreement (CETA) between the European Union (EU) and Canada. It offers some overarching reflections on the complex framing of energy as an environment-related question in trade agreements. More specifically, it acknowledges the systemic nature of energy regulatory concerns and outlines a necessary integrated approach of their content to understand the implications of CETA. Integrated stands for the need to move away from silo conceptualizations of energy (divided into energy sources and activities) toward connecting in policymaking all the activities structuring energy, as a physical force, into a useful social resource. Indeed, in CETA, energy not only appears as a commodity or a service, but also as a sector of investment and a regulatory concern. However, such extensive framing lacks explicit language in the deal. CETA is then alternatively promoted as a sustainable transition tool and denounced for its tacit support for fossil fuels. Faced with a difficulty to assess what CETA concretely means for Canadian energy systems, this chapter then seeks to answer two seemingly simple, yet highly representative, questions: where and how energy is featured in CETA, and what the spatial implications of this framing in Canada are. To answer these questions, the present study operates from a geographical angle. It draws on a methodology aiming to observe the texts and uses of law in situation, through their interactions with space. This approach first clarifies the wording of energy provisions in CETA, interpreting them in light of their context of negotiation and of incumbent geographic and regulatory dependencies. Second, it outlines trade agreements as instruments of territorial governance, examining them in the concreteness of their spatial workings. This chapter suggests that the energy vagueness of CETA raises several concerns related to the ambiguity of regulating fossil fuels without clear provisions, and in terms of interprovincial disparities. In saying so, this work serves to facilitate progression toward an analytical blueprint for thinking about a new model of energy norms in trade agreements, attentive to environmental concerns. This study is part of a funded research program led by the School of Environmental Studies at Queen's University, Ontario, and the École Normale Supérieure of Lyon, France, focusing on the effects of CETA on transatlantic waste and energy flows.

CETA AND ENERGY TRADE

Moving away from mostly focusing on trade of goods and on traditional border barriers, CETA addresses services, investments, norms, and regulations. As such, it designs a new generation of progressive economic and social governance tools, and complements the existing framework provided by the World Trade Organization (WTO). Started in 2017, the early, albeit provisional, implementation stage of CETA provides researchers with an opportunity to discuss CETA's novel implications on maintaining sustainable practices and facilitating environmental responsibility. Indeed, CETA is presented as both a broader governing tool, and a template for future international negotiations.

Reading through a Double Paradox

CETA provides an excellent case study to examine the tension behind integrating energy matters in trade law, in a context of global change. It especially reveals the complexity of phrasing bilateral fossil fuel standards in trade deals, due to their potential conflict with environmental efforts. Indeed, if CETA was initially designed at a time when most trade deals were thought as detached from climate concerns, its ratification and provisional implementation in the late 2010s took place in a context where climate action was recognized an urgent and integrated necessity – with trade deals being increasingly denounced as lacking environmental ambition. In this light, CETA's energy provisions present a double paradox.

Energy plays a key role in Canadian trade policies. It is the most emblematic example of North American specialization of Canadian trade, following the regional integration objectives pursued in the 1990s and embodied by the Canadian-US Free Trade Agreement (CUSFTA) (1988) and the North

American Free Trade Agreement (NAFTA) (1991). As of 2018, 98 per cent of all US natural gas imports came from Canada and 3.8 million barrels of oil crossed the Canada-US border per day (Natural Resources Canada, 2018), either by pipeline or by rail. In this context, the EU does not appear as the most strategic trade partner. Despite being the world's largest importer of oil and gas and largest standardized market – thereby being a significant diversification opportunity for Canada – the EU presents substantial limitations to importing Canadian energy. This situation can be attributed to several factors, including geographical contingency, lack of trans-Canadian and transatlantic transport capacity, high costs, regulatory conditions, and growing environmental ambitions. Moreover, taken prevalently as a good, energy appears mainly as residual in the commercial balance between Canada and the EU. Put aside trade in selected products such as uranium and services, Canada represents 0.7 per cent of European oil and gas imports and is the EU's 19th energy trade partner (Global Affairs Canada, 2019). These products benefited from low tariffs prior to CETA (up to 4.7 per cent for non-crude petroleum products, 8 per cent for liquefied propane for the two highest tariffs). From the outset, there was then less to discuss about energy trade in CETA than about other sectors. However, and this is the first paradox, it is evident that energy, including fossil fuels, was discussed during the CETA negotiations to the point that it became quite a controversial issue. It was particularly apparent in the tensions surrounding the European project of a fuel quality directive (FQD) in 2009 (Dir. 2009/30/EC). Following that event, energy became the catalyst for several environmental claims and a flagship for opposing free trade negotiations – as vocalized in Europe and Canada by various activists. And yet, despite these concerns, a second paradox is that energy appears to be rather unaddressed in the final text of CETA. At first read, one could almost believe that it is entirely absent from the deal.

Therefore, this chapter aims to clarify the ambiguous presence of energy matters within the treaty, in order to indicate reflection paths on the foreseeable implications of the agreement in Canada. It does not provide an analysis of the effects of CETA on energy trade, as it is too early to tell. Rather, this contribution challenges the widely held view that CETA would not have effects on energy issues, without embracing overly speculative claims. Its core argument is to demonstrate that energy matters are present in the deal albeit lacking explicit language. CETA treats energy as more than a traded commodity and such framing necessitates novel analyses. Notably, I argue that CETA maintains a regulatory vagueness around energy-environment issues which enables various, and sometimes opposed, claims, stretching from building trans-Canadian infrastructures to increase trade in fossil fuels, to lowering tariffs on green goods and increasing transatlantic climate cooperation.

After explaining the epistemological and methodological tenants of this research, this chapter is organized in three sections, each representing a deductive argument. The first one considers how CETA includes energy under four categories: goods, services, investments, and regulatory norms. The second section confronts the wording of the treaty – which tends to undermine energy's presence in CETA – with a story of the negotiations, during which energy appeared of constant concern, either in itself or to avoid stirring up tensions between the two parties. Finally, a third section highlights trends of spatial implications of CETA on energy systems in Canada. I notably suggest that CETA's indirect energy governance participates of a normative movement pushing for an upscaling of energy strategies in Canada.

AN INTEGRATED VIEW ON THE ENERGY-TRADE ENVIRONMENT NEXUS: GEOGRAPHICAL PERSPECTIVES

It is increasingly difficult to ignore the prominent role played by trade law on energy systems. In a conjunct regulatory movement since the 2000s, energy has entered environmental law in general (figure 12.1 gauges the incremental evolution of energy-related environmental law between 1870[1] and 2018) and has specifically contributing to include environmental provisions in FTAS (Morin, Dür, and Lechner 2018). The market was thought of as a place of regulation toward an attempt to reconcile climate action and economic growth (Dent 2018). That is why, leaving partially behind strictly trade-related objectives, FTAS have been recognized by some as tools for adapting to climate and environmental action, yet in need of critical understanding (Felli 2016).

Social science analyses of FTAS have therefore not been limited to quantifying changes in trade balances. Instead, a growing amount of literature has been questioning how FTAS and their judicial mechanisms could help attain decarbonization goals and regulate trade, but also how they would complexify responsibility models, and could create environmental regulatory chill (Tienhaara 2010, 2018). In geography, however, most scholarship has considered trade deals as regulatory backgrounds, and a penultimate dimension of regional cooperation through macro-scaled geopolitical lenses (Griller, Obwexer, and Vranes 2017; Harris 2016). Consequently, FTAS have been studied for their symbolism and not for their precise content. Focusing on the Canadian case, it is found that most of the geographic essays on trade deals emerged at the end of the 1990s and were

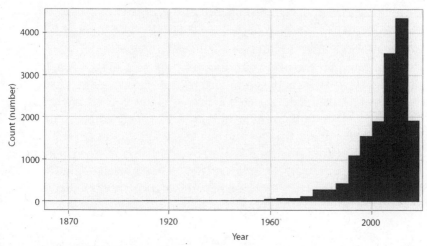

Source: Ecolex database (2019).

Conception/realization: Vaudor and Santoire (2019) for Santoire (2021).

Figure 12.1 Tracing the number of energy-related environmental laws, 1870–2018

characteristic of a strategic time for Canada. This scholarship was primarily case-based, enquiring on Canada-US treaties (Dalby 2019; Ryan 1991; Slowe 1991; Woudsma 1999) as catalysts for regional integration (Andresen 2010; Barlow 1993; Britton 2002). As such, despite these important references, there has been little discussion about trade deals as territorial governance tools. They yet raise a handful of geographical concerns such as place-making processes, entrenchment of fossil regimes, regional economy, uneven development, responsibilities over land, and scales of governance. Still, the usefulness of geographical insights on FTAs lacks visibility.

CETA serves as a topical example to remobilize geography to study trade deals. Indeed, CETA sets a precedent in terms of considering the energy-environment nexus in trade law, but it is also the by-product of evolving norms and regulatory tensions between market and environmental concerns. Emblematic of these tensions, the formal governance of energy, specifically fossil fuels, is done without much explicit content and the spatial implications of the deal seem particularly out of scope. As far as energy is concerned, CETA appears less as a precise legal document than as a political instrument, thus questioning the political will to engage in decarbonized changes. Finally, CETA is also original given its in-depth interest for local (provincial and municipal) governance through public procurement and services. Geographers, attentive to scales of power and practices, could thus inform the concrete consequences of these regulatory changes.

To investigate these novel concerns, this chapter distances itself from the geopolitical approach. Instead, it draws on a strand of literature called geo-legal (Forest 2010, 2009) questioning the co-constitution of space and law (Delaney 2010) to understand the role of norms in the spatialities of energy systems. This chapter consequently adopts an integrated view on energy to seize the interconnected nature of energy concerns in CETA. In doing so, it adheres to a movement that sees both geographers and legal scholars alike using the notion of energy system in their analyses (Bouzarovski, Pasqualetti, and Broto 2017; Bridge et al. 2013; Jenkins et al. 2014; Labussiere and Nadai 2018; Meadowcroft 2009; Selby, Cox, and Royston 2017; Talus 2016). These researchers insist on the value of inter-disciplinary protocols to explore contemporary energy issues.

METHODS

A combined quantitative and qualitative approach was used to achieve the research objectives. Firstly, preliminary text analysis was led to identify the structure of the agreement and clarify its energy content. Occurrences of the words "energy," "oil," "fossil," "renewable," and "electric" were documented throughout the text, helping to identify the annexes as a relevant section. This work yet appeared insufficient in understanding the extended purpose of CETA, its internal mechanisms, and its silences. That is why thirty-one semi-structured interviews were then completed throughout a four-month long fieldwork, in 2018 and 2019. These interviews were used to access information from three target groups: (1) academics and public advisers; (2) federal and provincial policymakers and politicians (with the difficulty of considering changing governmental majorities); and (3) activists and independent researchers. A fourth category of industrial stakeholders was originally considered but ultimately left out due to an absence of responses from the thirty-five companies contacted. Interviews were completed in Ontario, Quebec, and Alberta, as representatives of federal and sub-federal powers for CETA and energy. Prior to commencing the study, ethical clearance was personally sought from each interviewee and the content of each interview was anonymized.

ENERGY RE(DE)FINED: THE MANIFOLD DIMENSIONS OF ENERGY IN CETA

CETA includes energy systems in four trade-related ways. Firstly, energy falls under the General Agreement on Tariffs and Trade (GATT) framework.

Second, it falls under that of the General Agreement on Trade in Services (GATS). Hence CETA considers energy as a good (mostly oil and gas products) and as a service (services incidental to the production, transport, and distribution). Additionally, CETA foregrounds energy through investments and norms especially through government procurement and market access. Energy is finally referred to as a regulatory concern with regards to sustainability, as raised in the trade and environment chapter. However, two of the interviewed scholars agree that this chapter is aspirational in nature (Academics 1 and 5). Politician 1, who had participated in the negotiations noted that the environment chapter was consubstantial to trade goals, in a traditional trade-oriented vision of FTAs. They argued that environmental talks had to take place to make sure that they would not "disrupt the wider goals of CETA" (Politician 1).

The Explicit Mentions of Energy in CETA

Energy does not substantially stand out in the final text of CETA. The textual analysis echoes what one interviewee phrased as a "kind of here and there" (Politician 6) presence of energy in the treaty. Its few explicit mentions are summarized in table 12.1.

The analysis of energy occurrences in CETA reveals a large discrepancy between the extensive presence of energy concerns in the reservations to the agreement (102 occurrences) and its mere mentions in the main text (20 occurrences) (CETA 2016). Figure 12.2 represents this progression.

As indicated in figure 12.2, energy as a good is not found and energy services are only mentioned in the annexes, on the grounds of fostering collaboration on sustainable development. The Strategic Partnership Agreement (SPA) between Canada and EU (2016) signed alongside CETA and considered by several interviewees as the "real deal," targets energy issues much more directly in its Art. 12 on sustainable development than CETA itself.

In addition, all energy sources do not benefit from the same exposure. Specifically, green renewable energies are the only type explicitly mentioned (in Chapter 24, CETA 2016). By contrast, fossil productions only appear in the annexes, alongside other expected elements, such as production and transportation infrastructures. Those are reserved under a national treatment clause. The wording of CETA thus has a way to define, enhance, neglect, or even deny certain aspects of energy. It brings forward what seems to be a minimal liberalization of the sector. Yet, the understanding of its mechanisms leads us to indicate otherwise.

Table 12.1
Presence of explicit energy-related provisions in CETA and the Strategic Partnership Agreement (SPA)

Chapter	Section/Article	Provision/Content
Chapter 8: Investment	Section B: Establishment of investments Art. 8.4: Market access	Measures that would lead to the separation of the ownership of infrastructure from the ownership of the goods and services provided through that infrastructure to ensure fair competition. For example, in the field of energy
Chapter 24: Trade and Environment	Art. 24.9: Trade favouring environmental protection	Make efforts to facilitate and to promote trade and investment in environmental goods and services and especially remove obstacles to trade or investment in goods or services in **renewable energy goods and related services**
	Art. 24.12: Cooperation on environmental issues	Address adverse effects of trade on climate and **promote energy efficiency** and the deployment of low-carbon and other climate-friendly technologies Trade and investment in environmental goods and services incl. environmental and green technologies and practices; **renewable energy; energy efficiency**
Protocol on rules of origin and origin procedures	Section B: Rules of origin Art. 13: Neutral elements	No need to determine the origin of the energy and fuel **used in the production of a product**
Annex I	Schedule of Canada: Federal (applicable in all Provinces and Territories)	Investment: national treatment to hold an oil + gas production licence + share therein. Must be a corporation incorporated in Canada (in crude petroleum and natural gas industries, services incidental to mining)
	Schedule of Canada: Provincial and Territorial	60 results
	EU: Reservations applicable in the EU	22 results
Annex II	Canada: Federal	Reservation II-C-12: transportation services via pipelines, market access. Canadian right to issue certificates for the pipeline transportation of fuels
	Schedule of Canada: sub-federal	54 results
	EU	51 results (49 results electricity, 52 gas, 10 oil)

Table 12.1 (continued)
Presence of explicit energy-related provisions in CETA and the Strategic Partnership Agreement (SPA)

Chapter	Section/Article	Provision/Content
Strategic Partnership Agreement	Art. 12: Sustainable development, paragraph 6	Recognition by the parties of the importance of the energy sector for economic prosperity and international security. Mentioned dimensions: improvement and diversification of energy supplies; energy efficiency; energy affordability, sustainability and security; "high level dialogue on energy" and cooperation including scientific collaboration toward open and competitive markets

Source: Santoire (2021) using data from CETA (2016) and SPA (2016).

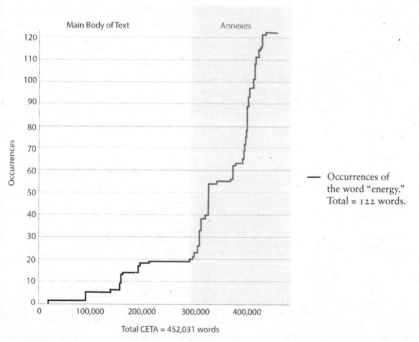

Source: CETA (2016).

Figure 12.2 Chart representing the progression of occurrences of the word "energy" in CETA

The Implicit Mentions of Energy in CETA

Three types of implicit energy references show that CETA deals with energy much more than what appears at the first glance. The first implicit mention concerns the non-systematic reference to energy matters as "energy" – specifically in the sectors of exploitation and export. Indeed, CETA approaches energy matters as silos, by sorting and governing energy sources differently. Forestry goods is one revealing example. As stated by Academic 12: "Europe uses biomass for electricity generation, significantly, increasingly. We have quite an abundant amount of biomass, so you can make a connection between our forestry, agricultural sector in terms of our production of biomass and the exports of this biomass: that's for energy use, right?" The second implicit mention is linked to the negative listing principle on which CETA is built. The investment chapter, for instance, does not mention energy per se, yet it is part of its scope, since liberalization is the default mode of operation in CETA. A third type of implicit energy mentions is found in the structure of the agreement itself. Namely, in a negative listed agreement, the restrictions addressed in the annexes are decisive. In CETA, 90 per cent of these restrictions are provincial and their study highlights substantial interprovincial differences (see for instance figure 12.3 on hydropower regulations under CETA). Following the negative listing logic and the subsequent reservations, it is then difficult to flatten every commodity chain and recompose a puzzle dispersed into different sections. These findings reveal the structural effects of CETA, but they also lead to a more critical understanding of what could be termed as a conundrum of energy silences in CETA.

Weighing Silences: Explaining the Absence of an Energy Chapter

In CETA, energy silences are significant. They tell the story of regulatory tensions between the two parties. One of the most striking finding to emerge from the data collection was indeed the variety of answers to the question, "Why is there no energy chapter in CETA?" (See table 12.2). What was first a configurational concern became an intriguing clue to understand CETA's energy vagueness.

The explanation given by Politician 2 about the potential divisive dimension of energy issues is particularly noticeable as it challenges the neutral reading made by most respondents. For him, the absence of an energy chapter directly relates to the FQD controversy, when CETA negotiations were at their pinnacle, along with the European regulatory project. This

Source: CETA (2016).

Figure 12.3 Hydropower regulatory regimes under CETA: broad overview of provincial reservations

example illustrates the necessity to move from a single textual analysis of the agreement to explore its context of production and the reasoning behind its silences.

OUT OF SIGHT, WELL IN MIND: ENERGY FROM THE NEGOTIATIONS TO THE IMPLEMENTATION

Results from the interview campaign reveal thought-provoking findings that add to our understanding of CETA's energy vagueness. They first manifest that energy gained traction in the negotiations as a potential divisive issue, despite initially limited interests. Then, they demonstrate how this vagueness now justifies using CETA as a flexible tool.

A Topical Issue: Energy Concerns during the Negotiations

It seems to be commonly accepted that fossil fuels are not a strategic object of trade between the two parties. The geographical distance and the

Table 12.2
Answers from the interview panel to "Why is there no energy chapter in CETA?"

Justification	Academics and researchers	Trade agents and politicians
Economic rationale	– "It wasn't necessary … Canada has now liberalized a lot of its energy market and so we don't require an energy chapter the way we should have at the time [NAFTA's time]" (A9) – "our energy trade with Europe is not significant. Hum, you know, in the context of all the other goods, hum, we have, you know, we trade with Europe." (A12)	– unnecessary because stabilized and liberalized Canadian energy market and no major supply security issue (P1) – "unlike our deal with the US which included an energy specific chapter, hum, there wasn't that much emphasis on energy just because it is not something that seen as high potential." (A2)
Legal rationale		– "so, the absence of an energy chapter is actually hum, the rule rather than the exception, hum, in trade agreements" (O3)
Political rationale	– "when the European Union gave up on that quality, hum, fuel quality directive, energy was not, in any way, in danger anymore" (A2)	– "The good and short answer is: 'it was a lot more necessary to have an energy chapter for the Americans' […] but in the end, it was 'an unnecessary chapter,' 'at the end of the day, energy issues were potentially divisive.'" (P2)

A: Academic; O: Organization; P: Politician
Source: Interview campaign, Santoire (2021).

infrastructure needed for their transportation represent an immediate material barrier to trade, both in terms of accessibility and costs – two constraints that are not found with the US. On the electricity side, 60 per cent of Canadian generation comes from hydropower (Natural Resources Canada 2018) – a sector historically conducted by state-lead monopolies which work as powerful lobbies. As evidenced by the lobbying registers, large hydro companies were present during the negotiations and pushed for protecting their activities, so that the complete liberalization of the sector was never considered (resulting in Reservation I-PT-157 for instance). Politician 1 affirmed that "nobody wants to face [name of energy company x] in such a negotiation … [x] often said … that their tender procedure was already largely international, that no one was discriminated against." Hence, if renewable energy compounds, energy services, skills sharing, and investments were finding a rationale under CETA, the same could not be said about major energy productions. Despite stringent concerns such as diversifying Canada's energy balance – Canada is heavily dependent on the US for its energy exports and imports – CETA was not primarily about energy.

And yet the interviews reveal that oil and gas became one of the main contentious matters during the negotiating rounds and a topic successfully pushed for by the Canadian delegation. As set forth by Academic 2: "There is no doubt that energy issues were at the core of the first tensions that emerged around CETA." The argument here is that energy became a key issue to secure in CETA due to the changing nature of the energy-environment relation.

Energy is the first item traded worldwide in value and its strategic interest regarding security of supply makes it an unavoidable object of negotiation, not only on tariffs and prices but also on regulatory conditions. Now, different evidence was gathered to show that as CETA was negotiated, Canada was looking into trade diversification to take a slight distance with the US and to change its environmental reputation. Negotiators had a mind to improve Canada's image on the international market and to enhance their trade balance with Europe. Securing common grounds on fossil matters was then necessary to discuss other concerns including agriculture, but also tariff elimination in environmental goods (mainly, manufactured renewables-related items), services, and investments.

Moreover, fossil productions were also relevant in themselves. As explained by Academic 9, Canada remains a resource-exporting country, "sort of good-based, we have so much of it! That we want to send it to everybody!" A federal civil servant (Politician 6) mentioned the port of Rotterdam as one of the main recipients for Canadian oil barrels, and data on the Canada-EU commercial balance reveals that mineral energy goods are a visible part of transatlantic exchanges (see figure 12.4 and table 12.3).

Yet, as this interviewee explained, if Canadian oil starts its journey in Alberta, then, a pipeline brings it down to the US to be refined. From there, it is put in a barrel and shipped to Europe. This passage through the US is key, since it should be remembered that for the EU, CETA was devised to be a gateway to an agreement with the US. What would be recognized in CETA in terms of carbon standards could therefore affect more than the mere Europe-Canada trade relationship. This point explains the Canadian action taken against the European 2007 FQD.

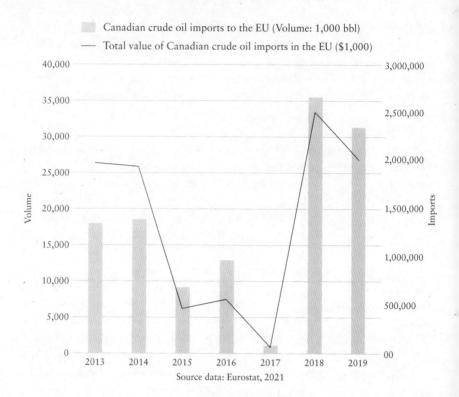

Figure 12.4 Evolution of Canadian crude oil exports to the EU: volume and total value, 2013–19

This domestic regulatory framework was meant to provide clarification to the Energy Charter Treaty (ECT) signed in 1994. In the wake of community-led climate action, the directive aimed to set out quotas for the amount of greenhouse gases (GHGs) emitted during the production, transportation, and combustion of fuels. It would thus regulate EU energy imports. Now, at that time, the European Commission was gathering expertise on the carbonated content of unconventional oil sand productions. For Academic 2, there is no doubt that the negotiations of the FQD were rapidly enmeshed with that of CETA in a sort of active give-and-take deal: "I think that was something Canada used in the negotiation as a tool, saying, 'well if you continue with that, we will give up on other sectors so we won't continue the negotiations,' as an effect, the fuel directive, um, just broke down." While direct energy trade with

Table 12.3
Canadian mineral ores, fuels, and oils exports to EU, October 2017 to September 2018

Recipient EU country	Type of export	Rank in top 5	Value ($M)	Δ% Oct. '17 to Sept. '18/Oct. '16 to Sept. '17
Belgium	Mineral Ores	3	448.9	−0.037
Denmark	Mineral fuels and oils	5	23.7	−0.317
France	Mineral Ores	2	653.4	0.051
Poland	Mineral fuels and oils	2	199.2	0.143
Italy	Mineral fuels and oils	2	607.3	0.178
Finland	Mineral fuels and oils	2	166.9	0.322
Romania	Mineral fuels and oils	1	59.8	0.568
Netherlands	Mineral fuels and oils	1	1200.1	0.869
Slovenia	Mineral fuels and oils	4	3.3	0.990
Croatia	Mineral fuels and oils	1	140.0	∞
Czech Republic	Mineral fuels and oils	3	27.0	∞
Ireland	Mineral fuels and oils	3	62.3	∞
Portugal	Mineral fuels and oils	1	117.9	∞

Source: Based on data from Global Affairs Canada (2018).

the EU might not have been the core issue, the regulatory consequences of this change on the oil value chain would thus have been significant in a context of looming negotiations with the US. Drawing on the FQD controversy, I thus suggest that explicit energy references were progressively elided in the deal and not simply forgotten as irrelevant.

The Discourses around Energy in CETA

Due to the absence of explicit language formally regulating energy concerns, CETA is the vehicle for energy discourses that go far beyond the interests articulated in the agreement. To understand the implications of CETA, it is then necessary to consider these political interpretations and their actors.

The collected data first presents an intriguing gap between the lack of binding provisions on sustainability in CETA and the discourse developed by federal authorities. Federal respondents spoke of CETA as an opportunity to set higher environmental standards and to improve Canada's image on the international stage. They claimed moving forward with "a world green agenda" (Politician 2) and focused on promoting renewable energies and an undefined category of "environmental goods." Politician 2 affirmed that "CETA certainly set up some new sort of gold standard in the 21st century ... to enhance co-operation but also to the use of clean technologies ... green growth." This green narrative produced at the federal level infused in the lower levels of government as a rhetorical instrument, to improve the level of trust between Canada and future investors. Academic 12 explained, "the energy that we use in a system serves as a political statement." That is why findings also suggest that this interpretation of CETA served a national strategy: to emphasize environmental issues as a national concern of federal jurisdiction. By enhancing its responsibility under treaties, the federal government gained an opportunity to highlight its beneficial unifying role, nationwide.

This discourse yet differs from the one displayed at the provincial level where energy is framed as a governance concern (Academic 6), a matter of provincial autonomy (Politician 4, Calgary) and a source of economic prosperity. Most of the politicians surveyed were interested in pragmatically guaranteeing a balanced economy for their province – concurrently reserving or opening energy-related services in CETA. They barely mentioned CETA as a green cooperation platform and only briefly cited potential benefits, focusing on growth and net exports increase in cleantech and renewable-related goods and patents.

By contrast, surveyed NGOs unanimously seized energy as an environmental symbol. They mentioned fossil fuels in the context of investment-state dispute settlement (ISDS) mechanisms. Organization 1 argued that "transnational companies will be served by these regulations." During the interview, activists shared their concerns about CETA which could hinder a sustainable transition in Canada, by propelling the privatization of public facilities, and generating losses in local governance and democracy. Energy represented a key segment of their defensive rhetoric and stood out in anti-CETA pamphlets much more than that in CETA itself (AITEC 2016; Cayley-Daoust and Girard 2012; Sinclair 2011; Trade Justice Network 2010; Trew 2017). As such, energy was incrementally enmeshed in a network of political claims engaging with power, governance, and resource responsibility issues.

IMPLICATIONS OF CETA
ON ENERGY SYSTEMS IN CANADA

Although it might be too early to document the precise effects of CETA on energy trade, this chapter demonstrates that CETA enhances select governing trends worth identifying by researchers and decision makers. This last section provides guidance to considering four changes in spatial and legal practices on energy.

Investments and Spatial Differentiation

A first trend fostered in CETA relates to investments and spatial differentiation, at the core of CETA's novelty. Politician 1 from Quebec defended: "French multinationals deciding to invest or not in Canada: there, you will find the heart of the energy relationship between Europe and Canada." Yet, increased foreign investments in the Canadian energy sector raise geographical issues of territorial equity and regional disparities, especially since CETA reservations substantially vary from one province to the other. Based on provincial standards, they reflect considerable trans-Canadian disparities concerning energy but also derive from an irregular commitment of sub-federal entities in CETA.

The Maritimes provide an excellent example for studying these disparities. New Brunswick is the only Maritime province that did not emit any limitation on fossil fuels investments, echoing ambitions to develop "responsible exploration and development" of oil and natural gas production and transportation means in the province (Nicholas 2013). By contrast, Prince Edward Island is the only province placing explicitly "renewable energy" in its future reserve of action. These regulatory variations multiply responsibility regimes, and they also lessen the federal government's capacity to deliver a unified Canadian energy strategy.

Finally, increased energy investments call to be attentive to the workings of the investment court system (ICS) set out in CETA. Indeed, if the ICS was to be used to judge cases with strong community implications, it seems essential to question whether such external jurisdiction would have the power to apportion environmental responsibilities; and discern whether an energy infrastructure should or not be built. The sense of proximity between energy undertakings and other elementary geographical variables (distance, terrains, water, human settlements, urbanization rate, etc.) and justice issues is not mentioned in the CETA, while preliminary economic impact assessments had identified them as conflict-conducive (Kirkpatrick et al. 2010). According to the activists interviewed, court mechanisms could also belittle the voice of local and regional entities by standardizing procedures at a higher administrative level.

The Political Economy of Energy Stakeholders

The second trend thus relates to the political economy of the deal. The interview campaign has revealed that political leaders, heads of state, and political and industrial lobbies have been key CETA contractors. But it also uncovers that environmental stakeholders played a significant part in opposing (most environmental activists) or interpreting the deal (renewable energy companies for instance) on environmental grounds. As such, this chapter suggests that deeper attention should be granted to the changing political economy of trade deals. Environmental stakeholders are a new element in the fights surrounding trade negotiations and their actions reveal the need for a new heuristic model for energy norms in FTAS.

Sub-federal governments are also key CETA stakeholders, and their role raises several jurisdictional issues. Specifically, during the negotiations, a tension emerged around the discrepancy between topics of provincial interest and of provincial jurisdiction. While the provinces had to be included when topics under their jurisdiction were discussed, this was not the case for topics of mere provincial interest, broader than provincial powers. Academic 4 thus mentioned that the provinces had to be present to exert a sort of "political buy-in" and avoid blockages and situations where some provinces would ultimately opt out of their commitment to implement the deal. Energy was one of those topics of provincial interest involved in several cross-cutting themes under mixed jurisdiction. For instance, Politician 4 mentioned uranium mining as a negotiating table on which the provinces, including Saskatchewan, primary stakeholder, were not sitting. As such, CETA highlights what Keefe has argued, namely that "the division of powers does not accurately reflect the changing nature of international trade agreements which are increasingly addressing areas of provincial responsibility" (Keefe 2008).

Enhancing Global Governance and Federal Competences

The third trend concerns the jurisdictional scale of environment-energy concerns. This study suggests that CETA takes place in – and supports – a governing trend that promotes large-scale governance of environmental matters and federal jurisdiction. A former federal adviser (Expert 1) indeed argued that CETA was "a high point for federalism." For him, CETA has participated to increase regulatory consistency across the country to boost investors' confidence. In so doing, it also worked as a "spur" for Canadian market policy, influencing the form and substance of the Canadian internal FTA. For that reason, several respondents have argued that Ottawa saw an opportunity to use the political momentum opened by CETA to advance a unified environmental policy.

Indeed, in Canada, energy issues are found under several titles of constitutional competences, most of which are shared between the federal and provincial levels. According to the existing literature, CETA came at a time of renewed "Canadian energy federalism" (Gattinger 2013), open to nation-wide propositions. Yet, environmental matters complicate this game, since "the Supreme Court has made clear many times that environment is not listed as a head of power" (Academic 13). Consequently, the interpretation of each jurisdictional boundary is still in the making and conflictual, as seen with the Greenhouse Gas Pollution Pricing Act (GGPA) which staged a piercing opposition between the federal and several provincial governments (Alberta, Ontario, and Saskatchewan; see for instance Court of Appeal for Ontario 2018). In this light, several respondents argued that CETA could enhance federal action, due to the necessity to work with the EU on progressive trade standards. They also mentioned that the ICS could be used to prevent environmental backtracking – thus, purporting that European companies would defend negotiated environmental standards. Nevertheless, the evidence gathered for the chapter shows that limitations pertain to considering CETA as influencing these domestic reforms.

CETA and Environmental Regulation

Concurrently, the last trend concerns CETA's regulatory reach. Mentioning the situation in Ontario with the governmental opposition to the GGPA and concurrent signature of the White Pines Wind Project Termination Act in 2018 (Government of Ontario 2018), Politicians 5 and 6 wondered if a European company could use CETA to indirectly strengthen environmental ambitions. These respondents close to federal circles, pondered third-party instruments such as CETA, as an option to protect commercial interests and advance a green federal agenda, following federal-provincial frictions. However, adopting a strictly legal perspective, another interviewee rejected that view, quoting the decision of the Court of Justice of the European Union (CJEU) made on 30 April 2019 (CJEU 2019). This decision states that arbitration mechanisms cannot be used to challenge a democratic government's decision made for public interest and related to the protection of the environment, health, or human rights (ibid.). As such, this decision reveals the difficulty of identifying CETA's perimeter as it necessitates to identify the political motives behind the Ontarian decision. Furthermore, only international law is recognized by the parties as applicable in the judgment of disputes and a ruling by the CJEU is considered domestic law. Therefore, it is not applicable as a right yet can only be used as a factual argument in a dispute. As Academic 9 then suggested: "the more an agreement is viewed as a governance agreement, the more likely it is to actually kind of result in those changes, even domestically." As for now, considerably more work will be needed to determine the territory of application of CETA.

CONCLUSION

This chapter set out to clarify the implications of the CETA on energy matters in Canada, from a geographical perspective. It demonstrated that the ambiguous presence of energy in the deal calls for a combined exploration of the legal provisions contained in the agreement, their interpretation by political actors, and their spatial and regulatory contexts of production and implementation. The key result of this study is that energy appears in CETA as more than a traded commodity. Consequently, this work calls to consider energy for its systemic implications in new preferential trade agreements. Although limited by the early stage of CETA's implementation in Canada, this chapter has raised many questions in need of further investigation.

Three main points can be highlighted. First, CETA broadens the parts of the energy system engaged in a process of liberalization as it encompasses goods, services, investments, and norms. Future studies could then continue to explore its role of changing energy spatialities, notably in terms of concentration of production sites, transportation networks, provincial diversification, consumption patterns and territorial equalization schemes in Canada. Issues of land access and energy justice will have to be considered. Second, it is clear that CETA will indirectly affect the energy sector, through higher demand rates. Consumption patterns of other industries, such as the agricultural sector, would thus need to be assessed in the future. As Academic 12 stated: "There is likely going to be an increase in the amount of natural gas that is consumed even though it is not directly for energy purposes." Finally, CETA participates to changing energy governing trends and multi-scale power relations in Canada. Thus, if the debate is to be moved forward, a better understanding of national and international energy jurisdictions will need to be developed, especially regarding scales of responsibility and incoming new regulatory actors.

The implication of these conclusions is twofold. On the one hand, they hope to convince readers that an integrated study of energy should question governance patterns, particularly those enclosed in international trade agreements. They are a growing concern in the changing landscape of global governing instruments and necessitate a clear and explicit framing. On the other hand, they state that the presence of environmental provisions in future trade agreements should be considered necessary, not merely because of political views or legal incentives to abide by carbon targets, but on account of the systemic nature of a problem that traverses all economic sectors.

NOTE

1   The first relevant year for environmental law is 1870. The first environmental texts can be found 1940 onward. The figure aims to capture these gaps.

REFERENCES

AITEC. 2016. "CETA maquette. Danger: CETA. Agir!" Campaign communication leaflet. Accessed 5 September 2020. https://aitec. reseau-ipam.org/

Andresen, Martin A. 2010. "Canada-United States Interregional Trade: Quasi-Points and Spatial Change." *The Canadian Geographer/Le Géographe Canadien* 54, no. 2: 139–57. https://doi.org/10.1111/j.1541-0064.2009. 00292.x.

Barlow, Max. 1993. "North American integration and Canada's geography." In *Canadian Transformations: Perspectives on a Changing Human Geography*, edited by Wayne Davies, 96–117. Wales: Crown.

Bouzarovski, Stefan, Martin J. Pasqualetti, and Vanesa Castan Broto. 2017. *The Routledge Research Companion to Energy Geographies*. London: Routledge.

Bridge, Gavin, Stefan Bouzarovski, Michael Bradshaw, and Nick Eyre. 2013. "Geographies of Energy Transition: Space, Place and the Low-Carbon Economy." *Energy Policy* 53: 331–40. https://doi.org/10.1016/j.enpol. 2012.10.066.

Britton, John N. H. 2002. "Regional Implications of North American Integration: A Canadian Perspective on High Technology Manufacturing." *Regional Studies*, no. 36:4, 359–74. https://doi.org/10.1080/00343400220131133.

Cayley-Daoust, Daniel, and Richard Girard. 2012. *Big Oil's Oily Grasp: The Making of Canada as a Petro-State and How Oil Money Is Corrupting Canadian Politics*. Ottawa: Polaris Institute.

CETA (Canada-European Union Comprehensive Economic and Trade Agreement). 2016. Accessed 21 July 2020. https://www.international.gc.ca/trade-commerce/trade-agreements-accords-commerciaux/agr-acc/ceta-aecg/text-texte/toc-tdm.aspx.

CJEU (Court of Justice of the European Union). 2019. Opinion 1/17 of the Court (Full Court), ECLI:EU:C:2019:341.

Court of Appeal for Ontario. 2018. File No: C65807 in the matter of a reference to the Court of Appeal pursuant to section 8 of the Courts of Justice Act, RSO 1990, c. C34, by Order-by-Council 1014/2018 respecting the constitutionality of the Greenhouse Gas Pollution Pricing Act, Part 5 of the Budget Implementation Act, 2018, No. 1, SC 2018, c. 12.

Dalby, Simon. 2019. "Canadian Geopolitical Culture: Climate Change and Sustainability." *The Canadian Geographer/Le Géographe canadien* 63, no. 1: 100–11. https://doi.org/10.1111/cag.12472.

Delaney, David. 2010. *The Spatial, the Legal and the Pragmatics of World-Making: Nomospheric Investigations*. Routledge-Cavendish.

Dent, Christopher M. 2018. "Clean Energy Trade Governance: Reconciling Trade Liberalism and Climate Interventionism?" *New Political Economy* 23, no. 6: 728–47. https://doi.org/10.1080/13563467.2018.1384456.

Ecolex database. 2019. Website. Accessed October 2019. https://www.ecolex.org.

European Court of Justice. 2019. Opinion of Advocate General Bot, 1/17 delivered on 29 January. ECLI:EU:C:2019:72.

Eurostat. 2021. Imports of oil and petroleum products by partner country dataset [NRG_TI_OIL__custom_1202982]. Accessed October 2021.

Felli, Romain. 2016. La Grande Adaptation. Climat, capitalisme et catastrophe. Paris: Le Seuil.

Forest, Patrick. 2009. *Géographie du droit: épistémologie, développements et perspectives*. Collection Diké. Quebec: Presses de l'Université de Laval.

– 2010. "Inter-local Water Agreements: Law, Geography, and NAFTA." *Les Cahiers de droit* 51, no. 3–4: 749–70. https://doi.org/10.7202/045732ar.

Gattinger, Monica. 2013. "A National Energy Strategy for Canada: Golden Age or Golden Cage of Energy Federalism?" Paper presented at the

2nd Annual Conference of the Canadian Political Science Association, 4–6 June, University of Victoria.

Global Affairs Canada. 2016. "CETA Benefits Already Visible a Year after Its Entry into Force." Accessed 23 September 2019.

– 2019. "Canada's State of Trade 2019." Report. Accessed January 2020.

Government of Ontario. 2018. White Pines Wind Project Termination Act, 2018, S.O. 2018, c. 10, Sched. 2.

Griller, Stefan, Walter Obwexer, and Erich Vranes. 2017. *Mega-Regional Trade Agreements: CETA, TTIP, and TISA: New Orientations for EU External Economic Relations.* Oxford University Press.

Harris, Jennifer M. 2016. "America, Europe and the Necessary Geopolitics of Trade." *Survival* 58, no. 6: 63–92. https://doi.org/10.1080/00396338.2016.1257181.

Jenkins, Kirsten, Darren McCauley, Raphael Heffron, and Hannes Stephan. 2014. "Energy Justice: A Whole Systems Approach." *Queens Political Review* 2, no. 2: 74–87.

Kirkpatrick, Colin, Selim Raihan, Adam Bleser, Dan Prud'homme, Karel Mayrand, Jean-Frederic Morin, Hector Pollitt, Leonith Hinojosa, and Michael Williams. 2010. "A Trade SIA Relating to the Negotiation of a Comprehensive Economic and Trade Agreement (CETA) between the EU and Canada." Final Inception Report, Commissioned by the European Commission.

Labussiere, Olivier, and Alain Nadai. 2018. *Energy Transitions: A Socio-Technical Inquiry.* New York: Springer International Publishing AG.

Keefe, Jennifer. 2008. "Canadian Federalism and International Trade Agreements: Evaluating Three Policy Options for Mitigating Federal-Provincial Conflict." Master's thesis, Simon Fraser University, Canada.

Meadowcroft, James. 2009. "What about the Politics? Sustainable Development, Transition Management, and Long-Term Energy Transitions." *Policy Sciences* 42, no. 4: 323–40. https://doi.org/10.1007/s11077-009-9097-z.

Morin, Jean-Frédéric, Andreas Dür, and Lisa Lechner. 2018. "Mapping the Trade and Environment Nexus: Insights from a New Dataset." *Global Environmental Politics* 18, no. 1: 122–39. https://doi.org/10.1162/GLEP_a_00447.

Natural Resources Canada. 2018. "Electricity Facts, Energy Sources in Canada." Webpage. Accessed 3 January 2020.

Nicholas, Graydon, Lieutenant-Governor. 2013. Speech from the Throne, Legislative Assembly of New Brunswick, 5 November.

Ryan, John. 1991. "The Effect of the Free Trade Agreement on Canada's Energy Resources." *The Canadian Geographer/Le Géographe canadien* 35, no. 1: 70–82.

Santoire, Emmanuelle. 2021. "Of space and law. Investigating the intervention
   of law in energy system spatialities (European Union, Canada)." PhD thesis,
   École Normale Supérieure of Lyon, France, under the supervision of Dr.
   Romain Garcier and Pr. Pascal Marty (NNT: 2021LYSEN058).
Selby, Jan, Emily Cox, and Sarah Royston. 2017. "The Impact of Non-Energy
   Policies on Energy Systems: A Scoping Paper." Report. Accessed
   23 September 2019. http://www.ukerc.ac.uk/publications/impact-of-non-
   energy-policies-on-energy-systems.html.
Slowe, Peter M. 1991. "The geography of borderlands: the case of the
   Quebec-US borderlands." *The Geographical Journal* 157, no. 2: 191–8.
Sinclair, Scott. 2011. *Tar Sands and the CETA*. Report. Ottawa: Canadian
   Centre for Policy Alternatives.
SPA (Strategic Partnership Agreement). 2016. Strategic Partnership Agreement
   between Canada and the European Union.
Talus, Kim. 2016. *Introduction to EU Energy Law*. Oxford: Oxford
   University Press.
Tienhaara, Kyla. 2010 [2011]. "Regulatory Chill and the Threat of Arbitration:
   A View from Political Science." In *Evolution in Investment Treaty Law and
   Arbitration*, edited by Chester Brown and Kate Miles, 606–27. Cambridge
   University Press.
– 2018. "The Fossil Fuel Era Is Coming to an End, but the Lawsuits Are
   Just Beginning." Accessed 23 September 2019. https://theconversation.com/
   the-fossil-fuel-era-is-coming-to-an-end-but-the-lawsuits-are-just-begin-
   ning-107512.
Trade Justice Network. 2010. "Top Ten Reasons Why CETA Is Bad
   for Canada." https://www.bilaterals.org/?10-reasons-why-ceta-is-bad-for.
Trew, Stuart. 2017. *From NAFTA to CETA: Corporate Lobbying Through
   the Back Door*. Ottawa: Canadian Centre for Policy Alternatives.
Wolfe, Robert. 2017. "Multiple trade negotiations offer tantalizing
   possibilities." *The Globe and Mail*, 27 December.
Woudsma, Clarence. 1999. "NAFTA and Canada-US cross-border freight
   transportation." *Journal of Transport Geography* no. 7: 105–19.

13

Taming Regulatory Cooperation for the Protection of Labour Rights: The Case of CETA

Isabella Mancini

INTRODUCTION

The Comprehensive Economic and Trade Agreement (CETA) between Canada and the European Union (EU) is one amongst the new generation of EU trade agreements that go beyond tariffs and aim instead at deeper legal and institutional integration. Emblematic of these aims is the incorporation of regulatory cooperation chapters. Regulatory cooperation is defined here as a set of institutional and procedural mechanisms at inter-, trans-, and subnational levels of law-making to bridge regulatory divergences and with broader aims of convergence. Regulatory cooperation is not new to international trade, yet CETA is particularly ambitious and novel in the scope of its application. For the first time, this trade agreement between two advanced economies – the EU and Canada – includes a chapter on regulatory cooperation which applies to the development and review of regulatory measures that are covered by the chapter on trade and labour.

As labour rights are not said to be protected, and neither is their protection to be enhanced via regulatory cooperation, much uncertainty exists about the relationship between these two chapters. Most importantly, little attention has been paid to how labour rights could be implicated in regulatory exchanges beyond the state. It is a voiced concern of regulators, particularly in the context of trade, that regulatory cooperation activities could lead to lower levels of protection than are appropriate (Eisner 2016, 22). Similarly, civil society has denounced endeavours to set global standards via regulatory cooperation, fearing that these activities would lead to "low cost" global standards (Corporate European Observatory 2017; Trade Justice Movement 2019). Past US-Canada regulatory cooperation activities provide examples of such downward pressure on the levels of protection for standards in worker safety, chemical labelling, and rail safety, corroborating these concerns (Trew 2019).

While the new generation EU free trade agreements (FTAs) have been concluded, and it is not possible to point at instances where EU regulatory cooperation activities have had an observable impact on labour rights, this chapter seeks to address the following questions: in this new era of deep integration and global reach of FTAs, how should we understand the place of labour rights in regulatory cooperation? How are labour rights called into question and intertwine in different elements of regulatory cooperation? Which voices and demands are being institutionalized in these processes (Bardutzky and Fahey 2017)?

The aim of the chapter is twofold: first, it enquires and warns against the wider scope of the regulatory cooperation chapter in CETA in light of the traditional understanding of regulatory cooperation as a means to address unnecessary costs that would otherwise arise in trade; second, it argues that this development could be welcomed insofar as regulatory cooperation were reconceived as a tool for enhanced protection and upwards convergence, above all for labour rights. Because civil society actors have embraced this vision, the chapter suggests that regulatory cooperation under CETA should be used as a platform by the EU and Canada, including civil society on both sides, to exchange views and table proposals on matters pertaining to trade and labour rights.

The chapter is structured as follows: it first provides an overview of regulatory cooperation in trade and its incorporation in CETA; it then explores the place of labour rights therein, highlighting potential challenges; and it concludes with an empirical account of the role of civil society actors to deliberations on labour rights in the implementation stage, and a discussion of their potential contribution to labour rights in regulatory cooperation activities.

THE INCORPORATION OF REGULATORY COOPERATION IN CETA

This section first provides an overview of how regulatory cooperation has developed in the context of trade, before turning to the specific case of the EU and Canada's cooperation on regulatory matters and the new regulatory cooperation chapter in CETA.

Regulatory Cooperation as a New Component
of Trade Agreements

In the context of international trade, regulatory cooperation has been understood as providing a space for addressing regulatory divergences that can "unnecessarily" increase the costs of trade exchanges (Lazo and Sauvé 2018). Different regulatory requirements can indeed amount to non-tariff barriers (NTBs) to trade, which nowadays represent the major impediment to trade. The World Trade Organization (WTO) is largely seen to have failed to work as a forum for negotiations on regulatory cooperation (Nakagaw 2016). Countries have resorted to bilateral, preferential, and free trade agreements. In recent years, several preferential trade agreements have incorporated specific chapters on regulatory cooperation and that search for deeper integration via regulatory cooperation in trade has grown (Krstic 2012). Regulatory cooperation represents a recent feature of trade agreements, which goes beyond the WTO and is liable to account for legal and institutional integration.

Regulatory cooperation is widely understood as a means to create a level regulatory field against a backdrop of regulatory divergence. However, its processes can vary in different agreements and forums, and its practices and results can differ. Regulatory cooperation activities can, for instance, take the form of exchanges of information and sharing of best practices, but also mutual recognition agreements (MRAs), and the more ambitious joint regulatory initiatives and standard-setting endeavours, to name just a few (Dunoff 2015). These activities can take place at the international level, but also at the bilateral level, and even at "transnational" or "hybrid" levels of regulatory activity, involving public and private bodies (among others), and trans-governmental networks of regulators (ibid.). Regulatory cooperation remains an undefined and over-inclusive concept that can encompass a panoply of mechanisms.

Although different modalities and degrees of cooperation on regulatory matters exist, regulatory cooperation can de facto imply an additional dimension of law-making beyond the state and the trade agreement itself. For instance, in the context of the EU-US negotiations for a transatlantic trade and investment partnership (TTIP) agreement, the regulatory cooperation activities envisaged therein were said to create a "postnational marketplace" (Bartl and Fahey 2014) and a "living agreement" (Meunier and Morin 2015, 1). Beyond the specific case of TTIP, it has been argued that institutionalized forms of regulatory cooperation can become veritable "vehicles for regulatory rapprochement," as the parties commit to "regulatory reform and changes to the regulatory culture" (Krstic 2012, 10). Trade agreements that include commitments to engage in regulatory cooperation activities can thereby channel closer legal and institutional integration. The EU emerges as one of the major proponents of these endeavours, through which it can enhance its global actorness in trade.

As a new component of the latest generation of EU FTAs, regulatory cooperation reflects the EU's new search for deeper integration via trade beyond the WTO. Consistently with the objectives of the "Global Europe: Competing in the World" strategy (European Commission 2006), the new generation EU FTAs have been advanced as strategic vehicles to externalize and globalize the EU's regulatory standards (Krstic 2012). Regulatory cooperation was conceived as a tool to both drive and shape globalization (European Commission 2017). While the strategy emphasized the EU's commitment to multilateralism, it envisaged bilateral FTAs be pursued as a way to go "further and faster in promoting openness and integration" (European Commission 2006, 8), particularly aiming at regulatory convergence by tackling NTBs. The bilateral trade relationship would have therefore become an outlet for negotiation of issues that were not ready for the multilateral discussions. Canada is one of the main strategic trade partners with whom the EU has agreed regulatory cooperation provisions as set out in the Global Europe strategy.

The EU-Canada Path toward the Regulatory Cooperation Chapter in CETA

The EU and Canada have been seeking closer regulatory cooperation since the 1990s. However, despite the early adoption of sectoral MRAs, the little progress in their implementation has been followed only by less ambitious political and voluntary commitments. Following the Framework Agreement for Commercial and Economic Cooperation to govern EU-Canada trade relations, the Declaration on Canada-European Community Transatlantic Relations (1990) established the beginning of a series of summits, leading to the adoption of the Canada-EU Joint Political Declaration and its Action Plan (1996), among other things. The trade chapter of the action plan paved the way for an MRA and several sectoral cooperation agreements. The dissatisfaction with the progress in the implementation of the agreements, and the recognition that regulatory barriers still represented major impediments to trade (European Commission 2003), led to consider further commitments on cooperation on regulatory matters. Following a summit in 2002, the EU and Canada adopted the Framework on Regulatory Cooperation and Transparency (2004).

The regulatory cooperation chapter in CETA replaces this framework. It contains a wider range of activities to be pursued: from exchanges of information during the regulatory process to ongoing bilateral discussions on regulatory governance; to conducting a concurrent or joint risk assessment, as well as post-implementation reviews of regulations (CETA 2016, Art. 21.4). CETA also contains provisions whereby the parties commit to take into consideration the other party's measures when developing new regulatory measures or amending existing ones; and to notify the other party on an envisaged regulatory measure (ibid., Arts 21.5, 21.4(f)). However, these activities appear to remain cautious in terms of regulatory convergence (ibid., Arts 21.4(f), 21.4(g)). Contrary to the ambitious rhetoric of the EU and its trade partners to address NTBS, the commitments to cooperate on regulatory matters have been eventually diluted in a number of ways.

First, under CETA, regulatory cooperation activities remain voluntary (ibid., Art. 21.2(6)).[1] This means that one party is not obliged to engage in regulatory cooperation with the other requesting party, even though it is expected to provide an explanation for not being willing to do so (ibid.). Second, a common feature is the reaffirmation of each party's regulatory autonomy, reflecting concerns of regulatory space. These are, for instance, provisions on the right to regulate and similar safeguard clauses recognizing that the parties are not restrained in their powers to pursue their public policy objectives (ibid., Art. 21.2(4)). Third, the parties are not bound to achieve a specific outcome or adopt certain standards, but they only commit to a certain kind of activities. Furthermore, some have argued that the commitments undertaken in the new generation of EU FTAs do not truly seek regulatory alignment, and therefore reflect a low level of ambition (Golberg 2019). Overall, it appears that much is left to the discretion of the parties as to what to engage in and to what extent.

Despite the limitations to regulatory cooperation, such commitments could in fact flow into more systematized forms of cooperation. Above all, the inclusion of regulatory cooperation in the FTAs, as opposed to other modalities outside the trade agreement, can have a stronger long-term impact than if it remained in the political realm (Bartl 2016). Furthermore, while the parties are not obliged to enter into regulatory cooperation with each other, they would still have the possibility to do so. Finally, even when activities took the form of mere exchanges of information, regulators from both sides would be able to build mutual trust, which is often recognized as one of the main elements for the success of regulatory cooperation (Hoekman 2015, 613). Regulatory cooperation is indeed a long-term project, which requires sustained commitment to engage in such exchanges. As long as the process might take, there is much potential for it to catalyze more sophisticated and ambitious activities whereby the parties would seek regulatory alignment (Golberg 2019).

It is therefore pivotal that these forms of regulatory cooperation, prone to become more institutionalized, emerge in ways that are consistent with fundamental rights. This is the more so since these activities are part of bilateral trade agreements between developed economies, likely to set regulatory standards that others will find difficult to disregard. While the inclusion of regulatory cooperation in trade agreements is said to be motivated by aims of global standard-setting and values projection, it is not clear what kind of global standards or values the parties should (or can) pursue via regulatory cooperation. The question then arises as to what kind of place fundamental rights occupy in the regulatory cooperation chapters of the EU FTAs. The next section turns to the complex relationship between regulatory cooperation and fundamental rights by looking at the place of labour rights in the regulatory cooperation chapter of CETA.

EXPLORING LABOUR RIGHTS IN REGULATORY COOPERATION UNDER CETA

Labour rights are not expressly addressed or mandated protection in the regulatory cooperation chapter of CETA. This is regardless of the fact that regulatory cooperation is usually held to impinge upon governments' traditional areas of domestic regulation and to delay, or even hinder, the future adoption of new regulations (Bank 2018; Corporate Europe Observatory 2017; Mertins-Kirkwood et al. 2016; Trew 2019). Civil society groups forcefully warned against the potential harming effects that regulatory cooperation activities could have for the levels of protection of public health and safety, among others. The argument was that "global standards" can come with costs for society if convergence of those standards is downward-sloped (Corporate European Observatory 2017; Trade Justice Movement 2019). This section explores labour rights in the scope of application and the objectives of regulatory cooperation in CETA, and then discusses the provisions on the right to regulate as alleged safeguards to labour protection.

The Place of Labour Rights in the Regulatory Cooperation Chapter of CETA

With regard to the scope of application, CETA's regulatory cooperation chapter differs from other regulatory chapters in new generation EU FTAS in that it expressly applies to "trade and labour" (CETA 2016, Art. 21.2). It is not totally clear, however, what this evolutionary change would imply in practice. As labour rights fall under the subject matter of regulatory cooperation chapters, they could become objects of regulatory cooperation exchanges between the EU and Canada. This would mean that regulatory divergences in rights standards could be addressed, by means of dialogues and exchanges of information, among others, or agreement on common standards and objectives via joint regulatory activities with the aim of harmonization or mutual recognition. The coverage of labour could become problematic insofar as other necessary conditions ensuring its protection were not met, such as objectives of enhanced protection and scrutiny mechanisms. Even where labour rights were not made part of the subject matter of regulatory activities, they could be discussed for regulatory initiatives on related matters. This situation would indirectly lead to the scenario described earlier whereby labour rights would be made the object of regulatory cooperation chapters. Alternatively, they could be indirectly affected without regulatory cooperation activity taking place to their respect. In this case, regulatory cooperation activities could disregard their salience in the subject matter at issue. In fact, there would be potential to reach higher standards via regulatory cooperation, but this would only be so under certain prerequisites and procedural safeguards relating to legitimacy and accountability. As rules could be made without taking into consideration potential negative spillovers affecting labour rights, the next paragraph considers more specifically the aims of regulatory cooperation.

With regard to aims, making sure that the objectives of regulatory cooperation chapters are not confined to aims of trade and investment liberalization is pivotal. Not only are the aims indicative of how the parties understand the purpose of regulatory cooperation; they also reflect the expectations of the parties toward the role of the actors involved in the implementation of the chapter. CETA reflects a balancing exercise of economic considerations of eliminating unnecessary divergent regulatory requirements on the one hand, and defensive rationales and normative issues on the other. The first objective in CETA is the contribution to the protection of "human life, health, or safety" (CETA 2016, Art. 21.3(a)), which is counterbalanced with aims of "trade and investment facilitation" and increased convergence, to avoid "unnecessary differences in regulation" and costs related to duplicative requirements (ibid., Art. 21.3(c)). The juxtaposition of these objectives begs a closer look into the hierarchy and compatibility of aims. Further objectives are more closely related to regulatory coherence, promoting a regulatory environment that is effective, transparent, and predictable, also by means of good regulatory practices (ibid., Art. 21.3(b)). CETA also seeks to build trust, mutual understanding, improvement of regulatory proposals and implementation, and regulatory impacts and compliance (ibid.). Looking at the objectives, it appears that regulatory cooperation would enable normative considerations and interpretations. At the same time, such purposes require that safeguards be in place to guarantee that labour rights are not undermined, and in the best scenario their protection enhanced.

The Right to Regulate for the Protection of Labour Rights

Despite the lack of express reference to labour rights in the regulatory cooperation chapter of CETA, two main provisions could represent a means to prevent potential undermining effects on the levels of protection of labour rights: the so-called non-lowering clauses, whereby the parties commit to maintain current/high levels of protection, and provisions on the "right to regulate," whereby the parties reaffirm their prerogative to introduce measures to achieve public policy objectives, thus precluding that those measures will become object of a trade dispute. While the non-lowering clauses are usually considered to be unenforceable (Araujo 2018, 240; Orbie, Van den Putte, and Martens 2017, 8), the provisions on the right to regulate have been pointed at as one way in which fundamental rights more broadly can be ensured protection: these provisions could indeed be invoked or relied upon by the parties to justify the adoption of measures that are necessary to protect and ensure respect of certain rights (Bartels 2017; Depaigne 2017). It is therefore useful to look at whether the grounds to which the right to regulate would apply do include labour rights.

In the regulatory cooperation chapter of CETA, the provision on the right to regulate states that the parties are not prevented "from adopting different regulatory measures or pursuing different initiatives for reasons including different institutional or legislative approaches, circumstances, values or priorities that are particular to that Party" (CETA 2016, Art. 21.5). Even though the grounds are not expressly listed, the EU-Canada Joint

Interpretative Instrument expressly states that CETA preserves the ability of the parties to adopt their own measures to achieve public policy objectives such as the protection and promotion of public health, social services, safety, public morals, or social or consumer protection (Joint Interpretative Instrument 2016, Point 2). The Court of Justice of the European Union (CJEU) also confirmed, in its Opinion 1/17, that CETA is to be interpreted as not restraining the regulatory autonomy of the parties.[2] Furthermore, the chapters on trade and sustainable development (TSD) and on trade and labour both contain provisions on the right to regulate where "levels of labour protection" are indicated as grounds on which the parties are recognized for the right to adopt or modify their laws or policies (CETA 2016, Art. 23.2).

The provisions on the right to regulate can be considered a means by which the lowering of standards as a result of regulatory cooperation activities could be prevented. However, while the right to regulate should remain a safety net in this context, it remains a unilateral action. It is arguable to what extent the recognition of this right would be able to ensure labour rights protection beyond borders. The right to regulate is rather artificial and left to the discretion of the parties. It implies no obligation to regulate, nor to proactively address potential breaches of labour rights. The reaffirmation of the right to regulate then emerges as a rather defensive, and not absolute, guarantee. These provisions appear to have been introduced by the parties because of a broader concern of being restrained in their regulatory space, no matter the specific object of the regulation. Under certain conditions, it would be possible to conceive of regulatory cooperation as a venue, or even a tool, to cooperate with another country to seek *upward* convergence of standards and practices, as opposed to downward convergence. Such a perspective would provide an alternative to the current approach which excludes and refrains from any discussion around labour rights altogether.

Labour rights could be discussed in the context of regulatory cooperation activities, yet it is not clear how this could develop. While regulatory cooperation betrays several shortcomings, scholars have provided insights to necessary elements and conditions under which full potential of regulatory cooperation could be achieved. There seems to be agreement that civil society input and involvement in all phases of regulatory cooperation could be such way of ensuring accountability (Hoekman and Sabel 2019; Shaffer 2002; Wiener and Alemanno 2015). The next section thus considers venues for civil society groups to monitor and inform the regulatory cooperation activities in the implementation of the agreement.

ACTORS FOR LABOUR RIGHTS IN REGULATORY
COOPERATION UNDER CETA

Regulatory cooperation usually involves exchanges between regulators on highly technical issues requiring technical expertise. While this could be problematic insofar as labour rights issues were overlooked, the institutional framework of the regulatory cooperation chapter set up in CETA (2016, Art. 21.6), the regulatory cooperation forum (RCF), which comprises a series of participatory mechanisms for civil society that could potentially contribute to deliberation on issues such as labour rights. CETA additionally provides for treaty bodies in charge of monitoring the implementation of the trade and labour chapter, which are considered as opening up to an additional possibility for discussions pertaining to labour rights, including in the context of regulatory cooperation activities.

Civil Society in the Implementation of the Regulatory
Cooperation Chapter in CETA

Regulatory cooperation has often been criticized for the closed nature of the decision-making process, and for excluding representation of broader constituencies with an interest in, not least liable to be affected by, the outcome (Bull et al. 2015, 13–14). In particular, many have expressed concerns as to the danger of regulatory capture by special interests, at the agenda-setting stage as much as at the deliberation stage (Benvenisti 2016, 62). Against this background, an assessment should be done of the mechanisms of participation, and special attention should be given to *who* is entitled, to provide *what kind of input*, and at *what stage* of regulatory activity. This section discusses available participatory mechanisms that would allow third parties to provide input, and thus potentially a more normative perspective to regulatory cooperation activities. Participatory mechanisms in CETA are clustered here around three main venues: (1) participation at meetings of the regulatory cooperation bodies; (2) consultations; and (3) comments in writing on regulatory measures.

Starting with the first, the parties may invite "interested parties" to participate in the *meetings of the RCF* (CETA 2016, Art. 21.6(3)). It is not specified further *whom* these interested parties would comprise, fuelling criticism that the operation of the forum would end up being subject to lobby by more resourceful organizations (Bartl and Irion 2017, 11). A slightly different approach had been taken in the EU's proposal for regulatory cooperation in TTIP, which specified (albeit in a footnote) that "no class of stakeholders should be accorded privileged treatment" (European Union 2016, Art. x5(2)), hence to an extent revealing the efforts to counter the concerns of regulatory capture by more resourceful actors. Regarding the *input* to be provided during the meetings, it is equally unclear what kind of contribution is expected by third parties as a result of their participation, or any follow-up duty on the regulatory bodies. By contrast, under the EU's position for TTIP, "natural or legal persons" may have submitted "concrete and sufficiently substantiated proposals" on "regulatory proposals"; the "progress of existing regulatory cooperation"; "new initiatives and activities"; as well as "priority setting" (ibid., Art. x6(1)(a)). The EU's proposal for TTIP also contained general transparency provisions on making third parties contributions publicly available, and committing each party to provide information on its assessment of the contributions received (Ibid., Art. 6x(2)(b)).

With respect to the second mechanism, CETA provides that *consultations* may be conducted with private entities, encompassing "stakeholders and interested Parties, including representatives from academia, think-tanks, non-governmental organisations, business, consumer and other organisations" (CETA 2016, Art. 21.8). While the aim is to have "non-governmental perspectives on matters that relate to the implementation of this Chapter" (ibid.), the parties are left the discretion to conduct consultations, and it is not specified at which stage this will happen. By contrast, the EU-Japan Economic Partnership Agreement (EUJEPA) goes one step further in this regard, as the relevant article on public consultations states that any person consulted should be allowed to provide comments at the stage of the preparation of regulatory measures, including drafts (EUJEPA 2017, Art. 18.7). It also requires that the comments (or a summary of the results thereof) be made publicly available and be taken into consideration (ibid., Arts 18.7, 18.7(1)(c)).

A final venue and opportunity for actors to provide input into regulatory cooperation activities is by means of *written comments on regulatory proposals*. In CETA, amongst the regulatory activities envisaged, interested parties are to be allowed sufficient time to submit "comments in writing" on a "proposed regulation" (CETA 2016, Art. 21.4(e)). As in the case of consultation, the input would come after a regulatory draft has already been provided, as opposed to *prior to* or *during* its definition. This can be contrasted with the relevant provisions for measures relating to technical barriers to trade (TBT) and sanitary and phytosanitary measures (SPS) which "may have an impact on trade with the other Party," the proposed measures for which shall be shared "at the earliest stage possible" in order for comments and proposals to "be taken into account" (ibid., Art. 21.4(d), Annex 5-D). While in CETA comments could be provided after a regulatory measure has been *proposed*, in EUJEPA this opportunity would only be available for measures already *in force*, hence at a later stage arguably undermining meaningful third parties' contributions.

Despite the different participatory mechanism available, it remains to be seen to what extent they can provide meaningful outlets for civil society groups' input that will be taken into consideration. The report of the first meeting of the RCF, in December 2018, identifies a series of issues for the RCF work plan: these issues are said to have been drawn from the consultations and to have received feedback from EU and Canadian regulators and agreement by EU and Canadian co-chairs (European Commission 2019). Labour issues largely emerge as a missing component of the contributions from the consultations, and also a missing component of the RCF work plan eventually. Importantly, the consultations held in Canada for the regulatory cooperation chapter of CETA have produced very deep insights as to the purpose of regulatory cooperation. The Coalition des Associations de Consommateurs du Québec (CACQ, Coalition of Quebec Consumer Associations) held that "upwards harmonisation should be seen as the main purpose of regulatory cooperation between the parties to the Agreement in the area of consumer protection" (CACQ 2018, abstract). According to them, regulatory cooperation should be approached "not with a view to eliminating some rules, but with a view to upholding trust, fostering transparency and reducing negative externalities" (ibid.). Similarly, for the Canadian Environmental Law Association (CELA) and Environmental Defence (ED), "The Regulatory Cooperation Forum should only be used to harmonize regulatory standards upwards to better protect the public interest in both jurisdictions" (CELA and ED 2018). These perspectives are largely absent from the work plan of the RCF (European Commission 2019).

At the time of writing, the second meeting of the RCF was to be held in early February 2020. The working agenda is based on the results of the consultations held in 2018 in the context of the first RCF meeting (European Commission 2020). Its results have been published online and are presented as the basis also for discussions of the second meeting (European Commission 2019). It appears that no additional consultations for the second meeting have been held. A "stakeholder debrief meeting" will take place the following day (ibid.). However, it is debatable how this meeting can be useful if no additional consultation will be held, in the future, on the direction of the work of the RCF.

Participatory Mechanisms under the Trade and Labour Chapter

Beyond the participatory mechanisms envisaged in the chapter on regulatory cooperation, CETA provides for several venues through which civil society actors would have the possibility to present their views on labour rights issues and thus contributing to discussions thereon. The focus here is on the involvement of civil society groups in the *implementation* of the trade and labour chapter and the monitoring thereof (CETA 2016, Chapter 23). If regulatory cooperation challenged certain commitments in relation to the labour chapter, this could arguably be a case to be questioned by the actors in charge of monitoring its implementation. Furthermore, participatory mechanisms for civil society groups would have the potential to contribute with on-the-ground perspectives as to the implementation of certain measures adopted in the context of regulatory cooperation activities, which could be monitored and assessed in their impact on labour rights. At the implementation level, the main institutionalized mechanisms enabling involvement of non-institutional actors are the domestic advisory groups (DAGs), in turn taking part in the EU-Canada Civil Society Forum.

The DAGs are a pivotal entity envisaged by the new generation of EU FTAS to deepen participation of civil society. They comprise civil society representatives, to be appointed by each party. On their own initiative, the DAGS may "submit opinions and make recommendations" on labour matters (ibid.). As the public can send submissions to the parties on labour matters, the DAGS are to be "informed" by the parties when this occurs (ibid., Art. 23.8(5)). One major concern as to the functioning of the DAGS relates to the limited scope of the mandate, as their monitoring function of implementation is only envisaged for the chapters on sustainable development, labour, and environment, as opposed to the agreement as a whole (European Economic and Social Committee 2018). Such limited scope could indeed constrain consideration of how and whether the implementation of other provisions would have an impact on the enjoyment of labour rights. Other shortcomings relate to: the composition, selection procedure and the degree of representativeness of interests; a limited budget; the lack of interaction with DAGS established by trade partners, or with EU institutions; and the concurrent need of a more structured and institutionalized consultation mechanisms as opposed to the informal and ad hoc nature of the current reporting modus operandi.

The EU and Canadian DAGS take part in the Civil Society Forum, together with civil society actors that do not necessarily belong to either DAGS. The forum created under CETA can be understood as a platform for civil society representatives and the DAGs to engage in a dialogue with the EU Commission and Canadian government officials (CETA 2016, Art. 22.5). In this way, not only would the forum be a venue for dialogue on the sustainable development aspects of CETA; it would also represent an important interlocutor of the main committee dealing with these issues and monitoring the implementation of the relevant provisions. Indeed, the TSD committee is required to *update* the Civil Society Forum on any matter related to the labour chapter, present the forum's views and opinions directly to the parties, and report annually on the follow-up to those communications (CETA 2016, Art. 22.4).

The EU-Canada Civil Society Forum met for the first time on 12 September 2018, featuring around 120 civil society actors (European Commission 2018a). On the agenda was an exchange of views on TSD, labour, and environment (European Commission 2018b). Regarding labour, the individual contributions largely omitted discussions on trade and labour, the topic having been sped up and merged into the agenda item on TSD (European Commission 2018a).[3] At the beginning of the meeting, one Canadian government representative stressed the backlash to globalization and the need to prompt "economic growth that is also inclusive growth," and observed how consultation is critical to this and to making CETA more inclusive. The following contributions yet omitted specific discussions on this matter, which is held here to be critical for the social acceptance of trade agreements and the linkages emerging with labour rights in a context of globalization and digitalization.

As to the specific contributions on trade and labour, Rosa Crawford, from the Trade Union Congress (TUC) of the EU, advocated for effective enforcement mechanisms to be put in place "to make sure the Parties uphold, and indeed businesses in both EU and Canada, uphold the obligations in the TSD chapter" as well as those in the joint interpretative instrument.[4] Crawford voiced how TUC had developed ideas on what enforcement would look like on the union's side, which would make sure there are consequences when there are violations of labour standards, for example, making sure that there is monitoring and that the EU and Canada uphold their obligations. The confederal secretary of the European Trade Union Confederation (ETUC), Liina Carr, cast attention on the scope and mandate of the DAGs, advocating for a larger mandate to monitor the whole agreement. While not mentioned explicitly, this could be a case in point for monitoring the implementation of the regulatory cooperation chapter, too, and specifically its impact on labour rights. However, beyond these contributions, no further discussion has started off regarding issues related to labour and trade, nor on labour in regulatory cooperation.

The meeting of the civil society forum was followed by, and was intended to inform, the meeting of the committee on TSD the next day (European Commission 2018c). It was furthermore stated, by one of the Commission officials, that representatives of the DAGs would have taken part in the TSD meetings *as a practice*,[5] albeit something not envisaged under CETA – which signals a positive practice institutionalizing the role of civil society in the monitoring of the implementation process. On the other hand, it is probably too early to judge the role of civil society in the implementation of the labour chapter, and to assess their role in its monitoring. Overall, the democratic character of these entities is limitedly operationalized in the provision of a "balanced representation of interests," with no indication as to how different interests will be eventually balanced (Mendes 2016). Furthermore, the legal embeddedness of these entities is limited, and left instead to informal mechanisms and voluntary practice of other actors. Certainly, so far, many meetings under different configurations have taken place, suggesting some prima facie change of practice in the inclusion of civil society at the implementation stage. It has to be seen, however, how civil society will understand the relationship between trade and labour, and between regulatory cooperation and labour. It is argued here that regulatory cooperation should be reconceived as a tool for enhanced protection and upwards convergence.

CONCLUSION: ON REGULATORY COOPERATION FOR LABOUR RIGHTS

The incorporation of a regulatory cooperation chapter in a trade agreement between two advanced economies, namely Canada and the EU, has been examined here in its intersection with labour rights. As discussed, regulatory cooperation encompasses the chapter on trade and labour, yet it is not clear however how the junction of regulation cooperation and labour will play out in practice. This uncertainty is particularly problematic in the context of a mechanism, namely regulatory cooperation, that is traditionally understood as a means to reduce a series of costs stemming from regulatory divergences. At the moment, when examining the implementation of the regulatory cooperation chapter and the discussions taking place at the civil society forum, the two chapters appear not to speak to each other, the priorities of regulatory cooperation being more technical issues.

What drives regulatory cooperation, its justification and purpose, needs a change in perspective. Trade agreements have now expanded the subject matter over which regulatory cooperation activities apply. There is a potential for regulatory cooperation to tackle not only NTBs, but also other issues *affecting*, and *affected by*, trade and investment. Particularly in a context of outsourcing and global competition, new challenges arise for social security and the protection of the labour market. Regulatory cooperation should be designed in such a way to make it the solution, and not the problem, to current challenges. To this aim, regulatory cooperation chapters should first of all embed *respect* for fundamental rights *in* the objectives, as a sort of negative obligation: regulatory cooperation activities should not happen when having a negative impact on the enjoyment of fundamental rights. To this respect, systematic impact assessments should be carried out as to the effect of cooperation on regulatory matters on labour rights, but also health and consumer protection, among others. Furthermore, regulatory cooperation chapters could envisage a more positive cooperation around labour rights. The protection of labour rights could be understood in itself a purpose of regulatory cooperation – something that could be reached *via* regulatory cooperation.

Enhanced protection could manifest in regulatory cooperation happening with an aim of upwards convergence of labour standards (which should not be lower to any of the parties). Especially for transborder problems that could hardly be addressed domestically or by unilateral action alone – and that would potentially jeopardize labour rights – the countries should understand the need to cooperate to achieve enhanced protection: for instance, in the field of business and human rights, rules could be agreed upon for the conduct of corporations and protection of the labour market. Re-conceiving the aims of regulatory cooperation allows expanding the subject matter of regulatory cooperation and address regulatory issues of global relevance, as opposed to merely seeking a reduction of costs to benefit economically, without considering important social interests at stake or redistribution issues deriving therefrom (Stewart 2014).

Starting from this stance, it is possible to espouse a broader perspective on regulatory cooperation, in its place and role in global trade today; its potential to both enable and circumscribe trade, as opposed to being a mere instrument of further market opening or costs reduction. Labour rights would not be excluded from discussions altogether, but their relevance and intersection with other objectives of regulatory cooperation activities would be recognized, acknowledged, and eventually addressed. At the same time, these objectives would need to be sustained with adequate procedural mechanisms and safeguards to ensure both input and throughput legitimacy. For this regulatory activity to emerge, an institutional design and set of practices would be needed that effectively sustained discussions on issues at the edge of regulatory cooperation and labour rights.

Civil society actors could play a major role in this, by monitoring the implementation of the regulatory cooperation chapter, particularly by assessing the effects on labour rights first, and by addressing issues pertaining to the trade and labour chapter. In a context of global challenges to labour rights, regulatory cooperation is ever more inevitable and necessary, and this chapter has argued that regulator cooperation could be tooled to address these challenges. By now, at the implementation stage, the RCF under CETA could provide a platform for regulatory exchanges whereby Canada and the EU, and civil society actors with on-the-ground knowledge, should prompt deliberation and table proposals on regulatory matters pertaining to trade and labour, with an aim of enhanced protection of labour rights.

NOTES

1 See also Point 3 of the Joint Interpretative Instrument (2017) OJ L 11/3.
2 CJEU Opinion 1/17 ECLI:EU:C:2019:341.
3 After an hour-long introduction by different members of the European Commission, civil society members were solicited to make brief interventions and topics were eventually merged and discussions hurried up, to be able to finish on time.
4 Intervention at 1h20 in CETA first Civil Society Forum Meeting (European Commission 2018b).
5 Intervention by Madelaine Tuininga at 1h40 in CETA first Civil Society Forum Meeting (European Commission 2018b).

REFERENCES

Araujo, Billy Melo. 2018. "Labour Provisions in EU and US Mega-Regional Trade Agreements: Rhetoric and Reality." *International & Comparative Law Quarterly* 67, no. 1: 233–53.

Bank, Max. 2018. "Submission on Regulatory Cooperation Activities in the Regulatory Cooperation Forum (RCF) under CETA." Accessed 21 July 2020. https://www.lobbycontrol.de/wp-content/uploads/LobbyControl-submission-on-the-work-of-the-RCF.pdf.

Bardutzky, Samo, and Elaine Fahey, eds. 2017. *Framing the Subjects and Objects of Contemporary EU Law.* Cheltenham: Edward Elgar.

Bartels, Lorand. 2017. "Human Rights, Labour Standards and Environmental Standards in CETA." Faculty of Law Research Paper No. 13/2017, University of Cambridge, Cambridge.

Bartl, Marija, and Elaine Fahey. 2014. "A Postnational Marketplace: Negotiating the Transatlantic Trade and Investment Partnership (TTIP)." In *A Transatlantic Community of Law: Legal Perspectives on the Relationship between the EU and US legal orders*, edited by Elaine Fahey and Deirdre Curtin, 210–34. Cambridge: Cambridge University Press.

Bartl, Marija, and Kristina Irion. 2017. "The Japan-EU Economic Partnership Agreement: Flows of Personal Data to the Land of the Rising Sun." Accessed 21 July 2020. https://papers.ssrn.com/sol3/papers.cfm?abstract_id=3099390.

Bartl, Marija. 2016. "TTIP's Regulatory Cooperation and the Future of Precaution in Europe." Amsterdam Law School Research Paper No. 2016-07, Amsterdam.

Benvenisti, Eyal. 2016. "Democracy Captured: The Mega-Regional Agreements and the Future of Global Public Law." *Constellations* 23, no. 1: 58–70. https://doi.org/10.1111/1467-8675.12202.

Bull, Reeve T., Neysun A. Mahboubi, Richard B. Stewart, and Jonathan B. Wiener. 2015. "New Approaches to International Regulatory Cooperation." *Law and Contemporary Problems* 78, no. 1: 1–29. https://scholarship.law.duke.edu/lcp/vol78/iss4/1.

CACQ (Coalition des Associations de Consommateurs du Québec). 2018. "Coalition des associations de consommateurs du Québec RCF submission." Accessed 21 July 2020. https://open.canada.ca/data/en/dataset/c45c4cda-7134-4e65-8e99-5214eb07bcf3.

CELA (Canadian Environmental Law Association) and ED (Environmental Defence). 2018. "Canadian Environmental Law Association & Environmental Defence RCF submission." Accessed 21 July 2020. https://open.canada.ca/data/en/dataset/c45c4cda-7134-4e65-8e99-5214eb07bcf3.

CETA (Canada-European Union Comprehensive Economic and Trade Agreement). 2016. Accessed 21 July 2020. https://www.international.gc.ca/trade-commerce/trade-agreements-accords-commerciaux/agr-acc/ceta-aecg/text-texte/toc-tdm.aspx.

Corporate Europe Observatory. 2017. "Regulatory cooperation: big business' wishes come true in TTIP and CETA." Accessed 21 July 2020. https://corporateeurope.org/en/2017/02/regulatory-cooperation.

Depaigne, Vincent. 2017. "Protecting Fundamental Rights in Trade Agreements Between the EU and Third Countries." *European Law Review* 42, no. 4: 562–76.

Dunoff, Jeffrey L. 2015. "Mapping a Hidden World of International Regulatory Cooperation." *Law and Contemporary Problems* 78, no. 4: 267–99. https://scholarship.law.duke.edu/lcp/vol78/iss4/11.

Eisner, Neil. 2016. "Facilitating Earlier Information Sharing and Cooperation Between the US Department of Transportation and the EU." In *Regulatory Cooperation: Lessons and Opportunities US-EU Final Report*, 12–49. Washington, DC: Regulatory Studies Center, Georgetown University.

EUJEPA (EU-Japan Economic Partnership Agreement). 2017. Accessed 21 July 2020. https://trade.ec.europa.eu/doclib/press/index.cfm?id=1684.

European Commission. 2003. "European Commission Communication on EU-Canada Relations." Accessed 21 July 2020. https://eur-lex.europa.eu/LexUriServ/LexUriServ.do?uri=COM:2003:0266:FIN:EN:PDF.

– 2006. "Global Europe: Competing in the World." Accessed 21 July 2020. https://eur-lex.europa.eu/LexUriServ/LexUriServ.do?uri=COM:2006:0567:FIN:EN:PDF.

– 2017. "Reflection Paper on Harnessing Globalisation." Accessed 21 July 2020. https://ec.europa.eu/commission/publications/reflection-paper-harnessing-globalisation_en.

– 2018a. "CETA 1st Civil Society Forum Meeting (12 September 2018)." Accessed 21 July 2020. https://webcast.ec.europa.eu/ceta-1st-civil-society-forum-meeting.

– 2018b. "EU-Canada Civil Society Forum: Trade and Sustainable Development under the Comprehensive Economic and Trade Agreement (CETA)." Accessed 21 July 2020. https://trade.ec.europa.eu/doclib/events/index.cfm?id=1901.

– 2018c. "Meeting of Committee on Trade and Sustainable Development: Agenda." Accessed 21 July 2020. https://trade.ec.europa.eu/doclib/docs/2018/august/tradoc_157266.pdf.

– 2019. "CETA Regulatory Cooperation Forum – Stakeholder Debrief Meeting." Accessed 21 July 2020. https://ec.europa.eu/growth/content/ceta-regulatory-cooperation-forum-stakeholder-debrief-meeting_en.

– 2020. "Proposed Agenda, 2nd Meeting of the CETA Regulatory Cooperation Forum 3–4 February 2020." Accessed 21 July 2020. https://trade.ec.europa.eu/doclib/docs/2020/january/tradoc_158565.pdf.

European Economic and Social Committee. 2018. "The Role of Domestic Advisory Groups in Monitoring the Implementation of Free Trade Agreements." Accessed 21 July 2020. https://www.eesc.europa.eu/en/our-work/opinions-information-reports/opinions/role-domestic-advisory-groups-monitoring-implementation-free-trade-agreements.

European Union. 2016. "TTIP - EU Proposal for Chapter: Regulatory Cooperation." Accessed 21 July 2020. http://trade.ec.europa.eu/doclib/docs/2016/march/tradoc_154377.pdf.

Golberg, Elizabeth. 2019. "Regulatory Cooperation - A Reality Check." M-RCBG Associate Working Paper No. 115, Mossavar-Rahmani Center for Business & Government, Harvard Kennedy School, Cambridge, MA. https://www.hks.harvard.edu/centers/mrcbg/publications/awp/awp115.

Hoekman, Bernard. 2015. "Fostering Transatlantic Regulatory Cooperation and Gradual Multilateralization." *Journal of International Economic Law* 18, no. 3: 609–24. https://doi.org/10.1093/jiel/jgv028.

Hoekman, Bernard, and Charles Sabel. 2019. "Open Plurilateral Agreements, International Regulatory Cooperation and the WTO." *Global Policy* 10, no. 3: 297–312. https://doi.org/10.1111/1758-5899.12694.

Joint Interpretative Instrument. 2016. Joint Interpretative Instrument on the Comprehensive Economic and Trade Agreement (CETA) between Canada & the European Union and its Member States. Accessed 21 July 2020. https://www.international.gc.ca/trade-commerce/trade-agreements-accords-commerciaux/agr-acc/ceta-aecg/jii-iic.aspx.

Krstic, Stanko S. 2012. "Regulatory Cooperation to Remove Non-tariff Barriers to Trade in Products: Key Challenges and Opportunities for the Canada-EU Comprehensive Trade Agreement." *Legal Issues of Economic Integration* 39, no. 1: 3–28.

Lazo, Rodrigo Polanco, and Pierre Sauvé. 2018. "The Treatment of Regulatory Convergence in Preferential Trade Agreements." *World Trade Review* 17, no. 4: 575–607. https://doi.org/10.1017/S1474745618000058.

Mendes, Joana. 2016. "Participation in a New Regulatory Paradigm: Collaboration and Constraint in TTIP's Regulatory Cooperation." IILJ Working Paper 2016/5 (MegaReg Series), Institute for International Law and Justice, New York University School of Law, New York, NY. https://www.iilj.org/publications/participation-in-a-new-regulatory-paradigm-collaboration-and-constraint-in-ttips-regulatory-cooperation/.

Mertins-Kirkwood, Hadrian, Scott Sinclair, Stuart Trew, Laura Große, Peter Fuchs, Anna Schüler, and Ines Koburger (eds). 2016. *Making Sense of CETA* (2nd edition). Berlin: Powershift.

Meunier, Sophie, and Jean-Frédéric Morin. 2015. "No Agreement is an Island: Negotiating TTIP in a Dense Regime Complex." In *The Politics of Transatlantic Trade Negotiations: TTIP in a Globalized World*, edited by Jean-Frédéric Morin, Tereza Novotná, Frederik Ponjaert, and Mario Telò, 173–86. Abingdon: Routledge.

Orbie, Jan, Lore Van den Putte, and Deborah Martens. 2017. "The Impact of Labour Rights Commitments in EU Trade Agreements: The Case of Peru." *Politics and Governance* 5, no. 4: 6–18.

Shaffer, Gregory. 2002. "Reconciling Trade and Regulatory Goals: The Prospects and Limits of New Approaches to Transatlantic Governance through Mutual Recognition and Safe Harbor Agreements." *Columbia Journal of European Law* 9, no. 1: 29–78.

Stewart, Richard B. 2014. "Remedying Disregard in Global Regulatory Governance: Accountability, Participation, and Responsiveness." *American Journal of International Law* 108, no. 2: 211–70. https://doi.org/10.5305/amerjintelaw.108.2.0211.

Trade Justice Movement. 2019. "Written evidence to the Joint Committee on Human Rights Inquiry on Human Rights in International Agreements." Accessed 21 July 2020. https://www.tjm.org.uk/documents/briefings/TJM-response-to-JCHR-inquiry-on-human-rights-in-international-agreements-Jan19.pdf.

Trew, Stuart. 2019. *International Regulatory Cooperation and The Public Good: How "Good Regulatory Practices" in Trade Agreements Erode Protections for the Environment, Public Health, Workers and Consumers.* Berlin: PowerShift.

Wiener, Jonathan B., and Alberto Alemanno. 2015. "The Future of International Regulatory Cooperation: TTIP as a Learning Process Toward a Global Policy Laboratory." *Law and Contemporary Problems* 78, no. 4: 103–36.

14

Conclusion: CETA Implementation Challenges and Trends

Robert G. Finbow

This volume has provided detailed investigations of several core aspects of the Comprehensive Economic and Trade Agreement (CETA) between Canada and the European Union (EU). CETA's lengthy and uncertain negotiation and ratification provide examples of the complexities inherent in the EU's contemporary economic and trade agreements. Post the Lisbon Treaty, and especially after the financial and Eurozone crises, the Commission pursued comprehensive economic and trade agreements to stimulate market access and competitiveness for European corporations, with flexibilization in labour markets. The EU's free trade agreements (FTAS) emphasized economic advantage, including regulatory coordination and investor protection. The Global Europe initiative advocated "activism in creating open markets and fair conditions for trade abroad" to stimulate economic changes in other countries, to strengthen the competitive position of the EU industry (European Commission 2006, 6). This meant broader economic arrangements, which included non-tariff barriers (NTBS), regulations on "intellectual property rights (IPR), services, investment, public procurement, and competition" (ibid., 7). Outlining ambitious negotiations with many states and regions, the report noted, "Completing our current agenda of competitiveness-driven FTAS remains a priority" (European Commission 2010). Alongside deals with South Korea, Singapore, Vietnam, and others, CETA was ambitious. Its final form retained breadth but not without complications.

The Treaty of Lisbon permitted the European Commission to act as one player in treaty negotiations where it held exclusive competence, with EU parliamentary ratification required for international agreements.

Nonetheless, fearing loss of competency, some member states remained reluctant to accept what they had agreed to and assert that most transnational economic agreements involved mixed competencies (Gatti and Manzini 2012). Hence the EU courts were asked to rule on the Singapore deal and determined EU competence did not extend to indirect investment and investor-state disputes settlement (ISDS). The EU acceded to mixed competency for the CETA requiring member state ratification. If CETA were to fall based on failure of ratification by a member state, especially a larger one, it could have profound consequences. It could challenge the EU's role as a unified actor in trade policy, overturn the longstanding system whereby qualified majority voting decided core commercial policy, and instead herald in a process "dependent on every veto point along the way" (Novotná 2017, 10). Eric White (2017) argues that the EU has to separate trade agreements where it has clear competence from other economic and political matters where competence is shared, such as investment.

Thus, in later Singapore negotiations, the EU settled on two parallel agreements: "a free trade agreement, which contains areas of exclusive EU competence and thus only requires the Council's approval and the European Parliament's consent before it can enter into force ... [and] an investment protection agreement which, due to its shared competence nature, will also have to go through the relevant national ratification procedures in all member states before it can enter into force" (European Council 2018). This approach was also employed in the negotiations with Japan where discussions of an investment court system (ICS) have been dealt with separately, though the EU insisted the ICS be agreed in parallel to the trade agreement. The Vietnam agreement followed a similar pattern (European Commission 2018). This model will permit future economic and trade agreements to be ratified expeditiously with the politically contentious issues of investor disputes systems removed and subject to member state ratification. While full ratification of CETA, including its ICS, remains possible, conversion to separate agreements for the economic and trade matters and an accompanying document for the ICS remains a potential future strategy to overcome any ratification roadblocks.

Yet there are complications beyond investment as our contributors demonstrate. Elements of the new committee machinery and delegated authority in raise issues of democratic legitimacy and accountability, given the role of EU and national parliaments in some competences covered in CETA. The CETA Joint Committee is granted broad authority to determine the structure of special committees and dialogues, and even to work out the arrangements for the ICS if this is ratified (indeed parameters for the investment court were developed in the joint committee in early 2021 – see table 14.1). As Stern notes, the delegation of authority, to be efficient, requires a high degree of discretion for CETA committees. This broad grant of authority "to interpret and adapt the content of the Agreement" may create challenges for balancing democratic legitimacy with efficiency in the transnational governance mechanism as the nature and purposes of committee is changed. This may require "legal solutions" which provide for "suitable control mechanisms" to restore the balance.

Weiß concurs that "CETA committees exercise significant public powers, by virtue of broadly drafted mandates." This may weaken the "legislative and treaty-making powers" of the European Parliament (EP), which is effectively excluded from substantial elements of the actual implementation of agreements like CETA. To restore a balanced executive-legislative relationship as intended by the Lisbon Treaty, existing and new mechanisms to involve the EP in decisions on treaties and to allow more effective supervision should be contemplated. While Weiß suggests the delegation of power maybe unconstitutional in some member states, notably Germany, courts in that country have ruled the provisional implementation of CETA legitimate, though high court cases remain pending, delaying ratification. The core issue of whether the surrender of powers to CETA bodies is unconstitutional remains the subject of numerous court cases in Germany at time of writing. "If the court finally issues an adverse ruling, Germany could still be compelled to withdraw from CETA" (Matussek 2021).

As the chapters in part 2 indicate, the regulatory elements of CETA are highly complex, with provisions in different chapters covering regulatory activity in specific economic sectors. In general, the parties pledged to engage in regulatory cooperation and conformity assessment to reduce NTBS to trade and to coordinate regulatory structures in an ongoing process. The regulatory cooperation forum (RCF) has been active in taking on some of the more common areas for action on matters such as cyber-security, cosmetics, pharmaceutical inspections, humane treatment of animals, pediatric medicines, and possible accommodations on product safety. Camilleri argues that there has been insufficient "ambition" in developing the regulatory cooperation process and that the RCF should be equipped with a secretariat to move forward more rapidly on efforts to address non-tariff regulatory barriers which are potential impediments to trade. The process must be open and fluid to permit engagements among regulators, industry, civil society, and individual businesses so that a "foundation of trust can be laid" and international regulatory cooperation via CETA can be expedited.

Table 14.1
Investment court system implementation

Provision	Purpose
Rules setting out the functioning of the appellate tribunal	Ensure an effective appeal function, the first such appeal function to become operational in international investment agreements;
A code of conduct for the judges of the ICS	Bolster the assurances of the highest ethics standards already contained in the agreement;
Rules for mediation	Mediation is an area which traditional investment agreements have largely overlooked
Rules for binding interpretations to be adopted by the CETA Joint Committee	Rules to allow EU and Canada to maintain control of the interpretation of the agreement

Source: CETA Joint Committee (2021).

The other contributors on regulatory matters noted potential obstacles to creating trust across all the affected stakeholders. Acconci notes that the existing commitments to ensure noneconomic social objectives are not disregarded in the search of regulatory integration and efficiencies are insufficient. Despite increased attention in economic and investment agreements to social considerations, more is required to safeguard the right to regulate and sustainable development objectives in deals such as CETA. Her preference would be to create a "multilateral regulatory instrument" to generate standards via interpretative declarations, guidelines, or "model clauses" to protect noneconomic interests and balance the right to regulate with regulatory cooperation. The EU has given hints of interest in such directions, though resistance from other actors might make such measures elusive for some time.

Van Rooy also notes that the inclusion of regulatory cooperation processes aimed at coordination and convergence can lead to issues of "democratic accountability, legitimacy of decision-making, and transparency." Such cooperation does have the potential to form a "policy laboratory" for optimal approaches in regulation which can potentially take account of legitimate noneconomic objectives. This can develop in a positive direction if checks and balances are sufficient and if stakeholders from civil society can participate in transparent processes to offset external pressures for changes in domestic policy which erode the right to regulate. To retain legitimacy and balance social and industry interests, national democratic checks and balances and judicial processes should not be marginalized. As regulatory collaboration develops in CETA, it will be interesting to assess this balance and determine if a foundation of trust among stakeholders is possible.

One of the EU's primary goals in CETA was opening up billion-dollar procurement markets to European bidders at all levels of government. The CETA framework includes a single access platform (SAP) through a new an electronic system for bidders which will be viewable by eligible contractors, suppliers, and service providers in Europe and Canada. Thresholds were retained but increased for small contracts eligible for local preferences. There were also exclusions for protection of national security or enforcement of measures regarding human, animal or plant health, public order, morals and safety; shipbuilding and repair; broadcasting program material; works of art and cultural industries (Quebec); preferences for Indigenous people and regional economic development in some "have not" provinces. There were also provisions whereby key sectors, such as education and health services, may be excluded (CETA 2016, Art. 19). The EU already has a central portal for procurement tender. To this point, Canada's SAP for public tenders remains under development which has slowed the ability of firms to take advantage of CETA provisions, though it was estimated to be completed by 2022.

Despite the exemptions, critical scholars and nongovernmental organizations (NGOs) expressed concerns that opening procurement could remove important instruments for local preferences in employment, for environmental or cultural or other policy objectives for provinces and municipalities. The two teams of researchers who contributed to this volume have not found evidence of restrictions on municipal governments in procurement decisions. Ruffat and Leblond note the problems of high transaction costs for small and medium enterprises (SMEs) which limit their ability to take advantage procurement opportunities. If these are overcome, the benefits of bidding in both directions will become evident via increased opportunities for business on both sides of the Atlantic as well as efficiencies and cost savings. Government needs to do more via the trade commission service to provide support for SMEs (SMEs have been a priority area for the joint committee). Assisted by financial measures based in part on EU initiatives and making use of programs such as the Greening Government Fund, Innovative Solutions Canada, Innovations for Defence Excellence and Security (IDEaS), and Build in Canada Innovation, Schwartz and Schwartz find that the municipal level impacts have been limited to date, since EU firms did not face much discrimination in the past, because municipalities were already looking for the best bids.

Given threshold levels, business for small local firms should not be significantly reduced. Prohibition of offsets for local employment or other benefits could be constraining, but carefully worded community benefit agreements (CBAs) could allow such public policy concerns to be factored into the contracting process.

After some resistance, CETA incorporated an investment chapter to protect investor rights and encourage removal of barriers to investment and capital mobility and clarification of legal requirements. Provisions included a higher threshold for review of takeovers by national regulators, common language on nondiscrimination, fair and equitable treatment (FET), and compensation for infringements or expropriations. To address civil society critiques of investor-state dispute settlement (ISDS) the EU proposed a bilateral ICS, with permanent judges to replace the ad hoc arbitrators used in existing international forums. The ICS would use transparent hearings with a right to intervene for interested parties and right to appeals. It would also end "forum shopping" for sympathetic arbitrators and frivolous claims which were forms of abuse in established ISDS systems. Gantz's wide-ranging chapter illustrates how distinct the system will be when put into practice compared to Canada's other major economic and investment agreements. Canada has taken risks by negotiating different investment disputes provisions in each of its major deals and removing it from the updated North American Free Trade Agreement (NAFTA) altogether. As a "taker" of larger states initiatives it was unsurprising the EU proposal for an ICS was accepted by Canada. While its provisions will be adequate for Canadian investors used to more conventional ISDS, its effectiveness remains indeterminant as ratification drags on. Gantz notes that while most of the EU states have adequate legal regimes for adjudicating investment disputes until ratification of the ICS, Canada will have to rely on bilateral deals with states, largely in Eastern Europe, where the rule of law on investment remains problematic.

Whitsitt addresses the legitimacy crisis surrounding ISDS and assesses whether the ICS system, once operational, will assuage these concerns. The concept of legitimacy requires careful delineation and has multiple normative and sociological aspects. Some of the proposed revisions to proceedings such as "adjudicator qualifications, provisions on conflict of interest, tenure and reappointment, and transparency" in the ICS design seem set to enhance its normative legitimacy. However, the deviation from the standard ISDS model has yet to be tested and could create problems, via the joint committee and Committee on Services and Investment (CSI), of state interference which past ISDS systems have sought to limit.

Researchers must carefully "design methodologies that acknowledge and measure the perceptions of the diverse constituencies involved in CETA's investment chapter," as the consequences could well be complex and differentiated by stakeholder constituency. It will take careful analyses to separate variables and assign import to various novel elements to determine which is most conducive to overcoming the legitimacy concerns. Overall CETA's more definitive "normative framework" in the ICS model specifies rights and obligations which can affect adjudicators deliberations and enhance legitimacy in the long run. But this depends on the eventual implementation of the ICS which awaits ratification across member states. The parties are moving forward with principles for ICS regarding functioning of the appellate tribunal, adoption of interpretations, code of conduct and rules of mediation (see table 14.1)

While it was being negotiated, CETA met with resistance as progressive critics and populist nationalists challenged its liberalized model. Under pressure from civil society and member states during CETA and TTIP negotiations, the EU adopted a revised approach to address increased politicization of trade negotiations. In the 2015 "Trade for All" strategy, responding to criticisms of weak commitment to the social dimension, the EU promised open transparent negotiations, worker and small business protections, and promotion of sustainable development, human rights, and good governance. (European Commission 2015). Both parties adopted a joint interpretive instrument, which affirmed the importance of the "right to regulate in the public interest" and changes to promote transparency, impartiality, favouritism, and consistency in disputes resolutions (Government of Canada 2016). The two parties highlighted the success of the open, transparent negotiation process: "We have responded to Canadians, EU citizens, and businesses with a fairer, more transparent, system" (ibid. 2016). The Commission claimed that CETA demonstrated its commitment to social responsibility in trade: "the Commission has taken social considerations into account in all policies, including its foreign trade policy – the Comprehensive Economic and Trade Agreement with Canada is an example thereof" (European Commission 2017).

The chapters in part 5 demonstrate the balance of enthusiasm and uncertainty about the potential of the sustainability, labour, and environment chapters of CETA. Bhardwaj argues that the success of the sustainability dimensions of CETA is "dependent on the interaction between public, private, and social actors," since such a large portion of international economic integration is conducted by transnational enterprises, whose activities are scrutinized largely by international NGOs. The sustainability chapter did address climate change, but its "effectiveness relies on the parties' efforts to meet the Paris obligations," which will ultimately resolve the "tension" between CETA's liberalization and sustainability goals. If political will is there, regulatory cooperation and cooperation-based dialogue could become significant to the attainment of the sustainability potential of CETA. Santoire shows how energy as a system is one of the principle aspects of the environmental impact of CETA which will test the boundaries of the sustainability chapter. Discovering the impact of liberalized energy flows versus sustainability constraints will require continued investigation of legal provisions in CETA and how these are interpreted in domestic law and affect fossil fuel production rates and environmental impacts.

Finally, Mancini considers the balance of labour rights and regulatory provisions in CETA, assessing the potential via civil society forums to implement regulatory cooperation "as a tool for enhanced protection and upwards convergence." CETA supporters speak of a "balance" of interests between civil society and corporate actors on regulatory integration to ensure appropriate attention to labour rights. Yet the specific implementation of these mechanisms is still evolving. From her investigations, it appears so far that regulatory cooperation and civil society forum "appear not to speak to each other." Efforts will be needed to ensure that there is adequate respect for fundamental labour rights, which may need to be backed up by regular "impact assessments" to determine the impact of regulatory collaboration on workers and their organizations. Future agreements should put these more explicitly into place, but the regulatory collaboration proceeding under CETA civil society actors with knowledge of impact on the ground should be taken seriously to promote enhanced labour protections. As these processes are just getting under way, it will take some time to determine if these socially-oriented components of the agreement will work well enough to assuage the concerns of civil society actors and ensure broad distribution of benefits in line with the progressive intentions expressed by both partners to CETA.

This project and volume covered a wide range of core CETA provisions and issues but did not address all components of this extensive economic agreement. Many of the provisions implemented since 2017 have produced substantial immediate results, with trade flows up substantially. The immediate tariff reduction for many products have brought gains as both parties' exports have risen, though with disproportionately greater benefits to the EU. The value-added mixture of the trade remains problematic. Post-CETA data suggests the Canada has exported US$933 million more in precious stones and minerals, US$2.7 billion more in crude oil and US$1.0 billion more in mineral ores. The EU has increased its exports of pharmaceuticals, motor vehicles parts, and machinery by some US$6 billion. Arnason (2020) suggests on this basis that Canada is trading "rocks for Audis."

Canadian government reporting indicates that increased exports, up 16.6 per cent versus pre-CETA levels by 2019, represent billions in new sales, even if benefits have been uneven. The official data indicates minimal gains, or even decreases in exports from Canada of high value-added goods such as machinery and aircraft components with most export gains in fuels, mineral ores, and the like (Global Affairs Canada 2020). Other reporting from Export Development Canada (2020) notes increases in motor vehicles exports, and potential in high-end manufacturing and service sectors once the agreement is fully utilized. While export gains have been quick where tariff reductions have been immediate (Jiang 2020), "Canadian companies must still create strategies that will help them benefit from CETA's potential" (Export Development Canada 2020) by taking steps to market products effectively and provide documentation demonstrating rules of origin. "While CETA is certainty benefitting Canada, the full potential of the trade deal is yet to be seen as the utilization rate of CETA preferences remains moderate" (ibid. 2020). Future studies will need to trace the evolution of this performance to trace the actual versus potential benefits over time.

Sectoral differentiation in benefits has the potential to becomes politically charged as they affect industries with strong regional political bases. Canadian complaints on agriculture have been particularly strong from exporters who note "an overall deterioration of Canada's agri-food trade balance with the EU" and a "lack of respect" by the EU for "the spirit of the CETA" (CAFTA 2020). The Canadian Agri-Food Trade Alliance (CAFTA) proposed a "Team Canada" trade delegation with producers and trade officials working on site to seek solutions to vexatious challenges from EU interpretations of CETA, to prevent a retreat to protectionism and fulfill the "win-win" benefits of this gold standard deal (2020). This could potentially raise political issues if it has distorting regional effects, for instance the perception that the Prairie provinces have been left out of CETA so far as agricultural exports lag (Arnason 2020). Compensation for dairy producers, concentrated in Central and Eastern provinces, is proceeding, but many agricultural sectors are still faring poorly. Producer groups have received non-partisan political support from high-profile former premiers, including original proponents of CETA such as Jean Charest, who call for an assertive effort to secure EU compliance with the spirit of the agreement (Ed White 2020). Management of such political tensions will be essential to making for optimal use of the agreement.

As ratification moves forward, the EU has had to overcome some challenges, often around similar narrow sectoral interests, especially in agri-food and geographic indications. The sub-national region of Wallonia in Belgium, led by a socialist leader at the time, initially refused to sign on because of concerns about the potential disruptions to health, social, and environmental policies, and the dairy sector (Van der Loo and Pelkmans 2016). Eventually Wallonia acceded with a four-page deal, the "Belgian Explanatory Amendment," which allowed provisional application of CETA while Belgium asked EU courts to clarify the legality of the arbitration and investment court provisions (Laird and Petillion 2017), which were eventually approved. Some 38 nonbinding statements and declarations from EU members and EU institutions provided interpretations of the EU on completion of CETA; "several member states adopted declarations to protect their specific interests" which added to complexity in the ratification process (Van der Loo 2016). Food products have continued to be contentious with the two sides haggling over tariff rate quotas (TRQs) for dairy in particular. Italy imposed country of origin labelling on imports of Canadian durum wheat while threatening not to ratify (Nicola and Scaccia 2021). The parliament in Cyprus voted against CETA for a range of issues, including labour and environmental protections, GMOs in food products, and a geographical indication for halloumi cheese (ITN 2020).

At time of writing, ratification in Ireland is stalled by a court challenge on CETA's constitutionality and the potential necessity of a referendum to ratify it (Kenny 2021). Similar issues have arisen in countries such as the Netherlands and France where opponents are seeking a greater NGO role on green and labour issues. The Commission has indicated ways in which it might work around such obstacles, though officially if a country notifies of failure to ratify because of judicial or legislative action to comply with a member state constitution, provisional implementation would be aborted in accordance with Art. 30.7(3)(c) of CETA (European Council 2016, 14). So, abandonment of CETA is not inconceivable, though these challenges have been parried so far and the process will be allowed to play out slowly, absent a major state rejection. As mentioned, uncertainty continues pending court challenges in Germany and potential obstruction from Italy etc. At time of writing, 15 of 27 member states had ratified CETA (excluding the UK on account of Brexit).

As CETA is implemented, unexpected contingencies also will arise, including business fluctuations and crises. The 2020 COVID-19 pandemic slowed uptake of CETA provisions and prompted some downturn in interactions, accentuated by lengthy public health closures, especially by SMEs already facing challenges of adjustment (Blanchet and Sekkel 2020). Potential tensions will need to be managed over time such as disruptions from public health or financial crises, or even possible vaccine or personal protective equipment (PPE) nationalism which some fear might bedevil relations during current or future pandemics. Canada is in a difficult position as a net importer of EU pharmaceutical and medical technologies – a gap which increased since CETA implementation (Global Affairs Canada 2020). The EU and Canada have pushed for transparency in any deviation from trade rules affecting supply chains, but it may be difficult to avoid tensions in a health crisis as EU states protect their citizens and EU medical technology patent holders (Finbow 2020). Additionally, if the US resumes its place as a full partner in the global economic and trading system, implications for CETA preferences will periodically arise (as with the Trump administrations pressure on the EU over Canadian lobster tariff preferences under CETA). If the US and the EU reach more trading accords, the benefits of CETA to Canada will be altered as competition increases. Brexit also affects the balance since some 40 per cent of Canada's trade with Europe was with the UK. Canada has reached transitional agreements with the UK to keep many CETA provisions in play but trade relations with the EU will be diminished in overall volume. But the two parties remain critical partners economically. Challenges from resurgent powers such as China or Russia could bring further retreat from the international liberal order or erode multinational economic and political institutions, so CETA will remain an important backstop for both partners and there will be a premium on making it work.

As the authors in this volume note, the results are preliminary as CETA is unevenly, though steadily, put into effect in the areas permitted by provisional implementation. Yet the assembled scholarly works have provided an important and innovative examination of how CETA is progressing as a comprehensive economic agreement. Additionally, they have revealed a range of potential outcomes in many aspects of the agreement, depending on the political will and effective leadership on both sides to make CETA economically mutually beneficial and as socially progressive as possible. Outcomes will become clearer over time once ratification and implementation is completed and officials and stakeholders learn how to make use of the complex provisions. Future analysis will need to focus on implementation of the investment components, progress on regulatory collaboration, and mutual recognition of standards and professional qualifications which will occur piecemeal with the assistance of nongovernmental associations and stakeholders. This volume illustrates the virtues – indeed the necessity – of an interdisciplinary and international set of investigators bringing their own scholarly techniques and insights to an understanding of future EU-Canada relations. Certainly, a combination of quantitative and qualitative methodologies, and insights from law, public policy, and economics have contributed to a multifaceted picture of the complexities, accomplishments, and challenges of implementation. Such diverse scholarship will be needed to inform future efforts to properly implement and understand the implications of the CETA agreement.

REFERENCES

Arnason, Robert. 2020. "We Export Rocks to Europe, they Sell Us Audis." *Western Producer,* 24 September. Accessed 15 March 2021. https://www.producer.com/opinion/blog-we-export-rocks-to-europe-they-sell-us-audis/.

Blanchet, Nancy, and Julia Sekkel. 2020. "COVID-19 Intensifies Challenges for Canadian Exporters." Accessed 15 March 2021. https://www.international.gc.ca/trade-commerce/economist-economiste/analysis-analyse/challenges-covid-19-defis.aspx.

CAFTA (Canadian Agri-Food Trade Alliance). 2020. "Canadian Agri-Food Trade Alliance (CAFTA) Open Letter to Ministers on Three Years of CETA." Accessed 15 March 2021. http://cafta.org/wp-content/uploads/2020/09/CAFTA-Letter-to-Ministers_3-years-of-CETA-Sept-21.pdf.

CETA (Canada-European Union Comprehensive Economic and Trade Agreement). 2016. Accessed 21 July 2020. https://www.international.gc.ca/trade-commerce/trade-agreements-accords-commerciaux/agr-acc/ceta-aecg/text-texte/toc-tdm.aspx.

CETA Joint Committee. 2021. "Decision No. 001/2021 of the CETA Joint Committee of January 29, 2021. Setting out the Administrative and Organizational Matters Regarding the Functioning of the Appellate Tribunal." Accessed 15 March 2021. https://www.international.gc.ca/trade-commerce/trade-agreements-accords-commerciaux/agr-acc/ceta-aecg/appellate-tribunal-dappel.aspx.

European Commission. 2006. "Global Europe: Competing in the World. A Contribution to the EU's Growth and Jobs Strategy." Accessed 11 January 2011. https://eur-lex.europa.eu/LexUriServ/LexUriServ.do?uri=COM:2006:0567:FIN:en:PDF.

– 2010. "Towards a Comprehensive European International Investment Policy." Accessed 15 March 2021. https://eur-lex.europa.eu/LexUriServ/LexUriServ.do?uri=COM:2010:0343:FIN:EN:PDF.

– 2015. *Trade for all: Towards a more responsible trade and investment policy.* Brussels: European Union. http://trade.ec.europa.eu/doclib/docs/2015/october/tradoc_153846.pdf.

– 2017. "Reflection Paper on the Social Dimension of Europe." Accessed 15 March 2021. https://ec.europa.eu/info/publications/reflection-paper-social-dimension-europe_en.

– 2018. "Overview of FTA And Other Trade Negotiations." Accessed 15 March 2021. http://trade.ec.europa.eu/doclib/docs/2006/december/tradoc_118238.pdf.

European Council. 2016. "Comprehensive Economic and Trade Agreement (CETA) Between Canada, of the one part, and the European Union and its Member States, of the Other Part – Statements to the Council Minutes." Accessed 15 March 2021. https://data.consilium.europa.eu/doc/document/ST-13463-2016-REV-1/en/pdf.

– 2018. "EU-Singapore: Council adopts decisions to sign trade and investment agreements." Accessed 15 March 2021. https://www.consilium.europa.eu/en/press/press-releases/2018/10/15/eu-singapore-council-adopts-decisions-to-sign-trade-and-investment-agreements/.

Export Development Canada. 2020. "CETA Trade Deal: Three years on." Accessed 15 March 2021. https://www.edc.ca/en/article/ceta-trade-in-eu.html.

Finbow, Robert. 2020. "Covid 19 Impacts on Trade and the Economy: Hard Choices for the EU." Accessed 15 March 2021. https://www.ecsa-c.ca/post/covid-19-impacts-on-trade-and-the-economy-hard-choices-for-the-eu.

Gatti, Mauro, and Pietro Manzini. 2012. "External representation of the European Union in the conclusion of international agreements." *Common Market Law Review* 49, no. 5: 1703–34.

Global Affairs Canada. 2020. "Canada's Merchandise Trade Performance with the EU after the Entry into Force of CETA." Accessed 15 March 2021. https://www.international.gc.ca/trade-commerce/economist-economiste/statistics-statistiques/eu-marchandise-ue.aspx.

Government of Canada. 2016. "Joint Interpretative Instrument on the Comprehensive Economic and Trade Agreement (CETA) between Canada & the European Union and Its Member States." Accessed 15 March 2021. http://www.international.gc.ca/trade-commerce/trade-agreements-accords-commerciaux/agr-acc/ceta-aecg/jii-iic.aspx?lang=eng.

ITN (Investment Treaty News). 2020. "CETA faces hurdle after Cypriot parliament fails to ratify the agreement." Investment Treaty News, 5 October.

Accessed 15 March 2021. https://www.iisd.org/itn/en/2020/10/05/
ceta-faces-hurdle-after-cypriot-parliament-fails-to-ratify-the-agreement/.

Jiang, Kevin. 2020. "Canada's Trade Performance under CETA." Accessed
15 March 2021. https://www.tradecommissioner.gc.ca/canadex-
port/0004919.aspx.

Kenny, Paula. 2021. "Irish parliament committees to examine CETA before
ratification." *Euractiv,* 11 March. Accessed 15 March 2021. https://www.
euractiv.com/section/politics/short_news/irish-parliament-committees-
to-examine-ceta-before-ratification/.

Laird, Ian, and Flip Petillion. 2017. "Comprehensive Economic and Trade
Agreement, ISDS and the Belgian Veto: A Warning of Failure for Future
Trade Agreements with the EU?" *Global Trade and Customs Journal* 12,
no. 4: 167–74.

Matussek, Karin. 2021. "EU-Canada Trade Pact Lawsuit Tossed by Top
German Court." *Bloomberg News.* 2 March. Accessed 15 March 2021.
https://financialpost.com/pmn/business-pmn/german-top-court-rejects-
case-over-lawmakers-role-in-ceta-pact.

Nicola, Fernanda G., and Gino Scaccia. 2021. "It's All About the Pasta:
Protectionism, Liberalization, and the Challenge for Quality and
Sustainability of Made in Italy." *Florida International University Law
Review* 14: 479–520. https://ecollections.law.fiu.edu/cgi/viewcontent.cgi?
article=1443&context=lawreview.

Novotná, Tereza. 2017. "The EU as a global actor: United we stand, divided
we fall." *Journal of Common Market Studies* 55, no. 51: 177–91.

Van der Loo, Guillaume. 2016. "CETA's signature: 38 statements, a joint
interpretative instrument and an uncertain future." Accessed 15 March
2021. http://aei.pitt.edu/80602/1/GVdL_CETA__II.pdf.

Van der Loo, Guillaume, and Jacques Pelkmans. 2016. "Does Wallonia's veto
of CETA spell the beginning of the end of EU trade policy?" Accessed
15 March 2021. http://aei.pitt.edu/80526/1/GVdL_and_JP_Wallonia_and_
CETA.pdf.

White, Ed. 2020. "Farmers fume over CETA failings." *Western Producer,*
1 October. Accessed 15 March 2021. https://www.producer.com/news/
farmers-fume-over-ceta-failings/.

White, Eric. 2017. "The Obstacles to Concluding the EU-Canada
Comprehensive Economic and Trade Agreement and Lessons for the
Future." *Global Trade and Customs Journal* 12, no. 5: 176–83.

Contributors

PIA ACCONCI is full professor of international law at the University of Teramo, Italy, where she has taught European Union (EU) law for more than fifteen years. Additionally, she has taught at several other universities and took part in many conferences both in Italy and abroad. Since 1 September 2018 she has been the academic coordinator of the three-year Jean Monnet Teaching and Research Module on EU Investment Law at Teramo. She has also taken part in several Italian and international research and study groups and contributed to the coordination of a few of them as a supervisor. She has a PhD in international economic law from the universities of Bergamo, Turin, and L. Bocconi, Milan, in 1997. Acconci is the author of many articles and two books, as well as the editor of four books. Her research activities are related to the fields of international organizations as protagonists of international law, investment, multinational enterprises, trade, and the protection of human rights, particularly of the rights to health and to food, from the perspectives of international and EU laws.

AAKRITI BHARDWAJ is a Marie Curie Early Stage Researcher and a PhD student in EU trade policy at the School of Law, University of Nottingham, UK. She has a master's in international trade law from the University of Turin, Italy. She has been an analyst at PricewaterhouseCoopers India and intern at the United Nations Economic and Social Commission for Asia and the Pacific (UNESCAP). Her research is funded under the EU Horizon 2020 program (grant agreement no. 721916) and analyzes the Comprehensive Economic and Trade Agreement (CETA) in the context of its sustainable development provisions. She is particularly interested in examining the role of law in promoting the regulatory governance of labour and environmental standards through trade.

MARK A. CAMILLERI is a Brussels-based lawyer with the law firm Camilleri Law. Mark has extensive commercial and regulatory experience and advises clients on a wide range of EU and Canadian legal and regulatory matters including trade issues, privacy and digital regulation, and natural resources. Prior to establishing Camilleri Law, he was a partner at the London office of a major Canadian law firm after starting his practice in the firm's Toronto office. Camilleri is qualified to practise law in the EU (Dutch Speaking Bar of Brussels), Canada (Ontario), and the United Kingdom (England and Wales). He holds a BA (Honours) in international relations from the University of Toronto, a combined LLB-MBA from Dalhousie University, and an LLM in EU law from the Faculty of Law, KU Leuven. Mark is the president and a founder of the Canada-EU Trade and Investment Association, a Brussels-based not-for-profit organization, focused on advancing and promoting Canadian and EU trade and investment interests through CETA and beyond. Camilleri is a member of the Faculty of Law, KU Leuven and is certified as an information privacy professional in Europe by the International Association of Privacy Professionals (IAPP).

ROBERT G. FINBOW is Eric Denis Memorial Professor of political science and deputy director of the Jean Monnet European Union Centre of Excellence at Dalhousie University. He holds an MA degree from York University and MSc and PhD from the London School of Economics and Political Science. His research focuses on the socially responsible elements of trade agreements, especially labour and social issues in the North American Free Trade Agreement (NAFTA) and the EU. He has published books, chapters, and articles on the CETA and TTIP negotiations, the EU social dimension and fiscal crisis, labour and environmental aspects of NAFTA, comparative health care and social policy, comparative North American political cultures, Atlantic Canadian regionalism, and comparative regional development in North America. His focus recently has been on CETA, especially the implications for social policy.

DAVID A. GANTZ is Samuel M. Fegtly Professor of Law emeritus, and director emeritus, International Economic Law and Policy Program at the University of Arizona. He is also Will Clayton Fellow for Trade and International Economics at the Center for the United States and Mexico/ Baker Institute Rice University He teaches and writes in the areas of international trade and investment law, regional trade agreements, public international law, and international environmental law. He has written extensively on World Trade Organization (WTO) and NAFTA trade law and dispute resolution issues, as well as a range of other international trade matters. Gantz is the author or co-author of four books and more than fifty law review articles and book chapters and has served as a consultant for the United Nations Development Programme (UNDP), the US Agency for International Development (USAID), and the World Bank.

PATRICK LEBLOND is CN-Paul M. Tellier Chair on Business and Public Policy and associate professor in the Graduate School of Public and International Affairs at the University of Ottawa. He is also senior fellow at the Centre for International Governance Innovation (CIGI), research associate at Centre interuniversitaire de recherche en analyse des organisations (CIRANO), and affiliated professor of international business at HEC Montreal. Leblond is an expert on economic governance and policy with a particular focus on Canada, North America, Europe, and, increasingly, China. He has published extensively on financial and monetary integration, banking regulation, international trade, data governance, and business-government relations.

ISABELLA MANCINI is a lecturer in law at Brunel University London. She holds a PhD from the City Law School (City, University of London), where she was a Marie Curie Early Stage Researcher on the EU-funded Horizon 2020 Network EU Trade and Investment Policy (EUTIP). Her research expertise and publications cover areas of EU external relations, EU trade policy, international trade law and policy, labour rights, data protection rights, and global economic governance. She also maintains a strong interest in UK-EU relations, and the role of parliaments and civil society. During her doctoral studies, Mancini has been a visiting fellow at the Egmont Institute (Brussels), at the Asser Institute (The Hague), and at the Amsterdam Centre for European Law and Governance (ACELG, Amsterdam). She has worked as a teaching assistant at the European University Institute (EUI) and as an intern at the European Parliament Liaison Office in London.

AGNÈS RUFFAT is an economist and a data strategist and analyst for Innovation, Science and Economic Development Canada at the Clean Growth Hub Cleantech policy department. She holds an MBA from l'Ecole des Ponts-ParisTech and, for over twenty years, she has worked in finance, financial technology, innovation, trade, and international affairs for both the private and public sectors. As a former economic and public diplomacy counsellor for the Embassy of the Kingdom of Belgium, as well as a private consultant, Ruffat facilitated trade and governmental relations between the EU member states and Canada, and developed her expertise on the CETA negotiations, and on the implications of this agreement implementation. Her project at the University of Ottawa's Graduate School of Public and International Affairs (GSPIA) focused on "Public Procurement in the International Free Trade Agreement CETA between the EU and Canada." Currently, Ruffat's research focuses on how the government supports businesses in their ecological transition.

EMMANUELLE SANTOIRE is a teaching and research assistant at the University Lyon 3 Jean Moulin. She holds a PhD in geography from the Ecole Normale Supérieure (ENS) of Lyon in France. Also at ENS, she obtained both her bachelor's and master's degrees in geography. Work experiences include a French lecturer position at the London School of Economics and Political Science (UK), a visit to the European Parliament Research Service in Brussels, and participation in a cross-funded French-Canadian research project on energy and waste issues in CETA. She specializes in the geography of energy and is particularly interested in geo-legal conversations, to study the role of law in the structuration of energy spatialities.

ELIZABETH SCHWARTZ is an assistant professor in the department of political science at Memorial University of Newfoundland and Labrador. She studies municipal politics and public policy, with particular emphasis on urban environmental and climate change policy. Her current research projects examine sustainable public procurement and municipal climate change policy in Canada.

SAUL SCHWARTZ is a professor at the School of Public Policy at Carleton University, Ottawa. Broadly speaking, his research involves the analysis of policies aimed at helping the poor. His work on government procurement, co-authored with Elizabeth Schwartz from Memorial University of Newfoundland and Labrador and Dmitry Lysenko from Deloitte, has been focused on the link between CETA and municipal efforts to promote the economic welfare of marginalized groups. With Barbara Allen from Victoria University of Wellington, New Zealand, and Pierre-André Hudon from Université Laval, he edited a special 2021 issue of *Canadian Public Administration* on public procurement.

FELIX STERN studied law and political science at the University of Munich, where he focused for the first time on European law, international law, and international relations. In 2012 he also studied at Istanbul

Bilgi University. After his two-state examinations in law, he completed LLM in European law at the University of Speyer in 2017/18. From August 2018 to September 2019 he was a research fellow at the chair for international and European law at Speyer. In January 2019 he was accepted as a doctoral student at Speyer where he was granted a doctoral scholarship of the Stiftung der deutschen Wirtschaft from June 2019 to May 2021. Since November 2021 he works for an international consulting firm.

CHARELL VAN ROOY is a PhD researcher at the School of Law and Politics at Cardiff University in Wales. She has been a research assistant and graduate tutor at this university since the start of her PhD in 2015. Her research interests lie in the areas of (comparative) constitutional and administrative law. Van Rooy completed her bachelor's and master's degrees in Dutch law at Groningen University in the Netherlands, where she specialized in constitutional and administrative law – with a special interest in the EU. During the final years of her bachelor's degree, she combined her studies with a research internship in constitutional law and a teaching assistantship in European law. Her keen interest and passion for European law propelled her to a second masters at Cardiff University, where she graduated in European law and governance. She has since taken on a research position at Cardiff where she is pursuing a PhD in law working on a comparative analysis of the integration of scientific expertise in regulatory cooperation between the United States and the EU.

WOLFGANG WEISS is full professor of public law, European law, and public international law at the German University of Administrative Sciences in Speyer/FRG and senior fellow at the German Research Institute on Public Administration. His expertise comprises EU constitutional and economic law, international economic law, and German public law. Previously, he was professor in international law at the Oxford Brookes University and at the University of Erlangen-Nuremberg. He is author of *WTO Law and Domestic Regulation*, Beck-Hart-Nomos 2020, and co-editor of *Global Politics and EU Trade Policy: Facing the Challenges to a Multilateral Approach*, Springer 2020. His most recent publications are "Adjudicating Security Exceptions in WTO Law: Methodical and Procedural Preliminaries" in the 2020 *Journal of World Trade*, 829–52; and "The EU in Search for Stronger Enforcement Rules: Assessing the Proposed Amendments to Trade Enforcement Regulation 654/2014," *Journal of International Economic Law* 4 (2020).

ELIZABETH WHITSITT teaches various courses in international law and dispute resolution at the University of Calgary, Faculty of Law. She received her LLM in international legal studies from New York University and completed her PhD in 2017. Her PhD research focused on the intersection of trade law and investment arbitration. Elizabeth has published and presented extensively in the areas of international trade and investment law. She has been appointed to Canada's USMCA (United States–Mexico–Canada Agreement) Chapter 10 Roster and is a Canadian Member of the USMCA's Joint Public Advisory Committee to the Commission for Environmental Cooperation. Whitsitt is also a scholar-in-residence at Wilmer Hale LLP (London Office).

Index